Anglais BTS/DUT

Global Network

Catherine BEAUCAMP

Professeur certifié
Enseignante en B.T.S. Comptabilité
et Gestion des Organisations
et en B.T.S. Assistant Secrétaire Trilingue
Lycée Aristide-Briand – Évreux

Frédérique CORBIÈRE-LÉVY

Professeur agrégé
U.F.R. de Sciences et Techniques
Université de Rouen

HACHETTE
Éducation

Maquette intérieure et réalisation : Agence Media
Couverture : N. Bossard
Dessins : C. Tarcellin et C.-H. Saunier
Iconographie : V. Delchambre

Photos : p. 9 : © Ian Hanning / REA ; p. 57 : © GettyImages / Image Bank / Francesco Ruggieri ; p. 139 : © Pierre Bessard / REA ; p. 181 : © Cosmos / SPL / Nasa.

www.hachette-education.com

ISBN : 2.01.16.8841.8

Foreword

L'objectif de ***Global Network*** est de permettre aux étudiants et étudiantes, futurs acteurs économiques :

- d'acquérir ou de consolider les éléments d'une communication à vocation professionnelle vivante et rigoureuse grâce à :
  - des exercices de communication écrits et oraux (techniques de recherche d'emploi, rédaction de CV, correspondance commerciale, activités relationnelles) ;
  - des cas pratiques (lecture et interprétation de données numériques, études de formulaires et de documents professionnels) ;
- d'approfondir leur compréhension du monde contemporain, notamment des aspects économiques et sociaux à l'aide d'articles de presse récents d'origines diverses, de difficulté graduée, accompagnés d'exercices de prononciation, d'aide à la compréhension et à l'exploitation ;
- de perfectionner leurs connaissances linguistiques. À cette fin ***Global Network*** est doté d'un lexique grammatical et d'aide à la communication (Tricks and Traps) ;
- de travailler de façon autonome en recourant à des textes très courts assortis d'exercices dont les corrigés détaillés figurent en fin de manuel ;
- de s'exercer à la compréhension audio grâce à des CD où figurent, outre des dialogues et articles du livre, des textes, documents et interviews dont la transcription n'apparaît pas dans le manuel.

Les auteurs

Tous nos remerciements à Ms Patricia Abbou pour ses précieux conseils.

« I had forgot(ten) how good it is to work » , *The Wild Palms* by W. Faulkner

Abréviations utilisées dans le manuel :

n. : nom
adj. : adjectif
adv. : adverbe
S : sujet
V : verbe
BV : base verbale
CO : complément
cf : voir
Ex. : exemple
= : synonyme
N.B. : remarque
GB : anglais britannique
US : anglais américain
sing. : singulier
pl. : pluriel
(C) : dénombrable
[U] : indénombrable
! : attention !
➔ : transformation

Global Network

Texte enregistré sur CD et figurant dans l'ouvrage.

Titre de la rubriqe avec repère dans l'unité.

Conseils pour une communication professionnelle et rigoureuse.

Exercices et **cas pratiques.**

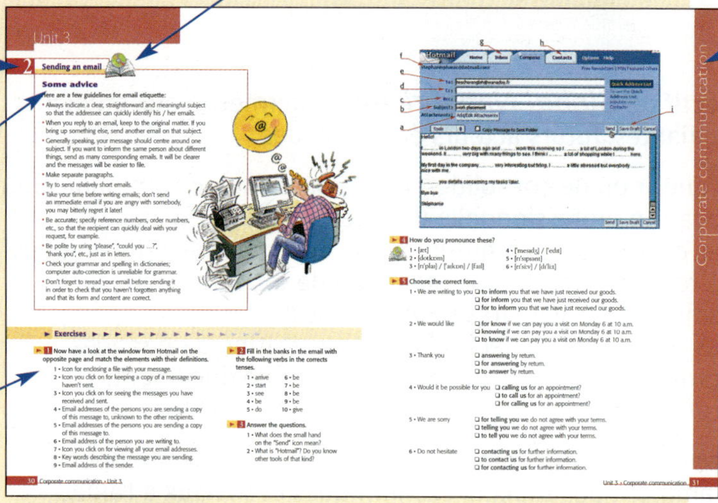

La première partie de l'ouvrage, **Corporate communication** est consacrée à la communication écrite et orale.

Enregistrements dont le script n'apparaît pas dans le manuel.

Les unités de **The business world, The working world** et **The world at stake** proposent chacune : A few landmarks, Warm-up, 3 textes suivis d'exercices et Checkup.

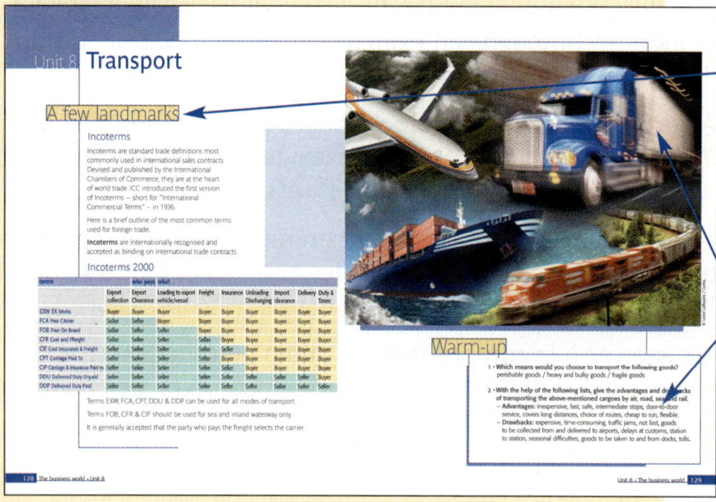

A few landmarks
Données de base à consulter tout au long de l'unité.

Warm-up
Un document iconographique accompagné de questions, introduit le thème de l'unité.

Texte enregistré sur CD.

Explications des difficultés lexicales.

Pair work

Exercices de communication orale à deux (ou plus : Group work).

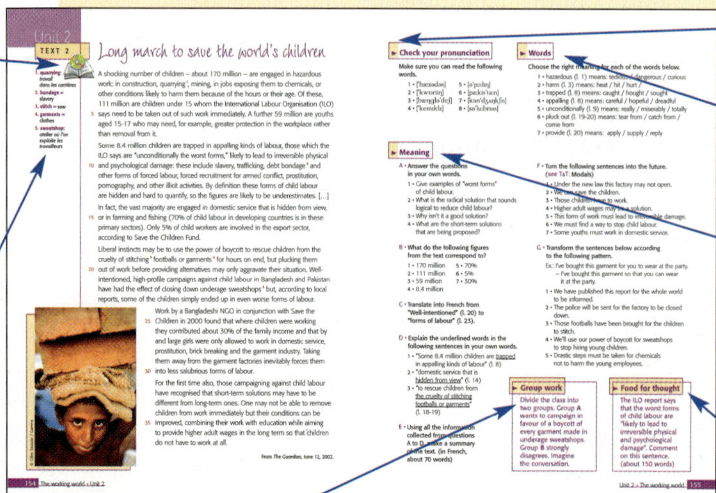

Check your pronunciation

Exercices de phonétique.

Words

Exercices portant sur les difficultés lexicales du texte.

Meaning

Exercices de compréhension et de grammaire d'une grande diversité.

Food for thought

Sujet de réflexion à rédiger.

En fin d'unité, **un texte court et simple** favorise le travail autonome (le corrigé figure en fin de manuel).

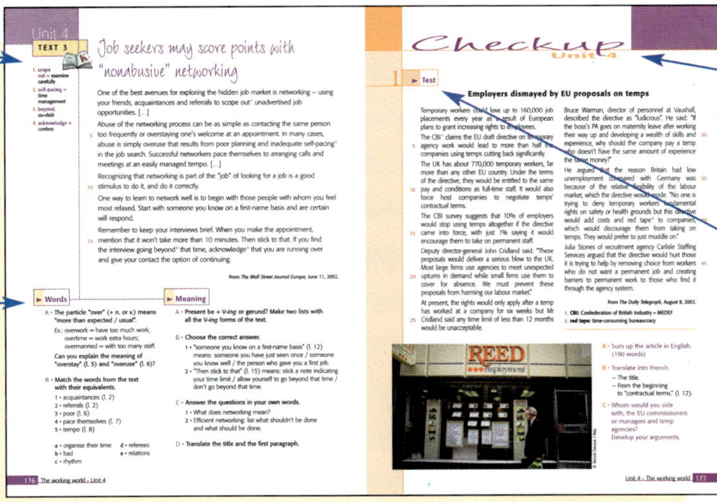

Bilan de l'unité.

1 ▶ Test

Sujet de préparation à l'examen.

Deux rubriques

▶ Words

▶ Meaning

contenant des exercices simples permettent l'auto-correction.

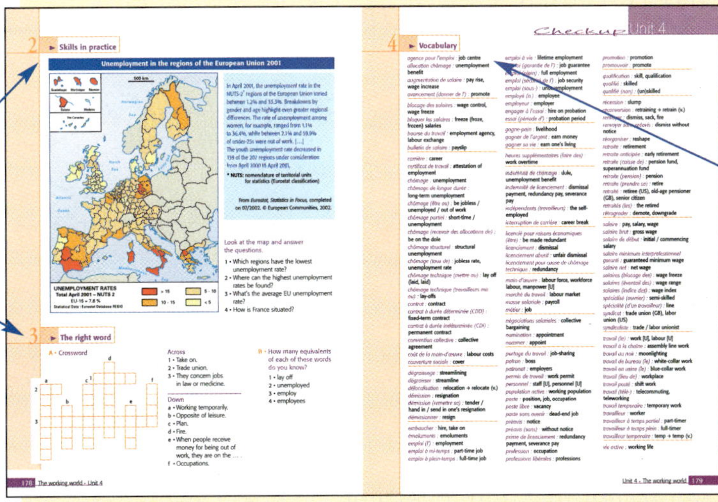

2 ▶ Skills in practice

Un cas pratique à résoudre.

3 ▶ The right word

Contrôle du vocabulaire acquis durant l'étude de l'unité (mots-croisés et exercices).

4 ▶ Vocabulary

Liste de vocabulaire spécifique à l'unité.

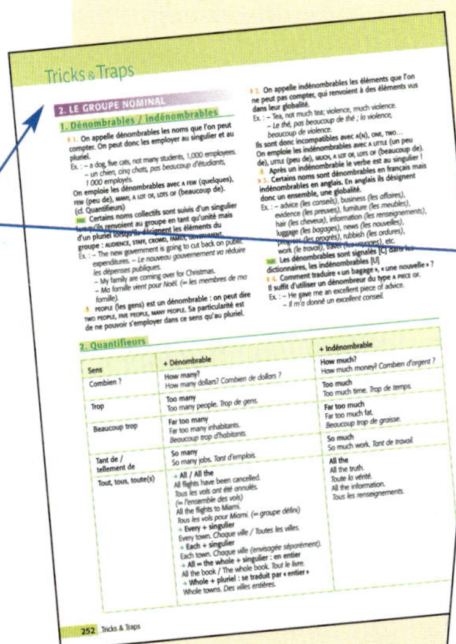

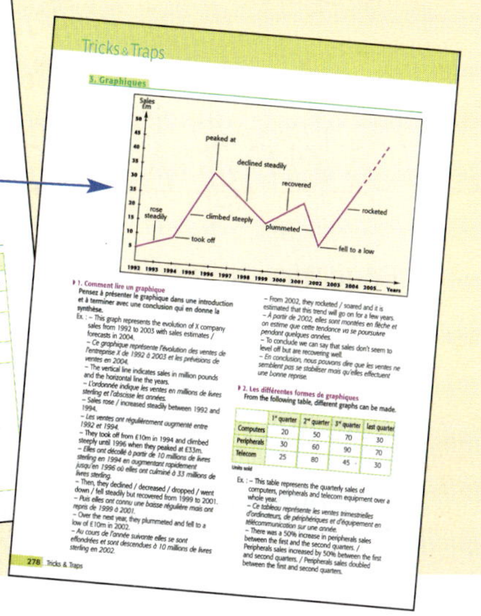

Tricks & Traps : les principaux pièges grammaticaux et des outils pour une pratique efficace de la langue.

En fin d'ouvrage, **Passport** propose des outils pour une meilleure approche du monde anglo-saxon.

Contents

Corporate communication

PART I The business world

PART II The working world

PART III The world at stake

Key to texts 3

Tricks & Traps

Passport to English-speaking countries

Corporate communication

Unit 1 Applying for a job

1 Job hunting

Whether you are looking for a work placement or for a job, you have to follow a number of steps before applying.

► Exercises

1 Among the following ways of job hunting, choose the ones you could opt for and explain how you could go about it.

Ex.: I could phone my uncle and ask him if the company he works for needs an assistant trainee.

Networking, i.e. contacting your friends and relations / looking up companies in the directory / making an Internet search / phoning companies you've heard of / going to companies you've heard of / contacting work placement or recruitment agencies / going to a temping agency.

2 Online search

Have a look at the window below and answer the following questions.

1 • What does the long list correspond to?
2 • Which category would you select?
3 • Can you choose a location apart from London? apart from Great Britain?
4 • Would you fill in the "keyword" heading? If so, what would you key in?
5 • Where do you have to click to get the answer to your request?
6 • Does this site offer to help you with your CV?
7 • Does it offer other career guidance / advice?
8 • Is this site only for job applicants?
9 • What is "My profile" box for?

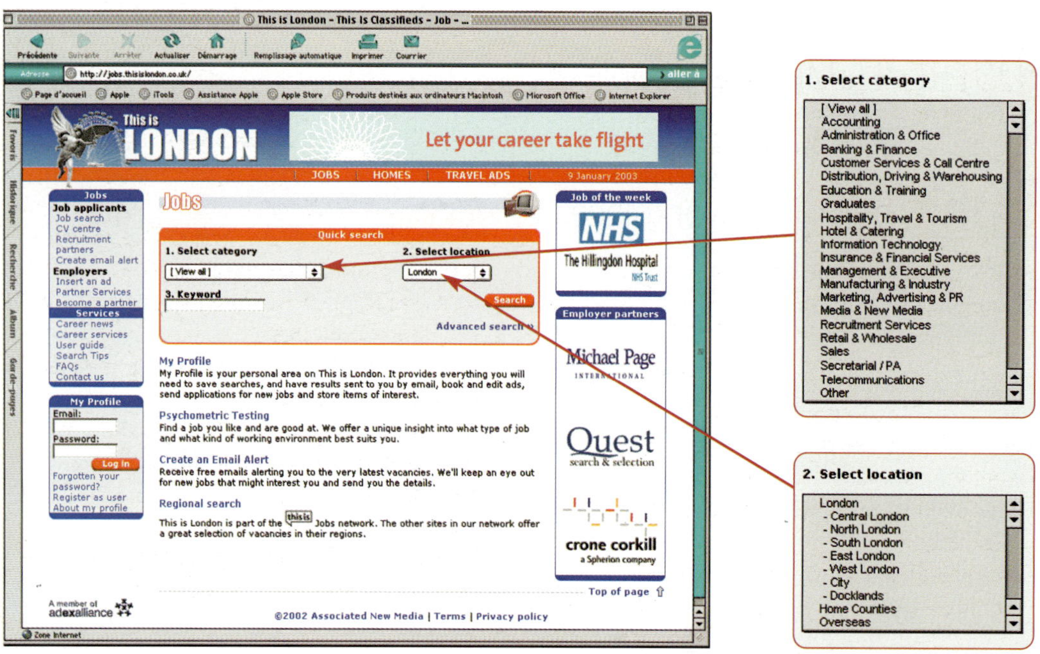

2 Going through the ads

You must learn how to go through the ads, i.e. you must understand what sort of job is advertised and which qualifications are needed. You should also be careful about ads that offer too much!

Exercises

1 Many abbreviations are used in ads. Can you decipher the following ones?

1 • P/T Exec. Sec. req. c. £14k pa. 50wpm+. MS Office ess.
2 • prev exp of business trips organisation ess. £9.00ph.
3 • French spkg switchboard op. £neg.
4 • Sales exp. English MT

2 Have a look at the ads on the following pages and study them.

A • Answer the questions below on the whole series of ads.

1 • Do all the ads offer jobs? If not, what do some offer?
2 • What positions are advertised?
3 • Would you apply for a job in a particular sector or would you answer several ads? Why?
4 • What skills and professional or personal qualities are often required?
5 • What is often proposed apart from a job?
6 • Are there any ads you would definitely not select? Why?

B • Choose an ad from the education section and say why you've chosen it.

C • Choose at least one job offer and say:

1 • which qualifications are required.
2 • what skills are needed.
3 • what the applicant is offered.
4 • what seems exciting (or dull) about this / these ad(s).
5 • why you think this job would (not) suit you.

D • Explain the different stages you follow in order to:

1 • find all the ads that suit you.
2 • select among them the ones you will answer.

3 Match each adjective in A with its equivalent in B.

A	B
1 • good at	a • effective
2 • important	b • impartial
3 • comprehensive	c • strong on
4 • pleasant	d • dedicated
5 • unbiased	e • major
6 • committed	f • extensive
7 • aspiring	g • secure
8 • brilliant	h • ambitious
9 • efficient	i • bright
10 • safe	j • attractive

4 Translate into English.

1 • *Nous recherchons un comptable qui devrait avoir au moins 5 ans d'expérience et être âgé de plus de 30 ans.*
2 • *Vous ferez partie d'une équipe d'hommes et de femmes extrêmement motivés.*
3 • *Il y a un poste libre à l'étranger pour un représentant motivé.*
4 • *C'est un travail prenant dans une entreprise juridique internationale.*
5 • *Vous vous occuperez de l'agenda du responsable export et assurerez la liaison avec les clients.*
6 • *Envoyez votre CV par email.*
7 • *Pour plus amples détails concernant le poste mentionné ci-dessus, téléphonez au…*

PUBLIC & COMMUNITY

VACANCIES AT BUSINESS SCHOOL

A busy international Business School based in London has the following vacancies:

- *Marketing officer • Salary £25K p.a. (ref. MO/08)*
- *Switchboard operator • Salary £23K p.a. (ref. SO/08)*
- *Data entry operator • Salary £23K p.a. (ref. DE/08)*
- *Junior administrator • Salary £21K p.a. (ref. JA/08)*

The school currently conducts a range of British and Australian degree programmes in business and IT. Candidates should have good communication skills, be articulate and willing to work under pressure. Interested candidates should send their CV to:

Professor Burt Beckman, 52 Better Street, London SE1 3QP

Please quote the appropriate reference number in your application.

ACCOUNTANCY

Graduate trainee management accountant

Kensington

Established group with diverse international operations seeks a graduate trainee management accountant to train for a senior position in the group's management accountancy team; relevant degree qualification essential; excellent communication and IT skills required; foreign language abilities useful. Salary: £22,000 pa.

Please reply in writing and send letter and CV to: Mr G Morrison, Charles Group, 10 Albert Road, London SW7 2BJ

P/T Bookkeeper / Administrator

for Design Company. 20 hours per week, flexible. General office admin., keeping financial records and reporting to director. Salary up to £14K depending on experience. Word / Excel / Sage essential. Apply in writing only to:

Mr Goodwick, Style Company
14 Apollo Street, London NW5 2SA

TRAVEL & TOURISM

Travel Assistant

London £15,000 OTE £25,000

Are you looking for work in a fast-paced, energetic, fun and sociable environment earning lots of commission and getting large discounts on exotic holidays?

If the answer is yes, this may be the position you have been waiting for. Working for this well-established high street travel agent, you will liase with agents and customers to arrange holidays for customers, negotiate deals and sell additional services. In return you will earn uncapped commission, receive excellent training and get huge discounts on holidays abroad.

Interested?
Contact me today: Jude on **0202 978 8666**

We are urgently in need of a **Guest Service Agent** *for our client based in Canary Wharf. Previous reception experience and knowledge of Fidelio would be an advantage but is not essential as training will be given to the right candidates. The emphasis of the role is on reception/reservations work and will involve late-early shift pattern (3 pm-11 pm and 7 am-3 pm) but staff accommodation is available for sleepover when changing shifts. Only seriously interested applicants who can commit to the shift pattern need apply.*

Send your CV to eva@staff.co.uk or call Eva on 020 7311 6072 for an initial interview.

London: E14
Skills required: reception, reservations agent, guest service agent, front office, hospitality, hotel, customer service, European languages.
This is a full-time permanent job. Contract starts ASAP.

SALES

Graduate commercial executive

£16-£18,000 West end

Working for an international market leader is a unique and fascinating specialist role. Unique, in that it combines your sales management skills with your interest in world affairs and current market trends. You will be dealing and trading in commodities, and a knowledge of French would be desirable. You will need to be enthusiastic, articulate and very ambitious. Full training will be given.

For more information, application only by telephone to David Grisham or Maureen Stilton in the first instance on:

020 7770 2129

Graduate sales

© GettyImages / Image Bank / Richard Drury.

- Looking for a career in the media, working for one of the UK's leading financial publishing companies.
- Successful candidates must have a desire to sell, good organisational skills, outgoing personality, coupled with the ability to work to deadlines.
- They will be enthusiastic, energetic and be able to demonstrate an entrepreneurial, go-get attitude.
- They must be excellent communicators and work well within a team. Spanish a plus.
- These are top level, professional organisations that offer a good office environment and excellent career prospects.
- This is an opportunity not to be missed. Call James Camden on 020 7248 1436 or email james@gsj.uk.com

MULTILINGUAL APPOINTMENTS

Telesales executives

You speak fluent English and either French, Spanish, Portuguese, Italian or German. We are currently expanding our European division and have a limited number of vacancies available in our telesales and telemarketing departments. No prior experience necessary as we will train and pay you during training.

Please call 020 7493 7151

Import / Export

Mature export admin. £20-23K
2nd job sec./admin.+export £18K
Export co-ordinator £17.5K
Export temps £10.00p/hour

T: 020 7734 9656
F: 020 7256 9051

© F. Boudon.

mail@people.co.uk
www.people.co.uk

EDUCATION

LEARN SAGE ACCOUNTING

Packages in under 18 hours and get a Pitman Certificate to prove it. 3 courses for the price of 2.
Call Pitman training on:
020 7962 4751 & quote ref: PLC946.

PITMAN TRAINING

Join the workforce with confidence.

Get qualified with the best training company in London.

We specialise in:
♦ MS Office ♦ Typing ♦ Shorthand ♦ Accounts ♦

Specialist diplomas:
♦ Legal secretaries ♦ Executive PA ♦ Workplace skills ♦
♦ Business skills ♦ Internet & web design ♦
♦ Fast track for graduates ♦ and many more ♦

Regent Street **020 7589 1142**
High Holborn **020 7362 4852**
City **020 7641 6000**

CITY AWARDS COLLEGE

Foreign & UK students welcome.
Courses and home study in English language, Business, Customer Service, Management, Marketing, Sales, Public Relations, Publishing, Secretarial Studies, Travel & Tourism. Oxford Cambridge RSA examinations & London Chamber of Commerce exams.

Call 020 7328 9986 or 020 8741 7555

HOTEL AND CATERING

Service staff

required for new concept cafes opening in **Soho, Islington and Portobello,** ranging from 50 to 100 seats.

European languages a plus. £7.00 to £8.00 per hour. Central London.
Please phone 020 8696 4872 between 9.00 am and 5.00 pm.

Receptionists

required to work 40 hours per week for busy hotel in Earls Court.
- *Speaking French, Spanish, German or Arabic ess.*
- *Previous experience preferred but not essential as training will be provided.*

For further information please contact Cindy on:
020 7323 7528

SECRETARIAL

PA / SECRETARY (SW8) up to £22,000pa

Property co. req PA/Sec. to join support services team. Your day will include typing, presentation work, extensive diary/meeting management, travel co-ordination & client liaison. Min 50wpm copy/audio & knowledge of W4W ess. French and Spanish a must.

Call Axe on 020 7808 7640
Email: axe@recruit.co.uk

Shipping & trading company in the City requires an

Evening Secretary

Hours 5 pm – 10 pm negotiable.
Good knowledge of Windows / Word / Excel is essential.
Should also be computer-literate.
Email your CV to jobs@tech.net

Import Assistant

D.R.

Major importer & distrib. loc. in NYC is seeking hands-on, exp'd import person to join their co. Applicant should possess exp in all areas of importing, incl L/C, purchase orders & entry of documents for in transit & receiving. Accuracy, speed & exp w/computer & PC is a must. Good bnfts & working conditions. Salary commens. w/exp.

Send resume showing sal, hist & reqs Attn Sham, Regent International, 11 E 26 St, 11th Flr, NY 10010 or fax: 221-649-2083.

Dynamic, new company specialising in executive search and IT are currently looking for a Secretary/PA

to work in their London City-based office. You will be involved in setting up the office, assisting with their office management and liasing with clients. This position will suit a confident, proactive and efficient candidate with excellent organisational and communication skills and a good level of French and German.

Contact address: **3 Waterloo Place, London SW7 2JE**
Contact: **Charlie Jones,**
Tel. 020 7324 1658 • Fax: 020 7324 2930
email: charlie@wa.com

Experienced job seeks interesting secretary...

At Action First, the best jobs come looking for you!

Right now, we've got a choice of long-term temp positions with leading companies just crying out for your unique input. £9.00p/hr – £12p/hr

Dynamic work environment.
Convenient Central London locations. **Immediate start!**

If you've got at least 2 years' experience in a secretarial/administrative role, fast typing speeds and excellent MS Office skills…

apply now!

lisa@actionplc.com 020 7581 5647 www.actionplc.com

3 Writing a curriculum vitae

Some advice

- A CV or résumé (US) should be accurate and in keeping with the post you are applying for.
- Its layout should be concise and clear.
- The character fonts must be unsophisticated and easily legible.
- You can use colours but make sure they are not too bright and aggressive.
- Avoid using clip art.
- Make your CV easy to photocopy.
- Check your grammar and spelling or have it checked by someone (avoid computer auto-correction).
- Put your name on each sheet (maximum 2) in case they get detached.
- If you email your CV, don't forget to type a covering note so that the addressee knows why he / she received your CV.

Have a close look at the CV on the next page with the help of the indications below.

❶ Personal details

In English you should always write your first name before your surname. Beware! It is not compulsory to indicate you are either male or female single, married, divorced or widowed, with or without children.

❷ Qualifications

Don't forget to start with your most recent diploma and continue the chronology in reverse order down to your "Baccalauréat". When possible, add the British / American equivalent but never try to translate them (a Baccalaureate has nothing to do with your Baccalauréat). Indicate the main subjects.
Here are some British equivalents of a few French diplomas:
Baccalauréat ≈ A levels (at least 3 subjects): Advanced levels
BTS ≈ HNC: Higher National Certificate
DUT ≈ HND: Higher National Diploma
DEUG ≈ two-year course degree in English, Spanish, etc.
LEA ≈ two-year course degree in business English, Spanish, etc.

❸ Experience

Again, start with your latest experience and end with your first one. Indicate the dates, type of experience (odd jobs, training, position), department or sector, tasks performed, the name and activity of the company you worked for, and its location (country). If you are applying for a particular post, insist on the qualities mentioned in the ad.

❹ Skills

According to your training and the post you are applying for, indicate your languages with your level of expertise (i.e. a few notions, basic, intermediate, advanced, fluent. Beware! Fluent means you are almost bilingual.) and / or your computer skills.

❺ Activities, interests, abilities

Once again, according to your training and the post you are applying for, show for example how dynamic you are in your private life. Your activities say a lot about your personality, so choose the ones you want to bring out to fit the post.

❻ References

These are the referees your prospective employer may need to contact. Again, select the ones for whom you carried out interesting tasks, in keeping with the post you are applying for. Don't forget to mention the name and / or position, address and phone number / email of each referee.

Exercises

1 Read the following words concentrating on the [aɪ] and [ɪ] sounds.

1 • trilingual **2** • bilingual **3** • studies **4** • dynamic **5** • children **6** • apply **7** • applicant **8** • file **9** • filing **10** • organise **11** • trip **12** • advertising **13** • typing **14** • site **15** • IT **16** • practising **17** • license **18** • child

2 Which syllable is stressed: the first one or the second one?

1 • applicant **2** • bilingual **3** • assistant **4** • secretary **5** • organise **6** • practising **7** • advertise **8** • dynamic **9** • accurate **10** • experience **11** • diploma **12** • languages **13** • computer

3 Pronounce the two series of words below and say which one corresponds to the sound [ʌ] and which one to [ɜː].

1 • London, mother, other, one, just, customer
2 • firm, work, learn, world, confirmed

4 Key in your own CV for a work placement in an English-speaking country.

CURRICULUM VITAE

❶
Élise BEAUJOUR
12, rue Lépouzé
27000 Évreux – France
Tel: +33 2 32 39 74 35 / Mobile: +33 6 56 48 97 23 / Email: elisebeaujour@wanadoo.fr

❷ Qualifications

- June 2003: BTS Assistant Secrétaire Trilingue – French / English / Spanish (the equivalent of HNC in Trilingual Secretariat) – Évreux.
- 2000-2001: first year in English studies at university – Rouen.
- July 2000: Baccalauréat STT (the equivalent of A levels: administration, commerce, management, economy, law, English, Spanish). Évreux.

❸ Experience

- June-Aug. 2003: **personal assistant** at Minnesota Rubber Europe – Évreux. *File updating, filing, mail, follow-up of orders.*
- Feb.-March 2003: **organising a trade fair** for Equipbureau (office equipment) – Vernon, France. *Mailshot, hotel and journey booking, layout of the stand, welcoming French and foreign visitors, assisting the marketing manager, follow-up of the prospects.* Two weeks + one day per week for 3 weeks.
- Nov.-Dec. 2002: 6-week work experience as a **trilingual assistant secretary trainee** at Airtime International (TV broadcasting) – London, UK. *Dealing with mail, emails and faxes, answering the phone, contacting customers, follow-up of orders, organising meetings and business trips.*
- May-Aug 2002: 6-week work experience as a **trilingual personal assistant trainee** at Filial del Groupe Giraudy (advertising agency) + 4 weeks as the PA substitute – Madrid, Spain. *Sorting the mail, answering the phone, typing letters, filing, laying out ads, contacting customers, attending meetings with the staff and with customers.*
- March-April 2002: **English translation work** for the creation of a Web site at Vidi Dixi Agency (communication agency) – Évreux. One day per week.
- Jan.-Feb. 2002: various **secretarial tasks** at GSK (pharmaceutical group) – Évreux. One day per week. *Filing, updating the customers' files, follow-up of orders.*
- Nov.-Dec. 2001: various **secretarial tasks** at Snecma (aeronautics) – Vernon. One day per week. *New layout of the in-house newsletter, preparation of transparencies and literature for the safety manager's conferences to the staff.*
- Jan.-May 2001: **waitress** in a bar in Rouen every weekend.
- 2000: **babysitting** regularly.
- 1999-2000: **activity leader** for a children's outdoor centre during the school holidays.

❹ Skills

Languages
- mother tongue: French
- advanced English
- intermediate Spanish
- basic Italian / a few notions of German

Software
- Word / Excel / Access / Powerpoint
- Some knowledge of the Internet
- Able to adapt to company computer networks
- I take shorthand and I can type 80 wpm.

❺ Activities, interests, abilities

- Children's activity leader certificate
- First aid certificate
- Reading, going to the cinema
- Tennis, downhill skiing, fitness training
- Driving licence

- Articulate, accurate, well organised, flexible
- Dynamic although a little reserved
- Enjoy: teamwork / practising foreign languages / travelling / handling responsibilities

References: Equipbureau …, Airtime International …, Filial del Groupe … ❻

4 Writing a letter of application

Some advice

- Your letter of application can be either handwritten (it must be legible), typed or emailed.
- Beware of grammar and spelling mistakes; have yourself helped by someone you can rely on.
- Don't use any abbreviations.
- Use block style, i.e.:
  - no commas after "Dear …" and "Yours faithfully / sincerely",
  - no indented lines at the beginning of the paragraphs,
  - line spaces between the paragraphs.
- Be as accurate, concise and straightforward as possible and don't
  - boast with sentences such as "This is exactly the kind of career I had hoped for",
  - use appalling flattery such as "I would be very pleased to work in your world-famous company",
  - make blunders with sentences such as "I am ready to do anything".

A letter of application explains the reasons why you are applying for the post and indicates that your qualities and experience correspond to the post requirements. In other words, it demonstrates that the company needs you. In no way should you repeat your CV; it would be clumsy, unhelpful and would lead to a negative answer.

© Bruno Boudon.

The contents of your letter

❶ Your name, address (+ country), phone numbers and email address.

❷ This is the most usual way to write a date in British English. In American English, it should be June 30, 2003. In both cases, it is pronounced June the thirtieth, two thousand and three. Be careful! 12/01/03 means January the twelfth in British English but December the first in American English.

❸ The addressee's name, position if possible and address (+ country).

❹ Repeat the name (and position) of the addressee.

❺ See "Writing business letters", I, 3 p. 29.

❻ Clearly indicate the subject of your letter (see "Writing business letters", I, 3 p. 28).

❼ Indicate the ad you are answering, with its reference (newspaper, date, ad number, …, job advertised).

❽ Briefly introduce the reason why you are applying for this job.

❾ Sum up your CV (without repeating it) in accordance with the qualities required for the post you are applying for. Use the nouns or adjectives mentioned in the ad (e.g.: "autonomous personal assistant" ➔ use the word "autonomous" in your letter) with examples. For instance, if "dynamism" is required you can write (only if it's true!): "I organised my sales manager's trip to Germany and prepared his conference there overnight."

❿ Close your letter by showing interest in further discussion.

⓫ Thank the addressee and finish with the usual letter ending (see "Writing business letters", I, 3 p. 28).

⓬ See "Writing business letters", I, 3 p. 29.

⓭ Don't forget to indicate that you've attached documents to your letter, either by the number of documents or by their names ("Enc. 1" or "Enc. CV"). For an email, use "Attached".

A few useful phrases

- I am currently preparing a BTS Assistant Secrétaire Trilingue.
- After I passed my …, I worked with … as a …
- On leaving school, I worked with …
- As indicated in my CV, I …
- As you will see from my enclosed CV, I …
- When I worked with X company, I dealt with …
  I was responsible for …
  I was in charge of …

Élise BEAUJOUR
12, rue Lépouzé
27000 – Évreux France
Tél: +33 2 32 39 74 35 ❶
Mobile: +33 6 56 48 97 23
Email: elisebeaujour@wanadoo.fr

Évreux, 30 June 2003. ❷

Mr David Williams
Personnel Manager ❸
Adlink International
...
London UK

For the attention of Mr David Williams, Personnel Manager ❹

Dear Mr Williams ❺

Application for the job of Personal Assistant ❻

In the "Evening Standard, classified week", 25-29 June 2003, I noted with interest your ad for a personal assistant with knowledge of English, Spanish and French as well as some secretarial experience and organisational skills. ❼

Since I have just passed my BTS Assistant Secrétaire Trilingue – French, English, Spanish – I would like to start in the working world with a company that would offer me the possibility to practise my language and secretarial skills. ❽

As you will see from my enclosed CV, until now I have undertaken odd jobs or work placements. However, not only did I perform basic secretarial tasks but I was also given the responsibility of organising managers' meetings and business trips. This, added to regular phone or one-to-one contacts with customers, has enabled me to be more self-confident and autonomous. ❾

Moreover, my work experiences abroad have improved my language abilities and have confirmed my eagerness to work with foreign partners. They have also revealed that I am quite flexible.

In addition, having worked with TV broadcasting, communication and advertising agencies, I believe my experience should meet your demand.

This is why I would be grateful if you could take my application into consideration and contact me for an interview at your convenience. ❿

I thank you for your attention and look forward to hearing from you soon. ⓫

Yours sincerely ⓬

Élise BEAUJOUR
Enc. 1 ⓭

Unit 1

▶ Exercises

▶ 1 The odd one out.

In each of the following series find the "*faux ami*" and translate it.

1 • actually / currently / at present
2 • possibly / eventually / perhaps
3 • lately / a long time ago / long ago
4 • realise / carry out / perform
5 • understanding / discerning / comprehensive
6 • stay / rest / remain

▶ 2 Crossword

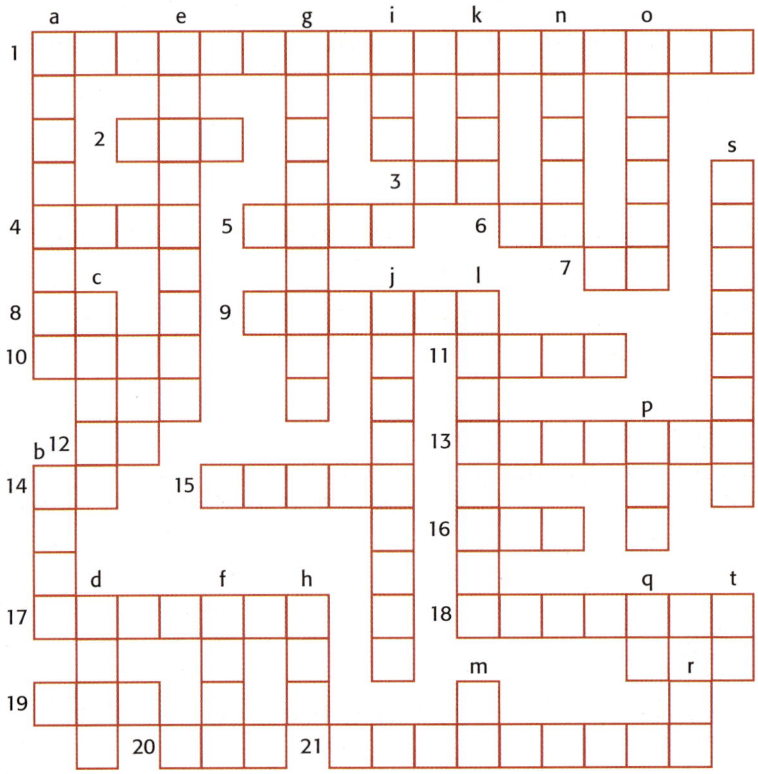

Across

1 • Sb who does secretarial and administrative work for a manager (2 words without any space).
2 • Full stop in email addresses.
3 • Indefinite article.
4 • Singular of those.
5 • Employ.
6 • Expressing condition.
7 • Job offer.
8 • Depend…
9 • Run a company.
10 • Midday.
11 • Principal.
12 • Expressing consequence.
13 • Seek (2 words without any space).
14 • Abbreviation of weekend.
15 • Expertise.
16 • However.
17 • Attach sth to a letter.
18 • Need.
19 • Representative.
20 • Reference.
21 • Able to carry out various tasks.

Down

a • Occupation.
b • Salary.
c • A sound sb or sth makes.
d • Necessity.
e • Writing with special signs.
f • One time.
g • Candidate for a post.
h • Conclusion.
i • Intention.
j • Vacant.
k • In a short time to come.
l • Person you work for.
m • Since.
n • Personnel.
o • Be present at an event or a meeting.
p • Responsible…
q • That is to say.
r • Subject of a letter.
s • Word or Excel for instance.
t • For example.

▶ **3** Translate into English. (see T&T: Present perfect / Preterite)

1 • *J'ai lu dans le* Guardian *de ce jour que vous recherchez une réceptionniste.*
2 • *Je viens d'obtenir mon BTS tourisme.*
3 • *J'ai effectué deux stages de 6 semaines à l'étranger.*
4 • *Ce travail m'a permis d'avoir plus d'assurance.*

▶ **4** *Since, for* or *during*? (see T&T: Present perfect / Preterite)

1 • – .... my training as an export assistant, I had the opportunity to work with the French car manufacturer Renault .... 2 months. .... then, I have been willing to work for an international company.
– .... I am still a student, I would like to find a job .... a short time.
– I have been working as an assistant accountant with the French bank Crédit Agricole .... I passed my *BTS Comptabilité et Gestion des Organisations.*

2 • **Now listen to the sentences, concentrating on stresses and tones. Underline the main stressed syllables and say whether the sentences' tone is rising, falling or falling-rising.**

▶ **5** Complete the covering note.

Dear Sirs

I read your .... for an experienced secretary in today's *Observer*
and wish to .... for the .... I .... my CV.
Please .... me know if there are any .... you require.
I look .... to .... from you soon.

Yours ....

▶ **6** Put the following words in correct order.

enquire / secretary / to / am / I / if / in / vacancies / are / for / there / a / dear / your / bilingual / office / sir / writing / any

▶ **7** *Vous êtes Ms Morrison du Service du Personnel de l'entreprise Apple & Peach. Vous écrivez à Miss Mary Anderson pour :*

1 • *la remercier de sa lettre de candidature du 12 juillet concernant le poste d'assistante trilingue,*
2 • *lui dire que vous lui joignez un formulaire qu'elle voudra bien compléter et renvoyer le plus tôt possible à l'adresse sus-mentionnée,*
3 • *lui dire qu'elle n'hésite pas à vous contacter si elle a d'autres questions à vous poser.*

N'oubliez pas les formules d'usage.

▶ **8** From the ads pp. 12-13, write a letter of application for:

1 • a training course,
2 • a job.

▶ **9** Now write your letter of application for your work placement abroad.

5 The job interview

The interviewer's point of view

"Interviewing a candidate is the most useful part of the hiring process. It enables you to get a clear picture of the individual that goes beyond the CV and letter of application." *(Encyclopedia Britannica)*

Some advice (see T&T: Sentences patterns)

- **The questions you will be asked can be either:**

– Yes / No questions, i.e. requiring a "yes" or "no" answer. They are generally used for simple factual matters but don't forget to develop your answer,
– or Wh- questions, i.e. which force you to elaborate an answer.

- **Remember that the same question can be either a Yes / No question or a Wh- question.**

Ex.: Can you learn quickly?
→ Under what conditions do you learn best?
Are you an ambitious person?
→ What is your own interpretation of success?

► **Tick the correct answer.**

1 • In the Yes / No questions, the tone is:
❑ rising ❑ falling

2 • In the Wh-questions, the tone is:
❑ rising ❑ falling

► **Find another three series of Yes / No questions and Wh- questions on the following topics:** Excel spreadsheets / teamwork / travelling abroad.

Carefully **preparing your interview** is essential whether for a work placement or for a job. Of course your preparation may also mean revising some vocabulary and grammatical points.

Concerning your CV

- Remember the key dates, e.g. "Three years ago I studied English at university for one year."
- Be prepared to justify why you preferred one subject to another.
- Keep in mind the key tasks you performed during other work placements, summer jobs, etc.
- Be able to give precise information on your skills, e.g. "My level of English at school was quite good but I have never spoken with English people, so it may be a little difficult for me at first but I'm really willing to try."
- Be ready to explain why you enjoy practising sports such as tennis or karate, playing the guitar, reading certain types of books or authors, why you passed the First Aid Certificate, etc.
- Be able to comment on your qualities and weaknesses.

Concerning your application

- Search for information on the company (activity, size, market share, …).
- Be prepared to give the reasons why you sent your application to this company.
- Think about how to describe what sort of tasks you would like to carry out.
- If it's for a work placement, be ready to define what you are expected to do for your exam.

Your behaviour during the interview will say a lot about you, so remember to:

- dress carefully,
- remain calm and relaxed, which should be easier if you have prepared your interview properly,
- smile and be polite. During the interview, you will have to develop the contents of your CV and letter of application, so don't say anything awkward such as: "Everything is in my CV" or "Haven't you read my CV?" for instance,
- listen carefully to the questions and ask your interviewer to repeat anything you are not sure you've understood correctly,
- avoid answering "no" or "I don't know",
- make frequent eye contact. If there are two people interviewing you, always look at both of them, whoever asks the question,
- ask questions about the firm and the tasks you will be required to carry out.

At the beginning of the interview

- You may be left the initiative of starting the interview either by introducing yourself or by asking questions about the firm / post.
- When you introduce yourself, you don't need to go into personal details (age, marital status, etc.). It is far more professional to start with your present situation (student, first job, etc.) and the reason why you applied for the post.

► Exercises

► Role play

1 Two friends are having a quick conversation before one of them has his / her interview. Student **A** gives advice to student **B** who replies briefly. Four pieces of advice should be chosen by each pair. (see T&T: A few phrases to express yourself)

2 Here is a list of subjects the interviewer wants to tackle.

hobbies / reading / films / sports / holidays / yourself / losing your temper / your strengths and weaknesses / being criticised / school subjects / schoolfriends / wage / too young

1 • Draw up the questions; there can be several for the same subject.
2 • Select three of them and reply. Be as straightforward as you can and remember the interviewer will judge you by your answers!

► Pair work

Matthieu is French and needs some help to prepare his job interview with an import-export company. Here is what he would like to say. Help him translate it and explain to him the preterite and the present perfect tenses with the graphs. For each sentence explain whether the action is over, whether it has consequences in the present time or whether it continues in the present time. (see T&T: Present perfect / Preterite)

Ex.: – *J'ai quitté cette entreprise il y 6 mois.* → – I quit this firm 6 months ago.

→ ***action passée terminée.***

1. – *J'ai travaillé comme vendeur il y a 3 ans.* → – ……………………………………………………

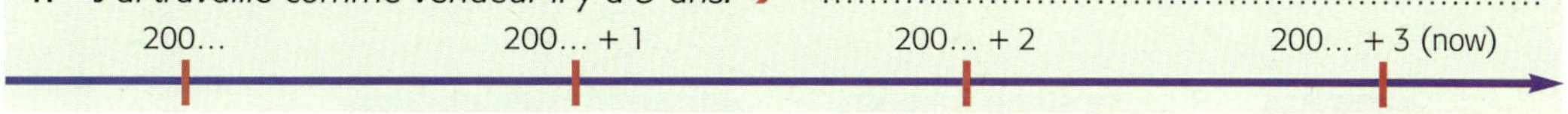

2. – *Pendant 2 ans, j'ai effectué des tâches de secrétariat de base.* → – ……………………………

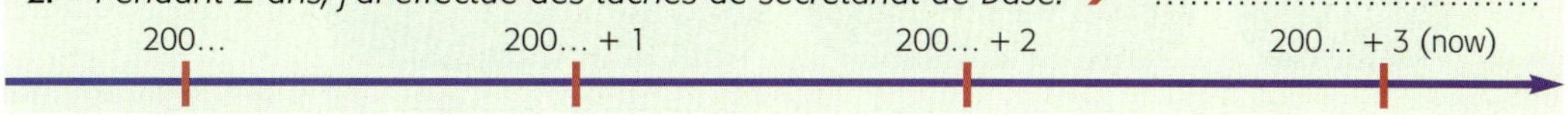

3. – *Je m'occupe du suivi clients depuis 1 an.* → – ……………………………………………………

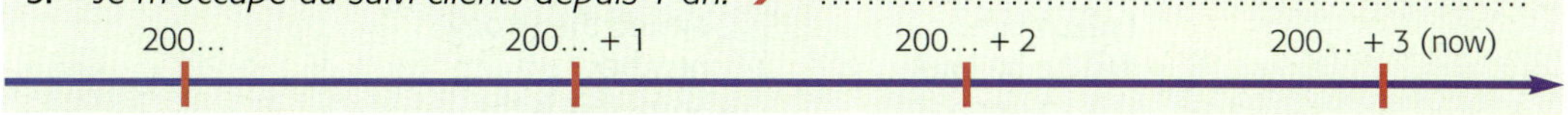

4. – *Mon séjour à l'étranger en juin 2002 m'a permis d'améliorer mes compétences en anglais.*
→ – ……………………………………………………………………………………………

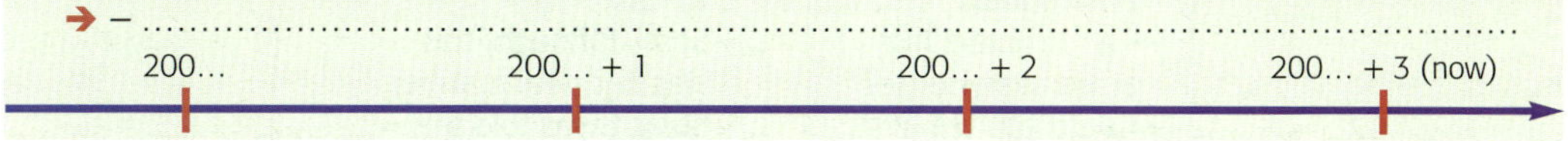

► Role play

You need your CV and letter of application to prepare the scene. Student **A** has applied for a work placement (or a first job) in the UK and has obtained an interview. Student **B** is the interviewer. Carry out the interview.

Listen to the job interview.

Unit 2 On the phone

Introducing yourself

You are calling

- Hello, Tony William calling.
- Good morning, Ms Simpson's office.
- Good afternoon, marketing department, Alice Dylan speaking.
- Hello, Office Equipment Ltd, personnel department.

You'd like to speak to sb

- Could I speak to Ms Jones, please?
- Is Mr Curtis there, please?
- I'd like to speak to Ms Hattaway. Is she in, please?
- Could you put me through to Ms Morrison, please?
- Could you please connect me with Mr Holmes?
- Can I have extension 504, please?
- Could you please put me through to the export department?
- Mr McEwan asked me to call him back.

OK

The person is not here

- When could I reach him?
- Will he be back this afternoon?
- Can I call back on Monday?
- Can I contact him at the warehouse?
- Could you tell him to call me when he's back? He can call me until 5 pm.
- Ok then, I'll call back tomorrow.

Wrong number

- Sorry, I must have dialled the wrong number.
- Sorry, this is the number I was asked to call.
- Sorry, I thought this was her new number.
- Sorry, I was told this was the purchasing department.
- Sorry, I was trying to get in touch with Mr Watson's assistant.

You are receiving a call

- Good morning, Ms Simpson's office. Can I help you?
- Good afternoon, marketing department, Alice Dylan speaking. What can I do for you?
- Hello, Office Equipment Ltd, personnel department. May I help you?

You give the information

- Yes, we received your order. Everything is all right.
- We're dealing with the shipment as agreed.
- I was expecting your call. etc.

You transfer the call

- Ok, I'm putting you through.
- Hold on, please, I'll see if he is in.
- Would you hold on, please? I'm checking.
- Hold the line, please. Sorry to keep you waiting.

Screening phone calls

- Who's calling, please?
- Can I ask who's calling, please?
- Who shall I say is calling, please?
- What is it about, please?

To your boss:

- Mr Holmes is on the line. Will you take the call?
- I have Mr Holmes on the line. He says it's a personal call.

You can't transfer the call

- I'm afraid he's still at the workshop. He told me you could call back in half an hour.
- Her line is busy at the moment. Can you call her back?
- Mr Holmes is not available right now. Shall I leave him a message?

Wrong number

- Sorry, you must have dialled the wrong number.
- Sorry, there is no one here by that name. What are you calling for?
- Are you sure you've dialled the right extension?

Ending the call

- Thank you very much, goodbye.
- Thank you for calling, goodbye.
- Thank you for your call. Have a nice day. Goodbye.

Unit 2

Advice on attitude

- Revise the key sentences (see "the balloons", p. 22-23).
- Always keep in mind what you are calling for.
- Plan your call: you can either note down the outlines of your call or create a flow chart (see "role play" p. 27).
- Use the name of the person you are calling, he / she will feel welcome. If you don't know his / her name, use "Sir" or "Madam"; never use "Mister" or "Ms" by itself.
- Make sure you understand what you are told by using phrases like "Could you repeat that, please?", "Could you spell your name, please?", "Is it a "p" or a "b"?", etc. (see "How to avoid misunderstanding").
- Be very polite. Avoid phrases such as "I want to"; use "I'd like to…", "Would you please…?", "Could you…?"
- End the conversation by reminding your correspondent of the main ideas, e.g. "So, I'll call him back tomorrow morning", "Well then, I'll check with Mr X to find out if he can come and see you on… and I'll email you his answer by tomorrow noon.", etc.

Your voice gives a picture of yourself. You should bear in mind that you are transmitting the company image. So don't shout but speak firmly and don't forget to smile!

How to avoid misunderstanding

- Sorry, would you mind repeating the address, please?
- Could you please speak more slowly?
- Sorry, I didn't catch what you said.
- Sorry, would you please repeat that last figure?
- I'm afraid it's a bad line. Could you speak up?
- How do you spell it, please?
- Is it her first name or her surname?
- Is he the personnel manager?
- Is that one word?
- Is it a "p" or a "b"?
- "G" for George.
- One hundred, one double O.

Exercises

1 Spelling

Make sure you know your alphabet and can count.

Student A dictates the following elements to student B who writes them down.

Write down the full details you are given.

2 Pronouncing

A • Pronounce and write down the words opposite.

[nəʊ] / [naʊ]
[θɔːt] / [θruː]
[letə^r] / [leɪtə^r]

B • Put the following words in the appropriate columns:

1 • [əʊ] or [aʊ]? : go / know / how / hello / hold
2 • [ɔː] or [uː]? : call / order / afternoon
3 • [e] or [eɪ]? : say / help / wait / ok

[əʊ]	[aʊ]	[ɔː]	[uː]	[e]	[eɪ]

C • How do you pronounce the modal auxiliaries in the following sentences? Choose the correct answer.

may / can / could / would / shall

1 • May I help you? ➔ [eɪ] – [e]
2 • Can I help you? ➔ [æ] – [ə]
3 • Could I speak to Ms Jones? ➔ [ʊ] – [ə]
4 • Would you hold on? ➔ [ʊ] – [ə]
5 • Shall I leave him a message? ➔ [æ] – [ə]

D • Pronounce the sentences below. Beware of the rising / falling intonations.

1 • Hello, Office Equipment Ltd, personnel department. May I help you?
2 • Is Mr Curtis there, please?
3 • Who's calling, please?
4 • Sorry, you must have dialled the wrong number.
5 • I'm afraid he's still at the workshop. He told me you could call back in half an hour.
6 • Thank you very much. Goodbye.

3 Vocabulary

A • Fill in the blanks with the following words in the appropriate forms.

toll free number / directory / reverse charge call / subscribers / area code / engaged / switchboard / extension / put through to / hold the line / enquiries / pick up / ring off / unlisted / dialling tone

1 • Before you call somebody, check the number in the ....
2 • The telephone is ringing. Why doesn't she .... the receiver?
3 • When you make a ...., the call is to be paid by the person called.
4 • Incoming calls to big firms are taken by a .... operator.
5 • You must have dialled the wrong ....
6 • In Great Britain, the .... is a series of bip-bip.
7 • For .... call 192 in the UK.
8 • If the operator is as unpleasant as yesterday, I'll ....
9 • – Is Mary Dylan there? – I'll see if she's in her office. .... , please.
10 • Mr Thompson is out. Shall I .... (you) his secretary?
11 • There must be something wrong. This line is .... all the time.
12 • I'm afraid I've been connected to the wrong ....
13 • The absent .... service.
14 • When you call a ...., you don't pay anything.
15 • I can't phone her; I haven't got her number and she is ....

B • In each pair, say which word is in British English and which one is in American English.

1 • engaged / busy
2 • directory / phone book
3 • ex-directory / unlisted
4 • collect charge / reverse charge call

► 4 Translate the sentences into French.

1 • *Ne quittez pas, je vous passe le poste 309.*
2 • *Je suis désolée, monsieur, Mr Holmes est absent jusqu'à lundi.*
3 • *Quand vous entendrez la tonalité, vous pourrez composer votre numéro.*
4 • *Merci de votre appel.*
5 • *C'est de la part de qui?*
6 • *Désolée, madame, Mr Parker est en conférence.*
7 • *Jane Eyre à l'appareil.*
8 • *Pourriez-vous épeler votre nom, s'il vous plaît?*
9 • *La ligne est si mauvaise que je peux à peine vous entendre.*
10 • *N'hésitez pas à m'appeler en PCV.*

► 5 Activities

A • Riceimport Ltd.

B • Listen to the dialogue and say what you have understood (type of document, number of people, male / female, what their conversation is about). Justify your remarks and put forward several hypotheses on their jobs, ages, etc. (see T&T: Modals)

C • You created this telephone memo so as not to forget to dispatch any information.

Listen to the two phone conversations and note down the two messages you've just received.

Tel. memo

Date: ....
Hour: ....
From: ....
....
To: ....
....
Tel / fax / email: ....
Message: ....
....
....
....

► Role play

1 • ***Étudiant A** : Vous êtes Mary Thomas, secrétaire de Mr Wilson, responsable des ventes. On vous téléphone.*
En anglais, vous allez :
– vous présenter ;
– expliquer que Mr Wilson n'est pas là, qu'il est absent pour la semaine ;
– demander à votre correspondant s'il veut laisser un message ;
– le prier de rappeler lundi prochain, votre patron sera là à partir d'environ 9 heures ;
– le remercier de son appel et prendre congé.
Étudiant B : vous improvisez les réponses.

2 • You sent Mr Thompson, Human Resources Manager for Philips, UK, an unsolicited letter of application three weeks ago for your work placement in two months' time and have not received an answer. You are calling them to find out if they received your letter and are prepared to take you on as a trilingual personal assistant trainee for six weeks.
Student A is the trainee who prepared the following flow chart.
Student B is the switchboard operator.
Student C is Mr Thompson.

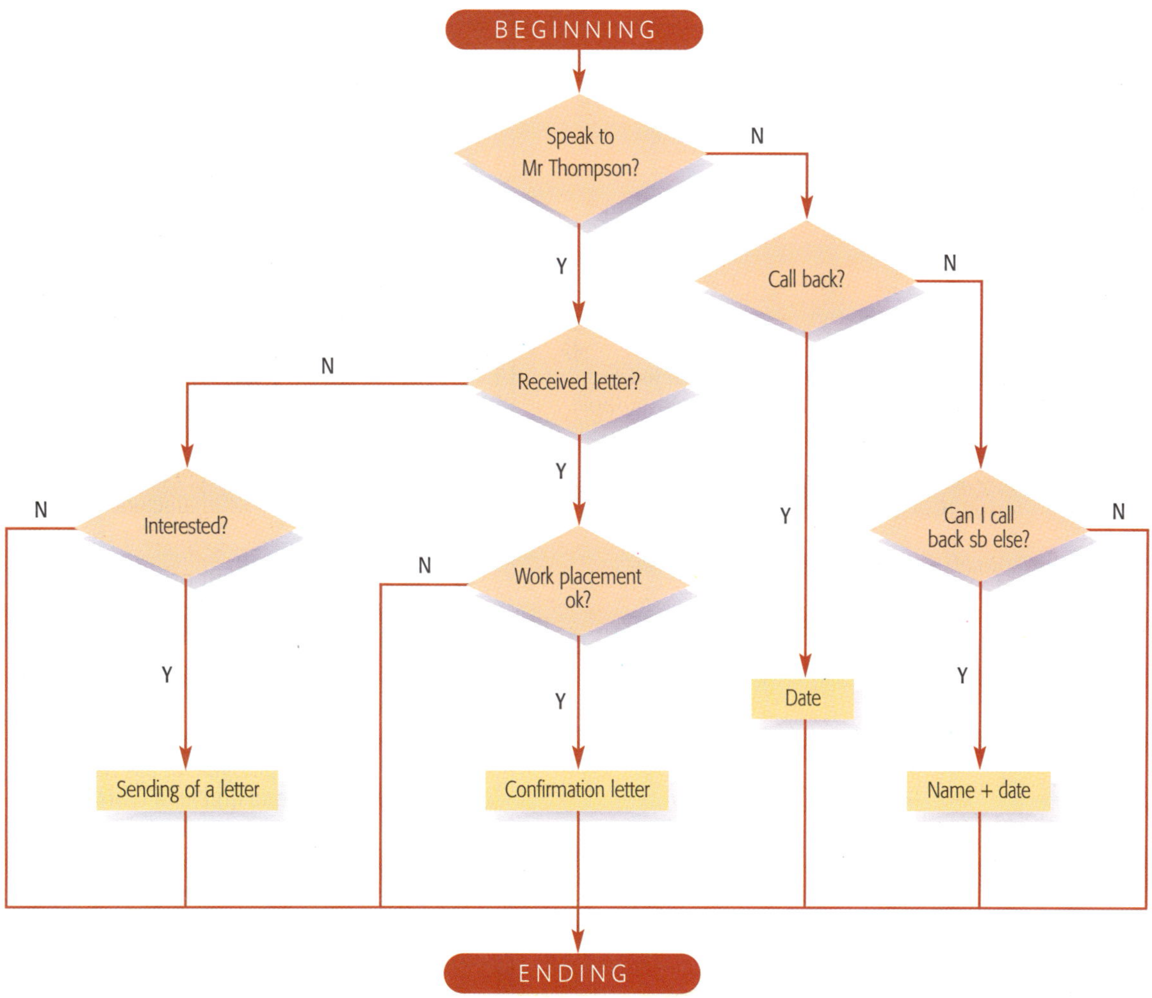

► 6 Thumbs do talking in Japan"
Listen, and answer the questions.

Corporate communication

Unit 3 Writing business letters

1 Letter layout

More or less formal layouts are adopted in companies. Here is a formal one that should be of some help for your exams and your first steps into the working world. Carefully memorise the following advice.

Lucy Bridgewood (1)
Marketing Department
Star Travel Agency (2)
23 King Street
Brighton BW2 5ER
UK

Personnel Manager
Artico Ltd (5)
74 Park Lane
London SW1 8NQ
UK

Your ref.: 02/03/MS (3)
Our ref.: LB302-SL

25 March 2003. (4)

For the attention of Mr Michael Steveman, Personnel Manager (6)

Dear Mr Steveman (7)

Literature for your personnel trips (8)

(9)

Further to your letter of 22 March 2003, we are pleased to send you the complete brochure of our wide range of products that we are sure will meet your personnel's demand.

You will also find enclosed our price list. Should your personnel be interested in package holidays, we can grant you special offers for company staff.

If you need any further details, do not hesitate to phone, fax or email us at the numbers and address mentioned below.

We thank you for having contacted us and look forward to hearing from you soon. (10)

Yours sincerely

L Bridgewood

Lucy Bridgewood (11)
Marketing Manager

Enc. 2 (12)

Star Travel Agency, 23 King Street, Brighton BW2 5ER, UK
Tel: +44 456 238 7935 Fax: +44 456 238 7930 Email: lbridgewood@startravel.co.uk (2)

1. Use **block style** (see "Writing a letter of application: Some advice" p. 16).
2. **The sender's address** is often already printed on **headed paper**. If it is not the case you can either centre it or type it on the left-hand side; indicate the name and department of the sender.
3. If you have **reference numbers,** type them below: "Your ref.: …" / "Our ref.: …".
4. Indicate the date: the most common form is 25 March 2003 (25/03/03) in the UK and March 25, 2003 (03/25/03) in the USA.
5. **The addressee's address** is typed on the right-hand side if you use a **window envelope** with at least the department or position of the addressee and if possible his / her name. If you don't use a window envelope, type it on the left-hand side beneath the date.
6. You may have to specify **"For the attention of …",** usually in bold characters.
7. See table opposite.
8. If you want **the content** of your letter to be quickly identified, indicate it either in bold characters or underlined. It can be preceded by "Re:". (Never use "Object" or "Subject").
9. **The body** of your letter.
10. To conclude your letter you should thank the addressee, apologise or ask him / her to contact you, and end with "I am looking forward to hearing from you (soon)".
11. Below "Yours …", write your signature (still on the left-hand side) followed by your name (which is usually in fact your manager's) and your department / position (same remark).
12. If you **enclose** documents, don't forget to indicate it under the form "Enc. 2" or "Enc. brochure and price list".

The addressee	Opening	Ending
Company's name / department	Dear Sirs	Yours faithfully
X manager	Dear Sir / Madam	Yours faithfully
Mr Thompson	Dear Mr Thompson	Yours sincerely
Mrs Arrow	Dear Mrs Arrow	Yours sincerely
Ms Silton[1]	Dear Ms Silton	Yours sincerely
Peter[2]	Dear Peter	Best regards / wishes

1 When you don't know whether or not the woman is married. This is used more and more, instead of Dear Mrs X.
2 When you know him / her well. Note that native speakers often quickly call people by their first name, so don't be surprised to be addressed by your first name, in which case your manner should nevertheless remain formal.

Exercises

1 Pronounce the following words and phrases.

1 • [staɪl] / [dɪ'pɑːtmənt] / [dɪəʳ sɜːʳz] / [fɔːʳ ði ə'tenʃᵊn əv]
2 • [mɪs] / [mɪz] / ['mɪsɪz]
3 • ['leɪaʊt] / [hedɪd peɪpəʳ]
4 • [ə'dres] / ['ædres'iː]
5 • [ɪn'kləʊzd] / [ɪn'kləʊʒəʳ]
6 • ['wɪndəʊ 'envələʊp] / ['refərəns 'nʌmbəʳ]
7 • [jɔːz 'feɪθfʊlɪ] / [jɔːz sɪn'ɪsəʳlɪ]

2 Decipher the words and translate them.

['lɪtrətʃəʳ] / ['brəʊʃəʳ] / ['fɜːðəʳ]

3 Rephrase the sentence.

"Should your personnel be interested in package holidays, we can grant you special offers for company staff."

4

Here are equivalents of words in the letter itself. Can you find those words?

Adjectives		Nouns	
full		discounts	
broad		staff	

5 You are working as the Personal Assistant of Mr William Jones, Sales Manager for Compucom, Birmingham. You will send letters to different companies. Compose only the layout of each letter, i.e. addresses, attention, subject, opening, ending, signature, enclosures.

1 • Rushton Connections, Linda Daniels. York.
2 • Osbourne House, Accounts Department. London.
3 • U.K.T. Dublin. You would like information on their latest computer microchips.
4 • The Loch Ness, Inverness. Bedrooms and conference room reservation.
5 • Meganet, Marketing Manager. Leeds. Open day. Schedule of the day enclosed.

6 Compose the letter in the correct order with the following elements.

1 • Peter Onslough
2 • 8 February 2003
3 • We are looking forward to hearing from you soon.
4 • Since this is a limited offer, please do not delay sending us your remittance.
5 • Newsmonth
Marketing Department
10, Kingscross Road
London SW3 9AL UK
6 • Dear Subscriber
7 • Signature
8 • On the enclosed invoice, you will note a special longer-term offer at a lower price per copy. You may, if you wish, extend your subscription.
9 • Penium ltd
54, rue Marbeuf
75008 Paris France
10 • Enc. 1
11 • Marketing Manager
12 • Thank you very much for your order. We hope that you enjoy receiving our magazine every month.
13 • Yours faithfully

2 Sending an email

Some advice

Here are a few guidelines for email etiquette:

- Always indicate a clear, straightforward and meaningful subject so that the addressee can quickly identify his / her emails.
- When you reply to an email, keep to the original matter. If you bring up something else, send another email on that subject.
- Generally speaking, your message should centre around one subject. If you want to inform the same person about different things, send as many corresponding emails. It will be clearer and the messages will be easier to file.
- Make separate paragraphs.
- Try to send relatively short emails.
- Take your time before writing emails; don't send an immediate email if you are angry with somebody, you may bitterly regret it later!
- Be accurate; specify reference numbers, order numbers, etc., so that the recipient can quickly deal with your request, for example.
- Be polite by using "please", "could you ...?", "thank you", etc., just as in letters.
- Check your grammar and spelling in dictionaries; computer auto-correction is unreliable for grammar.
- Don't forget to reread your email before sending it in order to check that you haven't forgotten anything and that its form and content are correct.

Exercises

1 Now have a look at the window from Hotmail on the opposite page and match the elements with their definitions.

1 • Icon for enclosing a file with your message.
2 • Icon you click on for keeping a copy of a message you haven't sent.
3 • Icon you click on for seeing the messages you have received and sent.
4 • Email addresses of the persons you are sending a copy of this message to, unknown to the other recipients.
5 • Email addresses of the persons you are sending a copy of this message to.
6 • Email address of the person you are writing to.
7 • Icon you click on for viewing all your email addresses.
8 • Key words describing the message you are sending.
9 • Email address of the sender.

2 Fill in the blanks in the email with the following verbs in the correct tenses.

1 • arrive	6 • be
2 • start	7 • be
3 • see	8 • be
4 • be	9 • be
5 • do	10 • give

3 Answer the questions.

1 • What does the small hand on the "Send" icon mean?
2 • What is "Hotmail"? Do you know other tools of that kind?

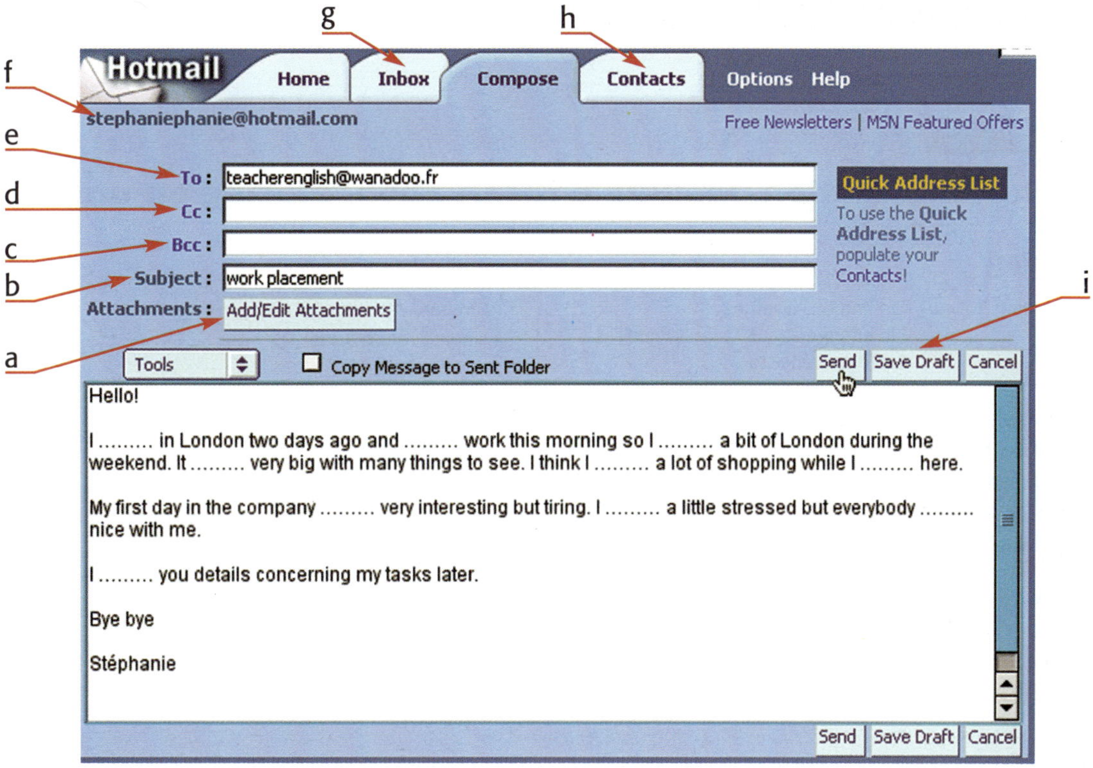

4 How do you pronounce these?

1 • [æt]
2 • [dotkɒm]
3 • [rɪ'plaɪ] / ['aɪkɒn] / [faɪl]
4 • ['mesɪdʒ] / ['edɪt]
5 • [rɪ'sɪpɪənt]
6 • [rɪ'siːv] / [dɪ'liːt]

5 Choose the correct form.

1 • We are writing to you
❑ **to inform** you that we have just received our goods.
❑ **for inform** you that we have just received our goods.
❑ **for to inform** you that we have just received our goods.

2 • We would like
❑ **for know** if we can pay you a visit on Monday 6 at 10 a.m.
❑ **knowing** if we can pay you a visit on Monday 6 at 10 a.m.
❑ **to know** if we can pay you a visit on Monday 6 at 10 a.m.

3 • Thank you
❑ **answering** by return.
❑ **for answering** by return.
❑ **to answer** by return.

4 • Would it be possible for you
❑ **calling us** for an appointment?
❑ **to call us** for an appointment?
❑ **for calling us** for an appointment?

5 • We are sorry
❑ **for telling you** we do not agree with your terms.
❑ **telling you** we do not agree with your terms.
❑ **to tell you** we do not agree with your terms.

6 • Do not hesitate
❑ **contacting us** for further information.
❑ **to contact us** for further information.
❑ **for contacting us** for further information.

3 Letter writing

Asking for information, making a reservation, placing an order

Vocabulary

- We are writing (to you) – to find out whether ...
  - – to enquire about ... [ɪn'kwaɪəʳ]
  - – with reference to ...
  - – further to ...
- We are contacting you to find out whether you could ...
- We would like to place an order for ...
- Could you please send us ... / tell us ...?
- We would be grateful if you could ... ['greɪtfl]
- We would appreciate it if you could ... [ə'priːʃɪeɪt]
- Would it be possible for you to ...?
- grant an X% discount / a discount for bulk order ['dɪskaʊnt]
- a price list
- a brochure / a leaflet / some literature
- single / twin / double bedrooms
- half-board / full-board
- a single / return ticket
- a season ticket
- a detailed estimate
- further details / information about ...
- as soon as possible
- Do not hesitate to contact us – for any further details.
  - – if you need any further information.
  - – should you need any information.
- We thank you – for your help.
  - – for faxing us your answer by return.
  - – for confirming our reservation.

Exercises

1 What form and tense?

1 • We .... a new product. (just / launched)

2 • We .... in acrylic fabrics for 10 years. (specialise)

3 • Our latest model .... now on display at our showroom. (be)

4 • You .... enclosed technical specifications together with the instructions for use. (find)

5 • Further details can .... on request. (obtain)

6 • You can also visit our website that .... (just / update)

2 The letter presented here contains many mistakes! Correct them.

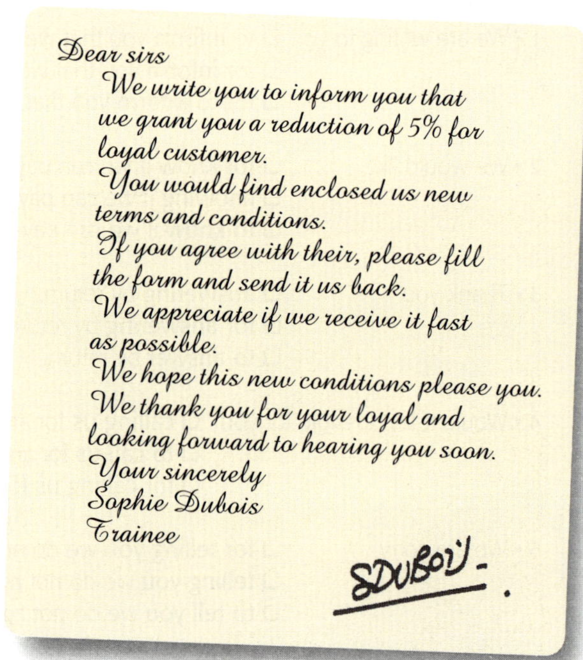
Dear sirs
We write you to inform you that we grant you a reduction of 5% for loyal customer.
You would find enclosed us new terms and conditions.
If you agree with their, please fill the form and send it us back.
We appreciate if we receive it fast as possible.
We hope this new conditions please you.
We thank you for your loyal and looking forward to hearing you soon.
Your sincerely
Sophie Dubois
Trainee
SDUBOIS

3 Write down the letter your boss is dictating.

4 For each of the following letters you have to put yourself in a different situation; having a look at exercise 4 in the next section may help you. Write the letters.

1 • **IMA, London**
You are a fruit import-export company that essentially works with Africa and southeast Asia. You want to know if IMA telemarketing services can help you with calls in African and southeast Asian languages.

2 • **British Airways, London**
You need to book a seat for a London-New York-London flight for your Managing Director, Mr Davidson (dates: 14-17 Jan. 2003), and you ask for a discount / season ticket for a business trip once a month for this destination.

3 • **The Central Hotel, Birmingham**
Reservation of bedrooms + half-board for a group of 10 executives for the Trade Fair.
Dates: 12-19 March 2003. As they intend to come several times a year, you ask if there is a conference room, a video conference room and / or bedroom suites (bedroom + office facilities).

4 • **Automotive Ltd, Liverpool**
You need a steel plate supplier for your car factory. Your web site: www.manucar.co.uk

5 • **Clear Service, Leicester**
You need maintenance service for your IT equipment (20 iMacs and printers, 4 laptops, 3 faxes, 8 phones, and 4 mobiles). Detailed estimate needed.

6 • **Office Furniture Ltd, Cardiff**
You are refurbishing your offices so you need 8 desks with chairs (ref. 53765) + 8 filing cabinets (ref. 59348). Delivery within 2 weeks. Place the order.

Writing positive or negative answers

Vocabulary

- With reference to / Further to } your letter / fax / email / order concerning ..., we ...
- We are pleased to tell / inform you that ...
- We are sorry for + N / V -ing
- We apologise for + N / V -ing [ə'pɒlədʒaɪz]
- Should you have any problems with your order, please let us know.
- owing to (for bad news) / due to / because of
- cancel
- a delay
- visit a company / pay a visit to a company / come and see sb
- make / obtain an appointment [ə'pɔɪntmənt]
- at your convenience [kən'viːnjəns]
- meet / suit the demand
- within a week
- in a month's time
- not until a month from now
- a regular / loyal customer
- fully booked / no vacancies

Exercises

1 [θ] or [ð]?

1 • within 3 • faithful 5 • thank
2 • month 4 • further 6 • although

2 **Put the following elements in the right order so as to write a letter correctly. Don't forget to add capital letters.**

Dear Ms Williams / we are looking forward to / Charles Wailes / thank you for / Personnel Manager / at 9 a.m. / and we would like you / yours sincerely / an interview / your completed application form / to come for / seeing you a week on Tuesday / your qualifications / interest us / at our office / and experience / on Tuesday 6 December

3 **Translate into English.**

1 • *Notre représentant peut passer chez vous pour une démonstration gratuite.*
2 • *Nous sommes heureux de vous informer que nous pouvons dorénavant assurer l'entretien 24 heures sur 24.*
3 • *Nous vous serions obligés de remettre la livraison à fin avril.*
4 • *Faites figurer votre numéro de compte client sur toute votre correspondance.*
5 • *Nous vous prions de nous adresser immédiatement un fax si cette modification vous convient.*
6 • *Recevez nos excuses pour ce dérangement.*

4 **Answer the letters you have just received (see previous section). Again, for each letter you have to imagine yourself in a different company.**

1 • *– Acceptation. Nombreux opérateurs de centres d'appels dont certains spécialisés dans les langues africaines, d'autres dans les langues asiatiques, tous en anglais.*
– Proposition d'aller visiter l'entreprise d'ici un mois pour mieux connaître la demande.
– Les contacter pour un rendez-vous.

2 • *– Réservation OK. Billets envoyés une semaine avant le départ.*
– Proposition d'abonnement sur vol Londres-New York-Londres pour client fidèle. Renseignements dans dépliant joint.

3 • *– Complet du 12 au 19 mars (Salon). Recommande le Princess Hotel (tel: 0594 324 785) qui a encore de la place.*
– The Central Hotel = 4 étoiles, de luxe, salle de visioconférence, ordinateurs, fax. Clientèle hommes / femmes d'affaires donc réservation de la salle un mois à l'avance.
– Excuses.

4 • *– Acceptation.*
– Rendez-vous à l'usine pour connaître les exigences.
– Le responsable du service ingénierie peut venir vous voir le mardi 16 février. Email ou fax par retour du courrier.

5 • *– Ci-joint devis.*
– Si pas réponse d'ici un mois, devis plus valable et annulé.

6 • *– Commande OK.*
– Grève des routiers donc livraison pas avant trois semaines.
– S'excuser et téléphoner dès que la date précise est connue.

Complaining

Vocabulary

- We acknowledge receipt of ... [ək'nɒlɪdʒ rɪ'si:t]
- the above-mentioned order / invoice / letter [əbʌv'menʃnd]
- We would be grateful if you could give us the reasons for this situation.
- We have no choice but to ...
- Would you be so kind as to replace this item?
- Very much to our regret, we must therefore cancel our order.
- unfortunately [ʌn'fɔ:tʃnətlɪ]
- unless
- instead of + N/V -ing

- duly ['dju:lɪ]
- damaged
- meet the delivery date
- behind schedule ['ʃedju:l]
- make up for
- ask for compensation
- refund
- the inconvenience caused
- faulty
- a hidden defect
- a dispute
- reservations

Exercises

1 Choose the correct word.

at / in / of / in / on / with / for

1 • This item is listed as No. 1234 .... our catalogue.
2 • The goods are to be collected .... our plant.
3 • We hope that you will grant us a 15% discount .... bulk order.
4 • Do not hesitate to place an order .... them.
5 • We hope your new range .... products will meet our requirements.
6 • We presume this is an error .... your part.
7 • Unfortunately, the goods have arrived .... bad condition.

2 How would you pronounce the following elements?

1 • 12/02/03 (GB date)
2 • 12/02/03 (US date)
3 • Ref. 584-ADSL/03
4 • # 98364
5 • 1.6 per unit
6 • US$30
7 • £13

3 Write the emails / faxes.

1 • – *Vous aviez passé commande de 3 classeurs de rangement. Commande N° 03-4672, réf. : B320 + B31 + B322. Or, vous avez reçu 3 chaises de bureau dont vous n'avez pas besoin.*
– *Vous demandez de procéder à l'échange dans la semaine.*

2 • – *Vous venez de recevoir votre facture N° 23/600.*
– *On vous avait consenti une remise de 5% sur catalogue avec port gratuit pour commande en gros qui n'apparaît pas sur la facture.*
– *Vous joignez le chèque du montant prévu et attendez facture correspondante par retour du courrier.*

3 • – *Vous deviez recevoir hier votre commande de pièces détachées (N° 3645).*
– *Allez-vous être livré cette semaine ? Sinon, risque de bloquer la fabrication de votre produit et d'entraîner des retards de livraison.*

4 • – *Vous accusez réception de votre commande N° AJ29.*
– *5 miroirs sont cassés. Échange avec réduction et livraison dans les 2 jours ou produits gratuits sur nouvelle commande ou bien remboursement ?*

Unit 4 Meeting people

1 Being introduced to each other

How to introduce yourself

Situation 1

– Good morning, Sir. May I help you?

– Good morning. Yes, I'm Harry Thornpike / My name's Harry Thornpike and I have an appointment with the Personnel Manager.

Situation 2

– Good afternoon, Sir.

– Good afternoon.

– You're Mr Sheridan, aren't you?

– Yes, that's right.

– And you've come to visit our plant, haven't you?

– Yes I have. You're the new secretary, aren't you?

– Yes I am, Mr Sheridan. Let me introduce myself. / May I introduce myself? My name is Bond, James Bond. Glad to meet you.

How to introduce someone else

– Ms Morrison, I'd like you to meet Ms Dylan. / Have you met Ms Dylan?

– How do you do, Ms Dylan. Pleased to meet you.

– How do you do, Ms Morrison. Nice to meet you.

© GettyImages / Taxi / Robert Brimson.

Meeting people you already know

Situation 1

– Nice to see you again.
How are you?

– Fine, thank you.
What about you?
How are you?

Situation 2

– Hello again.
How are you getting on?

– Very well, /
Fine, thanks.
How about you?

Saying goodbye

– Goodbye.
It was nice to have met you.
Have a nice trip / journey / evening.
See you soon / next month / in a few days.

– Thank you.
The same to you.
I'm so glad we've been able to meet.

► Exercises

1 Practise your pronunciation and intonation.

A • Listen to these dialogues again and say if the tone is rising or falling in the following series.

– May I help you?
– Have you met Ms Dylan?
– How are you?
– What about you?
– How are you getting on?

– Good morning.
– I'd like you to meet Ms Dylan.
– Pleased to meet you.
– Nice to see you again.
– Have a nice trip.
– See you soon.
– I'm so glad we've been able to meet.

Question tags (underlined)
– You're Mr Sheridan, <u>aren't you?</u>
– And you've come to visit our plant, <u>haven't you?</u>
– That's right. You're the new secretary, <u>aren't you?</u>

B • Among the following dialogues, which one suggests a formal relationship, a cool one, a warm one?

1 • – Hi John. How are you?
– Fine! Nice to meet you. I wanted to tell you about our new components. It happens that the delivery was delayed and …

2 • – Good morning, Miss Wilkes.
– Good morning, Mr Thompson. What can I do for you?
– I've an appointment with the Managing Director …

3 • – Hello Sarah!
– Hello Bob! What can I do for you?
– I'm trying to get in touch with Paul. Do you think you could call him on his bleeper?

► Role play

Each pair imagines a situation (hotel reception, bank counter, booking office, travel agency, etc.) and acts out the first contact. Use the dialogues above as a guide, and focus on your intonation.

2 Cultural differences

► Exercises

1 Listen to the recording and answer the following questions.

1 • What sort of document is it?
2 • Two main parts are developed. Which ones?
3 • Can you list the six points of the first part? Then explain them.
4 • Sum up what you have understood in the second part.
5 • What are the key words to understanding cross-cultural relationships?

2 Have you already been puzzled by a foreigner's attitude? Briefly describe the situation, analyse your attitude and draw a conclusion. (oral, or written in about 200 words)

3 Welcoming a visitor to the company

You don't know the visitor's name.

- Could I have your name, please?
- What can I do for you?
- Can I help you?
- Who gave you our name?

The visitor has given his / her name.

- Mrs Thornpike. Yes, that's right. You have an appointment with Miss Simpson, haven't you? I'm going to tell her you've just arrived and she will meet you in a minute. Please have a seat.
- Mr Melvis. Let me have a look. Oh yes, you phoned last week.

The visitor does not have an appointment.

- I don't know if Mr Ford will be able to see you this afternoon. He's very busy at the moment, but I'll do my best.
- Mr Ford would certainly have seen you if it had been possible, but unfortunately …
- I'm afraid it's going to be difficult for Mr Ford to see you this afternoon. Would you like to make an appointment with him next week? It'll be easier, I think.

The visitor has to wait

Try to make polite conversation.

- It's cold / sunny / rainy / windy this morning, isn't it?
- What a nice day it is today, isn't it?
- Did you find your way to our company easily?
- Can I get you a cup of tea / coffee?
- Would you like to have a look at our new brochure?

If the visitor has to wait for quite a long time, give an explanation. For instance:

- Mr Ford asked me to apologise. He's going to be late.
- Mr Ford called from his car. He's held up in a dreadful traffic jam.
- Mr Ford has missed his train. He is awfully sorry. He asked me to tell you how sorry he is. He won't be in until 5.
- Mr Ford was called away this afternoon. I'm afraid you'll have to wait. We do apologise for the inconvenience.

► Exercises

1 Complete the following dialogue.

– Good morning, ...?
– Good morning. I have an .... with Mr Carpenter.
– ....?
– Peter Martins.
– Mr Carpenter asked me to .... He is .... in a meeting with the General Manager. I am .... he .... be late.
– That's all right if he's not too long.
– Can I .... tea?
– No thank you.

2 Which question tags? (see T&T: Question tags)

1 • It's a bit complicated, ...?
2 • There was fog at Heathrow, ...?
3 • He doesn't really speak French, ...?
4 • You'll never forget that day, ...?
5 • We had a fright the other day, ...?
6 • They can't reserve a rented car, ...?
7 • She wants to fly to New York City, ...?
8 • Many people are always in a hurry, ...?
9 • It's been so nice, ...?
10 • I hardly know the Personnel Manager, ...?
11 • The police arrived too late, ...?
12 • Don't smoke in this room, ...?
13 • Let's have a drink, ...?

3 Translate into English.

1 • *Je vais me renseigner.*
2 • *Il vient de partir.*
3 • *Elle n'est pas encore arrivée.*
4 • *Elle est sur le point d'arriver.*
5 • *Je pensais que vous aviez pris rendez-vous.*
6 • *Je l'en informe tout de suite.*
7 • *Vous allez recevoir la confirmation dans une semaine.*
8 • *Je dois normalement la voir demain.*

► Role play

► 1 ***Vous êtes la secrétaire de Mr. Robinson. Vous accueillez un visiteur.***

- *Vous le saluez et lui demandez s'il a rendez-vous.*
- *Il vous répond que oui mais s'excuse d'être un peu en retard. Il se présente : Mr. Cheng, directeur de Beijing Computers.*
- *Vous lui répondez que ce n'est pas grave, car Mr. Robinson n'est pas encore revenu de son déjeuner d'affaires.*
- *Il vous demande où il peut l'attendre.*
- *Vous lui dites qu'il peut l'attendre à la réception si cela ne le dérange pas et vous lui demandez s'il veut une boisson.*

► 2 ***Votre patron, Mr. Clarks, vous a chargé d'accueillir Mr. Smith.***

- *Il vous demande de l'excuser car il a été retenu à l'usine pour un problème grave et ne pourra être à l'heure.*
- *Il vous demande de le faire patienter.*
- *Malheureusement pour vous, Mr. Smith n'est pas très enclin à la patience.*

Jouez la scène.

► 3 You are the new trainee. This is your first meeting with your tutor. You introduce yourself to him / her. Act out the dialogue.

4 Meeting a visitor at the airport / the station

► Exercises

► 1

Additional useful phrases

- Good morning. Are you Mr Karlsberg? I'm Pamela O'Connors. Pleased to meet you.
- Welcome to Ireland.
- How was your flight? / journey?
- Did you have a nice trip?
- We'll take a taxi. / My car is over there. / My car is in the car park (US = parking lot).
- I've booked a room for you at the X hotel.
- Would you like me to show you around?
- Is there anything I can do for you?

► Role play

You are to fetch Mr Esperanto, Production Manager for Goldco Ltd, Rio de Janeiro, Brazil, at the airport and drive him back to your company. You are thinking about the conversation you will have with him.
Formulate questions based on the following elements. (see T&T: Sentence patterns)
Other students will give the answers.

- his name
- his journey
- his company name
- his position within the company
- his home country
- the town where he works (name, size, location)
- the place where he lives (name, size, location, distance from work)
- his family
- the weather in his country
- first visit to London?
- the places he knows in London
- other visits to Europe?
- the frequency of his visits to Europe

► 2 Miscellaneous

© Pascal Sittler / Réa.

A • What would you answer to the following questions?

1 • What do you do?
2 • What are you doing?
3 • How are you?
4 • How are you getting on?
5 • How are you doing?
6 • How long have you been working here?
7 • How far do you live from your workplace?
8 • How long does it take you to get to the company?
9 • When did we last meet?
10 • How much is my return ticket?
11 • How many emails a day do you have to deal with?

B • Who's who? (see T&T: Adjectives)

1 • Mr Suhami is from Indonesia; he's an ....
2 • Mr Barak is from Hungary; he's a ....
3 • Ms Garcia is from Spain; she's a ....
4 • Miss Yamamoto is from Japan; she's a ....
5 • Mr Ben Jouli is from Morocco; he's a ....
6 • Mr O'Sullivan is from Ireland; he's an ....
7 • Mrs Cohen is from Israel; she's an ....

C • *A* or *an*? (see T&T: Articles)

1 • Argentinian 2 • Chilean 3 • Honduran 4 • Iraqi 5 • Uruguayan 6 • Yemeni

D • Check your general knowledge. (see Passport: World table)

1 • In order to link the capitals with their countries, ask as many questions as you can.
Ex.: What's the capital of Cambodia? Is Phnom Penh the capital of Cambodia? Phnom Penh is the capital of Cambodia, isn't it? Are you sure Phnom Penh is the capital of Cambodia? Etc.

Ottawa / Bern / Ankara / Amsterdam / Kuala Lumpur / Copenhagen / Pretoria / Vienna / Bogota / Cairo / London / New Delhi / Beijing

2 • Fill in the grid.

Capital	Country	An inhabitant	The inhabitants
	Austria		
	Canada		
	China		
	Colombia		
	Denmark		
	Egypt		
	India		
	Malaysia		
	The Netherlands		
	South Africa		
	Switzerland		
	Turkey		
	The UK		

► Pair work

Group A chooses six (2×3) countries from those listed below without telling the other group.
Group B is in charge of asking questions so as to guess the countries.
With the questions and the answers, try to make as long a conversation as possible, and don't turn to the Passport section too fast!

– 3 countries in the Middle East
– 3 countries in the EU
– 3 countries belonging to the Commonwealth
– 3 African states
– 3 NICs (Newly Industrialised Countries)
– 3 Asian countries
– 3 countries in the Far East
– 3 Latin American countries

► Group work

► Stereotypes
Look at the drawings on the next page.

A • **What is described?**

B • **Here are adjectives that might be of some help.**
Which ones are the synonyms, which ones the opposites?

1 • controlled → self-controlled / calm / restrained / irritated / annoyed / uncontrolled
2 • patient → eager / hot-tempered / composed / enduring / serene / impatient
3 • available → missing / free / absent / away / unavailable
4 • humble → discreet / conceited / vain / modest / reserved / proud
5 • humorous → funny / boring / sad / witty / serious
6 • talkative → voluble / reserved / silent / uncommunicative / loquacious
7 • generous → selfish / unselfish / benevolent / mean / charitable / avaricious
8 • famous → well-known / unknown
9 • organised → methodical / disorderly / orderly / confused
10 • discreet → ill-advised / discerning / inconsiderate / tactful / indiscreet
11 • flexible → monovalent / adaptable / versatile

C • **Give the stereotype implied in each drawing.**

D • Do you agree with these stereotypes?

E • Can you think of other well-known stereotypes concerning the inhabitants of the EU?

► **Role play**

► Socialising

You are in charge of driving Mr Cardigan, a Scot, from the station to your company and then to his hotel.
Of course, you will remember that you won't really "talk business", that you will avoid some topics and that you will essentially have a social conversation.

A • What topics should definitely be avoided?

B • Choose a few attitudes that you will try to compare (Great Britain / France / Spain / Germany).

Ex.: – food habits: cuisine, meal times, …
– work: office hours, what to wear, …
– entertainments: pub, cinema, …
– leisure: sport, holidays, …
– manners and temper: cold, warm, …

C • Act out the dialogue.

Unit 5 In the workplace

1 Company organisation

► Exercises

► 1 The premises

In your job, you will be in daily contact with people working in the same company as you do but into different premises. Here are the main terms you should remember.

Pronounce the following words and say which ones are synonyms. Then, try to match them with the drawings and explain how the differents elements can be associated.

1 • [ə'fɪlɪeɪt]
2 • [hed 'ɒfɪs]
3 • [plɑ:nt]
4 • [brɑ:nʃ]
5 • [hed'kwɒ:təz]
6 • [səb'sɪdjərɪ]
7 • [fæktrɪ]
8 • ['ɒfɪsɪz]
9 • ['weəhaʊs]

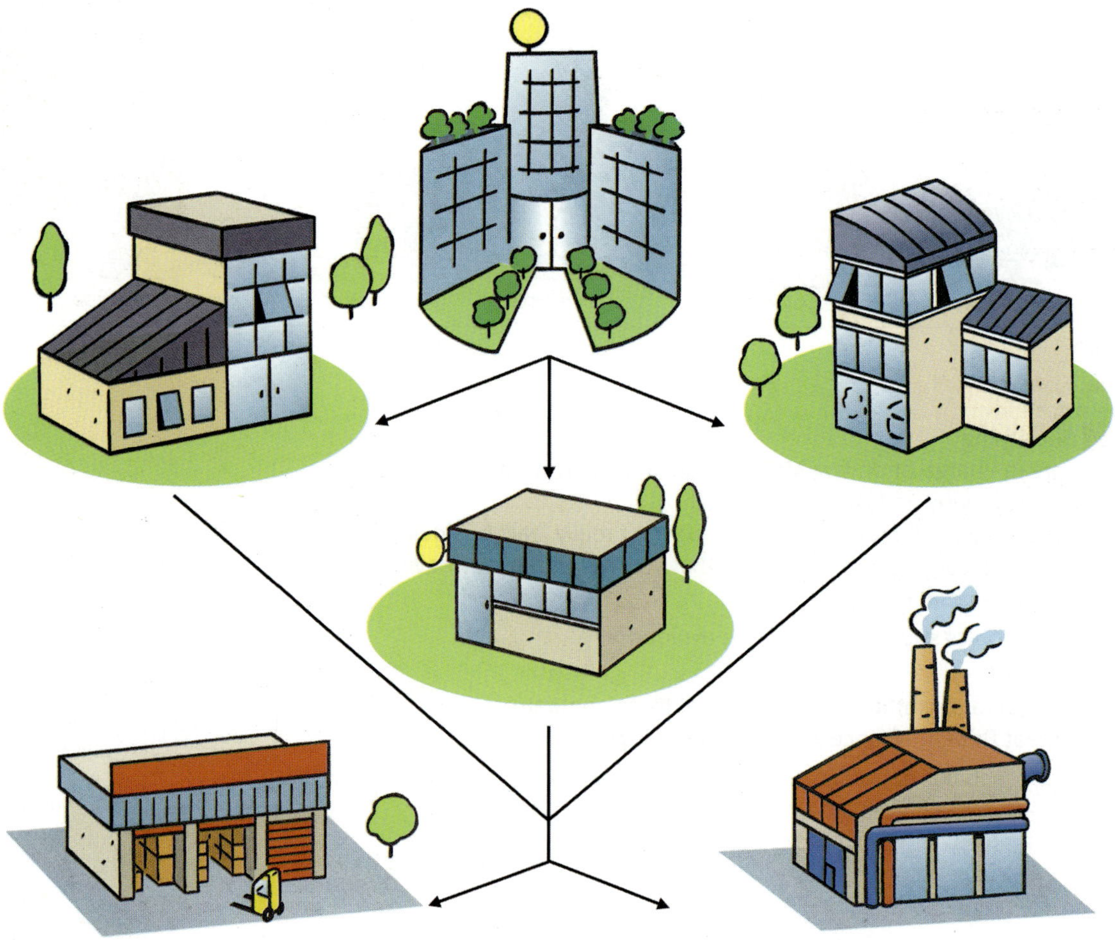

2 The departments

When you contact somebody within the company you are working for or in another company, you need to know what the main departments are in charge of.

A • Fill in the blanks with the following words.

research and development / sales / information technology / quality / human resources / safety / production / accounts / purchasing

1 • **The** .... **department** deals with invoices.
2 • **The** .... **department** is in charge of manufacturing products.
3 • **The** .... **department** collects all the company data.
4 • **The** .... **department** deals with the staff.
5 • **The** .... **department** buys all the goods the company needs.
6 • **The** .... **department** studies the prospective improvements of the company.
7 • **The** .... **department** ensures that the company cannot cause damage or harm.
8 • **The** .... **department** is responsible for what the company sells.
9 • **The** .... **department** checks if the products, the environment, safety, management, ... respect the highest standards.

B • Abbreviations are often used for three of these departments. Which ones?

2 Places and directions

Exercises

You very frequently have to direct visitors to departments or premises within the company.

1 Here is a company site map. Use the correct prepositions and adverbs to give directions to visitors who need to go to the following places:

Ex. : the delivery building
When you go .... the office, cross the main road. It's just .... . If you miss it, drive .... the roundabout to find your way .... .

1 • the factory
2 • the warehouse
3 • the shipment building

Unit 5

2 Have a look at the **office map** and explain to the visitors how to get to:

- the General Manager's office
- the Accounts Manager's office
- the toilets
- the lift

① Reception ② Personal Assistant
③ General Manager ④ Records
⑤ Accounts Manager ⑥ Photocopying
⑦ Lift ⑧ Canteen ⑨ Gents ⑩ Ladies
⑪ Stationery store

3 Office equipment

Office equipment has been on the move for some years. Yet the basics remain. You may often have to order stationery or furniture, and sometimes some of your best friends or worst enemies are office automation tools…

Exercises

1 Office stationery

A • **How many sorts of pens can you name in English? Make a list of them and translate.**

B • **You know that in English some nouns are countable whereas others are uncountable. If a quantifier is put before an uncountable noun, the phrase becomes countable. (see T&T: Countables / uncountables / Quantifiers)**

Ex.: advice → a piece of advice

What quantifier would you put with the following nouns? scissors / paper / glue / tape

C • **Which is which? Match the words with their corresponding translation.**

headed paper / a paper clip / a wastepaper basket / an index card / a rubber pen / a file / brown wrapping paper / staples / a folder / an out-tray / a note pad

un taille-crayons / une pochette plastique / une corbeille à courrier entrant / une enveloppe / une règle / un repositionneur / un intercalaire / une gomme / un timbre / du papier d'emballage / une agrafeuse / un calepin / un transparent

a ruler	
a rubber	
	un effaceur
a pencil sharpener	
a stapler	
	des agrafes
	un trombone
a self-stick note	
a notebook	
	un bloc-notes
	du papier à en-tête
wrapping paper	

	du papier kraft®
an envelope	
a stamp	
	une fiche cartonnée
a transparency	
a plastic folder	
a divider	
	une chemise
	un classeur
an in-tray	
	une corbeille à courrier sortant
	une corbeille à papier

2 Office furniture

Make sure you are able to use the correct prepositions.

1 • When I'm working ... my desk, I feel better ... a chair than ... an armchair.
2 • Where is Mr Stones's file? – It's ... the filing cabinet ... the second shelf ... the top.
3 • Remember you mustn't lean ... the pull-out flap.
4 • Could you please avoid putting important documents ... this pile of paper?
... the pile should be more logical, shouldn't it?
5 • As you don't often use this tray, don't you think that putting it ... the cupboard would make more room ... your desk?
6 • I'll spend some time tomorrow tidying up the place. My drawers are ... such a mess!
7 • The hanging files ... the bottom row should be replaced, they're really worn-out.

3 Office automation

Office automation (OA) corresponds to all the electronically-controlled tools that can be used in an office.

A • **Let's start with the smallest, in other words the pocket-sized or handheld devices. Do you know their English names?**

1 • We can send and receive calls with ....
2 • .... is used to send and receive documents electronically. It is sometimes coupled with a telephone.
3 • Your boss has dictated what he wants you to type on this device: ....
4 • When we need to calculate something or convert currencies we may use ....
5 • This palm-sized electronic tool is constantly evolving. Today it can offer an address book, a timetable, a translator, a dictionary, a note pad, mail and, in the case of the most sophisticated ones, a video, photo and music drive plus word processing and spreadsheet; it can also be connected to a computer. It works with keys and / or with an optical pencil. The simplest ones are called .... and the most sophisticated ones, ...

B • **Look at the following photos and give each element its English name.**

a mouse / a CD or a DVD / a laptop / a screen / a drive / a scanner / a printer / a video projector / a keyboard / a personal computer / (loud)speakers / a floppy or a floppy disk

C • What do these abbreviations stand for?

Ex.: PC stands for personal computer.

1 • CPU 2 • CD 3 • DVD 4 • CD-RW

D • Is "software" a countable or an uncountable noun? Use the word in a sentence.

E • Use the following words when translating the sentences below.

downloading / software / cordless / spreadsheet / network / processor / word processing / hard disk

1 • *De plus en plus d'ordinateurs sont équipés de souris sans fil.*
2 • *Quel processeur as-tu choisi ?*
3 • *Son disque dur semble saturé.*
4 • *Quel logiciel utilisent-ils le plus souvent : le traitement de textes ou le tableur ?*
5 • *Le téléchargement peut parfois être très long.*
6 • *Je suppose que vous travaillez en réseau.*

F • What do the two keyboards correspond to?

Even if you have a B keyboard, your computer enables you to type as if you had an A keyboard, so try to train yourself regularly with each.

Keyboard A

Keyboard B

G • Crossword

Across

1 • Tools used to project a transparency on a screen.
2 • Tool used to send information along a telephone line.
3 • Short time for relaxing.
4 • Part of a computer made of silicon and electronic circuits.
5 • Tool that can be connected to a computer.
6 • Information stored in a computer.
7 • Piece of furniture we work on.
8 • Typing and laying out documents on a computer.
9 • Relate, connect.
10 • Transmit information from an electronic tool to another one.
11 • Computerised office system.
12 • Meeting with people in different places made possible thanks to an audio and video system.

Down

a • OA.
b • Tool used to type.
c • Improved, promoted.
d • Letter sent by computer.
e • Cell phones.
f • Cordless.
g • PC.
h • Give a new version.
i • Key in information on a computer.
j • Building or room where we work.
k • Register information on a computer, a floppy or a CD.
l • Opposite of old.
m • Software used for calculation.

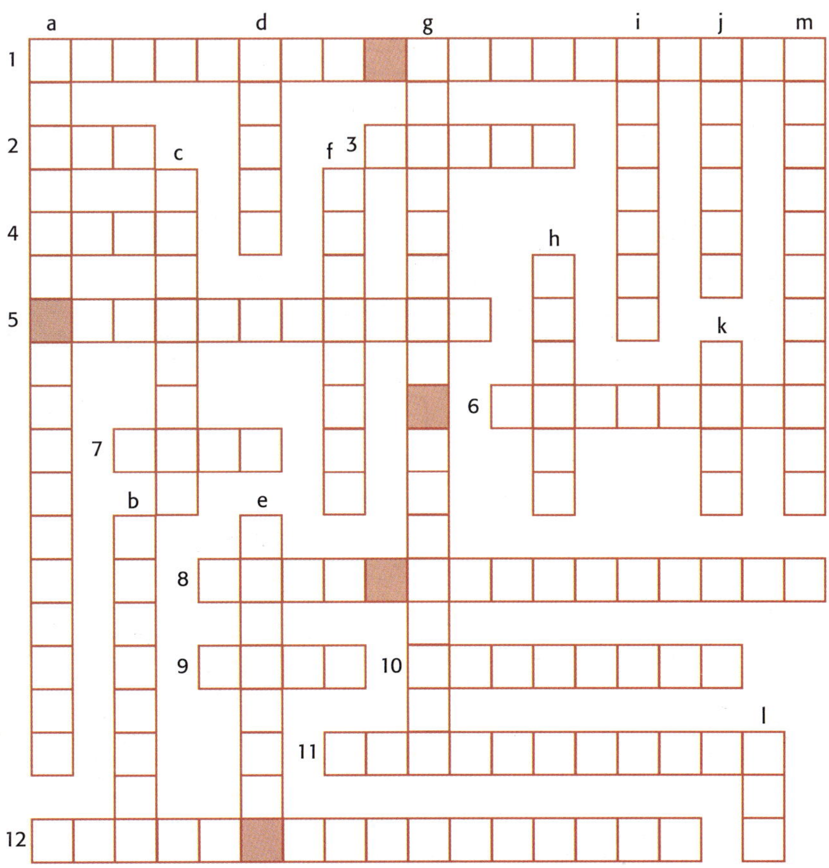

4 Office layout

Office layout refers to the arrangement of workstations, equipment and furniture in an office. A well-planned layout can make work flow more easily, help reduce employee fatigue and use office space more efficiently.

► Exercises

► 1 Refurbishing

A • This is the place you are currently working in: your office and your manager's office. As the two offices are not at all ergonomic, your manager has asked you to refurbish them both. First, you may need some of the following words. Can you decipher them and match them with their illustration?

a • [desk]	c • [tʃeəʳ]	e • [prɪntəʳ]	g • [plaːnts]	i • [fæks]	k • ['stɔːrɪdʒ 'juːnɪt]
b • ['telɪphəʊn]	d • [aːm'tʃeəʳ]	f • [kəm'pjuːtəʳ]	h • ['faɪlɪŋ 'kæbɪnɪt]	j • [læmp]	l • ['wɔːdrəʊb]

B • ► **Group work**

Students A and B try to find the best solution and then explain it to student C who will be the manager and who will give his / her point of view. Once all the groups have come to an agreement and outlined their projects, you can then decide which refurbishment is the best. You may need some phrases expressing suggestion, agreement, disagreement. (see T&T: A few phrases to express yourself)

► 2 Fitting out

Sometimes you need to fit out a meeting room for a conference or a stall at a trade fair, which requires preparation and organisational skills.

► **Group work**

Imagine the following situation.

The quality manager is to give a conference on the situation of the company in terms of environment and the improvements that could be made. Breakfast will be offered before the conference and refreshment will be proposed for the mid-morning break.
In the company, there is a meeting room that can hold 50 people. At the moment, it has tables and chairs for 50 people, a telephone-fax, an overhead projector, a filing cabinet with stationery, a cupboard with a computer and a video projector.
You are in charge of fitting out the room for 25 people, the quality manager and yourself.

For the conference, they will need:

– an overhead projector,
– a computer with a video projector,
– tables and chairs for all the participants,
– what is necessary for the breakfast and the mid-morning break.

Draw the layout of the room and explain your choices.

Vocabulary

abonné : subscriber
abonnement : subscription → subscribe (v.)
accéder à des données : access data
accord : agreement
accorder : grant
accueil : welcome → welcome (v.)
accuser réception de : acknowledge receipt of
actualiser : update
affaires (déjeuner / dîner) : business (lunch / dinner)
affranchir (main / machine) : stamp / frank
agence pour l'emploi : job centre (GB) / center (US)
agenda : diary
annuaire (tél.) : directory (GB), phone book (US)
annulation : cancellation → cancel (v.)
appel (entrant / sortant) : (incoming / outgoing) call
appeler en PCV : make a reverse charge call (GB) / a collect call (US)
appel urgent : emergency call
appeler (tél.) : call, ring up, phone
archives : records → record (v.)
assistée par ordinateur (conception), CAO : computer-aided design, CAD
assister à : attend
atelier : workshop
attendant vos instructions (en) : awaiting / pending your instructions
attendant avec impatience de (en) : looking forward to + V-ing
attention de (à l') : for / to the attention of
attirer l'attention de … sur … : draw sb's attention to
augmentation de salaire : pay rise, wage increase
automatisation : automation → automate (v.)
avancement : promotion → be promoted
avantage : advantage
avantages en nature : benefits, perks

base : basis (pl. bases)
base (de) : basic
bloc-notes : writing pad
bourse de l'emploi : employment exchange
bulletin de salaire : pay slip
bureautique : office automation, OA

cabine téléphonique : phone box
cadre (supérieur) : (senior) executive
candidat à un emploi : applicant → apply for (v.)
candidature : application
caractéristiques techniques : specifications
charger : load
chef d'entreprise : entrepreneur
chef de service : manager
chercher (emploi) : look for, seek
ci-dessous : below
ci-dessus : above
ci-joint : enclosed, attached
citoyen(neté) : citizen(ship)
classement : filing → file (v.)
comité d'entreprise : works committee / council
commande (en gros) : (bulk) order → order, place an order (v.)
comme convenu : as agreed
commission (à la) : on commission
compatible : compatible
compétence : skill, expertise
composer un numéro : dial
comptabilité (la) : accountancy , accounting
comptable (n.) : accountant
concernant : concerning, as regards, regarding
conditions : conditions
confirmer : confirm
conformément à : as per, in accordance with
connaissances : knowledge [U]
convaincus (nous sommes) : we trust that …
congé (être en) : (be on) leave
congé (jour de) : day off
congé maladie / de maternité : sick / maternity leave
congés payés : paid holidays (GB) / vacation (US), paid leave
conseiller (n.) : consultant
conseils : advice [U] → advise (v.)
contrat : contract
contrat à durée déterminée, CDD : fixed-term (work) contract
contrat à durée déterminée, CDI : permanent (work) contract
convivial (machine) : user-friendly
copier(-coller) : copy(-and-paste)
couper (tél.) : cut off
courrier : letters, mail [U]
courrier électronique : email
curriculum vitae, CV : curriculum vitae, CV, résumé (US)

dactylographe : typist
dactylographie : typing → type (v.)
date limite : deadline
décharger : unload
décrocher (tél) : pick up the receiver
délai de (dans un) : within

demande de : request for
demande (sur) : on request
demandeur d'emploi : job hunter / seeker
dérangement (en) : out of order
dérangement (occasionné) : inconvenience
détaillant : retailer → retail (v.)
dévoué: committed, dedicated
dictaphone : dictaphone
dicter : dictate
diplôme : degree, qualifications
diriger (une société) : run
documentation : literature (U)
donnée : datum (pl. data)
double (n.) : copy
dû à : due to, owing to (bad news), because of

---

effacer (traitement de texte) : delete
effectuer (tâche) : carry out, perform
embaucher : employ, hire, take on
employé (n.) : employee
employeur : employer
en-tête : heading
entreprise : business, company, concern, entreprise, firm
entreprise (d') : corporate (adj.)
entrée (de données) : input → input (v.)
entretien (machine) : maintenance → maintain (v.)
entretien (d'embauche) : (job) interview
équipement (installations) : facilities
ergonomie : ergonomics (U)
essai : test → test (v.)
essai (engager à l') : (hire on) probation
étranger (à l') : abroad, overseas
évaluation : assessment → assess (v.)
excuses : apologies → apologise (v.)
exemplaire (n.) : copy
exigeant : demanding → demand (v.)
exprime bien (qui s') : articulate

---

facture : invoice → invoice (v.)
flexible (personne) : flexible → flexibility
flexible (horaire) : flexitime, flextime
filiale : affiliate, subsidiary
fonctionnaire : civil servant
fonctionner : work
fonctionner (faire) : operate
forfaitaire : package
formation dans l'entreprise : in-house training
formation professionnelle : vocational training
formation sur le tas : on-the-job training
formulaire : form
fournitures de bureau : office supplies
frais : charges, costs, expenses

---

gérant : manager
gestion : management → manage (v.)
grossiste : wholesaler → wholesale (adj.)

---

héberger : host
heures de travail : working hours
heures supplémentaires (faire des) : (work) overtime
homologue (n.) : counterpart
horaire(s) : schedule
hors service : out of order

---

inconvénient : drawback
indemnité : allowance
informatique (n.) : computing , information technology, IT
informatique (n.) (traitement des données) : data-processing
informatiser : computerise
intérimaire : temp → temp (v.)
invité (n.) : guest, visitor
itinéraire : route

---

joindre (qqn) : contact, get in touch with

---

lettre de motivation : letter of application
lettre de relance : follow-up letter, reminder
liaison (contrat, collaboration) : liaison
liaison avec qqn (assurer la) : liaise
libre (chambre, poste) : available, vacant
lisible : legible
liste rouge (sur) : ex-directory (GB), unlisted (US)
livraison : delivery → deliver (v.)
local (n.) : premises
logiciel : software (U)

---

machine à affranchir : franking machine
machine à commande numérique : digitally-controlled machine
machine à écrire : typewriter
maison mère : parent company
matériel de bureau : office equipment
mémoire morte : read-only memory, ROM
mémoire vive : random access memory, RAM
mentionner : mention
menu : menu

micro-ordinateur : microprocessor
mise à jour : updating → update (v.)
mise en forme / en page : layout → lay out (v.)
mobilité : mobility
mode d'emploi : instructions for use
modem : modem
motivation : motivation → motivate (v.)
multiculturel : cross-cultural

nationalité (double) : (dual) nationality
négocier : negotiate
note : memo
numérique : digital
numériser : digitise
numéro vert : Freefone (GB), toll-free number (US)

occupé (tél.) : busy (US), engaged (GB)
octet (mega, giga) : (mega, giga) byte
offre : offer → offer (v.)
ordinateur de bureau : desktop computer
ordinateur personnel : personal computer, PC
ordinateur portable : laptop
ordre du jour : agenda
organigramme : organisation chart

panne (en) : out of order
panne (tomber en) : break down
papeterie (produits) : stationery
passeport (titulaire d'un) : passport (holder)
passer qqn à qqn (tél.) : put sb through to sb
patron : boss, employer, manager, owner
pause : break
performant : efficient
périphérique (n.) : peripheral
permis de travail : green card (US), work permit
personnel (adj.) : personal
personnel (n.) : personnel, staff
petites annonces : ads, classified advertisements/ads, classifieds
pièce jointe : enclosure
pirater : copycat
planning : schedule
pli séparé (sous) : under separate cover
police (de caractères) : (character) font
polyvalent : versatile
port dû : carriage forward
port payé : carriage paid
poste (téléphone) : extension
poste (emploi) : job, occupation, position, post
poste à pourvoir / vacant : vacant post, vacancy
poste de travail posté : shift
posté (travail) : shift work
préavis (donner son) : give notice
présenter (se) : introduce (oneself)
prime de rendement : incentive bonus
promotion : promotion → promote (v.)
proposer : offer
proposition : proposal
puce électronique : (micro)chip

raccrocher (tél.) : hang up, ring off
raison de (en) : due to, owing to (bad news), because of
rappeler (tél.) : call back
réception (dès) : on receipt
réception (lieu) : reception
recherche d'emploi : job hunting / seeking
réclamation : complaint → complain about (v.)
reconversion : retraining → retrain (v.)
référence : reference
relations publiques (un chargé des) : public relations (officer), PR(O)
relier à : connect to
rendez-vous (prendre) : (make) an appointment
renseignements : details, information (U)
renseignements (téléphoniques) : enquiries
réparation : repair → fix, repair (v.)
répondeur : answering machine
répondre aux besoins : meet the demand
réponse à : answer to, reply to → answer sb, reply to sb (v.)
réponse à (en) : in answer to, in reply to
reporter : postpone, put off
représentant de commerce : rep, representative, travelling salesman
reproduire un document : duplicate
réseau : network
retard : delay
réunion : meeting

saisie (de données) : capture, input, keyboarding → capture, input, key(board) in (v.)
salaire (brut / net) : (gross / net) pay, salary, wage
salon (exposition) : fair
sans fil : wireless
sauvegarder : save
sécurité sociale : National Insurance (GB), Social Security (US)

sélectionner : short-list
serveur : server
service : department
service (prestation) : service
société : business, company, firm, concern (GB), corporation (US)
sonnerie d'appel : ringing tone
stage : internship (US), work experience / placement (GB)
stagiaire : intern (US), trainee
standard(iste) : switchboard (operator)
sténodactylographe : shorthand typist
sténodactylographie : shorthand typing
sténographie (prendre en) : (take in) shorthand
suite à : further to, with reference to
suivi (n.) : follow-up

taper (ordinateur) : key
technique de pointe : hi-tech, high tech, high technology
télécharger : download
téléconférence : videoconference
télécopie : facsimile, fax → fax (v.)
temps utile (en) : in due course
ticket-restaurant : luncheon voucher (GB), meal ticket (US)
tonalité : dialling tone
tonalité de paiement : pay tone
touche (clavier) : key
traitement de texte (logiciel) : word processor (software), WP
traitement de texte (technique) : word processing
transmettre : forward
travail (le) : work [U]
travail (un) : job, occupation
travail au noir : moonlighting → moonlight (v.)
travail en équipe : teamwork
travail posté, par équipes : shift work
travail temporaire (le) : temporary work, temping
travailler à temps partiel / plein : work part-time / full-time
travailler en réseau : work within a network
travailleur à temps partiel / plein : part-timer / full-timer
travailleur temporaire : temp → temp (v.)

unité centrale : central processing unit, CPU

ventes : sales
veuillez agréer, Madame / Monsieur, l'expression de ... : Yours sincerely / faithfully
voiture de fonction : company car
voyage d'affaires (effectuer) : (make) a business trip
voyages : travel [U] → travel (v.)

Frequently used abbreviations

agy: agency
approx.: approximately
attn: for the attention of
av.: average
avail.: available
bens / bnfts: benefits
b/g: background
c.: circa: approximately
comm.: commission
conf.: confirm
enc.: enclosure
EMT: English as a mother tongue
eng.: engineer
exec.: executive
ex. sec.: executive secretary
exp.: experience / experienced
FAO: for the attention of
f/t: full time
hpw: hours per week
hq: headquarters
hrs: hours
inc.: income
jn / jnr: junior
K: kilo: thousand
Mon-Fri: from Monday to Friday
MT: mother tongue
neg.: negotiable
OTE: on-target earnings
p.a. / p/a: per annum
p/h: per hour
pkge: package
pls: please
PR: public relations
prev.: previous
p/t: part time
p/w: per week
req.: required
sae: stamped addressed envelope
sase: self-addressed stamped envelope
SME: small- and medium-sized enterprise
snr / sr: senior
w/: with
w/e: weekend
WP: word processing
wpm: words per minute
yrs: years

The business world

PART I

Unit 1

Launching, advertising, promoting

A few landmarks

Advertising

► **What are the purposes of advertising?**
- to increase sales
- to inform consumers about new products
- to promote a brand name (or trademark)

► **Who uses advertising?**
- firms
- charities
- the government
- the public

► **To whom is it important?**
It is important to manufacturers, suppliers and consumers.

► **Advantages of advertising**
- It informs.
- It encourages competition between firms.
- Firms sell more products, hence mass production lowers prices.
- It finances commercial radio and TV and keeps the price of newspapers low.

► **Drawbacks**
- It brainwashes people into buying what they don't really need or what they can't afford.
- It can be misleading.
- It appeals to the consumers' emotions.

• **The media**
- The medium is concerned with where the advertisement is to be placed.
- The different media: the press, free newspapers, commercial TV, commercial radio, posters, leaflets, handbills, cinema, shop display, points of sales, illuminated signs, telephone directories, trade exhibitions, sponsoring, carrier bags, packaging, labels, the sides and backs of buses and vans.

• **Themes to be found in advertising**
- ambition and success
- romance and escapism
- social acceptance
- hero worship
- easy life
- fairy tale world

• **The advertising campaign**
The target audience: four questions have to be asked.

1 • **How old is the target audience?**

2 • **Which income group do they belong to?**
Income groups: higher managerial or professional; intermediate managerial, administrative or professional; clerical and junior managerial; administrative or professional secretariat; skilled manual workers; casual or lowest grade workers.

3 • **Where do they live?**

4 • **Is the product right in terms of price, name and packaging?**

Warm-up

1 • Describe the ad.

2 • What is its target audience?

TEXT 1

Benetton man to create anti-smoking ads

Olivero Toscani, the controversial photographer behind Benetton's advertising campaign, has been hired by the World Health Organisation in its effort to combat smoking.

Mr Toscani will create hard-hitting advertisements for the organisation which is campaigning for a worldwide ban[1] on tobacco promotion.

As the former creative director of Benetton, Mr Toscani developed a reputation for his ability to shock. His campaigns for the fashion retailer[2] used controversial images such as depictions of Christ's crucifixion and photographs of real prisoners on death row[3] in the US.

"We are having ongoing discussions with Mr Toscani about doing something together and he's created a poster for our latest campaign," said a WHO spokeswoman.

Mr Toscani has already created a WHO poster which uses a graphic illustration of the effects of smoking on the human body.

The WHO is likely to enlist his help in its upcoming campaign against the promotion of tobacco at sporting events.

From *The Guardian*, April 8, 2002.

1. **ban:** *interdiction*
2. **retailer:** *détaillant*
3. **on death row:** *dans les couloirs de la mort*

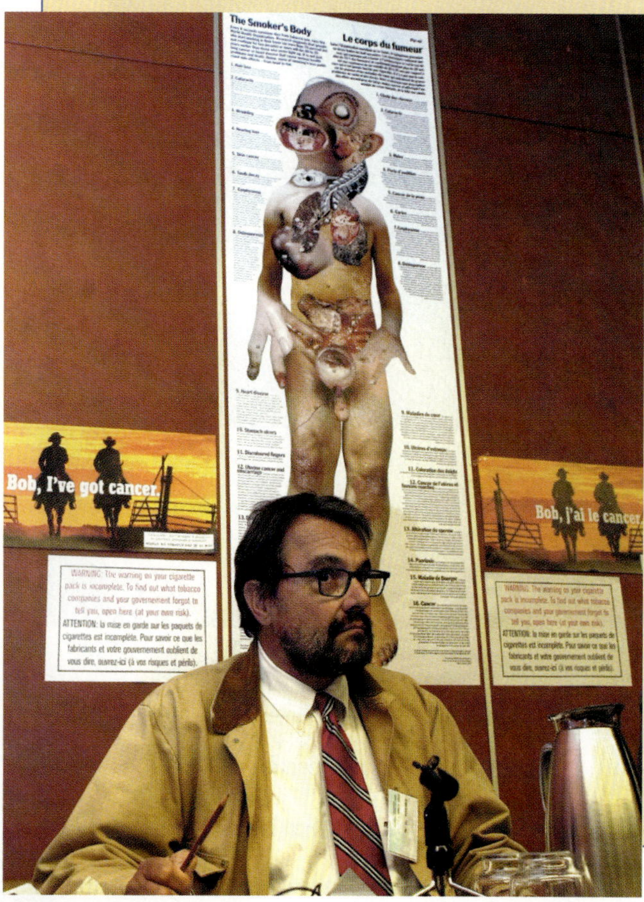

© OMS.

► Check your pronunciation

A • of the words ending in *-ion*:

1 • organisation
2 • promotion
3 • reputation
4 • depiction
5 • crucifixion
6 • discussion
7 • illustration

What conclusion can you draw?

B • of the following words:

1 • advertising
2 • effort
3 • combat
4 • image
5 • photograph

What do they have in common?

► Words

Match the following adjectives with their correct meaning.

1 • hard-hitting (l.4)
2 • former (l.6)
3 • ongoing (l.10)
4 • latest (l.11)
5 • upcoming (l.15)

a • continuous
b • uncompromising
c • newest
d • next
e • previous

© Robert Holmes/Corbis.

► Meaning

A • What does "its" (l. 2) refer to?
What does "he" (l. 11) refer to?

B • Read these two sentences. (see T&T: Present *Be* + *V-ing*)

1 • "the organisation which is campaigning … promotion" (l. 4)
2 • "we are having ongoing discussions" (l. 10)

What does the *Be* + *V-ing* form indicate about each action?

C • Reread the text and say which sentences are true.

1 • There has always been a consensus on Mr Toscani.
2 • Mr Toscani has just been employed by the WHO.
3 • Mr Toscani is known for his offensive ads.
4 • He is going to create his first poster for the WHO.
5 • The WHO is in favour of a ban on tobacco advertising at sporting events.

D • Fill in the blanks with *be to* (in the correct tense) or *must*. (see T&T: Modals)

1 • The Prime Minister .... visit Cambodia next month, his secretary declared.
2 • We .... put a ban on tobacco advertising before things get worse.
3 • You .... stop smoking unless you want to have more health problems in the future.
4 • The government .... back a bill that will ban all tobacco advertising.

E • Translate the following sentences into English.

1 • *En tant que directeur de cette société.*
2 • *Une interdiction de fumer.*
3 • *Le prisonnier dans les couloirs de la mort.*
4 • *Une campagne de publicité contre le tabac.*
5 • *Les effets du tabac sur la santé.*
6 • *Une discussion à propos de cette affiche.*
7 • *Le photographe à l'origine de cette publicité, sujette à controverse.*

► Pair work

Imagine a dialogue between **A** who is in favour of a total ban on tobacco advertising and **B** who is against.

► Food for thought

Advertising is a dream world. Comment. (about 200 words)

No sweat

1. can = tin
2. scent = perfume
3. downright = absolutely
4. breakthrough: *percée*
5. make it = succeed
6. shelf (pl. shelves): *rayon*
7. pester: *harceler*

[…] The Lynx effect is a classic example of a marketing campaign so effective that since its launch in 1983 the Lynx brand has become the olfactory equivalent of Nike. The world's best-selling deodorant for young men (it is sold as Axe in most countries abroad), half of all British teenage boys use it and one in three men of all ages has a can[1] in their bathroom.

These are astounding figures particularly when you consider that only 30 years ago men liked nothing better than the smell of their own sweat. […]

In 1980 fewer than half of men used a deodorant or anti-perspirant. The norm until the seventies was to wash, possibly apply a little talc and … well, that was about it. Although it was acceptable to splash on a bit of Old Spice for a special occasion (Old Spice, the first mass-market aftershave, arrived with the GIs), scents[2] for men were generally viewed as rakish or downright[3] homosexual.

The market opened up in the seventies, with such marvels as Hai Karate and Denim, but the big breakthrough[4] came with Brut 33. […]

Brut opened the door to the next generation of products which still dominate today: body spray deodorants targeted directly at the group who needed to be perfumed above all others – teenage boys. And it is teenage boys who have propelled the current market leader, Lynx, into its position of unassailable ascendency. […]

"We focus on 18-year-olds – most men want to be 18 even if they're not," says Joanna Teasdale, Lynx brand manager. But she also points out that it is crucial that the marketing doesn't alienate women, who still make 40 per cent of purchases, often at supermarkets (Lynx was one of the first products to make it[5] on to supermarket shelves[6]). "If we do our job properly it should work like pester[7] power does with children," says Teasdale.

From *The Independent on Sunday*, 9 June 2002.

▶ Check your pronunciation

A • Among the following words, spot underlined syllables which are pronounced [eɪ].

1 • sweat
2 • target
3 • rakish
4 • age
5 • leader
6 • spray
7 • unassailable
8 • breakthrough
9 • today
10 • dominate

B • Can you stress the right syllable in the following words?

1 • deodorant
2 • unassailable
3 • astounding
4 • figure
5 • teenage
6 • properly

► Words

Match the adjectives from the text with their synonyms.

1 • effective (l. 1)	a • essential
2 • astounding (l. 6)	b • successful
3 • rakish (l. 12)	c • dissolute
4 • current (l. 18)	d • amazing
5 • unassailable (l. 18)	e • firm
6 • crucial (l. 20)	f • present

► Meaning

A • What does "these" (l. 6) refer to?

B • Fill in the blanks.

(§1) Definition of the Lynx effect: ....
Date of launch: ....
The Lynx effect now: ....
(§2) 30 years ago:
Deodorant consumption ....
(§3) Scents for men viewed as ....
(§4) Development of the deodorant market: ....
(§5) Target: ....
(§6) But also: ....
Why? ....

Now use all these elements to sum up the text in about 70 words.

C • Put the verbs between brackets in the correct form and tense.
(see T&T: Present perfect / Preterite)

1 • Brut .... (dominate) the market since it .... (be launched) in 1983.
2 • I .... (start) on deodorants when I .... (go) to upper school at 11, says Simon.
3 • Since its launch the Lynx brand .... (become) the best-selling deodorant for young men.
4 • The deodorant market .... (open up) in the 1970s.
5 • I .... (use) this deodorant for ages.

D • Translate from "The norm" (l. 8) to "about it" (l. 9).

E • Explain Joanna Teasdale's viewpoint in a few words.

F • Translate into English.

1 • *Un adolescent sur trois.*
2 • *La moitié de tous les hommes britanniques.*
3 • *Les années 1970.*
4 • *Les jeunes âgés de 18 ans.*
5 • *Jusqu'aux années 1980.*
6 • *Plus de 25 % des achats.*

► Pair work

A thinks that admen can tune consumers' tastes to the products they have to sell. B strongly disagrees. Imagine their dialogue.

► Food for thought

There are more and more products targeted at teenagers. Comment. (about 150 words)

TEXT 3

1. **ploy:** *stratagème*
2. **fat:** *graisse*
3. **fizzy:** *gazeux*
4. **dramatic =** spectacular

"Don't eat too much of our food," warns McDonald's

McDonald's in France has been testing an unusually frank marketing ploy[1] – running adverts advising people not to eat too much of its food.

The American fast food giant has run "advertorials" in women's magazines in France featuring comments about diet from two independent nutritionists.

One of the experts said eating too much McDonald's food was not recommended, especially for children, as it would not constitute a balanced diet.

The comments go against the line McDonald's has always put forward – that its food is a nutritious part of a balanced diet.

To put across the company's point of view, the ads include descriptions of what McDonald's sees as the health benefits of its products – that its burgers are 100% meat, that no fat[2] is added in the grilling of the meat, and orange juice was being offered as an alternative to fizzy[3] drinks.

"The advertorials talk about McDonald's, children and nutrition, and the need for a balanced diet and exercise. There is nothing new or dramatic[4] in this," said a McDonald's spokeswoman. "The key part of the message was that you shouldn't do anything too often and it was one nutritionist's personal opinion. We printed it because it was that nutritionist's opinion and they wanted to open up the debate," she said.

From *The Guardian*, May 31, 2002.

► Words

You won't find the word "advertorial" in a dictionary.
From what you have understood of the text can you guess what it means?

► Meaning

A • Translate into English.
(see T&T: Compound nouns)

1 • *Des conseils de marketing.*
2 • *Le géant de la restauration rapide.*
3 • *Des bienfaits pour la santé.*
4 • *Du jus d'orange.*
5 • *De la viande de bœuf.*
6 • *Le message clé.*
7 • *Une alimentation de régime.*

B • Answer the following questions.

1 • Why is McDonald's advice to French people unusual?
2 • Why does it go against the line of McDonald's?
3 • What are the "health benefits" of McDonald's food?
4 • According to a McDonald's spokeswoman why did McDonald's print the nutritionist's point of view?

C • Translate the first paragraph into French.

1 ► Test

What's in a name?

[...] However good the product, rebranding is never cheap. When Airtours decided to change its name to My Travel it had to refit all its high street shops at a cost of £18m. Last week it announced losses of £45m. Guinness spent £250m to become Diageo, though that has had some good results, with the company being praised for good relations with city investors.

Rita Clifton, the chairman of Interbrand, which was involved with the Guinness rebranding, says: "The Guinness name no longer reflected the company's true scope. The rebranding worked because it was preceded by the company taking its staff and customers with it. Some companies think that rebranding is the same as rebadging or renaming. It has to be more than that. You have to have a business plan and you have to carry the staff and customers with you." [...]

She explains the use of exotic names thus: "We were involved with naming the demerged part of ICI Zeneca. It was a name that gave the impression of scientific excellence. You have to remember that when you're looking at 50,000 trademark applications in the course of a year, the search for a new name is particularly tough. Sometimes you have to go for a name that is unusual because you have to register it quickly with a board meeting looming."

But the business world is full of rebrands that have not solved the underlying problems. The rebranding of Ondigital as ITV Digital coincided with a slump in its fortunes. The National Lottery's £72m makeover as Lotto has yet to show that it has significantly changed the image of the twice-weekly game or significantly improved ticket sales.

Rita Clifton says: "When you rebrand, you've got to be prepared for a bit of teasing."

From *The Independent*, 14 June 2002.

ALTERED IMAGES

GUINNESS DIAGEO

- **When was the name changed?**
  October 1997, after the merger of the drinks companies Grand Metropolitan and Guinness.
- **Why the new name?**
  "Every day, all around the world, millions of people enjoy our brands. Based on the Latin word for "day" and the Greek word for "world", Diageo captures what this company is all about." (company statement)
- **What was the effect?**
  Although it was roundly ridiculed at the time, Diageo shares have risen by about 50 per cent since the name was changed.

CONSIGNIA

- **When was the name changed?**
  January 2001, apparently to better reflect the Royal Mail's global ambitions.
- **Why the new name?**
  "To consign means 'to entrust to the care of', which is what each of our customers does every day. The new name describes the full scope of what the Post Office does in a way that the words 'post' and 'office' cannot." (John Roberts, chief executive)
- **What was the effect?**
  The new name failed to reverse the company's fortunes, staff disliked it and the chairman, Allan Leighton, couldn't wait to see the back of it. Like the name, John Roberts is on his way out.

A • Sum up the article in French in about 50 words. You will insist on the consequences of rebranding.

B • Carefully analyse the two examples given in ALTERED IMAGES and say how far they illustrate the article (you will insist on the reason for and effects of rebranding). (about 60 words)

C • Translate the first paragraph.

D • Advertising creates artificial needs. Do you agree? (about 200 words)

2 ► Skills in practice

The Formula One car: "The most powerful advertising space in the world"

A recent study in the United States found that there were almost 6,000 sightings or mentions of tobacco company names or logos during a 90-minute broadcast of a major-racing event. It is difficult to get precise Formula One figures, but a 1994 advertisement in a tobacco industry journal claimed that it was now possible to sponsor a Formula One racing car "for a fraction of the cost often associated with Formula One and you can sponsor it on a race-by-race basis that suits your marketing strategy... This Formula One car is the most powerful advertising space in the world. It will carry your brand to viewers in 102 countries."

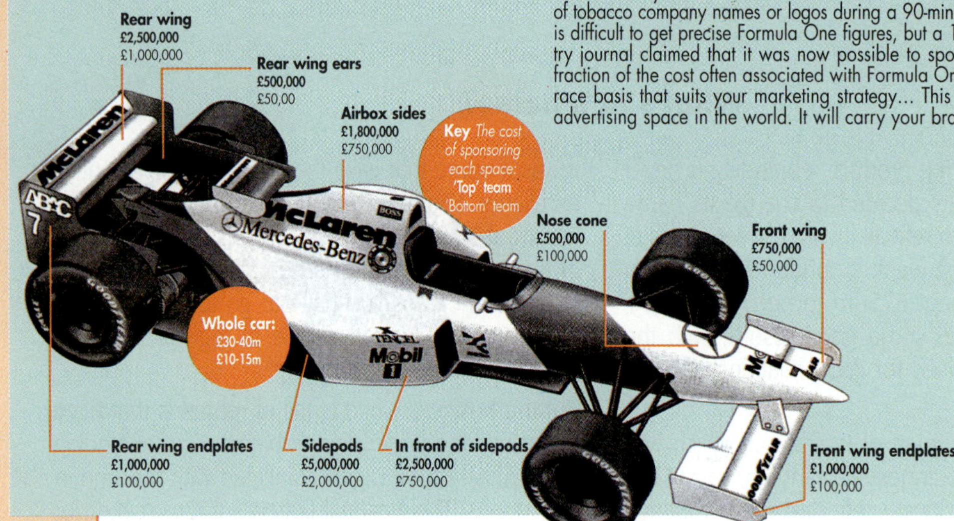

How to reach your audience

Formula One TV audiences are growing and desirable, according to the consultancy Sports Marketing Surveys:

- 57 per cent of ABC1 males in Europe, aged 18-55, watch Formula One.
- UK TV audiences have grown by 43 per cent in five years.
- Demographics are "stable but getting younger".
- Formula One shows the biggest growth in general sport programmes.

From *The Guardian*, November 6, 1997.

Carefully study the document and answer the following questions.

1 • Which part of the car is the most expensive?
2 • The cheapest?
3 • Is there a big difference between the cost of sponsoring a top team and a bottom team?
4 • How many sightings or mentions of tobacco brand names are there during a motor-racing broadcast?
5 • How many countries will be able to see the advertising space during a Formula One programme?

3 ► The right word

A • Crossword

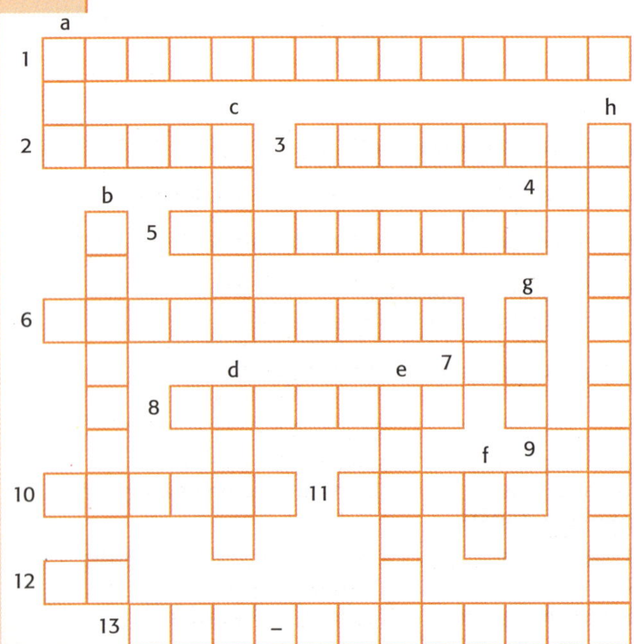

Across

1 • Announcements in a newspaper or on a billboard about a product.
2 • Television, the radio and the press.
3 • A study.
4 • Onomatopoeia indicating hesitation.
5 • The container that something is sold in.
6 • An ad on TV or the radio.
7 • Stands for Los Angeles.
8 • When a firm tries to get people buy its own products rather than another's.
9 • The news... controversial.
10 • Make a product available.
11 • Version of a product made by a particular manufacturer.
12 • Stands for Extraterrestrial.
13 • That draws attention.

Down

a • Goal.
b • Transmit on TV or the radio.
c • Conscious.
d • One time.
e • Aim.
f • Expression of refusal.
g • Exploit.
h • Forcing somebody to believe that something is true by means of repetition.

B • Fill in the blanks with words from the following list and make the necessary adjustments.

ad / advertising / at stake / broadcast (v.) / feature (v.) / focus (v.) / launch (v.) / target (v.) / test (v.)

1 • This commercial which will be .... on Channel 1 and 2. It will .... middle-aged executives.

2 • We have had this new washing powder .... by more than 50,000 consumers before we decide to .... it on the Dutch market.

3 • Huge sums of money are .... in the detergent market.

4 • We have decided to .... on the "green" concept.

5 • Six prizes have just been won by British .... agencies.

6 • Have you seen the latest Benetton's .... ?

7 • This commercial .... a businessman who is working on a laptop.

4 ► Vocabulary

affichage : bill posting
affichage (panneau d') : hoarding (GB), billboard (US)
affiche : poster
agence publicitaire : advertising agency
analyse du marché : market analysis
annonceur : advertiser
attaquer un marché : tap a market

battage publicitaire : hype
brochure : brochure, leaflet

campagne publicitaire : advertising campaign
catalogue : catalog (US), catalogue
catégorie socio-professionnelle : socio-economic group, income group, income bracket
cibler : target → a target
concevoir : design
conditionnement : packaging
courbe : graph
créneau : niche
critère : criterion (pl. criteria)
croissance : growth

dépliant : leaflet
devise : motto
diffuser (à la radio ou à la TV) : broadcast
documentation : literature

enjeu : stake
en jeu (être) : be at stake
enquête : survey
enseigne lumineuse : neon light
espace publicitaire : advertising space
essai (faire des) : test → a test
étude de marché : market research
étude de marché (faire une) : make / perform / carry out / conduct a market study
étude de marché (faire effectuer une) : commission a market study
étude de motivation : motivation research
exposant : exhibitor
exposition commerciale : trade exhibition

fiche technique : spec / specification / technical sheet
film publicitaire : commercial

hall d'exposition : show hall
heure de grande écoute : prime time

image de marque : brand image

lancement (prix de) : introductory / launching price
lancer : launch → a launch

marque : brand name
mener (une opération, une campagne) : conduct
message : message
message publicitaire chanté : jingle
mettre l'accent sur : emphasise
modèle déposé : trademark, TM

numéro vert : toll-free number

objectif : aim, goal, objective

point de vente : outlet, point of sale
présentoir : display stand, display unit, showcase
prévision : forecast, estimate
profil : profile
promotion : promotion
promouvoir : promote
prospectus : handbill
publicitaire (n.) : adman
publicité (la) : advertising
publicité (une) : ad, advert, advertisement
publicité comparative : comparative advertising
publicité (directeur de) : advertising manager
publicité mensongère (la) : deceptive / misleading advertising
publipostage : mailing, mailshot

revue professionnelle : trade journal

salon : show, trade fair
segment : segment
slogan : catch phrase, slogan
sondage : poll
sponsoriser : sponsor
spot publicitaire : commercial
stand : stand, stall, booth (US)
support publicitaire : medium (pl. media)

tendance : trend
test : test, trial, try out
tester : test, test market, try out

Unit 2 Distribution

A few landmarks

- **Retailing** consists in selling products to the public. **Retailers** sell from **shops** or **stores** (also called **outlets**). Big retail **chains** are organised in many countries. They sell a standardised selection of products. Their outlets are mostly **shopping centres,** also called **shopping arcades** or **malls** (US).
  Hypermarkets (over 30,000 sq metres) or **superstores** (under 30,000 sq metres) are out-of-town outlets with parking facilities.
  Department stores such as Harrods in London are large shops which sell a wide variety of products. They are usually situated in city centres. They are organised in departments, each with its own manager.

- **Franchising** is a business system in which a company, called a **franchiser**, sells a person (the **franchisee**) the right to operate a business using the franchiser's system. The franchisee pays an initial sum of money as part of the franchise agreement. This sum of money is the **franchise fee** also called **front end fee**. He also agrees to pay the franchiser a **management services fee** for advice and assistance. This fee is usually calculated as a percentage of turnover. He may also pay an advertising fee to contribute to the franchiser's advertising cost.
  The franchiser provides the franchisee an **operation manual** containing all the information necessary to run the business.
  A **master franchisee** may be appointed by the franchiser to supervise the business in a particular field.

© Pascal Sittler / Réa.

© Daniel Besson/ Réa.

© Reportdigital / John Harris / Réa.

Warm-up

1 • What food, motor-trade and clothing franchises have you heard of?

2 • Do you know in which country they were first launched?

3 • Where are they most famous?

Unit 2

TEXT 1

1. **expletive =** swear word
2. **bowlderise:** *expurger*
3. **a throw =** each
4. **coarse:** *grossier*
5. **weed:** *mauvaise herbe*

Cleaning up Hollywood is a profitable business

Basic Instinct without Sharon Stone controversially crossing her legs, *Saving Private Ryan* without expletives[1] and without some of the more violent scenes, *Titanic* without Kate Winslet in the nude, *Schindler's List* stripped of its most painful scenes, and *Gladiator* with almost no gore are examples of the kind of movies that right-thinking Americans can view without risking any moral contamination.

Videos bowdlerised[2] in that way can be rented from a chain of stores called CleanFlicks, which was set up 18 months ago in Pleasant Grove, Utah, near Salt Lake City, by a Mormon, Ray Lines.

He has been surprised by the scale of his success. At $12-$15 a throw[3], the cost of renting a CleanFlicks video is more than twice what competitors charge. That has not prevented the company from opening 65 sales outlets in the western United States. It hopes to have one in each state by the end of the year.

The CleanFlicks catalogue already includes almost 500 "cleaned up" films that contain no coarse[4] language, no sentences in which the word "God" is mentioned, and no sex scenes – and the list is getting longer by the week [...].

"We're growing like a weed[5]," says Lines. "I'm a businessman. I satisfy the demand of customers whose values I share. I have great respect for James Cameron, the director of *Titanic*, and Steven Spielberg, who made *Schindler's List*. It's just that I want my seven kids to view great movies, and I don't think they need to watch all that sex, to listen to all those insults and to look at all that gore." [...]

From *The Guardian Weekly*, 20-26 June 2002.

► Check your pronunciation

Are you sure you can pronounce the following words correctly?

1 • profitable
2 • controversially
3 • bowdlerised
4 • outlet
5 • coarse
6 • demand

► Words

A • **Make sure you have understood the meaning of "up" in the title. Can you think of other verbs that can be followed by *up* to convey the same meaning?**

B • **Match the following words with their definitions.**

1 • rent (l. 6)
2 • chain (l. 11)
3 • charge (l. 10)
4 • outlet (l. 6)
5 • catalogue (l. 13)
6 • demand (l. 16)
7 • customer (l. 17)

a • number of shops owned by the same person
b • need
c • someone who buys something especially from a shop
d • shop
e • price you have to pay for a service or something you buy
f • some money you pay every week or month in order to be able to use something
g • list of things you can buy from a particular company

C • **Fill in the blanks with the right prepositions from the following list (some may be repeated several times).**

at / by / during / for / from / in / of

1 • Those films can be rented .... the video store round the corner.
2 • A lot of TV channels .... the US have .... years taken the liberty .... removing scenes of a sexual or violent nature .... films shown .... prime time.
3 • "It's a breach .... intellectual property," says Professor Wheeler Winston Dixon, a film specialist .... the University .... Nebraska .... Lincoln.
4 • "Mutilating a movie .... removing the violence that forms an integral part .... its message can have the effect .... reducing the impact and substance .... its message."

► Meaning

A • **The journalist writes "the more violent scenes" (l. 2), why does he use "the more" and not "the most"? (see T&T: Comparatives / Superlatives)**

B • **Each of the following sentences could be written a little differently by using a relative clause. Find the right words.**

1 • "Sharon Stone .... controversially crossing her legs" (l. 1)
2 • "*Schindler's List* .... stripped of its most painful scenes" (l. 3)
3 • "Videos .... bowdlerised in that way" (l. 6)

C • **In the sentence "I satisfy the demand of customers whose values I share" (l. 16-17), why can't we replace "the demand of customers" by "the customers' demand"?**

D • **Answer the following questions.**

1 • Why does the journalist speak of "bowdlerised" films?
2 • What is the name of the company which rents such films?
3 • Where was the company set up?
4 • Do they charge the same price as ordinary videos?
5 • What shows that the company is quite successful?
6 • How many "cleaned up" films do they have on their catalogue?
7 • What kind of public is targeted?

E • **Translate into English.**

1 • *Cela ne nous empêchera pas de voir ce film.*
2 • *Tu peux louer* Titanic *dans n'importe quel magasin de vidéo.*
3 • *Je n'accepterai aucune grossièreté.*
4 • *Ce film ne contient aucune scène qui pourrait choquer de jeunes enfants.*
5 • *Cet homme d'affaires ne fait que répondre à la demande de ses clients.*

F • **Explain Ray Line's point of view. (about 25 words)**

► Pair work

A is in favour of "cleaning up" films, **B** strongly disagrees and says it amounts to mutilating them. Imagine their dialogue.

► Food for thought

Write a short paper on the Mormon community in Salt Lake City. (about 100 words)

Unit 2

TEXT 2

Warehouse woes[1] strike again at Mothercare

1. woe = misfortune
2. hold-up = delay
3. invoice sb for sth: *facturer qqch à qqn*

Mothercare, the embattled mother and baby products retailer, has been hit by further logistical problems, which have forced the retailer to suspend deliveries in its warehouse because it cannot handle any more volume.

The hold-up[2] comes only three weeks after Alan Smith, chairman, told shareholders that the group's distribution woes had been resolved, a crisis which has contributed to the retailer's flagging reputation in the City.

One Mothercare supplier, who did not want to be named, said: "[...] Their buyers are useless. We've got numerous orders that we have invoiced[3] Mothercare for, but they have not been picked up for a month."

He said Mothercare's warehouse had told his company that its buyers had ordered too many products and to ignore any future orders placed. Mothercare denied the claim.

The retailer has issued three profit warnings in the past year following disappointing sales and distribution problems at its Daventry warehouse, which is run by Tibett and Britten, the logistics group.

A Mothercare spokesman said: "This is our highest-volume period. It is a short-term action to ensure the proper flow through the warehouse. We expect to be back to normal next week."

He claimed the move was not unusual for retailers during product changes between seasons, although that theory was rejected by retail analysts.

Rhys Williams, analyst at Seymour Pierce, said: "That is what you have sales for. When you get the offer incorrect, you get a lot of stock left over. I do not believe the company's stock position is as clean as it is stating."

From *The Daily Telegraph,* August 8, 2002.

© GettyImages / Taxi / Denis Felix.

► Check your pronunciation

A • Make sure you can read the following words correctly.

1 • woe
2 • embattled
3 • further
4 • issued
5 • through

B • How do you pronounce the -*s* endings in the following words?

1 • woes
2 • products
3 • problems
4 • deliveries
5 • shareholders
6 • buyers
7 • orders
8 • profits
9 • sales
10 • changes
11 • analysts
12 • stocks

What can you conclude on the pronunciation of plurals?

► Words

A • **Tick the correct meaning.**

1 • "Flagging reputation" (l. 6) means: failing / rising / uneven.
2 • "Their buyers are useless" (l. 7-8) means: Their buyers are hopeless / Their buyers can't be used / Their buyers are helpful.
3 • "They have not been picked up" (l. 9) means: They have not been written / They have not been collected / They have not been left.
4 • "To ignore any future orders" (l. 11) means: to deal with any future orders / to place any future orders / to disregard any future orders.

B • **Translate the following adjectives from the text.**

1 • useless (l. 8)
2 • unusual (l. 19)
3 • incorrect (l. 22)

Then think of other adjectives on the same pattern and translate them.
Ex.: hopeless: *désespéré* **(see T&T: Word formation)**

C • **Find synonyms for the following words in the text.**

1 • many
2 • beset
3 • stop
4 • continuity
5 • declare

► Meaning

A • **Answer the following questions.**

1 • Introduce the company (name, products, type of distribution).
2 • What sort of problems is this company going through?
3 • Who is complaining?
4 • What is the company's answer?
5 • What is the point of view given by an analyst?

Use your answers to make a short summary of the text in English. (about 80 words)

B • **Translate into English.**

1 • *Tous nos problèmes ont été résolus.*
2 • *Nous sommes contraints de suspendre nos livraisons.*
3 • *Ceci est dû à quelques problèmes logistiques.*
4 • *La situation redeviendra normale la semaine prochaine.*
5 • *On s'attend, hélas, à d'autres problèmes de distribution dans les mois à venir.*

D • **Translate into French.**

1 • "Mothercare denied the claim" (l. 11-12)
2 • "That is what you have sales for" (l. 21)

C • **Fill in the blanks with *during* or *for*. (see T&T: Present perfect / Preterite)**

1 • They have been going through logistical difficulties .... a while.
2 • .... the conference the company's spokesman said that everything was all right.
3 • Delivery problems are normal .... product changes.
4 • We are quite busy .... the sales season.
5 • I haven't picked up my mail .... a fortnight.
6 • We placed a few orders .... the summer.
7 • The company's troubles led to speculation about its future .... a few weeks.

► Pair work

A is a Mothercare spokesman who would like to calm things down. **B** is one of Mothercare's suppliers who is complaining. Imagine their dialogue.

► Food for thought

Do you think that the evolution in retailing will bring about the end of the small shops?

TEXT 3

1. **handset:** *combiné*
2. **cut-throat:** *coupe-gorge*
3. **freefall:** *chute libre*
4. **niche:** *créneau*
5. **steady** = regular

Carphone sends brighter message

Carphone Warehouse […], Europe's largest independent mobile phone retailer estimates that 1,200 mobile phone shops – 28% of the market – have closed in the past six months as sales of handsets[1] slowed dramatically. Alongside the closure of small independent retailers unable to compete in the cut-throat[2] market, many supermarket chains which started selling pre-pay phones over a year ago have reallocated their shelf space to faster selling goods such as DVDs. […]

The dramatic drop in mobile phone sales recorded across the country last year was caused by the decision of the mobile operators to stop heavily subsiding new phones, especially pay-as-you-go packages. Many of the operators raised handset prices. […] With sales of new handsets in freefall[3], Carphone Warehouse has been concentrating on replacement handset sales and after-sales services such as insurance and customer care for the mobile operators. […] Including its own niche[4] network, Fresh, Carphone Warehouse services more than 1m subscribers in the UK and France, giving it a steady[5] stream of recurring revenue.

© Réa / Ian Hanning.

From *The Guardian,* June 7, 2002.

► Words

Complete the following sentences using the words in the list below to show what changes have occurred.

doubled / fallen / increased / rise

1 • Subscribers last year: 1.5 million
Subscribers this year: 2 million
→ There has been a .... in subscribers.

2 • Price last year: $50
Price this year: $40
→ The price of this product has ....

3 • Franchisees last year: 380
Franchisees this year: 760
→ The number of franchisees has ....

4 • Employees last year: 45
Employees this year: 98
→ The number of employees has .... this year.

► Meaning

A • Right or wrong?

1 • The mobile phone business is booming.
2 • Supermarket chains are increasingly giving up selling mobile phones.
3 • Selling DVDs is simpler than selling mobile phones.
4 • Handset prices have increased.
5 • This is due to a decision of not subsidising new phones any more.
6 • Carphone Warehouse now just concentrates on after-sales services.
7 • It services only British subscribers.

B • Translate into English.

1 • *L'entreprise se concentre maintenant sur le service après-vente.*
2 • *Nous avons commencé à vendre de nouveaux produits tels que des DVD.*
3 • *Le plus gros détaillant européen en matière de téléphones portables.*
4 • *Une chute spectaculaire des ventes.*

Checkup Unit 2

1 ► Test

Fresh ideas from young guns

A dynamic new generation of entrepreneurs who don't fit the traditional franchising mold is charting its way to success.

Chance Miller and Jon Paul Martin made a deal: they decided that if they didn't get fantastic jobs upon graduation, they would go into business together and open their own Smoothie King[1] franchise.

After Martin graduated in 1993, he got a high-pressure, low-gratitude job as a stockbroker. A year later Miller got his diploma and took an $18,000-a-year position selling duplicating services to lawyers.

Before long, Smoothie King started looking pretty good to them, and soon they were scouting potential franchise sites around the University of South Florida in Tampa, Martin's hometown.

With borrowed funds from various sources, including a $50,000 bank loan cosigned by their parents, Miller and Martin secured more than the $130,000 they needed to buy a turnkey franchise, and they opened their first Smoothie King in early 1995. It was store No. 59 for the New Orleans-based company, and it set the record for first-year gross revenues for Smoothie King franchises.

The following year, the pair opened another store 130 miles away on the University of Florida campus in Gainesville. Now Mil-Mar Enterprises Inc. has five Smoothie King franchises in the two cities, and three of the stores are among the chain's top 5 percent in gross revenues. [...]

Dara Craft's goal in launching Babies 'N' Bells Inc., based in Carrollton, Texas, was not to build a franchising concern. She started the business in 1997, after the birth of her second child, as a way to parlay her experience in commercial printing into an income-producing activity that would allow her to stay at home.

But Craft, 30, soon realized that other stay-at-home moms wanted the same opportunity to sell personalized birth announcements and party invitations, and she quickly adapted to franchising. She now has 29 franchisees, more than double the number she had a year earlier.

"My goal is to make them feel they're really part of something that's professional and just like a retail business," Craft says. "It just doesn't happen to be in a retail location."

Miller, Martin, Craft, and others among the growing crop of young players in franchising today, are turning the field upside down.

Not long ago, the ranks of franchisees expanded to include many down-sized middle managers. Now, franchising is attracting a dynamic new generation of entrepreneurs. They are young – many enter the field directly out of college. Increasingly, they are armed with MBAs. And they are largely unhindered by the traditional notion that people turn to franchising only after years of working in a conventional business.

The new-generation franchisees and franchisers – having seen middle-aged corporate refugees enter the field successfully after being turned out of good jobs – have concluded there was no reason to be down-sized themselves before starting their own companies.

From *Nation's Business,* January 1999,

1. Smoothie King is a fresh-blended fruit juice chain based in New Orleans, Louisiana.

A • Create two identity cards, one for Miller and Martin and one for Craft. Give their university and / or professional backgrounds, the dates they started their businesses, the name and location of their companies, their status (franchiser or franchisee) and the current state of their businesses.

B • Compare what the franchisers / franchisees looked like a few years ago and what they are now (age, background, qualities). (30-40 words)

C • Translate from "A dynamic new generation" (l. 1) to Martin's hometown" (l. 15).

D • Write about the advantages and drawbacks of being a franchisee. (about 150 words)

2 ► Skills in practice

You have to prepare and test a questionnaire that will be used for a customer survey in a hypermarket. The following information has to be collected.

1 • Customer profile (resident or visitor / professional and social background / income / regular or occasional customer / average level of spending)

2 • Customer satisfaction (service / product range / prices / suggestions)

3 • Attitudes to e-commerce (experience and opinion)

Work in pairs and prepare the questions to include in your survey. (your questions should be multiple-choice, closed or open).

NB: Examples:

– **multiple-choice:** How much do you spend when you do your shopping here?
  a • £1 - £10
  b • £10 - £50
  c • more than £50

– **closed:** Do you live in the city centre?

– **open:** Where do you live?

3 ► The right word

A • Crossword

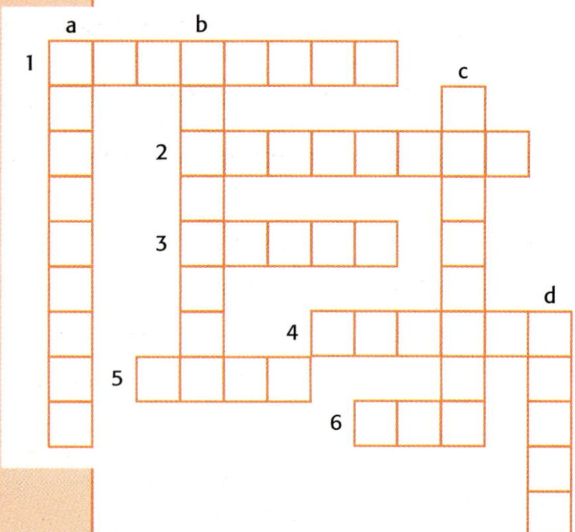

Across

1 • Counter where you have to pay for the things you have bought.

2 • Person or firm that provides you with something such as goods or equipment.

3 • It is sometimes special.

4 • Person or company that receives a service from a professional person or organisation in return for payment.

5 • When you have nothing to pay.

6 • Short for "do-it-yourself".

Down

a • Sale in which the goods in a shop are sold at reduced prices because the shopkeeper wants to get rid of them or because the shop is closing down.

b • Someone who buys something from a shop.

c • The bringing of letters, parcels or goods to someone's house or office.

d • The activity of buying or exchanging things.

B • Fill in the blanks with words from the following list and make the necessary adjustments.

discount / network / outlet / out-of-town / retail / sample / shelf / store (n.) / store (v.) / warehouse

1 • This supermarket is now offering free .... of shampoo.

2 • A .... is a place where goods are stocked.

3 • A .... price is the contrary of a wholesale price.

4 • After Christmas the .... in the toy department of this store were practically empty.

5 • I think we'll have to increase our distribution ....

6 • Hypermarkets are generally built on .... locations.

7 • The wholesaler .... goods in a warehouse.

8 • A .... is a reduction in the usual price of a product.

9 • Harrods is London's smartest department ....

10 • Lots of companies are now looking for .... in Eastern Europe.

4 ► Vocabulary

abandonner (un produit) : drop (a product)
achat à domicile : home-shopping
acheteur : shopper, buyer, purchaser
agent exclusif : sole agent

boutique franchisée : franchised operation / outlet
brader : sell off / out

caddie : trolley (GB), cart (US)
caisse : cash desk
caisse de supermarché : checkout
centre commercial : shopping centre / arcade / mall (US)
chaîne de magasins : chain store
chef de rayon : shopwalker
chiffre d'affaires : turnover
circuit de distribution : distribution channel
client : client (services), customer (shops)
clientèle : clientele (services), customers (shops)
commerçant : shopkeeper, shop owner, storekeeper (US)
commerce : business, trade
concessionnaire : dealer
coopérative : cooperative

débouché : outlet
démarcher : sell door-to-door, canvass
détail : retail
détaillant : retailer
distributeur automatique (de boissons par exemple) : (automatic) vending machine

échantillon : sample
échantillon gratuit : free sample
échantillonner : sample
échelle internationale (à l') : worldwide
échelle nationale (à l') : nationwide
entrepôt : warehouse
éventail de marchandises : range of goods
exclusif : sole
exclusivité de la vente : exclusive right of sale

fabricant : manufacturer
filiale : subsidiary
fournir : supply, provide
fournisseur : supplier
fournitures : supplies
frais d'expédition : delivery charges
franchise : franchise
franchisé : franchisee
franchiseur : franchiser

gamme : range
gondole : shelf (pl. shelves)
grands magasins : department stores
gratuit : free (of charge)
gros : wholesale
gros (acheter / vendre en) : buy / sell in bulk
gros (magasin de) : wholesale shop
grossiste : wholesaler
groupement d'achat : purchasing group

hypermarché : hypermarket, superstore

implanter (s') : set up
imputer : charge
intermédiare : middleman, intermediary
inventaire : inventory

libre-service : self-service
liquidation : clearance sales
livraison : delivery
livraison contre-remboursement : cash on delivery, COD
livraison (modalités de) : delivery terms
livrer : deliver
livreur : delivery man

magasin à marge réduite : discounter, discount store
magasin à succursales : multiple, multiple chain store, chain store
magasin de bricolage : do-it-yourself shop, DIY shop
magasin de conception standardisée : standard-format store
magasin de détail : retail outlet
magasin de proximité : convenience store, neighbourhood shop
magasin d'usine : factory outlet store
magasin (grand) : department store
marchand : trader, merchant
marché : market
modèle : model

offre : offer
offre (l') et la demande : supply and demand

point de vente : outlet
prévision des ventes : sales forecast
prévoir les ventes : forecast sales
prix brut : gross price
prix de vente : selling price
prix fort (au) : at full price
prix net : net price
producteur : 1) producing (adj.)
2) producer (n.)
produit : 1) produce *(non manufacturé)*
2) product *(manufacturé)*
produit (chef de) : product manager
produit d'appel : loss leader

rayon : department
réassortiment : replenishment, restocking
réassortir : replenish, restock
relance : follow-up
remise : discount
remise (faire une) : discount
représentant de commerce : commercial traveller
réseau : network
retard : delay
retirer progressivement du marché : phase out of the market

service après-vente : after-sales service
soldes : sales
sous-traitant : subcontractor
sous-traiter : subcontract
stock (être en rupture de) : be out of stock
stockage : stocking, storing
stocker : stock, store
succursale : branch
supermarché : supermarket
surface commerciale : floor area

télévente : teleshopping, TV-shopping, television selling

vendeur : 1) shop assistant *(magasin)*
2) seller *(marchand)*
vendre : sell (sold, sold)
vendre à perte : sell at a loss
vente : sale
vente (analyse des) : sales analysis
vente (force de) : sales force
vente par correspondance : mail order (selling)
vente (prévisions des) : sales forecast
ventes (promotion des) : sales promotion
vente promotionnelle : bargain sales
vente (réseau de) : sales network
ventes (volume des) : volumes of sales, sales volume
vol à l'étalage : shoplifting
voleur à l'étalage : shoplifter

Unit 3 Consumption

A few landmarks

Consumption

In economics, the final using up of **goods** and **services**.
The term excludes the use of intermediate products in the production of other goods (e.g., the purchase of buildings and machinery by a business). Economists use statistical information on income and purchases to trace trends in consumption, seeking to map **consumer demand** for goods and services. In classical economics, consumers are assumed to be rational and to allocate expenditure in such a way as to maximise total satisfaction from all purchases. Incomes and prices are seen as consumption's two major determinants. Critics of the model point out that there are many exceptions to rational consumer behaviour – for example, the phenomenon of **conspicuous consumption**, in which the high price of a product increases its prestige and adds to demand.

Consumer goods

Any tangible commodity purchased by **households** to satisfy their wants and needs. **Durable goods** (e.g., cars, furniture, and appliances) have a significant **lifespan**, often defined as three years or more, and consumption is spread over this span. **Nondurable goods** (e.g., food, clothing and petrol) are purchased for immediate or almost immediate consumption and have a lifespan ranging from minutes to three years.

© Corbis / Peter Aprahamian.

Consumer credit

Short- and intermediate-term loans used to finance the purchase of commodities or services for personal consumption. The loans may be supplied by lenders in the form of cash loans or by sellers in the form of sales credit. **Instalment loans**, such as those for cars and credit card purchases, are paid back in two or more instalments; **noninstalment loans**, such as the service credit extended by utility companies, are paid back in a lump sum. **Consumer loans** usually carry a higher rate of interest than business loans.

Warm-up

1 • Try to guess where this photo was taken?

2 • Why does it look so smart?

Unit 3

TEXT 1

Fowl[1] play

1. **fowl =** chicken
2. **breast:** *blanc*
3. **thigh:** *cuisse*
4. **gizzard:** *gésier*
5. **slab:** *pavé*

Europe is big on breasts[2]. The Japanese prefer thighs[3]. Feet are a big of a fetish in China. Gizzards[4] go to Russia. But smooth, damp slabs[5] of white flesh are what we British buy when we want chicken. That leaves the carcasses, and skin, mountains and mountains of it – pale, flaccid, pimply, raw, ripped off by 100,000 shift workers' hands from Thailand to Brazil, from the Netherlands to Norfolk. The skin goes around the world for chicken nuggets. […]

The rise of the nugget has been dizzying. We bought 42 million packs of them – that's £79m worth, or 21,000 tonnes – in the UK last year, just to eat at home, according to analysts Taylor Nelson Sofres. British adults also ate 73 million meals of them away from home in the same period. Children probably ate more. Served in school dining halls, fast-food outlets, at hospital bedsides, and on the tables of harassed parents, nuggets have become ubiquitous. Mass production has created a homogeneity in our diets at a time when the origins of your food are more varied than ever.

© Réa / Ludovic.

From *The Guardian*, 8 July 2002.

► Check your pronunciation

A • Read the following words.

1 • fowl
2 • foul
3 • fuel
4 • full

What can you remark?

B • Pronounce the following adjectives.

1 • [smu:ð]
2 • ['flæksɪd]
3 • ['pɪmpli]
4 • [rɔ:]
5 • [ju:'bɪkwɪtəs]

► Words

A • Choose the right meaning of the following adjectives.

1 • "smooth" (l. 2): even / rough / straight
2 • "damp" (l. 2): cold / dry / wet
3 • "flaccid" (l. 4): soft and loose / hard / cold
4 • "pimply" (l. 4): soft / even / spotty
5 • "raw" (l. 4): exported / uncooked / processed
6 • "ubiquitous" (l. 17): numerous / omnipresent / rare

B • Circle the correct meaning.

1 • "Europe is big on breasts" (l. 1) means: Europe is keen on breasts / Europe produces chickens with big breasts / Europe's consumers do not really care about what they eat.

2 • "The skin goes around the world for chicken nuggets" (l. 5-6) means: The skin is thrown away around the world / The skin is processed into nuggets in many parts of the world / The skin is looking for chicken nuggets.

3 • "The rise of the nugget has been dizzying" (l. 7) means: Nugget consumption has been steadily increasing / Nugget consumption has been skyrocketing in an amazing way / Nugget consumption has been steady in an amazing way.

4 • "Harassed parents" (l. 15) means: Parents who are quite tired when they come back home / Parents who are fed up with eating nuggets / Parents who are pestered by their kids.

5 • "Nuggets have become ubiquitous" (l. 16-17) means: Nuggets can be found everywhere / Nuggets are now edible / Nuggets can be found nowhere.

► Meaning

A • What do those figures correspond to?

1 • 100,000
2 • 42 million
3 • 79m
4 • 21,000
5 • 73 million

B • What tense is used in the first paragraph? Why?

C • Complete the following sentences. (see T&T: Adjectives)

1 • Someone who lives in China is a ....
2 • Someone who lives in Spain is a ....
3 • Someone who lives in .... is a Moroccan.
4 • Someone who lives in the Netherlands is a ....
5 • Someone who lives in .... is an Italian.
6 • A man who lives in .... is an Irishman.
7 • Someone who lives in Scotland is a ....
8 • A man who lives in .... is a Welshman.

D • Questions on the text.

1 • Which part of the chicken is the British consumers' favourite?
2 • Which part of the chicken is turned into nuggets?
3 • Do the British only have nuggets away from home?
4 • Are children keen on nuggets?
5 • Where are nuggets served?
6 • Are our diets varied?

E • Translate into English.

1 • *Je préfèrerais une cuisse, s'il vous plaît.*
2 • *Ces montagnes de viande blanche et flasque ne me disent rien du tout.*
3 • *J'ai acheté moins de poulet cette année que l'an dernier.*
4 • *Je déteste la viande crue.*

F • Translate the last sentence of the text into French (l. 17-21).

► Pair work

The western world is increasingly keen on junk food. Discuss.

► Food for thought

"Mass production has created a homogeneity in our diets". Do you agree? (about 200 words)

TEXT 2

1. **mainland:** *territoire continental*
2. **caution =** warn
3. **make up for =** compensate

European mobile phone ownership nears 75%

The latest survey of European mobile phone ownership by *Mobile Communications* magazine shows that penetration in Europe reached 74.5 per cent at the end of June with the total number of subscriptions across the region at 289.7m.

The rise in new subscribers is slowing rapidly, putting pressure on mobile operators to deliver revenue growth through selling more services. New subscribers have been growing at a rate of less than 0.5 per cent a month this year, according to the survey, a marked slowdown on previous years. In 2000, monthly growth peaked at 5.1 per cent.

As a result, analysts said mobile operators were concentrating their future efforts on increasing average revenues per user (ARPU) in the light of the expected slowdown in new connections.

"The maturity of the subscriber base means the top line growth needs to come from ARPU growth," said Simon Weeden, analyst at Goldman Sachs.

"To achieve this operators are concentrating on new data services such as camera phones. If operators can get enough volumes, it could be a camera phone Christmas."

Western Europe's most saturated market, according to the survey, is Luxembourg, reflecting the country's wealth and the large number of workers who commute to Luxembourg from neighbouring countries.

Many of these workers buy their mobile phones in Luxembourg, contributing to the high market penetration figure of over 99 per cent.

© Réa / Mario Fourmy.

Of Europe's largest markets, penetration is highest in Italy and Sweden with levels of 89 per cent and 84 per cent respectively.

With less than 44 per cent population penetration, Gibraltar has the lowest level of mobile phone ownership in Europe, partly reflecting the fact that some users buy their mobiles in mainland[1] Spain.

Shani Raja, editor of *Mobile Communications*, cautions[2] that there is an element of double counting in the survey as significant but unknown numbers of adults in Europe possess more than one mobile.

Eastern Europe is making up for[3] much of the slowdown, with new subscribers up more than 50 per cent in the year to the end of June. Total mobile subscribers in eastern Europe now exceed 48m, or almost a quarter of the population.

From *Financial Times*, August 5, 2002.

► Check your pronunciation

All the following words are also used in French, can you pronounce them correctly?

1 • region
2 • mobile
3 • penetration
4 • communication
5 • total
6 • population
7 • Europe
8 • magazine

► Words

Match each word with its correct meaning.

1 • latest (l. 1)
2 • slowdown (l. 7)
3 • achieve (l. 14)
4 • commute (l. 18)
5 • significant (l. 30)
6 • exceed (l. 35)

a • reduction
b • noteworthy
c • succeed in doing
d • go over
e • travel every day between home and place of work
f • most recent

► Meaning

A • **Which of the following statements are true?**

1 • Mobile phone owners are unlikely to grow.
2 • New subscribers are fewer and fewer.
3 • Hence the necessity to concentrate efforts on increasing the number of subscribers.
4 • The camera phone could be another niche.
5 • Italy's market is the most saturated one.
6 • The lowest penetration market for mobile phones is Spain.
7 • The survey may not be totally significant.
8 • Only 25 per cent of the population are mobile subscribers in eastern Europe.

B • **What do the following percentages correspond to?**

1 • 74.5%
2 • 0.5%
3 • 5.1%
4 • 99%
5 • 89%
6 • 84%
7 • 44%
8 • 50%

C • **Briefly explain what ARPU means.**

D • **Read the following sentence aloud in order to check you have understood it and then translate it: "To achieve this operators are concentrating on new data services such as camera phones."**

E • **Translate into English.**

1 • *La croissance approche les 25 %.*
2 • *Presque un quart de la population.*
3 • *Le marché le plus saturé.*
4 • *Le nombre des consommateurs dépasse maintenant 50 millions.*
5 • *Respectivement 50 % et 51,8 %.*
6 • *L'augmentation des abonnements.*
7 • *Le nombre de gens qui travaillent au Luxembourg est en train de baisser rapidement.*
8 • *Le nombre d'utilisateurs croît depuis le début de l'année.*

► Pair work

Imagine a dialogue between **A** who would like to increase average revenues per user (ARPU) and **B** who would like to concentrate on developing population penetration of mobile phone ownership (by making people buy a second mobile phone, for example).

► Food for thought

When the penetration is high for a product, what efforts can be made to increase average revenues per user (ARPU)? Give examples.

Billion bottle record for scotch whisky

Scotch whisky is proving more popular than ever, with more than 1bn bottles of the spirit exported from British distilleries. [...] The UK Chancellor[1] takes about 70% in tax on the price of a bottle of scotch bought in Britain where 115m bottles were drunk last year, making it the third largest whisky market behind Spain and France. In France drinkers prefer low-price brands, often mixed with a cola to become "le whisky coca" – now more popular than pastis. It is the Greeks, however, who consume the most scotch per head, with whisky accounting for more than 42% of the country's combined alcohol consumption. The chairman of the Scottish Whisky Association (SWA), Ian Good, said 1bn bottles had been sold last year to more than 200 countries, making scotch the most widely exported spirit in the world. "It is a feat that both the industry and the country can be proud of," he said. "Not bad for a nation of just 5 million people." [...] Ian Grist, commercial director for Chivas Brothers, which makes Chivas Regal, said the success of scotch overseas, particularly in Asia and parts of Latin America, was down to careful marketing designed to position the ancient Highland spirit as a fashionable and highly aspirational luxury brand, popular among a wealthy and trendy set.

From *The Guardian Weekly,* June 20-26, 2002.

1. **Chancellor (of the Exchequer) =** British minister who makes decisions about finance and taxes

► Words

A • Try to guess the meaning of the following words.

1 • "spirit" (l. 2) means: mind / alcohol / state
2 • "feat" (l. 11) means: fact / act / exploit
3 • "aspirational" (l. 15) means: ambitious / expensive / popular
4 • "trendy" (l. 16) means: fashionable / funny / lively

B • Fill in the blanks with the right prepositions.

1 • A decline .... tea consumption has recently been observed in Great Britain.
2 • French drinkers are more and more drawn .... low-price whisky mixed with cola.
3 • There is a sudden explosion .... scotch consumption in Asia.
4 • In Greece whisky accounts .... over a third of the country's alcohol consumption.

► Meaning

A • Right or wrong?

1 • Scotch whisky has never been so popular.
2 • Great Britain is Europe's number one scotch consumer.
3 • French people are keen on cheap scotch.
4 • Greece is Europe's number one scotch consumer.
5 • Scotland can be proud of its whisky exports.
6 • Scotch appeals to Latin America and Asia thanks to a successful marketing campaign.

B • Translate into English.

1 • *Le whisky est plus populaire en France que le cognac.*
2 • *Les buveurs asiatiques sont de plus en plus attirés par le scotch.*
3 • *L'an dernier on a vendu 3 millions de bouteilles.*
4 • *Le whisky est l'alcool le plus exporté au monde.*

1 ► Test

Shoppers "confused" by food quality logos

Food logos designed to reassure people about what they eat are confusing consumers, who are unsure what the plethora of different schemes signify, a report published yesterday said.

More than 20 "food assurance" signs operate in Britain, using a range of different logos on packaging for products from milk and eggs to beef and lamb.

The Food Standards Agency (FSA) found producers failed to explain why their goods had been approved, and it identified wide differences in standards between different schemes.

Thousands of products in Britain are allowed to use the stamps of approval, even though they adhere only to minimum legal standards.

The FSA said that the confusion left customers unable to make proper decisions over what they should buy, and could push up prices.

It called for reforms to make the schemes work better, including an independent regulatory body to oversee those carrying the red tractor logo.

It is the biggest scheme of its kind, but is recognised by only 30 per cent of people; and even they are confused by what it means.

Products can carry the mark only after inspectors have checked all aspects of the production process, including how animals are kept and fed and the way producers care for the countryside.

Sir John Krebs, chairman of the FSA, said: "[...] Consumers are not sure whether the red tractor logo has to do with country of origin, better standards of production or better quality of food."

The FSA's review looked at 18 schemes with about 78,000 members between them, covering more than 85 per cent of production in eggs, milk, chicken, pork and crops, and more than 65 per cent of beef, lamb and horticultural produce. It wants minimum standards, more involvement from customers, and better cooperation between the schemes.

The red tractor appears on more than 550 items, produced under 11 different schemes, which fall under the umbrella of Assured Food Standards, an independent body that oversees how they operate. [...]

Another of the schemes, Lion Quality, covers eggs. Its logo appears on eggshells and boxes. The qualification requirements for that scheme include compulsory vaccination against salmonella, improved traceability of eggs and a "best before" date stamped on the shell. [...]

Peter Jenkins, senior public affairs officer at the Consumers' Association, said: "All too often these schemes offer little more than what producers are supposed to be doing anyway, but they can be more expensive, suggesting to customers that they are receiving something extra."

From *The Independent*, 10 July 2002.

A • Sum up the text in French.
You will insist on what food logos were designed for, the reasons for their being confusing and the necessary steps that should be taken. (about 80 words)

B • Translate into French from "Another of the schemes" (l. 45) to "on the shell (l. 50).

C • Essay (about 150 words): Do you think shoppers are too often "confused"?
If so, what should be improved?

2 ► Skills in practice

Carefully study the figures in the chart and then fill in the blanks with words or figures from the following list (do not forget to make the necessary adjustments).

products / buy / sales / average / shoot up / almost / 73% / 30% / 18% / top

1 • In Italy, sales of non-disposable razors jumped by ....
2 • In France, bubble baths and shower gels are at the .... of the list of fastest-growing ....
3 • In Germany, sales of air fresheners jumped by ....
4 • In Great Britain, sales of creams and lotions rose by ....
5 • Britons .... 16% more diet aids.
6 • In Spain, ... of sugar substitutes .... by 174% and sales of deodorants rose by .... 30%.
7 • In France, Italy and Germany cereals and muesli sales increased by an .... of 15%.

What price beauty?

Personal grooming and hygiene products are the fastest-growing categories in the five largest markets in Europe.

UK	% change
oral analgesics	38.6
antacids	33.3
dishwasher detergent	24.3
cough/cold medicine child	23.1
skin creams/lotions	18.1
hot sauces	18.0
cough/cold medicine adult	17.7
infant milk	17.7
slimming aids	16.2
chewing gum	16.0

SPAIN	% change
sugar substitutes	174.1
pre-packed sliced meat	115.4
dry dog food	45.0
non-processed cheese	41.1
colas	33.6
mayonnaise/salad dressing	32.4
deodorants	29.1
ice cream	26.7
frozen prepared meals	21.9
furniture polish/cleaner	21.9

ITALY	% change
non-disposable razors	72.7
non-carbonated soft drinks	31.2
ice cream	28.4
cereals/muesli	22.2
port/Sherry/Madeira	20.0
razor blades	19.6
frozen pizza	18.9
dry dog food	18.8
crackers	18.1
baby food	16.7

FRANCE	% change
bath/shower additives	9.5
plastic foil/wraps	9.4
toothbrushes	8.9
cereals/muesli	6.9
colas	5.6
toothpaste	4.1
hair conditioners	3.1
instant coffee - premium	2.8
chewing gum	1.7
infant milk	1.4

GERMANY	% change
dehydrated soup	36.4
air fresheners	30.0
panty liners	21.8
nuts	19.6
dishwasher detergent	18.1
instant coffee - premium	17.7
tampons	16.4
instant coffee	16.2
lipsticks	14.9
cereals/muesli	14.5

Source : Nielsen

3 ► The right word

A • Crossword

Across

1 • People who buy things or use services.
2 • When you ask for something that you'll pay for to be brought or sent to you.
3 • Something manufactured by a company.
4 • Small piece of paper or plastic attached to an object giving information such as price on it.
5 • Consumer.

Down

a • Variety.
b • Regular.
c • Not dear.
d • Soar.

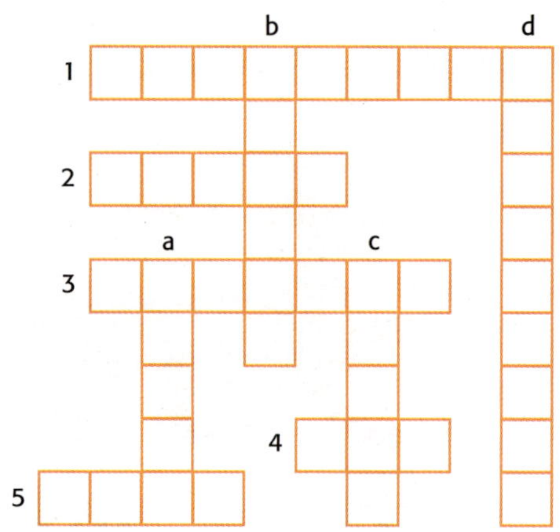

B • Fill in the blanks with words from the following list (remember to make the necessary adjustments).

booming / brand name / buyer / consumer / fall / increase / sales / soar / tumble

1 • Home computers, camcorders, microwaves are expensive .... goods.
2 • It seems that the British .... is quite receptive to new technology.
3 • The consumption of spirits seems to be .... in Europe and in the US. It is then difficult to .... profits when consumption is ....
4 • When it is very hot, sales of beer are ....
5 • The sales of the Louis Vuitton classic handbag are still ....
6 • Rémy Martin, the French Cognac producer, relies on Japan for a great part of its ....
7 • Dior perfumes and Dom Perignon champagne are two famous .... goods.

4 ► Vocabulary

acheter : buy (bought, bought), purchase
annuler (une commande) : cancel (an order)
arrhes : deposit
article défectueux : faulty article / item
article de première qualité : first-rate article
augmenter : increase, rise (rose, risen)
authentique : genuine

baisser : decrease
biens de consommation : consumer goods
biens d'équipement : durable goods, durables
bon marché : cheap

chef de produit : product manager
cher : expensive, dear
chuter : fall (fell, fallen)
code-barre : bar code
commande : order → order (v.)
commande (bon de) : order form
commande (sur) : on order
confiance du consommateur : consumer confidence
consommateur : consumer → consume (v.)
consommation : consumption
consommation des ménages : household consumption
consommation (habitudes de) : consumer habits / patterns
consommation (société de) : consumer society
consumérisme : consumerism
contrefaçon (la) : counterfeiting [U], faking [U], forgery [U]
contrefaçons : counterfeit goods, forged products, bogus goods, fake goods
contrefaire : counterfeit
contrefaire (impossible à) : forgery-resistant
copies (faire des) : counterfeit, pirate
courbe : graph
croître : grow (grew, grown)

dégringoler : tumble
demande : demand
dépenses : expenses, expenditure [U]
doubler : double
durée de vie (d'un produit) : lifespan (of a product)

échantillon gratuit : free / complimentary sample
effondrer (s') : plummet
étiquette : label
étiquette (prix) : tag

faussaire : falser, defrauder, forger, cheater, copycat
foyer : household

gamme : range, line
gamme (bas de) : downmarket

haut de gamme : upmarket

image de marque : brand image
indice des prix : consumer price index / CPI

luxe (objets de) : luxury items / goods

marque: brand name, trademark
monter en flèche : skyrocket, rocket up

nouveau (tout) : (brand) new

payer qqch : pay for sth
pouvoir d'achat : purchasing /spending power
produit à forte marge : high-profit product
produit à forte valeur ajoutée : high-value-added product
propriétaire : owner
propriété : ownership

qualité : quality
qualité (faire des contrôles de) : exercise quality controls
qualité (satisfaire aux normes de) : meet the quality standards

ralentir : slow
rapport qualité / prix : quality / price ratio / value for money
réduction : cut
remboursé (être) : be refunded / reimbursed, get one's money back
revenu : income

stable : steady
statut : status
stimuler : boost
sur mesure : custom-made (GB), customized (US)

tendance : trend
tripler : treble
troc : barter
troquer : barter, swap

utilisateur : user

valoir : be worth (+ V-ing)
vogue : craze, fad, vogue

Unit 4 **Big business**

A few landmarks

Forms of business organisation

- The **sole trader** or **sole proprietor**: one person provides the capital, controls the business, keeps all the profits or bears all the loss and has **unlimited liability**. Unlimited liability means that if a business fails then all the private wealth of the owner can be used to pay back the creditors.
- A **partnership** (of at least 2 people and maximum 20) may be formed to increase the amount of money invested in a business in common. Each partner is responsible for the debts of the partnership. Profits and losses are shared. A partnership has **unlimited liability**.
- A **private limited company** has at least 2 but usually not more than 50 members who provide the capital which is divided into **shares**. This type of company is controlled by a **board of directors** elected by the **shareholders**. A **director** and a **company secretary** are appointed. The profit is distributed in proportion to the number of shares that are owned by each shareholder. A private limited company has **limited liability** (this is indicated by the letters **Ltd** after its name), which means that if the business fails the owners will only lose the money they have invested in the company and no more). In the US such companies are **incorporated** (registered) in the state where they have their headquarters (this is indicated by the letters **Inc.** or **Corp.** after their names).

- **There are several ways to strengthen a company's operations in order to remain competitive:**
  - The **joint venture** is when two or more companies jointly invest in a separate business project.
  - The **merger** is when two companies join together under the name of one of them or as a new company.
  - The **takeover** or acquisition is when one company has accumulated enough shares of another company to take over control and ownership.

Sforsail Cy
ORGANISATION CHART

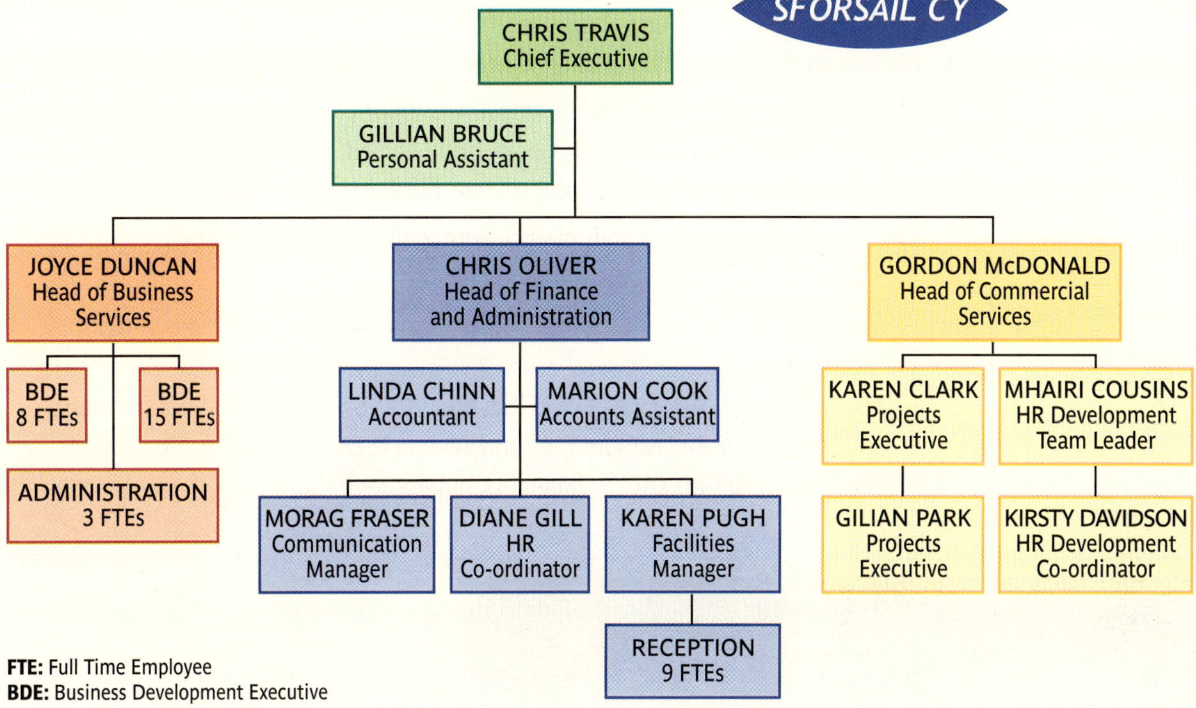

FTE: Full Time Employee
BDE: Business Development Executive

Warm-up

1 • **To whom will the following people report?**
- the Accountant
- the Facilities Manager
- the PA
- the Head of Commercial Services

2 • **Who's chief executive?**

3 • **What's his PA's name?**

4 • **How many FTEs report to the Facilities Manager?**

5 • **What is Morag Fraser in charge of?**

6 • **Pair work:**
A asks as many questions as possible on the structure of Sforsail Cy, and B answers.

Ex.: Who is in charge of .... ?
Who is in responsible for .... ?
Who reports to .... ?
Who is in charge of .... ?
Etc.

TEXT 1

Levi Strauss and Co

1. **apparel =** clothing
2. **casual =** informal
3. **strength:** *solidité*
4. **share:** *action*

Founded in 1853 by Bavarian immigrant Levi Strauss, Levi Strauss & Co. (LS&CO) is one of the world's largest brand-name apparel[1] marketers with sales in more than 100 countries. There is no other company with a comparable global presence in the jeans and casual[2] pants markets. Our market-leading apparel products are sold under the Levi's® and Dockers® brands.

In 1873, Levi Strauss and Nevada tailor Jacob Davis patented the process of putting rivets in pants for strength[3], and the world's first jeans – Levi's® jeans – were born. Today, the Levi's® trademark is one of the most recognized in the world and is registered in more than 160 countries.

The company is privately held by descendants of the family of Levi Strauss. Shares[4] of company's stock are not publicly traded. Shares of Levi Strauss Japan, K.K., the company's Japanese affiliate, are publicly traded in Japan.

The company employs a staff of approximately 1,400 people at its San Francisco, California, Headquarters.

Levis Strauss & Co. is a worldwide corporation organized into three geographic divisions:

– Levi Strauss, the Americas (LSA), based in the San Francisco headquarters;
– Levi Strauss Europe, Middle East and Africa (LSEMA), based in Brussels;
– Asia Pacific Division (APD), based in Singapore.

From www.levistrauss.com

© Corbis Sygma / James Andanson.

► Check your pronunciation

A • of the *-ed* word ending. (see Passport)

1 • patented
2 • recognized
3 • traded
4 • organized
5 • based

B • of the following words.

1 • apparel
2 • casual
3 • strength
4 • headquarters
5 • worldwide

► Words

Match the words from the text with their definitions.

1 • a marketer (l. 2)
2 • patent (l. 6)
3 • held by (l. 10)
4 • stock (l. 11)
5 • an affiliate (l. 12)
6 • staff (l. 13)
7 • headquarters (l. 14)
8 • a corporation (l. 15)

a • shares in the ownership of a company
b • a large business or company
c • give the right to make or sell an invention
d • employees
e • owned by
f • a subsidiary
g • a seller
h • main offices

► Meaning

A • Find the questions corresponding to the following answers.

1 • in 1853
2 • Bavarian
3 • 100 countries
4 • Levi's® and Dockers®
5 • in 1873
6 • in more than 160 countries
7 • descendants of the family of Levi Strauss
8 • in Japan
9 • 1,400 people

B • Translate into English. (see T&T: Compound nouns)

1 • *Le siège social de Bruxelles.*
2 • *L'immigrant venu de Munich.*
3 • *Un tailleur du Nevada.*
4 • *La famille Levi Strauss.*

C • Complete the sentences: use a superlative. (see T&T: Superlatives)

1 • It's a very old brand. It's .... in the USA.
2 • He was a very clever man. He was .... in his family.
3 • It is a very good brand. It's .... in the store.
4 • They are very large marketers. They are .... in Europe.

D • Turn into the passive. (see T&T: Passive form)

1 • They will organise the company into several geographic divisions.
2 • Jacob Davis patented the process.
3 • We've held the company for 150 years.
4 • We are now employing 1,400 people.

► Pair work

Imagine a dialogue between **A** who would like to set up his / her own business and **B** who tries to talk him / her out of it.

► Food for thought

Where would you rather carry out your internship: in a small or a large company?

1. **in the pipeline:** *en chantier*
2. **fuelled on:** *alimenté par*
3. **on the shelves:** *en rayon*
4. **price tag:** *étiquette*
5. **sinkhole:** *cloaque*

The battle for the video games market

© Reuters / Max PPP.

These are nerve-racking times in the video console business. Just listen to Satoru Iwata, who took over as president of Nintendo last week. One might have expected him to brim with optimism about the great games the company has in the pipeline[1], or the prospects of Nintendo's GameCube console muscling in on its rivals from Microsoft and Sony.

But this is what he actually said yesterday, to a group of analysts in Tokyo: "We can't be optimistic about the game market. No matter what great product you come up with, people get bored."

That's quite an admission in a business that has long since been fuelled on[2] soaring optimism for the future. Just two weeks ago, at the Electronic Entertainment Expo in Los Angeles, Nintendo's representative Peter MacDougall was happily predicting that the current dominance of Sony's PlayStation 2 machine would prove to be short-lived. "I think they know that the battle is on," he announced.

The battle is indeed on, and has been ever since Nintendo and Microsoft raced into the market to try to catch up with Sony, whose PlayStation 2 had a whole year on the shelves[3] to itself.

Nintendo has already worried publicly that the price war is going to eat into its future profits – it predicts a 15 per cent drop for the coming year. That's not surprising, given that all the Big Three can now expect to lose money on every console they sell.

Sony, which enjoys an 80 percent market share, was the first to slash its price, bringing the PlayStation 2 down from $299 to $199 in the United States. Microsoft followed suit with an identical drop two days later on its Xbox®, even though it had previously admitted that it could not make a profit even at the $299 price tag[4]. Nintendo, which already had the cheapest console, dropped the price on the GameCube from $199 to $149 to stay ahead of the game.

It's easy to conclude that the video game industry is becoming a vast commercial sinkhole[5], a market sector that refuses to grow at the anticipated pace and turns out to be all take and no give.

From *The Independent,* Friday 7 June 2002.

► Check your pronunciation

A • Stress the following words from the text.

1 • optimism
2 • optimistic
3 • identical
4 • commercial
5 • rival

B • Make sure you can pronounce these words correctly.

1 • video
2 • console
3 • Los Angeles
4 • Tokyo
5 • Sony
6 • Nintendo

► Words

Match the following words from the text with their synonyms.

1 • nerve-racking (l. 1)	a • fall
2 • actually (l. 10)	b • speed
3 • soaring (l. 14)	c • alarming
4 • current (l. 17)	d • contrary to expectation
5 • drop (l.23)	e • rising
6 • slash (l. 26)	f • present
7 • pace (l. 33)	g • reduce.

► Meaning

A • Complete each sentence.

(§1) 1 • An attitude expected from Nintendo: ....
(§2) 2 • A link word showing there was a clash between what was expected and what was actually declared: ....
(§3) 3 • One word belonging to the vocabulary of war: ....
(§4) 4 • The Big Three are ...., ... and ....
(§5) 5 • Find the prediction common to the Big Three: .... (expressed in one phrase) .
(§6) 6 • The marketing decision taken by the Big Three concerning the prices of their consoles: .... prices.
(§7) 7 • A word that sums up the current state of the video game industry: ....

B • Now use the words you've found in A to sum up the text. (maximum of 60 words)

C • Underline the correct forms of the words in bold, then translate the sentences. (see T&T: Present perfect / Preterite)

1 • When Satoru Iwata **took over / has taken** over as president, he was expected to be optimistic.
2 • Yesterday he **actually admitted / has actually admitted** that people are getting bored with the game products.
3 • Two weeks ago his rival **predicted/ has predicted** a long war with Sony and Microsoft.
4 • The battle **was / has been** on since Nintendo and Microsoft started to catch up with Sony.
5 • Sony **slashed/ has slashed** its price before the Los Angeles Expo. It **was / has been followed** by Microsoft. And then Nintendo **dropped / has dropped** the price of its GameCube.

► Pair work

A Sony representative is discussing with a Nintendo and a Microsoft representative. They are comparing their results and speak about their prospects. Imagine the conversation.

► Food for thought

Can you try to think of other marketing "wars" between rivals?

Unit 4

TEXT 3

Boots plans £100m revamp for stores

1. **spruce up** = dress up, be neat and smart
2. **refurbishment** = renovation
3. **put off** = dissuade

Boots, the healthcare and pharmaceuticals company, is next week expected to announce a multi-million-pound plan to spruce up[1] its stores. Analysts are eagerly awaiting news on whether Boots is going ahead with the refurbishments[2] when the company reveals its full-year results, this Thursday. City investors have been concerned that the dated stores are putting off[3] shoppers. "There is no doubt that its stores look tired, particularly in London," said one analyst. More than £100m is expected to be spent on the programme, which is likely to take more than a year. The proposed refurbishment is believed to involve Boots' 14,000 stores getting a lick of paint, with more colours, particularly blue, used to brighten up the general ambience. However, one analyst said that the business needed other investments aside from the refurbishing of the stores. "If you just spend the money on stores, it won't be money well spent," he said. "For example, they are often out of stock, and they seem rather demotivated as a group, so perhaps they could increase the staff wages or bring in new managers."

From *The Independent on Sunday*, 26 May 2002.

© Réa / Pierre Bessard.

► Words

Match each word in bold with its meaning.

1 • "Analysts are **eagerly** awaiting news" (l. 23).
a • impatiently b • stupidly c • patiently

2 • "City investors have been concerned that the **dated** stores are putting off shoppers." (l. 4-5).
a • old-fashioned b • recent c • ancient

3 • "The proposed refurbishment is believed to **involve** Boots' 14,000 stores" (l. 8).
a • exclude b • include c • omit

4 • "The business needed other investments **aside** from the refurbishing of the stores." (l. 10-11).
a • except b • apart c • after

► Meaning

A • Fill in the blanks with verbs from the following list. Remember to make the necessary adjustments.

brighten up / bring in / bring in / put off / spruce up

Boots stores need to be .... Indeed, they are so outdated that they .... a growing number of shoppers. That's why refurbishment is planned in order to .... the general ambience. Yet the business needs other changes. New managers could be .... All these investments would .... a lot of profit in the years to come.

B • Rewrite the following sentences using a passive form. Omit the agent if unnecessary. (see T&T: Passive form)

1 • The business needed other investments.

2 • It will give shareholders the benefits of future growth prospects.

3 • One expects the group to announce a 9-per-cent increase.

4 • The dated stores are putting off shoppers.

Checkup
Unit 4

1 ► Test

Just the small question of no added value

It is 18 months since Glaxo Wellcome merged with SmithKline Beecham to create Europe's biggest pharmaceuticals group.

It was their second attempt to merge and investors almost universally welcomed the union.

The organisation – based in London but run from Philadelphia by French-born Jean-Pierre Garnier – looked good on paper and its senior executives had a record of delivering the goods. It was Glaxo's second big merger – it had pulled off an audacious deal with Wellcome in 1995, which had been designed to convert Glaxo from a one-product company dominated by ulcer drug Zantac to a pharmaceutical world leader. Buying Wellcome brought in key Aids drugs, and most analysts thought Glaxo would repeat the trick with the SmithKline deal.

GSK has 107 manufacturing sites in 40 countries producing 1,200 brands. Every minute more than 1,100 prescriptions are written for GSK drugs and every hour the company spends nearly £300,000 searching for new blockbuster medicines.

But the merger has so far failed to add any value or to produce any big new drugs, and the firm has been beset by a series of problems.

There have been image issues sparked by GSK's intransigence over cutting the price of its HIV drugs in South Africa. There is also the matter of a damaging investigation by Munich police into allegations of bribing German doctors between 1997 and 1999.

The company is also in trouble with patents on two of its biggest sellers – anti-depressant Seroxat and antibiotic Augmentin. Both drugs are approaching the end of their patent protection and last month GSK lost a court case which is likely to result in Seroxat facing cheap competition earlier than expected. GSK has seen potential blockbusters fail at the final hurdle and is now scouring the world to license in products from rival firms, prompting criticism that it is now a marketing company rather than a drugs group. GSK is now believed to be considering a merger with Bristol Myers Squibb.

From *The Guardian*, June 12, 2002.

A • Introduce Glaxo company insisting on its headquarters, its sites and its products. (about 30 words)

B • Complete the following grid.

Mergers	With	In	What for?
1st merger	....	....	....
2nd merger	....	2001	....
3rd merger	....	unknown	unknown

C • Sum up the text in French. (maximum of 100 words)
You will insist on its mergers and the various problems Glaxo has recently come across.

D • Translate into French.

1 • "It was Glaxo's second big merger" (l. 9-10) to "world leader" (l. 14).
2 • "But the merger" (l. 23) to "problems" (l. 25).

2 ► Skills in practice

Read the following newspaper headlines. Try to guess what they mean.

1 • Oil opportunities
2 • A company is going to replace a chief executive
3 • A group of people fighting a company
4 • A company is considering a bid for another one
5 • A boss turns down an offer
6 • Taxpayers will have to stump up an extra sum of money
7 • A company becomes number one and raises capital from the public

BAA chief spurns £75,000 pay rise

Public foots £150M Railtrack bill

BHS targets Woolworth

Maxi tops mobile floats

ABBEY SET TO OUST FAILED BOSS

Bookies at odds with Lotto

Falklanders see a future in black gold

3 ► The right word

A • Crossword

Across
1 • Regular and essential expenses of a business.
2 • Opposite of gain.
3 • In difficulty.
4 • Rhythm.
5 • List of items to be discussed in a meeting.
6 • Firm.
7 • Short for incorporated.
8 • When someone buys enough shares in a company to gain control of it.
9 • Subdivision of a company.

Down
a • Yield.
b • President.
c • Part of a larger company.
d • Shared.
e • Associate.
f • Joining of two companies.
g • US for share.

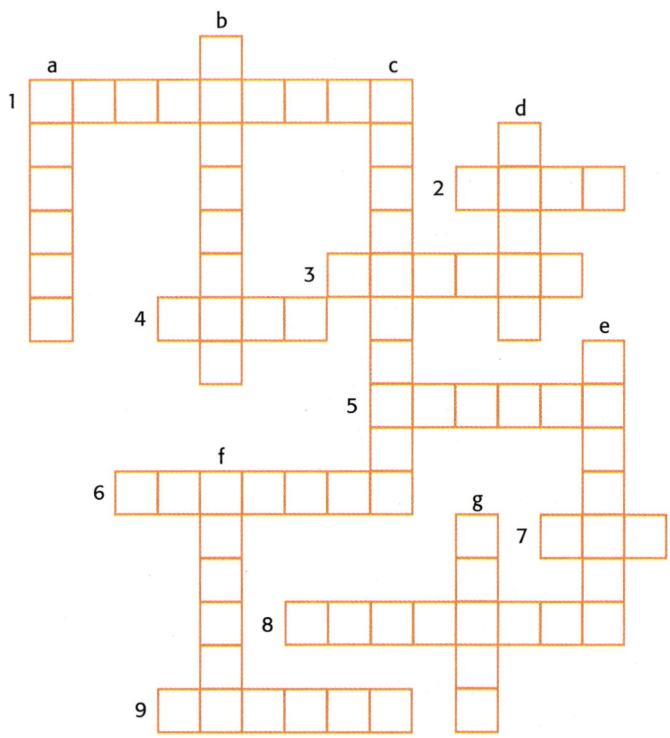

B • Fill in the blanks with words from the following list.

chairman of the board / company secretary / headed / liabilities / limited company / limited partnership / memorandum of association / privatised / self-employed / shareholders

1 • Lawyers and sole traders are ....
2 • A .... is a document drawn up when a company is set up.
3 • The sales department is .... by the sales manager.
4 • .... will see from the directors' report that an increase of 2 per cent in the final dividend is proposed.
5 • This company is going to undertake very heavy ....
6 • The .... is the nominal head of the company.
7 • In a ...., the owners' or shareholders' liability is limited to the amount of their contribution.
8 • The .... keeps the company's statutory books.
9 • In Great Britain, British Telecom, British Gas and British Airways are the most important .... companies.
10 • In a ...., the partners bring a financial contribution to the company but they don't manage it.

4

► Vocabulary

acte constitutif : memorandum of association
actionnaire : shareholder
administrateur : director
archives : records
assemblée générale des actionnaires : general shareholders' meeting
associé : partner
atelier : workshop

capital : capital
capital social : equity
chargé des relations publiques : Public Relations Officer, PRO
chef comptable : accounts manager
chef d'entreprise : entrepreneur
chef de production : production manager
chef des ventes : sales manager, head of sales
chef du personnel : personnel manager
co-entreprise : joint venture
commanditaire : limited partner, sleeping partner, silent partner (US)
comptable : accountant, book-keeper
compte (à son) : self-employed
conseil d'administration : board of directors
constitué (être) : be set up / incorporated
contrôleur : supervisor

dépendre de : report to
directeur commercial : sales manager
directeur général : managing director
dirigé (être) : be headed, be run

étendre (s') : expand

fermer (définitivement) : shut down
filiale : subsidiary, affiliate
fonder une société : form a company
fusion : merger → merger (v.)

homologue : counterpart

maison mère : parent company
majorité relative : plurality

nationalisé : state-owned, nationalised

ordre du jour : agenda
organigramme : organisation chart

P-D-G : chairman and managing director
président du conseil d'administration : chairman of the board
privatisé : privatised
procès-verbal : minutes
propriétaire : owner
propriété : ownership

responsabilité (sens juridique) : liability
réunion : meeting

séance : meeting
secrétaire : company secretary
service : department
service comptable : accounts / accountancy department
service de la production : production department
service de la recherche et du développement : Research and Development department, R&D
service des ressources humaines : Human Resources Department, HR department
service des transports : transport / packing and shipping department
service des ventes : sales department
service informatique : data-processing department, IT department
service juridique : legal / law department
service publicité : advertising department
siège social : headquarters, head office
société : company, corporation (US), business, firm
société anonyme, SA : public limited company, PLC, plc
société à responsabilité limitée, SARL : private limited company / corporation (US)
société en commandite : limited partnership
société en nom collectif : partnership
société par actions : joint stock company, limited company, Ltd Co
statuts : articles of association

vote : vote
vote prépondérant : casting vote

Unit 5 World trade

A few landmarks

- When countries exchange goods and services, this is called **international trade** and it depends on what countries produce and need. **Exports** are products or raw materials which are sold and sent to another country. **Imports** are products or raw materials which are bought from another country.

- Governments control international trade with tariffs (also called duties) and quotas. A **tariff** is a tax on imported products and a **quota** is the maximum quantity of a product allowed into a country over a certain period of time. Those measures are called **protectionist** measures as they raise the price of imported goods so as to protect goods produced in the country.

- **A few international organisations**

– WTO or World Trade Organisation
– EFTA or European Free Trade Association
– NAFTA or North America Free Trade Agreement
– OPEC or Organisation of Petroleum Exporting Countries
– ASEAN or Association of South East Asian Nations
– LAIA or Latin American Integration Association
– MERCOSUR or Mercado Comun del Sur
– CACM or Central American Common Market
– COMESA or Common Market for Eastern and Southern Africa
– CEMAC or Communauté Économique et Monétaire de l'Afrique Centrale

They regulate tariffs and reduce trade restrictions between member countries. Other organisations are the OECD or Organisation for Economic Co-operation and Development, the EU or European Union.

Warm-up

1 • What does WTO stand for?

2 • What are those people doing?

3 • What are they wearing? What for?

Unit 5

TEXT 1

A complex and enduring globalisation

1. **reversal:** *renversement*
2. **upfront:** *payé d'avance*
3. **be bent on =** be eager to
4. **shorthand:** *formule consacrée*
5. **bind (bound, bound):** *lier*

The fiery denunciations of globalisation, free trade and the US model of capitalism, while common and politically alluring, have yet to produce the wholesale political reversals[1] called for by critics. Instead, countries are scrambling either to join the World Trade Organisation or to become more active participants in it and are doing all they can to attract foreign investment. China has just become the world's fourth largest trader (after the US, Europe and Japan). Despite the important upfront[2] costs, difficult entry conditions and political risks of joining the WTO, the Russian government is bent on[3] gaining acceptance as soon as possible. Countries such as Jordan and Turkey are overcoming huge domestic obstacles to open their economies and to become more integrated with the rest of the world. [...]

Consider the widely held view that globalisation is shorthand[4] for international trade and investment, or what multinational corporations do. Thanks to Al-Qaida, everyone knows that globalisation goes well beyond the links that bind[5] corporations, traders, financiers and central bankers. It is used not just to spread ideas but also for communication by terrorists, politicians, religious leaders, anti-globalisation activists and bureaucrats. Governments are working with counterparts worldwide more closely than ever. September 11 showed political globalisation is as powerful a phenomenon as the globalisation of the economy.

From *Financial Times*, August 5, 2002.

© The Image Bank / Ian Mckinnell.

► Check your pronunciation

A • Can you stress the right syllable in the following words?

1 • denunciation
2 • globalisation
3 • anti-globalisation
4 • communication
5 • condition
6 • corporation

B • Now check you can pronounce the following words.

1 • fiery
2 • bind
3 • phenomenon
4 • Jordan
5 • Turkey
6 • bureaucrats

► Words

A • Choose the correct meaning.

1 • "enduring" (title) means:
lasting / long / hard

2 • "fiery" (l. 1) means:
proud / passionate / stupid

3 • "alluring" (l. 2) means:
interesting / attractive / dull

4 • "scrambling" (l. 3) means:
rushing / trying / refusing

5 • "overcoming" (l. 9) means:
defeating / refusing / cancelling

6 • "counterpart" (l. 17) means:
enemy / friend / equivalent

B • Complete the following sentences. (see World Table)

1 • Someone born in Turkey is ....

2 • Someone born in Jordan is ....

3 • Someone born in Russia is ....

4 • Someone born in China is ....

5 • Someone born in the Netherlands is ....

► Meaning

A • Fill in the following blanks with words from the text.

1 • Those who criticise globalisation also criticise .... and ....

2 • Those who criticise globalisation have failed to produce examples of ....

3 • Globalisation appeals to countries. The proof is lots of them desperately want to ....

4 • This is the case for ...., ... and ....

5 • Globalisation is not only limited to .... and ...., it also enables ....

6 • Hence globalisation is also ....

B • Would you say that the writer of this article is…

– totally in favour of globalisation?
– dead against globalisation?
– undecided about what to think of globalisation?

Justify your answer.

C • Translate into English.

1 • *La Russie est désireuse d'adhérer à l'OMC.*

2 • *Ce pays est le troisième plus grand producteur de cacao.*

3 • *Notre président travaille en étroite collaboration avec son homologue britannique.*

4 • *Ce pays vient de décider d'ouvrir son économie au reste du monde.*

5 • *La Chine attire de plus en plus les investissements étrangers.*

D • Translate into French from "Instead, countries" (l. 3) to "investment" (l. 5).

E • Pick out all the nouns in the singular without articles (in the first paragraph) and explain why they have this form. (see T&T: Articles)

F • Find a synonym for "while" in the expression "while common and politically alluring" (l. 2).

G • Make sure you can translate the following expression: "Consider the widely held view" (l. 11).

► Pair work

A is in favour of globalisation whereas **B** is dead against it. Imagine their arguments.

► Food for thought

List a few "domestic obstacles" that can prevent countries from joining the WTO.

Unit 5

TEXT 2

Trade spats[1] over garlic[2] imports

1. **spat (coll.) =** quarrel
2. **garlic:** *ail*
3. **stem the tide:** *enrayer la marée*
4. **backfire:** *effet inverse*
5. **misgiving =** fear

Despite emergency legislation, shipment seizures and gigantic tariffs, America is drowning in a sea of Chinese garlic.

Although garlic imports from China have to be transported at considerable expense across the Pacific and are subject to an enormous 400 per cent duty, they still sell in the supermarkets for less than US farmers' similarly aromatic crops.

No measure the US government has tried appears able to stem the tide[3] of low-priced goods, which is also damaging America's domestic apple and honey industries. US consumers are thought unlikely to show their patriotism: Chinese garlic is considered better quality and is less than half the price of domestic produce.

The flood started with China's entry into the World Trade Organisation (WTO) last December, and represents a colossal backfire[4] of US trade policy. In California, farmers have been forced to cut garlic cultivation for the first time in nearly 40 years. Just three years ago, Californian authorities were only too glad to embrace normalised trade with China. Sensing the opportunity to sell pistachios and almonds into the huge Chinese market, Californian growers actively pushed for China's entry into the WTO.

© Corbis / Wolfgang Kaehler.

Any farmers who did have misgivings[5] were soon silenced by the then booming technology industry, which was also eyeing the great potential of the Chinese market.

But it is now clear that when it comes to agriculture, the US has lost more than it gained. More than half of China's 1.4 billion population work on farms; the country has enormous resources, and the whole growing process is centrally planned. Commodities analysts are now predicting that garlic is just the vanguard of a major trade assault by China that could see the US market dominated by Chinese crops within 10 years.

China's actions are under heavy fire from the US International Trade Commission, which is now accusing importers of breaching "anti-dumping" laws by selling goods below home market costs.

From *The Independent,* 20 June 2002.

► Check your pronunciation

A • Can you stress the right syllable in the following words?

1 • emergency
2 • unlikely
3 • misgiving
4 • dominated
5 • considerable
6 • colossal
7 • agriculture
8 • enormous
9 • cultivation
10 • population

B • Remember a pronunciation rule and read the following words.

1 • guard
2 • guardian
3 • vanguard
4 • guarantee
5 • guarantor

► Words

A • Choose the correct meaning.

1 • "unlikely" (l. 8) means: improbable / not liked / eventual
2 • "embrace" (l. 14) means: kiss / adopt / comprehend
3 • "grower" (l. 16) means: worker / people / farmer
4 • "commodities" (l. 24) means: articles / stuff / convenient things
5 • "breaching" (l. 29) means: obeying / respecting / breaking

B • Find synonyms of the following words in the text.

1 • improbable
2 • reduce
3 • include
4 • forefront

► Meaning

A • Join the sentence halves below.

1 • Despite emergency measures…
2 • Although garlic imports are very expensive…
3 • In spite of the present recession…
4 • In spite of rising costs of shipments…
5 • Even though US growers are furious…

a • economists remain optimistic.
b • the US is flooded with garlic.
c • the Chinese will keep their prices low.
d • there is nothing they can do against those imports.
e • they sell well in US supermarkets.

B • Link the pairs of sentences using an expression of contrast. (see T&T: Adverbs / Clauses of contrast)

Ex.: Our sales fell. Our reputation is still good.
In spite of a fall in sales our reputation is still good.

1 • We have taken emergency measures. People still continue to smoke a lot.
2 • Pollution is rising in this river. Tourists enjoy swimming there.
3 • Prices have increased. Consumption has been steady.
4 • I would like more spare time. I do enjoy my job.
5 • The recession is looming. We'll achieve good profits.

C • Which of the following statements are true?

1 • The US is flooded with Chinese garlic.
2 • Importing garlic from China is not really expensive.
3 • Chinese garlic sells well in the US because of huge import duty.
4 • The garlic flood has been continuous since China's entry into the WTO.
5 • Californian farmers used to cheer China's entry into the WTO.
6 • Those who in the past had misgivings about China's entry into the WTO clashed with the bosses of the technology industry.
7 • US agriculture has enjoyed lots of advantages since this entry.
8 • China is forecast to dominate the US agricultural market in a few years.
9 • US importers are now charged with dumping.

► Pair work

Imagine a short dialogue between **A** who thinks China's entry into the WTO will develop the country and **B** who thinks it is going to be a catastrophe for the global economy.

► Food for thought

Can you think of a few advantages and drawbacks of protectionism?

D • Translate into English.

1 • *Ces importations sont soumises à des droits très élevés.*
2 • *Il semble que les agriculteurs américains aient plus gagné que perdu à l'adhésion de la Chine dans l'OMC.*
3 • *Les produits chinois continuent de bien se vendre dans les supermarchés américains.*

E • Translate into French from "No measure" (l. 6) to "honey industries" (l. 8).

TEXT 3

1. **blend:** *mélanger*
2. **waiver =** exemption
3. **bulk =** large quantity

Sri Lanka plans tea venture in Pakistan

The Sri Lankan industry, which excels in tea packaging and other forms of adding value to the beverage, is planning to form joint ventures in Pakistan for the blending[1] and marketing of teas. Pakistan's move to allow duty-free imports of teas from Sri Lanka has encouraged some producers there to explore the possibility of forming alliances with Pakistani businessmen.

Industry officials said the proposed duty waiver[2], which will be part of a new trade arrangement between the two south Asian countries, will boost Sri Lankan tea exports to Pakistan, the world's third-largest tea importer after the Commonwealth of Independent States and the UK. The customs waiver will create goodwill for Pakistan in Sri Lanka, much to India's discomfort. Pakistan imports annually between 58m and 67m kilos of tea from Kenya and its next biggest supplier is Indonesia with 12m kilos. "The Pakistani market is big enough to accommodate a third major supplier. And, unlike the other producing countries, Sri Lanka is planning investment in Pakistan for value addition to bulk[3] tea," said an Indian trade official.

From *Financial Times,* August 6, 2002.

► Words

Circle the correct answer.

1 • "will boost Sri Lankan tea exports" (l. 7-8) means:
will raise / will decrease / will cancel

2 • "will create goodwill" (l. 9) means:
will create kindness / will create anger / will create fear

3 • "much to India's discomfort" (l. 10) means:
India is very happy / India feels very nervous / India feels uneasy

4 • "The Pakistani market is big enough to accommodate a third supplier" (l. 12-13) means:
The Pakistani market is big enough to welcome a third supplier / to eliminate a third supplier / to strike a deal with a third supplier

► Meaning

A • The two partners and the plan:

– Country number 1: ....
– Country number 2: ....
– Industry at stake: ....
– The plan is ....
– Consequence for country number 1: ....
– Two major suppliers for country number 2: ....
– Another country is not happy with the decision: ....
– Major advantage of the plan for country number 2: ....

B • Make sentences expressing opposition. (see T&T: Adverbs / Clauses of contrast) You may use *unlike / whereas / contrary to.*

Ex.: Tom is small. Peter is tall.
– Unlike Peter, Tom is small.
– Tom is small whereas Peter is tall.

1 • Pakistan is a big tea importer. Sri Lanka is not.
2 • Customs duties were cut for Sri Lanka. they were not for India.
3 • Sri Lanka excels in tea packaging. Indonesia doesn't.
4 • The customs waiver will create goodwill for Pakistan in Sri Lanka. It won't for India in Sri Lanka.

Checkup Unit 5

1 ► Test

In Asia, balance of economic power shifts to China's favor

From South Korea to Indonesia, China is rapidly strengthening its economic presence across Asia, gobbling up foreign investment and chipping away at the United States' position as the region's economic engine.

As it buys up goods, parts and raw materials from its neighbors as never before, China has accompanied its new heft* with diplomatic efforts to assure them it wants to offer cooperation, not competition. […]

The United States still remains an essential trading partner for Asian countries but is becoming somewhat less important in the face of China's rise, analysts say. Some see China's economic thrust, more apparent now under its newly minted membership in the World Trade Organization, as the beginning of an inescapable process of China replacing the United States as the dominant power in Asia. […]

China is grabbing much of the new foreign investment in Asia, leaving its neighbors with crumbs compared with the record $50 billion China is expected to gain this year. China – a hungry importer – is forcing its Asian neighbors to adjust.

Singapore's exports to China surged by 69 percent in April over the previous April, mainly because of petrochemical and pharmaceutical sales. Malaysia's exports to China have increased by more than 30 percent in the last three months, driven mostly by electronic products.

As a sign of the new circumstances with respect to China, ASEAN members agreed last November to trade talks with China. The idea for the trade zone came from China, acting to alleviate resentment in the region over its new membership in the World Trade Organization.

A mutual courtship has emerged between China and its neighbors. "I look at China and its neighbors as a friendly force," said Indonesia's minister of trade and industry. […] Until recently, Indonesia had viewed China as a hostile power. […]

The sudden economic influence of China on the region is evident almost daily. […]

South Korea and Taiwan, as well as Malaysia and Singapore, will have to adapt cleverly by going further upscale. For example, with its well-educated work force, Singapore plans to spend billions of dollars to reinvent itself as the biomedical center of Asia.

Adapted from *The New York Times* (from *Le Monde*), July 7 and 8, 2002

* **heft (US)** = importance.

A • Complete the following blanks.

1 • The two rivals present in Asia are .... and ....
2 • The country about to become dominant is ....
3 • Give three examples of this country's neighbours:
.........................., ... and ....
4 • This country's offer to its neighbours: ....
5 • The reason why this emergence is more now dominant than ever:
....
6 • Attitude the neighbours were forced to adopt: ....
7 • Give an example: ....
8 • Decision taken by ASEAN members: ....
9 • Previous attitude of one country (reflecting the other neighbours'):
....
10 • New attitude shared by this country and its neighbours: ....
11 • What the dominant country buys from its neighbours: ....

B • Translate the last paragraph into French.

C • Translate into English.

1 • *Ce pays demeure notre principal partenaire commercial.*
2 • *Les membres de l'association se sont mis d'accord le mois dernier pour accroître leurs exportations de 20 %.*

2 ► Skills in practice

Answer the following questions concerning the four trade organisations.

1 • Which one is the oldest?
2 • Which one is the newest?
3 • Three of them have almost the same goal. Give their names and try to say what they have in common.
4 • Which organisations only concern a geographical area?

GATT (General Agreement on Tariffs and Trade)	Set of multilateral trade agreements aimed at the abolition of quotas and the reduction of tariff duties among the signing nations. Originally signed by 23 countries at Geneva in 1947, GATT became the most effective instrument in the massive expansion of world trade in the later 20th century. By 1995, when GATT was replaced by the WTO, 125 nations had signed its agreements, which governed 90% of world trade.
WTO (World Trade Organisation)	International organisation based in Geneva that supervises world trade with the intention of making it flow as smoothly, predictably, and freely as possible. It was created by 104 members in 1995 to replace the GATT. Like its predecessor, it aims to lower trade barriers and encourage multilateral trade.
NAFTA (North American Free Trade Agreement)	Trade pact signed by Canada, the U.S., and Mexico in 1992, which took effect in 1994. Inspired by the European Community's success in reducing trade barriers among its members, NAFTA created the world's largest free-trade area.
ASEAN (Association of South East Asian Nations)	International organisation established by the governments of Indonesia, Malaysia, the Philippines, Singapore, and Thailand in 1967 to accelerate economic growth, social progress, and cultural development and to promote peace and security in the region. Brunei became a member in 1984, Vietnam in 1995, Laos and Myanmar in 1997, and Cambodia in 1999. ASEAN became a leading voice on regional trade and security issues in the 1990s; in 1992 member nations created the ASEAN Free Trade Area.

From *The Britannica Concise.*

3 ► The right word

A • Crossword

Across

1 • Goods sent to another country.
2 • Someone who arranges business for someone else.
3 • Opposite of home.
4 • The whole world.
5 • Short for General Agreement for Tariffs and Trade.

Down

a • Order made by a government to stop trade with another country.
b • Commerce.
c • Act of reaching a decision acceptable to everyone.

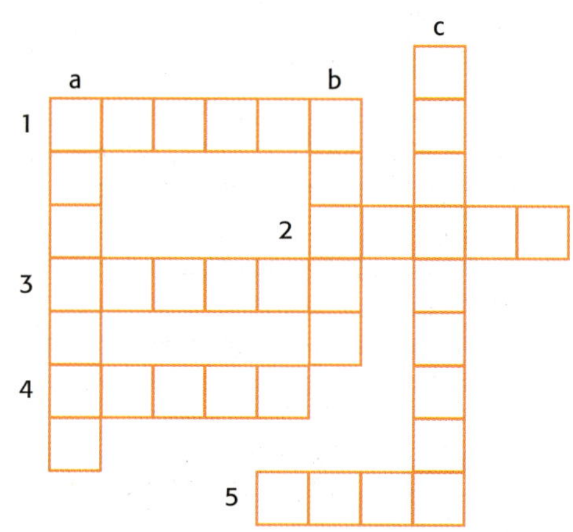

B • Match each of the following words with its proper definition.

1 • retaliate
2 • global
3 • tariff
4 • dumping
5 • trade (v.)
6 • standard
7 • balance of payments
8 • agreement
9 • quota
10 • flood (v.)

a • Practice of selling abroad at prices far below those charged at home.
b • Buy, sell or exchange.
c • Difference between the payment made for imports and the payment received from exports.
d • Limited quantity of something which is officially allowed.
e • Reaching a decision acceptable to everyone involved.
f • Saturate.
g • Tax that a government collects on goods coming into a country.
h • Harm in return.
i • Norm.
j • Worldwide.

4 ► Vocabulary

accord bilatéral : bilateral agreement
accord commercial : trade agreement
accord (conclure un) : strike a deal
accord général sur les tarifs douaniers et le commerce : General Agreement on Tariffs and Trade, GATT
accord multilatéral : multilateral agreement
accord (parvenir à un) : come to an agreement
accord (passer un) : enter into / conclude an agreement
accord tarifaire : tariff agreement
acte unique européen : Single European Act
agent exclusif : sole agent
atteinte à la liberté du commerce : restraint on trade

balance commerciale déficitaire : adverse / unfavourable trade balance
balance commerciale excédentaire : favourable trade balance
balance de paiements : balance of payments
barrière commerciale : trade barrier
barrière douanière : customs barriers / walls
barrière tarifaire : tariff barrier / wall

clause de la nation la plus favorisée : Most Favoured Nation clause, MNF clause
commerce extérieur : foreign trade / commerce
compétitivité : competitiveness
concurrence : competition
concurrence acharnée : harsh / fierce competition
concurrence déloyale : unfair competition
concurrence illicite : unlawful competition
concurrencer : compete
concurrent (adj.) : competitive, rival
concurrent (n.) : competitor, rival
concurrentiel : competitive
contingent : quota

déficit (combler un) : bridge a deficit, bridge a gap
déficit commercial : trade deficit / gap
droit de douane : customs duty
dumping : dumping

échanges commerciaux : trade / trading exchanges
échanges (faire des) : trade, exchange
embargo : ban, embargo
état membre : member state
étranger (adj.) : foreign, overseas
étranger (à l') : abroad, overseas
excédent commercial : trade surplus
excédent (dégager un) : show a surplus
exportateur : exporter
exportation : export
exporter : export

fond Monétaire International, F.M.I : International Monetary Fund, IMF

guerre commerciale : commercial war

importateur : importer
importation : import
importer : import
internationalisation : internationalisation, globalisation

libre-échange : free trade
libre-échangiste : free trader

marché acheteur : buyer's market
marché extérieur : foreign / overseas market
marché intérieur : home / domestic market
marché mondial : world / global market
marché réglementé : regulated market
marché (saturer le) : flood / glut the market
marché unique européen : single European market
mondial : global, worldwide

négociations commerciales : trade negotiations / talks
norme : standard, norm
norme de qualité (satisfaire aux) : meet quality standards
norme de sécurité : safety standard

pacte : pact
pourparlers : talks, discussions
protectionnisme : protectionism

quota : quota

représailles : retaliation → retaliate (v.)

sanctions : sanctions, penalties

traité commercial : trade treaty

unifié : unified, united, consolidated, integrated

zone franche : free zone

Unit 6 Banking

A few landmarks

Taking the stock of the Stock Exchange

If you are starting a new business you will need money. You might have enough money yourself but it is far more likely that you will need to obtain some from other people. This sort of money is known as **financial capital** and the people or organizations who provide it are called **investors**.
The reason they are willing to invest is that they hope the company will become a success and they will then get a share in the profit. Another name for this process is to say a person has bought **shares** in the company.
Shares do not always stay at the same price. If the company does well other people start to want the shares because they can see the profits will be good. People who own shares can then charge more than they paid and the share price goes up. This process also works in reverse with the **share price** dropping for companies which are not doing very well. At least once during a year if the company is doing well it will share out the profit among its **shareholders**. This payment is made per share and is called a **dividend**.
When companies get big enough they almost always want to sell shares to the public but they cannot just sell them and the public cannot just buy them: deals have to be done through a **stock exchange**.
Important stock exchanges can be found in London, New York, Hong Kong and Tokyo.
Ordinary people cannot walk into a stock exchange and buy shares. They have to do it through a firm of **stockbrokers**. The staff will buy and sell shares for you and charge you a commission (a percentage of the price).
Individual stocks and shares rise and fall with the fortunes of the company and those of other companies which affect it. But the whole **market** may move as a result of world events such as political changes and wars.
When lots of people want to buy shares most share prices go up and a **bull market** is said to exist. But share prices may fall; this is called a **bear market**. When shares prices fall very quickly a **crash** is said to have occurred.

© GettyImages / The Image Bank / M. J. Cardenas.

© Masterfile / Damir Frkovic.

Warm-up

- Describe the photographs and say what changes have recently occurred in the way clients can now manage their bank accounts.

Unit 6

TEXT 1

Financial exclusion

1. **take sth for granted:** *tenir pour acquis*
2. **bill:** *facture*
3. **the penny dropped:** *ça a fait tilt*
4. **overdraft:** *découvert*
5. **charges:** *frais*
6. **no-frills =** unsophisticated
7. **upgrade:** *améliorer, revaloriser*
8. **benefit:** *allocation, prestation*

Most people take having a bank account for granted[1], but up to 23 per cent of people don't have one. This means major disadvantages in settling bills[2], handling cheques, getting access to credit, and obtaining information about financial products. "Having a bank account is the gateway," says Sue Edwards, a social policy officer at the National Association of Citizens Advice Bureaux.

The penny really dropped[3] for the Government with the 1999 report Access to Financial Services. This found that traditional accounts, with overdraft[4] facilities and high charges[5], often don't meet the needs of those on low income.

Since then the Government has cajoled the often reluctant high street banks into providing no-frills[6] bank accounts designed to meet the needs of those living on between £51 and £150 per week.

According to the British Bankers' Association, there are now 3 million of these bank accounts, and they are becoming more popular. During 2000, 254,000 such accounts were opened, while 104,000 were upgraded[7] to normal accounts. The BBA says that the figures should rise significantly.

Basic accounts have many of the facilities of normal bank accounts, but do not normally provide a chequebook, or a conventional overdraft facility. They have been given a boost by plans to pay benefits[8] by automated credit transfer starting in 2003. This will include a benefits encashment option at post offices. Although there is more choice, it is difficult to get hold of a basic account, Edwards says. "Customers are often given wrong information. Banks are not advertising their basic bank accounts and information is kept under the counter, often only available for those who ask."

Sharon Collard, from the Personal Finance Research Centre at Bristol University questions whether they will be effective in reducing long-term financial exclusion: "The issue is whether people 'unbanked' in the past actually do use the account, whether they progress to other accounts, or whether the account is left dormant."

Some progress has been made in allowing individuals without passports or driving licences, such as the homeless, to open a bank account.

From *The Observer,* June 16, 2002.

► Check your pronunciation

Can you stress the following words?

1 • disadvantage	5 • significantly	9 • advertising
2 • government	6 • benefits	10 • available
3 • access	7 • automated	11 • research
4 • facilities	8 • option	12 • issue

► Words

Find the right meaning for each of the following sentences.

1 • "[It] is the gateway" (l. 4) means:
- It is the end.
- It gives an opportunity to progress.
- It sounds like paradise.

2 • "The Government has cajoled the [...] banks" (l. 9) means:
- The Government has coaxed banks.
- The Government has had a row with banks.
- The Government has come to an agreement with banks.

3 • "Basic accounts [...] have been given a boost" (l. 16) means:
- There has been a great deal of information about basic accounts.
- Basic accounts have been given some sort of stimulation.
- Their number has increased.

4 • "It is difficult to get hold of a basic account" (l. 20) means:
- It is difficult to obtain a basic account.
- It is difficult to understand what a basic account is.
- It is difficult to turn down a basic account offer.

© Réa / Benoit Decout.

5 • "Information is kept under the counter" (l. 22) means:
- Information is to be found everywhere.
- Information is open to bank employees only.
- Information is hidden from the public.

6 • "People 'unbanked'" (l. 26) means:
- Faithful clients
- People who do not have bank accounts.
- Homeless people.

7 • "The account is left dormant" (l. 27) means:
- People never use their bank accounts.
- People overuse their bank accounts.
- People do not get informed on this type of account.

► Meaning

A • Match the following figures from the text with the information they provide.

1 • 23	a • Number of basic bank accounts opened in 2000.
2 • 1999	b • The year when automated credit transfer will be possible.
3 • 254,000	c • The year the Government issued a report on bank accounts.
4 • 104,000	d • Number of basic bank accounts turned into normal ones.
5 • 2003	e • Percentage of people who do not have a bank account.

B • Complete the following blanks with information from the text.

Traditional bank accounts	Basic bank accounts
– Overdraft	– No ....
– High	– No .... facilities

C • Turn the following sentences into the passive form. Be careful! Two solutions are possible for each sentence! (see T&T: Passive form)

1 • The bank clerk gave some wrong information to those customers.
2 • Plans have given a boost to those basic bank accounts.
3 • The bank is offering promotion to this efficient employee.
4 • Has anybody shown our new chequebooks?
5 • The accountant will pay you an extra £200 for your expenses.

► Pair work

A is a bank manager and supports the idea that bank charges are justified.
B is a client and complains about those charges.
Imagine their dialogue.

► Food for thought

It is often said banks lend money only to the wealthy. What do you think of this statement?

Unit 6

TEXT 2

1. graduate: *diplômé de l'université*

2. custom: *clientèle*

3. freebies = gifts

4. fresher = first-year student

5. voucher: *bon*

6. tier: *disposer en niveaux*

University will leave your child with debts of £10,000

The terms offered by banks on their student and graduate[1] accounts have become increasingly generous over the years because if banks can attract students at 18, they should have a good chance of keeping their custom[2] through most of all their working life. [...]

Among the tempting freebies[3] offered to last year's freshers[4] was a four-year railcard or £50 in cash from HSBC. NatWest offered a handheld TV or £60; those signing up to Lloyds TSB received £50.

If you opted for an Abbey National student account, you had the choice of a personal CD player, a 15-month magazine subscription or £40 in cash. Royal Bank of Scotland gave students a mobile phone plus money off CDs, videos, DVDs and concert tickets.

Meanwhile, Barclays' account holders received a £20 voucher[5] for books, CDs or videos and further discounts from Waterstones and HMV.

But don't just go for the account offering the best freebies. As a student loan is unlikely to be enough, you may well need an overdraft, so see what interest-free overdraft facilities are available.

Most banks tier[6] the amount by which students can be overdrawn so that it rises with each year of study. Unless you are very disciplined, opting for a tiered overdraft system is a better idea than going for one that is fixed for three years.

While a fixed overdraft may enable you to borrow more in the early years, and is therefore attractive to first-year students, unless you have the means to repay it each year, you could easily find yourself in financial difficulties later on, with no way of getting any more money.

From *The Independent on Sunday*, 26 May 2002.

► Check your pronunciation

Check your pronunciation of the following words.

1 • freebies
2 • subscription
3 • mobile
4 • voucher
5 • available
6 • tiered

► Words

A • Match each word below with its correct meaning.

1 • custom (l. 3)	a • increase
2 • through (l. 3)	b • portable
3 • handheld (l. 6)	c • during
4 • further (l. 13)	d • clients
5 • unlikely (l. 15)	e • additional
6 • rise (l. 17)	f • improbable

B • Complete these sentences using the verbs below in the correct imperative form (affirmative or negative). (see T&T: Imperative)

decide / opt / look / remember / sign up

1 • .... at the terms of your contract closely.
2 • .... immediately on your bank.
3 • .... to consider the location of bank branches.
4 • .... to NatWest and you'll be offered a handheld TV.
5 • .... for this bank, they will only give you £40.

C • Complete the following sentences using the link words below.

because / once / unless / until

1 • Banks are more and more generous .... they want to attract students.
2 • I will never sign up to this bank .... they offer me the best overdraft facilities.
3 • .... you are in Oxford, you'll find out about NatWest branches there.
4 • If I were you, I would wait .... you receive another offer.

► Meaning

A • Four main points have to be considered by a student who would like to open an account. Reread the text carefully and complete the grids below.

1 •

1st point to be considered	Banks	Offering
Freebies	....	4-year railway card or .... in cash
	....	handheld TV or ....
	Lloyds TSB	....
	....	personal CD player or .... or ....
	....	mobile phone + ...
	Barclay's	a £20 .... for books, CDs, etc. + ...from 2 stores

2 •

2nd point to be considered				
....	2 possibilities: .... /	advantages: rises .... / possibility of	weak points: .... / risk of	

B • Translate the first paragraph into French.

► Pair work

A's bank doesn't give him any overdraft facilities whereas **B** may be overdrawn. They discuss on the pros and cons of overdrafts.

► Food for thought

Are freebies a good idea to attract new clients?

Unit 6

TEXT 3

G7 issues warning to Swiss banks

1. **crackdown:** *mesure sévère*
2. **laundering:** *blanchiment*
3. **haven =** paradise
4. **chancellor =** minister in the British government who makes decisions about finance and taxes.

The world's leading economies are considering economic sanctions against Switzerland unless it reforms its secretive banking laws, which are hampering the global crackdown[1] on money laundering[2], tax evasion and the financing of terrorism. G7 finance ministers issued a warning to the Swiss that time is running out for them to cooperate in international exchanges of financial information. "We expect to have visible progress this year and we are ready to think about sanctions this autumn if we see no results," said Germany's finance minister, Hans Eichel. The global campaign against tax evasion and money laundering has intensified in the wake of September 11, 2001. The leading economies have accused secretive financial centres of providing a haven[3] for terrorist funding, a charge which the Swiss reject. The chancellor[4], Gordon Brown, said G7 finance ministers were determined to "move forward quickly to achieve an effective exchange of information to end banking secrecy". He added: "It is our determination that countries outside this are shown to be isolated from the international community."

From *The Guardian,* June 17, 2002.

► Words

Find the synonyms of the following words.

1 • "hampering" (l. 2) means:
developing / stopping / limiting

2 • "time is running out" (l. 4) means:
there is no time left / there is a lot of time left / it is time things changed

3 • "in the wake of September 11, 2001" (l. 8-9) means:
during the September 11, 2001 events / following the September 11, 2001 events / before the September 11, 2001 events

4 • "providing a haven" (l. 10) means:
supplying a safe place / warning against a tropical paradise / trapping into same sort of paradise

5 • "a charge" (l. 10) means:
a thought / an accusation / a burden

6 • "determined" (l. 11) means:
hesitating / resolved / sure

► Meaning

A • Make a list of the G7 members. What does G stand for? We also speak of G8 countries. Why?

B • Complete the following blanks.

1 • G7 countries all agree to fight three global blights:
....
....
....

2 • Accusation made against Switzerland: ....

3 • What the leading economies would like to put an end to: ....

4 • What the leading economies are looking forward to:
....

C • Complete with *unless / if / provided* (one word is repeated twice).

1 • .... the Swiss banks put an end to banking secrecy, we'll be forced to consider economic sanctions.

2 • .... the Swiss banks accept to cooperate, we won't be forced to take sanctions.

3 • Switzerland won't suffer any economic sanctions .... it complies with international laws.

4 • They won't put an end to banking secrecy .... they are forced to.

Checkup
Unit 6

1 ► Test

Fly away from your old bank

Switching current accounts is no longer the hassle it used to be, which is why a growing number of people are making the move. And with banks offering a new range of accounts that provide different services, it is becoming easier to find something tailored to your particular needs.

Research by ICM for the telenet bank Intelligent Finance shows more than 2.75 million adults have switched current accounts in the past 12 months, up from 1.6 million in the previous year. And the rise is set to continue, with five million saying they planned to move in the next 12 months.

There are many advantages to switching, particularly if your current account is with one of the "Big Four" high-street banks: Barclays, NatWest, Lloyds TSB and HSBC. Some 70 per cent of the UK's current accounts are held at these banks, even though they pay a paltry 0.1 per cent interest on balances and charge between 15 and 19 per cent on authorised overdrafts.

If you compare these rates with the 4 per cent Cahoot customers receive on balances or with Halifax's 8.9 per cent rate on authorised overdrafts, there is clearly a case for switching. "There is quite a dramatic increase in people switching away from the Big Four as they are realising they are not getting a good deal," says Richard Popper, marketing director at Zurich bank. "In the past there was nothing better to switch to, while it was also physically difficult to do so. This situation is changing."

The process of switching has become easier since the introduction of an industry code requiring banks to swap information about customers' direct debits and standing orders to reduce the hassle involved in moving.

From *The Independent on Sunday*, 9 June 2002.

A • What is the new tendency among bank clients?

B • Why? (Give two reasons.)

C • Complete the following sentences.

1 • The "Big Four" are ...., ..., ... and ....

2 • Percentage of current accounts at these banks: ....

3 • 0.1 % interest paid on ....

4 • 15% to 19% .... on authorised ....

5 • Name of two other banks mentioned in the article: .... and ....

6 • Number of people who have "flown away" from their banks: ....

7 • 5 million is the number of people ....

8 • 4% interest paid by .... on ....

9 • ....% rate on authorised .... paid by ....

D • Translate the last paragraph (l. 32 to l. 36) into French.

© Réa / Pascal Sittler.

2 ► Skills in practice

Summary of balances

1 • How many operations
– have credited the account?
– have debited the account?
Give their nature.

2 • What would have happened if the $4,500 hadn't been paid into the account?

3 • Why were they transferred on August 7?
– because the money was available?
– because it was necessary?
Justify your answer.

4 • What do the $1,374.14 and the $577.70 correspond to?

CITICORP CITIBANK

PO 5870 GRAND CENTRAL STA 015
NEW YORK, N. Y. 10163

3739/R5/02
001

3 JEAN RAULT
16 BOULEVARD DE CHAMBEAUDOIN
EVREUX FRANCE 27000

ACCOUNT
58384385
AS OF 08/24/0
PAGE 1 OF 2

THIS REPORTS YOUR BALANCES AND ACTIVITY FROM JULY 26 TO AUGUST 24, 2003.

SUMMARY OF BALANCES

YOUR CITI-ONE ACCOUNT
CITI-ONE CHECKING
REGULAR CHECKING 58384385 AS OF 08-24 $ 1,374.14

YOUR CITIBANK INVESTMENT PORTFOLIO
SAVINGS ACCOUNTS
SAVINGS 58384385 577.70

CITI-ONE ACCOUNT

CHECKING ACTIVITY
YOU STARTED WITH $ 404.14
FUNDS ADDED 4,500.00
AUGUST 7, TRANSFER FROM SAVINGS $ 4,500.00
Citicard Banking Center 01503, 123 E 86 ST, NY, NY

CHECKS PAID 3,030.00

Check #	Date Paid	Amount	Check #	Date Paid	Amount
128	08-07	3,030.00			

OTHER WITHDRAWALS 500.00
AUGUST 8, GOT CASH 500.00
Citicard Banking Center 01502, 123 E 86 ST, NY, NY

YOU ENDED WITH 1,374.14

RUNNING BALANCES

Date	Balance	Date	Balance	Date	Balance
07-26	404.14	08-07	1,874.14	08-08	1,374.14

FUNDS AVAILABILITY INFORMATION
CHECKS AS CASH: YOUR BALANCES IN THE FOLLOWING ACCOUNTS COVER WITHDRAWALS YOU MAKE BEFORE YOUR CHECK DEPOSITS CLEAR.
SAVINGS, AS OF 08/24/03 $577.70

3 ► The right word

A • Crossword

Across

1 • Arrangement with a bank which allows you to keep your money in the bank and to withdraw it when you need it.
2 • It can be Blue, Gold or Visa for example.
3 • Short for "Bills Receivable".
4 • Money in the form of notes and coins.
5 • Holder.

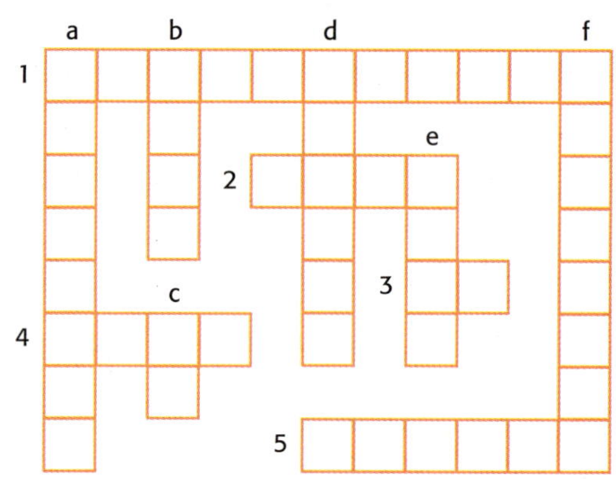

Down

a • The money you have in your bank account.
b • Piece of paper used as money.
c • Short for Stock Exchange.
d • The price you have to pay for a service or for something you buy.
e • Sum of money you owe someone.
f • Now it can be electronic.

McScrooge Bank

Dear Mrs Duck
Thank you for your interest in McScrooge Bank's currency deposits. This type of deposit allows you to benefit from the high levels of interest in other countries and gives you a large .... on your investment.
The enclosed brochure tells you about McScrooge Bank and how to become a .... of the bank. McScrooge Bank specialises in receiving deposits from non-residents, and upwards of 40,000 customers, from more than 150 countries, have already taken advantage of our favourable offers to improve the return on their ....
The enclosed interest table shows you the return on .... in various currencies. From this you can decide your own .... of interest, dependent upon the exchange rate risks you are prepared to run.
These are your .... when opening a currency deposit:
– a high return on your deposit,
– no .... maintenance fee,
– no Swiss taxation of your interest ....
Diversification into several .... deposits provides you with a certain protection against individual exchange rate and inflation fluctuations, thus providing the potential for increased .... in the long term.
Make use of this favourable offer and send us the opening form with your initial deposit today.

Yours sincerely,
McScrooge Bank

B • Fill in the blanks with words from the following list.

1 • account
2 • yields
3 • deposits
4 • earnings
5 • assets
6 • rate
7 • customer
8 • benefits
9 • return
10 • currency

4 ► Vocabulary

action : share (GB), stock (US)
actionnaire : shareholder (GB), stockholder (US)
agios : bank charges
arrérages : back interest

bénéfices : profits
bénéficiaire : payee
billet : note
bon du trésor : bond
bourse : Stock Exchange (GB), Stock Market (US)
brut : gross

caisse d'épargne : savings bank
carnet de chèques : chequebook
chèque : cheque (GB), check (US)
chèque sans provision : dud / bad cheque
chiffre d'affaires : turnover
comptant (payer) : pay cash
compte courant : current (GB) / checking (US) account
compte de dépôts : deposit account
cours : quotation
coût : cost
créance : debt
créancier : creditor
crédit : credit
crédit personnel : personal loan

date d'échéance : redemption date
découvert : overdraft
dépôt : deposit
détenteur : holder

devise : currency
distributeur automatique de billets : cash dispenser (GB), automatic teller (US), ATM
dividende : dividend
dû : outstanding
dû à : due to

effets de commerce : commercial papers
émettre : issue
emprunt : loan
encaisser un chèque : cash a cheque
endos : endorsement

faillite : bankruptcy
faillite (faire) : go / run bankrupt
falsifier : forge
fonds : funds

gage : pawn
guichet : counter

honorabilité : credit worthiness
hypothèque : mortgage

impayé : dishonoured

lettre de change : bill of exchange, draft

marché à la baisse : bear / bearish market
marché à la hausse : bull / bullish market
monnaie (menue) : cash
monnaie (pièces de) : coins

négocier : trade
net : net

obligations : stocks (GB), bonds (US)
offre d'achat : bid

payer comptant : pay cash
portefeuille : portfolio
porteur (au) : bearer
prélèvement automatique : standing order (GB), direct debiting (US)
prêt : loan

reconnaissance de dettes : I.O.U., I Owe You
régler : settle
relevé de compte : bank statement
rembourser : pay back, pay off, refund, reimburse, settle
rendement : yield
retrait : withdrawal
revenu : income
revenu du capital : capital return

solde créditeur / débiteur : credit / debit balance
souscripteur : subscriber
succursale : branch

taux : rate
tiré (n.) : drawee
tireur : drawer
traite : draft, bill of exchange
trésorerie : cash

versement : remittance
virement : transfer
virement automatique : standing order

Unit 7

Accounting and investing

A few landmarks

Accounting

- **The cash cycle**

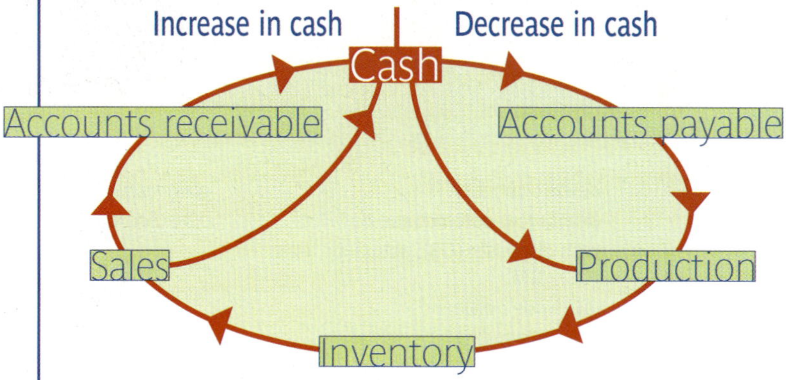

Insuring

- An insurance contract is a contract whereby a person or company, known as **the insurer**, agrees in return for a price known as the **premium**, to pay a sum of money to another person or company, known as **the insured**, on the happening of a certain event, or to indemnify that person against loss caused by the risk which has been insured against.

- **A few types of insurances:**
  - all-risk insurance (all-in insurance)
  - fire insurance
  - luggage insurance
  - motor car insurance
  - public liability insurance
  - theft insurance
  - third-party insurance
  - unemployment insurance

© GettyImages / Stone / L. Dutton.

© GettyImages / Hulton Archive.

Warm-up

- Here are two photos that could be entitled "the new way" and "the old way". Why?

TEXT 1

Surrey: an end to quick killings

Graphic designer Tom Howe has just bought a two-bedroom flat, in Surbiton, Surrey, as a short-term investment, but fears it may end up as a long-term commitment[1].

He made £35,000 in 14 months out of his previous, one-bedroom flat in Putney, after spending £5,000 on refurbishing it, installing a new boiler, laying wooden floors, and stripping the wallpaper. He had hoped for an equally profitable experience with his new flat.

All the indications were good. The previous owner[2] had made a killing[3], buying the flat for £128,000 in December and selling it for £175,000 six months later. Even in the few days since completing his purchase, Tom has received details of identical flats selling for £10,000 more.

But now he says: "Almost as soon as the deal went through I heard on the radio that property prices were going to stabilise and could even dip[4] slightly."

This should not prove a disaster. If things don't work out, he could always rent out the second bedroom. Either way he is prepared to convert his interest-only mortgage[5] to a repayment one and stay in the flat until he makes a decent profit.

From *The Observer*, 16 June 2002.

1. **commitment:** *engagement*
2. **owner:** *propriétaire*
3. **make a killing:** *ramasser un joli paquet*
4. **dip =** decrease
5. **mortgage:** *emprunt-logement*

► Check your pronunciation

All words from the following list but ONE are stressed on the same syllable. Can you find it?

1 • previous
2 • profitable
3 • purchase
4 • property
5 • prepare
6 • profit

► Words

All the verbs on the left below are followed by *out*. Make sure you can translate them.

1 • put out
2 • make out
3 • let out
4 • go out
5 • work out
6 • set out
7 • rent out

a • *s'entraîner*
b • *présenter*
c • *éteindre*
d • *s'en tirer*
e • *louer*
f • *donner libre cours à*
g • *passer de mode*

► Meaning

A • A flat with two bedrooms is a two-bedroom flat. Make your own compounds with the following elements. (see T&T: Compound nouns)

1 • a house with four rooms
2 • a child who is 7
3 • the train at 4.30
4 • a purchase that costs £1,000
5 • an investment of £128,000
6 • the accounts for 2001
7 • a cut of 50 per cent

B • The following figures are important in Tom Howe's story. Why?

1 • £35,000
2 • £5,000
3 • £128,000
4 • £175,000
5 • £10,000

C • Transform the sentences below using the following pattern: *after* + *V-ing*:

Ex: – After he had spent two years in London he decided to buy a flat in Oxford.
– After spending two years in London he decided to buy a flat in Oxford.

1 • After he had refurbished the house, he decided to rent it.
2 • After he had heard on the radio about property prices, he decided not to sell his house.
3 • After he had rented out his first bedroom, he decided to rent out the second one.
4 • After he had made a killing when buying his flat, he started investing his money on the Stock Exchange.

D • Translate into French.

1 • "He had hoped for an equally profitable experience with his new flat." (l. 5-6)
2 • "This should not prove a disaster." (l. 13)

E • Tom Howe seems to be making profitable investments. But does the future look bright? What are his new plans?

► Pair work

Bargaining: **A** is selling his / her car for £50,000. **B** finds this car wonderful and is desperate to buy it but he / she cannot afford such a sum. Imagine the dialogue.

► Food for thought

Buying and selling with a profit: have you heard of profitable experiences in fields other than the property business?

Unit 7

TEXT 2

British boffins[1] are boosted by bankers

1. **boffin:** *expert*
2. **pinstripes =** (here) investors
3. **drive:** *offensive*
4. **spawn =** multiply
5. **strike (struck, struck):** *conclure*
6. **stake:** *participation*
7. **be hot on sb's heels:** *être sur les talons de qqn*

As universities across the UK respond to growing pressure to commercialise the technologies arising from their laboratories, they are finding a ready supply of keen investors from the City.

An increasing number of these emerging technologies – from the fields of biochemistry, computer science and engineering – end up being "spun-out" as small companies, and the pinstripes[2] are keen to get in at the earliest possible stage.

Oxford, Cambridge, Imperial College and Southampton University have been at the forefront of the drive[3] to commercialise their research. [...]

The pace of commercialisation has now reached the point where, between them, Britain's universities are spinning out companies at the rate of about one every week.

The city is desperate to get in on this act, and the "spin-out" culture is spawning[4] a new wave of deals between financiers and universities.

One of the earliest groups to recognise the huge commercial potential locked into the universities was the investment bank Beeson Gregory. In a deal struck[5] with Oxford's chemistry faculty, the bank provided £20m of investment in return for a 50-per-cent cut of anything the department managed to convert into profits.

Beeson later created a separate division, known as ip2ipo. Last week ip2ipo gained a 19-per-cent stake[6] in its third Oxford spin-out, a biotech company with a revolutionary approach to disease research.

Other investment houses are hot on Beeson's heels[7]. Two weeks ago, the investment fund of the Fleming merchant-banking family structured a deal in which it gained a 21-per-cent stake in any companies that are spun out of Imperial College.

From *The Independent on Sunday*, 26 May 2002.

► Check your pronunciation

A • Can you read the following words.

1 • [juːnɪˈvɜːsətɪ]
2 • [prɪˈfɜːʳ]
3 • [baiəuˈkemɪstrɪ]
4 • [endʒɪˈnɪərɪŋ]
5 • [faiˈnænsiəʳz]

B • Check you can stress the right syllable in the following words.

1 • commercial
2 • industrial
3 • social
4 • special
5 • commercialise
6 • industrialise
7 • socialise
8 • specialise
9 • commercialisation
10 • industrialisation
11 • socialisation
12 • specialisation

► Words

Find a synonym for each of the following words (they are all to be found in the text).

(§1)	1 • react	(§4)	5 • speed	(§6)	9 • transform
(§1)	2 • eager	(§5)	6 • determined	(§7)	10 • bargain
(§2)	3 • growing	(§6)	7 • enormous		
(§3)	4 • vanguard	(§6)	8 • discount		

► Meaning

A • Complete the blanks with words from the following list.

commercialise / division / emerging / investment / keen / merchant / pace / potential / recognise / stake

The Government directly encourage universities to .... more of their scientific research especially in the field of .... technologies. A lot of companies are now .... to get in as soon as possible. Indeed, new technology commercialisation is developing at an amazing .... Beeson Gregory, an .... bank was one of the first to .... that universities represented a huge .... market. Beeson has even created a ...., called ip2ipo. Now other investment houses are following his example: for instance, the Fleming .... bank which has recently gained a .... in companies that are spun out with Imperial College.

B • Translate the following sentences into English. (see T&T: Present perfect / Preterite)

1 • *Depuis quelques mois le gouvernement encourage les universités à commercialiser leur recherche scientifique.*

2 • *Il y a deux semaines un accord a été conclu entre une banque et une université.*

3 • *Des universités telles que Oxford ou Cambridge encouragent depuis longtemps leur chercheurs à avoir le sens des affaires.*

4 • *Le rythme de la commercialisation augmente depuis le début de l'année.*

C • Make sentences with the following elements.

1 • has / Oxford University / investment bank / with / this / struck / just / a deal

2 • number / willing / increasing / universities / to / an / are / commercialise / research / their / of

3 • hot on / bank / was / two years ago / our heels / this

4 • don't we / growing / respond to / from / why / the banks / pressure / ?

5 • potential / locked / huge / there / a / commercial / into / Universities / is

D • Translate the first paragraph into French.

► Group work

If you had a lot of money to spend, what would you invest it in: equity, property, antiques, jewels, gold, etc? Discuss.

► Food for thought

Universities are encouraged to think about their research from a more entrepreneurial position. Can you think of a few advantages and drawbacks of such a stance? (about 200 words)

Insurance giants

1. **thinktank:** *groupe de réflexion*
2. **recovery:** *reprise*
3. **brakes:** *freins*
4. **shipping:** *transport*
5. **highlight =** underline
6. **withstand (withstood, withstood):** *résister à*
7. **premium:** *prime*

Some insurance giants would go bankrupt if the world suffered a repeat of the attacks of 11 September 2001, a global thinktank[1] warned yesterday. The consequences of the assaults on New York and Washington could inflict major damage on the world economy despite the initial strong recovery[2], the Organisation for Economic Co-operation and Development said. It said rises in insurance costs, larger government spending on defence, and barriers to international trade could all put the brakes[3] on growth. It did not put a figure on the potential impact but said trade volumes alone could fall by 3 per cent because of higher shipping[4] and insurance costs. In its assessment, the OECD said: "Even though the short-term recovery from the terrorist attacks has been faster than expected, negative medium-term consequences through various indirect channels cannot be excluded." It highlighted[5] the impact on the insurance industry as one of the most serious impacts. It said that despite losses estimated at between $30bn and $58bn as a result of the attacks, no major bankruptcy had occurred. "Nevertheless, the capital base of many insurance firms has been hit, and it is likely that several companies would not be in a position to withstand[6] another shock of similar magnitude," it said. The OECD said the rises in insurance premiums[7] of as much as 30 per cent had already hurt the aviation industry as well as the transport, construction and energy sectors.

From *The Independent,* 7 June 2002.

► Words

Match one noun from each group to form a compound noun.

1 • insurance 2 • insurance 3 • insurance 4 • aviation 5 • trade
a • volumes b • giants c • sector d • premiums e • industry

► Meaning

A • Now use the compound words to complete the blanks below.

1 • The rises in .... has already hurt the ....
2 • No major bankruptcy has occurred in spite of the fact the .... has been seriously hit.
3 • .... are likely to fall by 3 per cent because of the tragedy of 11 September 2001.
4 • .... would go bankrupt if another terrorist disaster was to happen.

B • Carefully read the text and complete the following blanks.

1 • An event: ....
2 • The economic consequences of this event: ....
3 • Three reasons: ... / ... / ...
4 • A possible consequence: ....
5 • The OECD conclusion: short-term recovery but possible.................... .
6 • Serious impact on the insurance industry but no ....
7 • Consequence of another tragedy: ....
8 • Reason why certain sectors have already been hurt: ....

Checkup Unit 7

1 ► Test

Staying longer than expected? You'll be glad you're covered

Around 200,000 18- to 25-year-olds will go on a gap adventure this year, according to insurer Primary Direct. And whether you travel on a shoestring as a student or in a more luxurious style with money saved up from your job, it's important to get comprehensive insurance. Research from Primary Direct shows that 36 per cent of all gap year travellers are affected by a medical problem, while around 38 per cent make a baggage claim. And some 14 per cent of backpackers also have to claim for lost cash during their time overseas.

Despite this, insurance is rarely top of the agenda. "Young people and students travelling the world are likely to leave travel insurance to the last minute, which can lead to costly mistakes," says Richard Mason at Moneysupermarket.com, a website that compares different financial products. "Many assume an annual travel insurance policy will cover them – but it won't. These polices are designed for people taking multiple trips abroad each year, and cover is usually limited to trips that do not exceed 30 days."

The longer you are away and the more offbeat your destination, the greater will be the chance of something going wrong. And the costs incurred if you don't have insurance can be considerable: Primary Direct says a head injury and concussion can set you back £3,000 in Thailand, while even a case of diarrhoea can cost more than £1,000 to treat in the Far East. […]

Even for those on a budget, there are certain essentials that really must be covered. These include medical care; bringing you home in an emergency or flying a friend or relative out to you; replacing lost luggage or a mislaid passport; cancellation or curtailment of your trip; personal liability; and search and rescue.

From *The Independent on Sunday*, 9 June 2001.

A • Answer the following questions.

1 • Who is concerned by this article?
2 • What is the age bracket of those people?
3 • What is often wrong with them?
4 • What should they do?

B • Translate the last paragraph into French.

C • Apart from those mentioned in the text, what are the different policies that can be taken out? What for?

2 ► Skills in practice

Group work

- A is the insurer and B to F are the clients. They phone A in order to have further information on Direct Line's holiday insurance. A answers.
- B is 67.
- C is going to Australia on a 30-day trip.
- D is 22 and is leaving on a gap year.
- E would like to know if he could have a discount if he and his wife bought a policy.
- F is going to Spain, France, Italy and Greece on a 3-month trip.

3 ► The right word

A • Crossword

Across

1 • Inspection of the accounts.
2 • Sum of money.
3 • Amount of money you have to pay to a government.
4 • People you owe money to.

Down

a • Opposite of liabilities.
b • When you have the right to some money.
c • Government department dealing with the country's finances in Great Britain.
d • Opposite of "opened".
e • State of owing money.

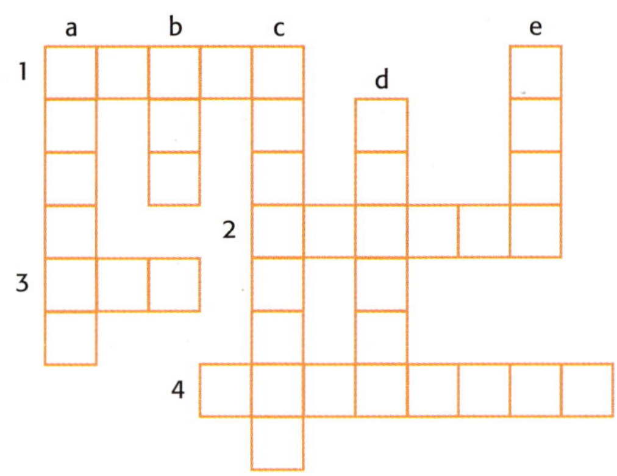

B • Fill in the blanks with words from the following list and make the necessary adjustments.

settle / refund / snap audit / liabilities / tax-deductible / stocktaking / amount / bills payable / record / debtor / debit balance / tax inspector

1 • When you have a ...., you are "in the red", it means you have spent more money than you have in your bank account.
2 • When you .... a bill, you pay the amount that you owe.
3 • A .... is a person who owes money.
4 • If you are at all dissatisfied, we will .... you your money.
5 • The accountant .... the various credit and debit operations of a firm.
6 • A chartered accountant generally carries out .... when he checks the accounts.
7 • .... belong to the liabilities of the balance sheet.
8 • If you want to buy a business, assets and .... have to be carefully studied.
9 • In French supermarkets .... takes place every year at the beginning of January.
10 • The total .... of his taxes were fixed at £5 million.
11 • Charitable contributions are .... up to a certain amount.
12 • My .... agreed to spread my payment over three months.

4 ► Vocabulary

actif immobilisé : fixed assets
actifs : assets
amortissement : depreciation
année civile : calendar year
annuler : cancel
annuler une écriture : write off
apport : allowance
approbation des comptes : approval of the accounts
apurement de comptes : audit
arrhes : deposit
assurance : insurance
assurance responsabilité civile : public liability insurance
assurance au tiers : third party insurance
assurance tous risques : all-risk policy, all-in policy
assurer : insure → the insured
assureur : insurer, insurance broker

barême des impôts : tax scale
bénéfice : profit, return
bénéfice net : net earnings
bilan : balance sheet
bilan consolidé : consolidated accounts
bilan (déposer son) : file a petition in bankruptcy
brut : gross

capital circulant : circulating capital
capital entièrement libéré : capital entirely paid up
capital immobilisé : fixed capital
cessation de paiement : act of bankruptcy
chiffre : figure, digit
chiffre d'affaires : turnover
clause : provision
clôture : close, closing
commissaire aux comptes : auditor
comptabilisé (non) : not reported above
comptabilité : bookkeeping, accountancy → an accountant
comptabilité en partie double : double-entry bookkeeping
constatation de sinistre : ascertainment of damage
contracter une police d'assurance : take out an insurance policy
contrat : contract
contribuable : taxpayer
contrôle : audit
contrôler : check
contrôleur des impôts : tax inspector
courant, en cours : current
couvrir : cover → a cover, a coverage
créance : debt
créancier : creditor

date d'échéance : due date
débit : debit
débiteur (solde) : debit balance
déclaration d'impôts : income tax return
décliner (responsabilité) : disclaim
dédommager qqn de : compensate sb for → compensation
déductible des impôts : tax-deductible
déficit : deficit
dégats : damage
dégressif : declining
dégrèvement d'impôts : tax relief
dépenses d'exploitation : operating expenses
dépôt de bilan : statement of affairs
dépréciation : depreciation
disponible (actifs) : available assets
durée de validité de la police : currency of the policy

échéance : due date
écriture rectificative : correcting entry
écriture de fin d'année : closing entries
effet : bill
effets à payer : bills payable
effets à recevoir : bills receivable
équilibrer : balance
espèces : cash
état : return
évasion fiscale : tax evasion
exercice : period
exercice social : company's year
exonéré d'impôts : tax-exempted
expert-comptable : chartered accountant
expertise des dégâts : damage survey
expirer : expire

faillite : bankruptcy → bankrupt (adj.)
faillite (faire) : go bankrupt
feuille d'impôts : tax card, tax sheet
fisc : Inland Revenue (GB), Internal Revenue (US)

honoraire : fee

immobilisation : fixed assets
impayé : dishonoured
imposable : taxable
imposition : taxation
impôt prélevé à la source : PAYE, Pay As You Earn
impôt sur les plus-values : capital gains tax
impôt sur le revenu : income tax
impôt sur les sociétés : corporate tax
indemniser : indemnify → an indemnity
inscription au Grand Livre : posting to ledger
insolvabilité : insolvency → insolvent (adj.)
inventaire : inventory, stocktaking
inventaire (faire l') : take stock

liquidation : liquidation, winding up
liquidation d'actifs : administration of assets
livre de caisse : cash book
lucratif (à but) : profit-making

maquiller (des comptes) : falsify the books, tamper with the books, fiddle the books
marge de profit : profit margin
modification (d'un contrat) : alteration
moyen (adj.) : average → an average

omettre : pass

paiement (retard de) : overdue (adj.)
paradis fiscal : tax haven
passif : liabilities
percepteur : tax collector
perte sèche : dead loss
plan comptable : accounting system
plus-value : capital gains
police : policy
poste comptable : entry
présentation : format
présentation fallacieuse : window-dressing
prime : premium

rappel d'impôts : tax reminder
rapport annuel : annual report
reçu : receipt
réel : actual
rembourser (une dette, un emprunt) : pay back
rembourser (une somme déjà versée) : refund
renouvellement : renewal
résilier : cancel
responsabilité : liability

solde créditeur : credit balance
solde débiteur : debit balance
solde de tout compte (pour) : in full settlement
surplus : excess

tiers (un) : third party
total général : grand total
Trésor public : Treasury

vigueur (en) : operative

Unit 8

Transport

A few landmarks

Incoterms

Incoterms are standard trade definitions most commonly used in international sales contracts. Devised and published by the International Chambers of Commerce, they are at the heart of world trade. ICC introduced the first version of Incoterms – short for "International Commercial Terms" – in 1936.

Here is a brief outline of the most common terms used for foreign trade.

Incoterms are internationally recognised and accepted as binding on international trade contracts.

Incoterms 2000

terms		who pays	what						
	Export collection	Export Clearance	Loading to export vehicle/vessel	Freight	Insurance	Unloading Discharging	Import clearance	Delivery	Duty & Taxes
EXW EX Works	Buyer	Buyer	Buyer	Buyer	Buyer	Buyer	Buyer	Buyer	Buyer
FCA Free CArrier	Seller	Seller	Buyer	Buyer	Buyer	Buyer	Buyer	Buyer	Buyer
FOB Free On Board	Seller	Seller	Seller	Buyer	Buyer	Buyer	Buyer	Buyer	Buyer
CFR Cost and FReight	Seller	Seller	Seller	Seller	Buyer	Buyer	Buyer	Buyer	Buyer
CIF Cost Insurance & Freight	Seller	Seller	Seller	Seller	Seller	Buyer	Buyer	Buyer	Buyer
CPT Carriage Paid To	Seller	Seller	Seller	Seller	Buyer	Buyer	Buyer	Buyer	Buyer
CIP Carriage & Insurance Paid to	Seller	Seller	Seller	Seller	Seller	Buyer	Buyer	Buyer	Buyer
DDU Delivered Duty Unpaid	Seller	Seller	Seller	Seller	Seller	Seller	Seller	Seller	Buyer
DDP Delivered Duty Paid	Seller	Seller	Seller	Seller	Seller	Seller	Seller	Seller	Seller

Terms EXW, FCA, CPT, DDU & DDP can be used for all modes of transport.

Terms FOB, CFR & CIF should be used for sea and inland waterway only.

It is generally accepted that the party who pays the freight selects the carrier.

Warm-up

1 • **Which means would you choose to transport the following goods?**
perishable goods / heavy and bulky goods / fragile goods

2 • **With the help of the following lists, give the advantages and drawbacks of transporting the above-mentioned cargoes by air, road, sea and rail.**
- **Advantages:** inexpensive, fast, safe, intermediate stops, door-to-door service, covers long distances, choice of routes, cheap to run, flexible.
- **Drawbacks:** expensive, time-consuming, traffic jams, not fast, goods to be collected from and delivered to airports, delays at customs, station to station, seasonal difficulties, goods to be taken to and from docks, tolls.

Unit 8

TEXT 1

1. **meter:** *compteur*
2. **cabby** = taxi driver
3. **reel off** = repeat information from memory quickly and easily

"By the time I rounded Trafalgar Square it was £8 on the meter[1]. Normally it's £4"

Alan Fleming is in the very best tradition of London cabbies[2]. [...] He spends a good part of his day queuing at traffic lights, inching forward each time the red light turns green, often for only a few seconds, before it turns back to red for several minutes.

"You used to have to wait 90 seconds, maybe, for lights to turn green again. Now it's two to three minutes," said Mr Fleming, chairman of the London Cab Drivers' Club. "And it's only green for eight or nine seconds. You only get two vehicles across."

He reeled off[3] a list of ten junctions he was convinced had shortened the amount of time for cars. *The Independent on Sunday* passed the list to Transport for London (TfL), the body in charge of major roads and traffic lights, which confirmed all junctions had changed its phasings in recent times – for a variety of reasons. TfL says it is impossible to give details of what timings were and what they are now because the situation is too complex.

"It's a complete nightmare," commented Mr Fleming. "I have just taken a passenger from Victoria, down the Mall and by the time we got around Trafalgar Square it was £8 on the meter. Normally it would be £4. And that's due to waiting at traffic lights."

Paul Robinson, another cabby, said: "The Government seem to cause a lot of traffic problems in London. They set up all these problems by narrowing the streets and widening pavements for pedestrians. It's got so bad that I can't even use *The Knowledge** I studied when I sat the test 30 years ago."

* *The Knowledge* is a very difficult test which requires cabbies to know by heart more than 450 London routes.

From *The Independent on Sunday*, 9 June 2002.

► Check your pronunciation

Are the underlined sounds to be pronounced [ɪ] or [i:]?

1 • green
2 • list
3 • minutes
4 • give
5 • detail
6 • meter
7 • complete
8 • reeled
9 • traffic

► Words

A • Choose the correct meaning of the following words.

1 • "inching forward" (l. 2) means: moving carelessly / driving a small car / moving very slowly
2 • "junction" (l. 7) means: crossroads / tunnel / roundabout
3 • "set up" (l. 17) means: shorten / create / delete
4 • "I sat the test" (l. 19) means: I passed the test / I failed the test / I took the test

B • Continue the list of verbs.

1 • make narrow → narrow
2 • make wide → widen
3 • make deep → ....
4 • make long → ....
5 • make light → ....
6 • make straight → ....

► Meaning

A • Transform the following sentences using the pattern given below. (see T&T: Preterite)

Ex.: When I was young there was a roundabout here. It has disappeared.
– When I was young there used to be a roundabout here.

1 • I went to work by car. I no longer do; now I take a taxi.
2 • London's taxis were the best in the world only a few years ago. They no longer are.
3 • New York taxis offered hair-raising rides. They no longer do.
4 • Black cabs had to park, with their "to hire" signs lit, at designated places only. This rule has been relaxed.
5 • He charged £4 for the journey. He now charges a lot more.
6 • Those streets were wide when I first visited the town. Now they are narrower.
7 • The situation was complex. It is simpler now.

B • Which statements are true?

1 • Mr Fleming is furious because
– there is a growing number of traffic lights in London.
– the amount of time for cars at junctions has been shortened.
– the amount of time for cars at junctions has increased.

2 • It is true that
– phasings have changed at junctions, which is confirmed by the TfL.
– phasings have changed but waiting time is in favour of cars.
– phasings have not really changed.

3 • This situation is
– nightmarish for cabbies.
– too complex to be understood by cabbies.
– a good thing for cabbies.

4 • TfL admits
– phasings have changed.
– phasings are out of control.
– timings are longer for drivers.

5 • Paul Robinson blames it on
– the Government.
– the pedestrians.
– London streets.

© Jeremy Horner / Corbis.

C • Translate into English.

1 • *Il vient de prendre un passager.*
2 • *Le feu est vert pendant seulement 10 secondes.*
3 • *Il n'y a que deux voitures qui passent.*
4 • *Ce chauffeur de taxi passe sa journée à attendre aux feux.*
5 • *Les trottoirs ont été élargis, ce qui est une bonne chose pour les piétons.*
6 • *Les rues de Londres sont de plus en plus étroites ; cela est dû à la nouvelle politique du gouvernement en matière de circulation.*

► Pair work

A cabby phones TfL in order to complain about the traffic problems in London. Imagine the conversation.

► Food for thought

What can be done to persuade people to use transport facilities?

Unit 8

TEXT 2

The Port of Liverpool

1. **carve:** *tailler*
2. **enhanced** = increased
3. **gantry crane:** *grue à portique*
4. **gateway:** *entrée, porte*
5. **ro-ro:** *roulage*

The Port of Liverpool has been undergoing the biggest investment programme since the Royal Seaforth Dock, with its container, grain and forest products terminals, was built in the late 1960s and early 1970s.

Container Terminal investment

At nearby Gladstone Dock, a £2m rail-linked terminal, including an 8,300 sq m warehouse, was completed in the first half of 2000. 1999 saw the commissioning of new silos to boost by 300,000 tonnes the potential annual storage capacity of the Port's Royal Seaforth Grain Terminal.

© GettyImages / Stone / Jason Hawkes.

The Mersey Docks and Harbour Company's new Chief Executive Peter Jones summed up the Port's outlook: "Liverpool has carved[1] a powerful position for itself over a decade and a half of development across a range of trades. Implementation of the current programme of investment is the latest phase of a strategy to drive the Port forward. The next decade will mark an exciting new era of further expansion and growth."

Increasing volumes

Liverpool's position among North Europe's top ten container ports was strengthened as volumes handled by the Royal Seaforth Container Terminal rose in 2000 from 515,000 TEUs to 540,000 TEUs, reflecting increased carryings by established shipping lines, which were joined late in 1999 by Independent Container Line (ICL) and its weekly service to the East Coast of the US. This latest arrival strengthens Liverpool's position in the North Atlantic container trade. The Port now handles some 25% of all box traffic crossing between the UK and North America.

Container Terminal

With the Royal Seaforth Container Terminal already enjoying recognition among shipping lines and shippers alike, as one of Europe's most efficient operations, its performance is being substantially enhanced[2] by the various elements of the £22m programme of investment. The combination of new ship-to-shore gantry cranes[3] and sophisticated computer systems, along with substantial development of terminal facilities, is producing a quality of ship-side and land-side service unequalled in the UK and Continental Europe.

Irish Sea Gateway[4]

As Britain's major gateway for trade with Ireland, Liverpool has enjoyed an average of over 10% growth in Irish Sea Trade, year-on-year for the past decade. Ro-ro[5] cargo rose by a third in 1999 and 17% in 2000. In response to the quality, capacity and frequency of services between Liverpool and Ireland, the number of passengers using the Port now exceeds 600,000.

From merseydocks.co.uk

► Check your pronunciation

A • Can you pronounce the following words?

1 • Liverpool
2 • Europe
3 • East
4 • North America
5 • Irish Sea
6 • Ireland

B • Read the following words aloud. What do they have in common?

1 • commission
2 • position
3 • implementation
4 • expansion
5 • recognition
6 • operation
7 • combination

► Words

A • Circle the right meaning for each of the following words.

1 • "undergo" (l. 1) means:
experience / suffer / go under
2 • "boost" (l. 7) means:
boast / raise / decrease
3 • "outlook" (l. 10) means:
appearance / past / prospect
4 • "strengthened" (l. 18) means:
made weaker / made stronger / made steadier
5 • "recognition" (l. 27) means:
remembrance / admission / acknowledgement

B • What is the difference between a port and a harbour?

► Meaning

A • Translate into French.

1 • "a £2m rail-linked terminal" (l. 5)
2 • "The Mersey Docks and Harbour Company's new Chief Executive Peter Jones" (l. 9-10)
3 • "Liverpool's position among North Europe's top ten container ports" (l. 17)
4 • "in the North Atlantic container trade" (l. 23-24)

B • Make a list of all the sectors in which the Port of Liverpool has been expanding since the investment programme began.

C • Make a list of all the improvements mentioned in the text (in French).

D • Translate into English.

1 • *Le commerce a augmenté d'un tiers.*
2 • *Un service hebdomadaire.*
3 • *Sur une décennie.*
4 • *Un système informatisé.*
5 • *Plus de 25 % de croissance annuelle.*
6 • *Le nombre actuel de passagers.*
7 • *Un programme d'investissement s'élevant à 30 millions de livres sterling.*

E • Translate from "Liverpool has carved" (l. 10) to "growth" (l. 15).

► Pair work

Give a talk on the evolution of the Port of Liverpool. You may use the following table as a guide:

– late 1960s-early 1970s	....
– 1985-2000	....
– 1999	....
– late 1999	....
– 1999-2000	....
– 1990-2000	....
– 1st half of 2000	....
– 2000-2010	....

► Food for thought

What other important ports have you heard of? What do you know about them? Are they all undergoing changes?

TEXT 3

UPS Internet Shipping

Whether you send one package a month or several packages a day, UPS Internet Shipping is your fastest and most convenient shipping solution on the Web. Access the industry's widest array of shipping options right from your computer. All you need is an Internet connection, a MY UPS.COM registration, and either a credit card or a UPS Account for billing.

After registering with MY UPS.COM, you can immediately start creating labels for your shipments. Simply provide the address and service information, and you're ready to print the label. […] UPS offers a variety of ways to get your shipments to UPS:

– regular "Daily Pickup" customers can give Internet Shipping packages to their UPS driver.
– hand the package to a UPS driver. Whether they're making deliveries to you in the morning or […] in the afternoon, UPS drivers accept Internet Shipping packages.
– take your package to an Authorized Shipping Outlet or a UPS Customer Counter.

Air and International Shipments only:

– Over 50,000 UPS Drop-Off boxes are conveniently located near you (letters and small packages only).
– Schedule a UPS On Call Air Pickup to have a UPS driver collect your Air and International shipments.

If you're registered with MY UPS.COM, simply log in and get started with UPS Internet Shipping! If you're not yet registered with MY UPS.COM, then register now!

► Words

Find the equivalents in the text of the following words.

1 • largest
2 • range
3 • directly
4 • invoicing
5 • shipping
6 • give (2 verbs)
7 • deposit
8 • plan
9 • pick up

► Meaning

A • Rephrase the sentences with "whether … or …". (see T&T: Links words)

1 • You are a regular customer or a new one / UPS can deal with your packages.
2 • UPS drivers come to your company or you go to an Authorized Shipping Outlet / your packages will be well looked after by UPS.
3 • Your packages are sent within the USA or to any other country / you can rely on UPS.

B • Look at l. 4-5 "All you need … billing" and translate the following sentences.

1 • *Nous pouvons apporter nos colis soit à un magasin d'expéditions homologué, soit à un guichet client UPS.*
2 • *Soit on dépose les colis à l'international dans des conteneurs UPS, soit un chauffeur vient les récupérer.*
3 • *Ou vous souscrivez maintenant ou vous vous connectez.*

C • Answer in your own words.

1 • What are UPS and UPS Internet Shipping?
2 • How can you give your shipments to UPS?
3 • If your goods need to be shipped by plane or to any country except the USA, what should you do?
4 • Describe the steps to follow for a new customer who wishes to use UPS Internet Shipping.

Checkup
Unit 8

1 ► Test

Pay per drive

Britain is too fond of the car – traffic has grown by 80% over 20 years. According to a poll by the Commission for Integrated Transport, 54% of car users already experience regular congestion in towns, while 34% routinely spend time in jams on motorways. Gridlock is becoming a way of life in Britain. Most organisations agree that doing nothing is not an option.

The government's transport guru, professor David Begg, complains that the taxation system on motoring has barely changed since the early days when the automobile was the preserve of the few. Drivers pay for their travel through an annual disc, and fuel duty. [...]

Many transport strategists suggest motorists should pay for each journey the way that they pay for a trip by bus, train or plane. Road charging, however, is controversial.

Three approaches to charging are under consideration. Motorists could pay motorway tolls; they could be charged for entry to towns and cities; or, most radically, they could be billed for every mile they travel on Britain's road system.

Motorway tolls initially appear the simplest option – most drivers have experienced paying at giant booths that straddle major roads on the continent. But our road system works against this. Britain's network has dozens of by-passes and link roads constructed incrementally over decades. Faced with a motorway toll, many vehicles will take A and B roads, as the gap in quality is often marginal.

The government has paved the way for urban charges, passing legislation two years ago that allowed local authorities to apply to levy fees on cars entering specified areas. London mayor, Ken Livingstone's scheme has been given the go-ahead. Politicians in Edinburgh and Bristol are considering congestion charges, but most are likely first to see if the London plans succeeds in raising £130m a year to spend on upgrading buses and tubes.

The most overarching solution, a national charging scheme, was proposed earlier this year by the commission for integrated transport – a government think-tank. It put forward a £180bn proposal under which every car would be fitted with satellite technology to register the distance, type of road and time of each journey.

Motorists would be billed according to a sliding scale of fees, with the highest rate for rush-hour journey on major trunk roads. An average weekday journey along a motorway would cost 3.5p a mile – which would mean £7.40 to travel from Manchester to Birmingham. The commission believes the plan would cut congestion 44%, with average speeds up 3%. The plan involves a dramatic cut in fuel duty and car tax, so that the overall burden would be barely different.

From *The Guardian*, June 14, 2002.

A • After summing up the present state of car traffic in Britain, you will explain the current taxation system on motoring (in French, about 40 words).

B • Then you will introduce the three solutions that have been considered (in French, about 50 words).

C • Using information from the text and your personal experience, you will discuss the advantages and drawbacks of the three solutions. (in English, about 150 words)

D • Translate into French from "The government's transport guru" (l. 9) to "fuel duty" (l. 14).

2 ► Skills in practice

A • Match the words with the drawings.

van / fork-lift truck / crane / chain / hook / padded envelope / packing case / carton / barrel / bale / drum / carboy / parcel / polystyrene mould / pallet / rope / metal bands / nails / screws / string / hand truck

B • You are working in the export department of a French firm and your Australian customer has just placed an order with you for some of your goods. An unscrupulous trainee has mixed up all the main tasks to be carried out except the first and the last ones. Put the tasks back into the order that your Australian customer, on the one hand, and you, on the other hand, have to follow.

1 • My customer placed an order.
2 • I contact the forwarding agent.
3 • I have to export the goods.
4 • The cargo is checked and cleared by the customs authorities.
5 • My customer has to import the goods.
6 • The goods are transported from the port to the customer.
7 • I fill in the bill of lading.
8 • The goods are shipped to the port of arrival.
9 • My customer wants the consignment to be made by sea freight.
10 • The customer acknowledges receipt of the goods and pays the invoice.

3 ► The right word

A • Crossword

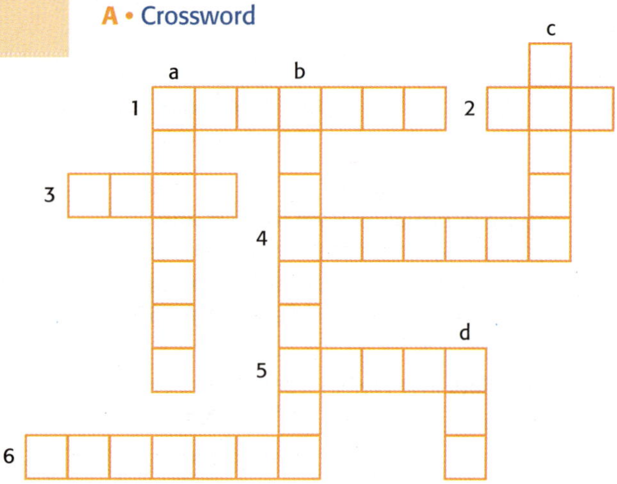

Across

1 • Checkpoint when leaving a country.
2 • Short for Free on Board.
3 • Sth which is being carried somewhere.
4 • Ship, truck or railway vehicles used for transporting large quantities of gas or liquid.
5 • A large machine that moves heavy things by lifting them in the air.
6 • Long journeys on a ship.

Down

a • Plane or boat hired by a particular person or a group.
b • US for breakdown trucks.
c • Area in a port where ships are loaded, unloaded and repaired.
d • Short for ex-works.

B • Fill in the blanks with words from the following list.

barges / bunk / ex-works / FOB / Shuttle / ro-ro / sidings / stalling / toll-houses / traffic

1 • If you want to go to England you can take the .... from Calais.
2 • Yesterday, because of the cold weather my engine kept ....
3 • The .... was jammed by a truck that could not start.
4 • With an .... price the goods are collected and transported at the buyer's expense.
5 • .... includes transport and loading aboard the ship.
6 • In summer holidaymakers queue up at the .... on the motorways.
7 • The carriages that are not being used are left on ...., that is to say on short railway tracks.
8 • A ferry for lorries is called a ....
9 • .... are used on rivers for carrying heavy loads such as coal for example.
10 • The lorry driver was so exhausted that he threw himself on the cabin .... and fell asleep at once.

4 ► Vocabulary

affréter : charter
agent transitaire : forwarding agent
aller-retour dans la journée : day trip
armateur : shipowner
arrimer (une cargaison) : stow
autoroute : motorway (GB), highway (US)
avion cargo : freighter

banlieusard : commuter

camion : truck (US), lorry (GB)
camionnette de livraison : delivery van
cargaison : cargo
cargo : cargo ship
charger : load
code de la route : Highway Code
colis : parcel
commande en provenance de l'étranger : indent
connaissement : Bill of Lading, B/L
conteneur : container
contrebande (passer en) : smuggle
Coût, Assurance, Frêt, CAF : Cost, Insurance, Freight, CIF
Coût et Frêt : Cost and Freight, C/F
Covoiturage : high occupancy vehicle

décharger : unload
dédouanement : customs-clearing
dédouaner : clear goods through the customs
dépanneuse : tow truck
départ usine : ex-works
destinataire : consignee

documents contre acceptation : Documents against Acceptance, D/A
documents contre paiement : Documents against Payment, D/P
documents relatifs au transport : shipping documents
douane : customs
droits de douane : customs duties

embargo : embargo
embouteillage : traffic jam
étranger (adj.) : foreign → foreigner
étranger (à l') : abroad, overseas
exempt de droits : duty free
expédier : despatch, dispatch (US), ship
expéditeur : consigner
expédition : shipment, consignment
exportation : export

facture consulaire : consular invoice
facture pro forma : pro forma invoice
flotte : fleet
« fragile » : "handle with care"
franco à bord : Free On Board, FOB
franco à quai : Free alongside Ship
frêt : freight

gazole : diesel
gros porteur : jumbo jet

heures de pointe : peak hours

importation : import
itinéraire : route

lettre de voiture : waybill

manutention : handling
moteur : engine

parc (de voitures) : fleet
péage : toll
péage (barrière de) : toll-house
port maritime : maritime / sea port
prix (billet de train, bus, etc.) : fare

quai (être à) : dock
quatre-voies : dual carriageway

remorqueur : tug
roulier : roll-on roll-off, Ro-Ro
routier : haulier

semi-remorque : semi-trailer
souffrance (en) : held up in transit, awaiting delivery
sous-douane : in bond prices
sous-douane (entrepôt de) : bonded warehouse
station service : filling station

train de marchandises : freight train
transbordement : transshipment
transborder : transship
transitaire : transit
transporteur : carrier

vitesse : speed
voie de garage : siding
voyage en mer : voyage

wagon de marchandises : goods truck (GB), freight car (US)

The working world

PART II

Unit 1

Education and training

A few landmarks

Education

Education and training are the cornerstones of a successful career. When you leave high school, you enter **higher education** that is provided by a **college**, a **university** or a specialised school, a college being a part of a university that offers a specialised group of **courses**.

During your studies, you can follow different **curricula** (sg. curriculum), i.e. sets of courses, and you **sit for** (or **take**) **exams**. If you **pass an exam** you obtain a **degree** that will be made official by a document called a **diploma**. Before getting a degree, you are an **undergraduate**. Once you get your first degree, you become a **graduate**. If you pass your third-year or fourth-year exam you obtain a bachelor's degree; then, you can get a master's degree and finally a doctorate.

Here are some of the most famous and prestigious schools:

British universities	American universities
– Oxbridge = Oxford (12th c.) and Cambridge (13th c.) universities. – Edinburgh University (16th c.)	– The "Ivy League" universities (in New England) = Harvard (17th c.), Yale (18th c.) and Princeton (18th c.). – MIT = the Massachusetts Institute of Technology. – Berkeley = the University of California. – UCLA = the University of California in Los Angeles.

Training

The Open University enables the students who are often employed to receive lessons and lectures at home, partly by correspondence courses and partly by television (BBC2) and radio broadcasts. It now includes students from the EU.

Concerning workers, those who need training can attend **evening classes** or be part-time students in **continuing education**. Those who haven't been training for their jobs have to learn about them on their own while working; this is called **on-the-job training**. Sometimes, they get **retraining** or **job training**, that is additional or new training, in order to upgrade their skills or to change their jobs.

Londoners' Job Fair 2002

© Atlantic Syndication Partners.

How they stand and where to find us

HOW TO GET THERE

The Evening Standard Londoners' Job Fair takes place on Wednesday 18 and Thursday 19 September at the New Connaught Rooms, Great Queen Street, Kingsway, WC2.

Doors open each day at 11am and remain open until 7 pm.

Admission is free.

The nearest Tubes are Holborn (Piccadilly and Central lines) and Covent Garden (Piccadilly line).

The following buses take you there: 1, 8, 19, 22B, 25, 38, 55, 68, 91, 96, 168, 171, 188, 501, 505, 521.

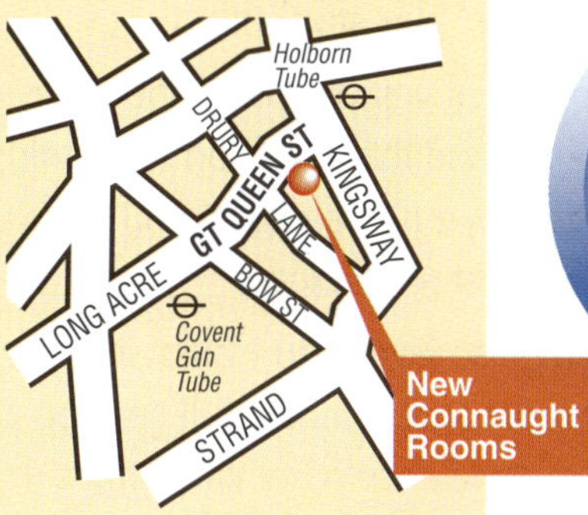

02
Londoners' Job Fair 2002

HOW THEY STAND

Stand	Company
31	Access Storage Solutions
28	Anchor Trust
27	Army
24	Barclays
14	Brighthouse
32	Caretech Community Services
03	Debenhams
30	Enterprise Rent A Car
15	Gadget Shop
13	Habitat
23	Hertfordshire Constabulary
18	HSS Hire Shops
29	London Borough of Camden
01	Loot
04	Monsoon/Accessorize
17	Moorfields Eye Hospital
21	Nationwide Building Society
26	RAF Careers Service
25	Royal Navy
12	Lambeth, Southwark and Lewisham Pct
19	Sussex Police
22	Teacher Training Agency
02	Tie Rack
11	Toys R Us
20	William Hill

Education – courses & CV Clinic

Stand	Company
B4	Brittania Training
B12	CV Clinic – Rebecca Fuller
B6	Elite College
B3	Fern Training & Development
B8	Joskos
B7	Pitman Training, Love & Tate
B1	TBG Learning
B2	Thisislondon
B5	Westminster Kingsway College

From *Evening Standard*, September 16, 2002

Warm-up

1 • What is a job fair?

2 • Where and when did this fair take place?

3 • What are the opening hours and conditions of admission?

4 • What is the use of the list on the right-hand side?

5 • Which stands would you visit? Why?

Unit 1

TEXT 1

1. **glamour:** *prestige*
2. **retail:** *vente au détail*
3. **harm** = hurt
4. **the odd letter** = any letter

Last-minute jobs that will serve your career well

You might want to work while planning your future career. And there are many jobs that can enhance your skills and prospects even if they lack glamour[1]. Try these for size:

Retail[2] positions

"Time management, self-motivation, tight deadlines and excellent customer service skills. These are all things that someone who's looking for an office manager might look for," says Asela Ali, development manager with Read Graduates recruitment consultancy.

You could easily develop these skills working in a burger bar, she says. "It might not provide an obvious opportunity to gain transferable skills, but working in McDonald's is not going to harm[3] someone who wants to work in an office. And someone who has worked in a fast-paced retail environment might also do very well in sales."

Filing / Administration

"A lot of graduates don't like the idea of filing or typing the odd[4] letter or invoice but that's how you learn how business works," says Asela.

"Even something like data entry requires attention to detail, working to targets and quite often customer service," she says.

© Benoit Decout / Réa.

"Temp work gives you the opportunity to find out about the nitty-gritty. And that leads on to learning more about yourself." This, she says, is essential if you're going to make any sound long-term career choices.

Temping also gives you insight into the company you're working for and should a full-time position arise, you have an advantage over other candidates. [...]

"Ultimately it's not so much about the type of job, but about the skills you gain," says Asela. "The most important question to ask is, will it enhance my employability? It's not the nature of the work, it's what you're going to get out of it. Any work is valuable – it's just a matter of how you view it."

From *The Guardian*, September 7, 2002.

► Check your pronunciation

The "o" vowel in these words is pronounced [ɒ], [ə] or [əʊ]. Classify them.

1 • job 2 • prospect 3 • consultancy 4 • motivation
5 • over 6 • office 7 • going 8 • obvious 9 • position
10 • also 11 • odd 12 • most

► Words

Match each word from the text with its equivalent.

1 • enhance (l. 2) 3 • obvious (l. 9) 5 • sound (l. 19)
2 • tight (l. 4) 4 • temp (l. 17) 6 • ultimately (l. 24)

a • temporary b • clear c • finally d • strict e • improve f • reasonable

► Meaning

A • Select the correct meaning.

1 • "in a fast-paced retail environment" (l. 11): in a dull environment / in a peaceful environment / in a speedy environment
2 • "working to targets" (l. 15): meeting the goals / meeting the deadlines / meeting the demand
3 • "find out about the nitty-gritty" (l. 17-18): understand the essentials / understand the details / understand what is not for you
4 • "Temping gives you insight into the company" (l. 21): temping is a barrier to getting to know the company / temping is useless for getting to know the company / temping is useful for getting to know the company

B • Rewrite the sentences using another modal auxiliary. (see T&T: Modals)

1 • You will perhaps first look for a job that has nothing to do with your future career.
2 • Perhaps this job will not sound attractive to you.
3 • It is possible for you to find an odd job that will boost your CV.
4 • Are you unable to see a temping agent?
5 • I advise you to accept this odd job.
6 • They will certainly take you on for your dynamism.

C • Choose the appropriate link word.

if / even if / even / even though / should

1 • I advise you to accept this job as a bar tender .... you want to become a recruiter.
2 • .... you analyse all the tasks carefully, you'll increase your skills.
3 • Any sort of job, ... the less glamorous, is useful experience.
4 • You know, temping is often rewarding .... you don't want to hear about it.
5 • .... he call you back, tell him you are available for an interview.

D • Rephrase the following quotations from the text.

1 • "Try these for size" (l. 2)
2 • "Time management, self-motivation, tight deadlines and excellent customer service skills." (l. 4)
3 • "This [...] is essential if you're going to make any sound long-term career choices." (l. 19-20)
4 • "Should a full-time position arise, you have an advantage over other candidates." (l. 22-23)

E • Answer the questions.

1 • To what extent is working as a waiter / waitress helpful for a retail career?
2 • What are the advantages of performing tasks such as filing, typing and data entry?

F • Translate the last paragraph and sum it up in English. (30 words)

► Pair work

A is being interviewed for a job as sales assistant manager. Apart from his / her work placements, his / her experience includes basic secretarial tasks and working as a waiter / waitress in a restaurant. **B** is the interviewer. Imagine the interview.

► Food for thought

Weigh the pros and cons of temping.

Unit 1

TEXT 2

1. **spreadsheet:** *tableur*
2. **package:** *progiciel*
3. **SME =** small- and medium-sized entreprise

A lesson e-learned

Training can be an expensive business. Not only do you have to pay for a tutor and usually travel and accommodation, but it can also be difficult keeping a business running when key people are in a classroom somewhere.

Alison Stanley, a director of Stanley's, a small family-run jewellery business in the West Midlands, believes she has found an answer. Rather than book places on traditional training courses, she has embraced online learning to help improve her accounting skills. "I use it for advanced spreadsheets[1]. When I get five minutes, I get my laptop out and learn a little every day. It's the flexibility which I find very useful."

She is encouraging her staff to use web-based learning packages[2] as well. "There are lots of courses you can do. I just think it's the way to go. The courses don't rush you. Everything is explained clearly and it tells you whether or not you're correct."

E-learning organisations now have UK-based SMEs[3] firmly in their sights. They see them as ideal candidates for flexible web-based courses. The government-backed University for Industry recently announced that it is making a whole range of e-learning programmes available to SMEs through Chambers of Commerce up and down the country. [...]

[Cameron Beard, head of sales for the University for Industry] says the e-learning courses that are being made available to SMEs are intended to solve day-to-day business problems. And the idea is that company directors can contact their local chambers of commerce in order to work out which packages would be most likely to make a difference to their competitiveness and productivity. "Some of the courses are very comprehensive. Some are quick hits and you can do them in your office," he says, pointing out that if you are interrupted by a customer you can log straight back to the place where you left off. He says the e-learning packages can cost anything from £20 to £250 and cover essential business skills such as communication and marketing.

From *The Guardian,* May 30, 2002.

▶ Check your pronunciation

List the words according to their "u" pronunciation: either [juː], [ɪ], [ə] or [ʌ].

1 • productivity
2 • tutor
3 • industry
4 • interrupt
5 • usually
6 • business
7 • UK
8 • customer
9 • use
10 • such
11 • university

▶ Words

Pick out in the text the equivalents of the following words.

1 • hurry (§3)
2 • all over (§4)
3 • complete (§5)
4 • doses (§5)

▶ Meaning

A • Several compound nouns are used in this article. (see T&T: Compound nouns)

1 • Find and translate them.
2 • Translate the following expressions using compound nouns:
– *un chef de PME.*
– *des plans de formation.*
– *des connaissances en informatique.*
– *des programmes d'apprentissage en ligne.*
– *un audit sur les compétences en mercatique.*

B • Look at "web-based packages" (l. 9). It means the packages are based, i.e. located, on the web. (see T&T: Adjectives) Find other compound adjectives in the text with the same pattern (n. + p.p.) and explain their meaning in English.

C • Answer the questions in your own words.

1 • What can the drawbacks of training be for a company?
2 • What skill does Alison Stanley need to improve?
3 • What option has she chosen to upgrade this skill?

D • Right or wrong?

1 • Alison Stanley considers e-learning is only efficient for bosses.
2 • E-learning organisations do not want to work with SMEs all over the UK.
3 • The University for Industry has made e-learning courses that can be followed by SMEs in their Chambers of Commerce.
4 • These courses aim at providing SMEs with in-depth theoretical knowledge.
5 • The Chambers of Commerce lack a choice of courses.
6 • Online courses should be studied outside working hours.
7 • When you are interrupted in an exercise, you then have to start again from the beginning.

E • Look at the sentence in §1 "Not only … somewhere." (see T&T: Sentence patterns) Make sentences using the same pattern and the following elements.

1 • E-learning / less expensive than traditional training / the staff stays on the spot
2 • A. Stanley uses it for herself / she recommends it to her personnel
3 • You can correct your mistakes / it is possible to interrupt your exercises.
4 • I needed to revise a few points / I learnt complete courses.

F • Translate the first paragraph.

▶ Pair work

Group **A** notes down the advantages of traditional training (evening classes or part-time) and group **B** those of e-learning. Imagine their debate.

▶ Food for thought

You are working in the UK. You need to learn more about how to use Excel and you would also like to improve your time management skills. You've heard of e-learning and so you write a letter to your Chamber of Commerce for advice and information on their e-learning programmes.

TEXT 3

Reaching one and all

Thompson, a film-school graduate who cut his teeth[1] working on educational videos before specialising in information technology for a management consultancy[2], and then producing and directing training packs, now runs his own company, Supernova, based in Hove.

"Rick's operation struck me as a perfect opportunity for a training video, an inspiring case study of what it takes to motivate a team, day in day out. As the business has grown and diversified, the restaurant, the bistro, the deli[3], the cookery school, the hotel, so managing his 150 or so staff has become more and more important. Rick has had to learn the art of delegation [...]. What he has to say is useful for all managers, whether they are younger team leaders or more experienced professionals taking on management responsibility."

Thompson's resultant video, *Recipe For Success*, comes with a guide and a CD-Rom, which acts as a kind of workbook reminding viewers of the points raised and how they can be related to the individual's own situation.

From *The Evening Standard,* 16 September 2002.

1. **cut one's teeth =** make a start
2. **management consultancy:** *cabinet conseils*
3. **deli / delicatessen:** *épicerie fine-traiteur*

► Words

Match the words with their equivalent.

1 • information technology (l. 2)
2 • operation (l. 5)
3 • day in day out (l. 6)
4 • manage (l. 8)

a • run
b • every day
c • enterprise
d • IT

► Meaning

A • **How far did you understand the text?**

1 • **What is the subject of the verb "runs" (l. 3)?**
2 • **What is the subject of the verb "has become" (l. 8)?**
3 • **Translate "so managing his 150 or so staff" (l. 8).**
4 • **Look at l. 2: Thompson worked on educational videos "before specialising in information technology" which means "before he specialised in information technology". (see T&T: Gerund) Rephrase the sentences on the same pattern.**
– Before he diversified, Rick was a restaurant owner.
– Make a list of the points you want to improve before you view the video.
– After I saw the video I was again full of hope.
5 • **Does "as" in l. 6 and l. 13 have the same meaning? What does each word express? Give their equivalents and write down what sort of words follows them.**

B • **Answer the questions in your own words.**

1 • What is Thompson's current job?
2 • Give his CV.
3 • Who is Rick?
4 • What does Rick's job now consist in?
5 • What is *Recipe for Success*?

C • **Sum up in English what this method is for. (15 words)**

D • **Explain the pun in the title of the video. (30 words)**

E • **Translate the last paragraph.**

F • **How do you understand the title? (40 words)**

Checkup Unit 1

1 ► Test

Getting down to business

"Business studies graduates are seen as having good employment prospects," says Carl Gilleard, chief executive of the Association of Graduate Recruiters (AGR).

"They have generally done quite rounded degrees and they will have picked up a lot of skills, as well as knowledge that can be applied in the workplace. They are going on to a wide range of jobs both in the private and public sector."

A survey of 10,500 men and women with business studies degrees in 1999 showed that 78% got jobs within six months of graduating. Of these 13% were in marketing, sales and PR; 23% in the commercial, industrial and public sector; 7.5% in business and finance; almost 5% in IT; and 18.5% in clerical and secretarial. [...]

Business studies graduates are sought after by employers. The kind of person who enrols on business studies courses quite often knows what they want from a course and has career goals in mind. While getting a degree is important, it is as important to develop skills, get some work experience and be able to demonstrate personal qualities such as leadership and taking responsibility. [...]

"You can develop skills in almost any experience. Something as mundane as working in the students' union bar will help you to develop skills in how to deal with customers. When the bar shutters come down, you need some very good skills, diplomacy and tact in handling people who are desperate to get another pint before the bar shuts." [...]

Birmingham offers the bachelor of commerce a generalist, broadly-based, three-year business degree. It also offers a bachelor of commerce with language, which involves a year's study abroad, and a joint honours* language with business course in which students can spend half their time studying business and the other half studying language and literature. [...]

Some students also have the opportunity to study abroad in their second year at one of the City's exchange institutions: Emory University in Atlanta, the University of Illinois, City University Hong Kong, University College Dublin and the National University of Singapore. Competition for these places is stiff – there are five applicants for each exchange. [...]

International business studies degree students can go abroad for a year to work. Many students go on company internships during the summer holidays; others take part in student exchange programmes. All students have a chance to take a year out if they wish.

From *The Guardian*, August 19, 2002.

* **honours:** *licence*

A • Sum up in English the passage from "Business studies graduates" (l. 1) to "before the bar shuts" (l. 31). (100 words)

B • Give an account in English of what British business schools can offer. (120 words)

C • Translate §5 (l. 25-31).

2 ► Skills in practice

A • Insert the following words in the text below.

minorities / rose / discriminatory / poor / growth / performance / score

The proportion of young people awarded bachelor's degrees .... from 2% in 1900 to 19% in 1950 [...] to 32% in 1999. The .... of higher education after WWII was accompanied by increasing emphasis on admission based on merit rather than ability to pay, merit being measured mainly by high school grades and .... on tests, including the SAT*. But by the late 1980s the merit principle was colliding with affirmative action, the practise of giving special consideration to .... and women. Affirmative action in higher education had roots in the Civil Rights Act of 1964, which disallowed the use of tests that had a .... effect. It soon became apparent that Asian-Americans and white females had little need of special treatment, as they tended to .... well on the SAT. Because the average SAT scores of black, Mexican-American and Native American applicants were well below that of non-Hispanic whites – by 19, 14 and 9% respectively in 1999 – they were held to a lower test-score standard to compensate for .... schooling.

* **SAT** = Scholastic Aptitude Test

From scientificamerican.com, March 21, 2000.

B • Comment on the chart. (see T&T: Comparatives / superlatives + Graphs)

Minorities and Bachelor's degrees in the U.S.

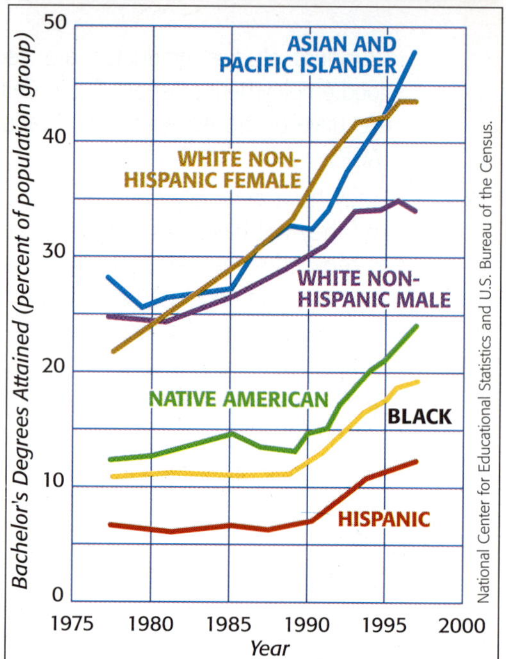

Data are annual estimates of the percentage in each group that were awarded bachelor's degrees, calculated by dividing the number of degrees conferred by the number of 22-year-olds in the corresponding group.

3 ► The right word

A • Crossword

Across

1 • Document attesting the success of a course of study.
2 • Occasional (for jobs).
3 • US noun for a mark.
4 • Give knowledge.
5 • Short for examinations.
6 • Percentage or proportion.
7 • Teach.
8 • Breeding.

Down

a • When you pass exams, you get them.
b • I need further training to go .... in the hierarchy.
c • Law voted in Parliament.
d • My training includes ....-to-one sessions.
e • Receive knowledge.
f • The fact of receiving knowledge.

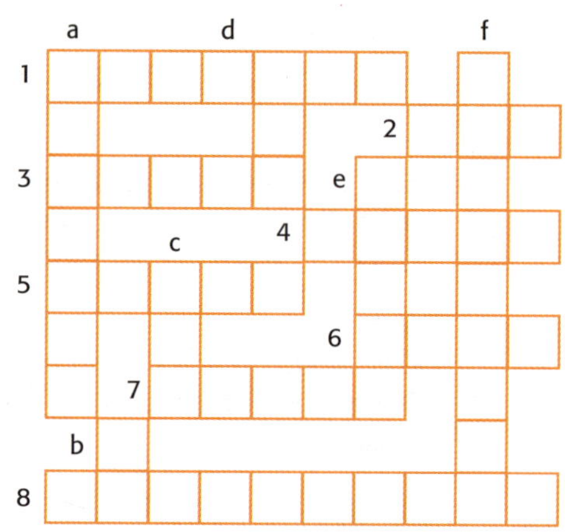

B • Fill in the blanks with words from the following list.

graduate / job market / education / training / leadership posts / business school / curricula / decision-making / job-training / trainee / academic / skills / abilities / flexibility / training courses

It isn't always easy for a .... to find a job but it depends on your .... Indeed, your university may have had .... proposing .... in several enterprises. You can also have been in a .... offering you the possibility to get acquainted with ....
As a ...., you are asked to develop your .... as aptly as you can, which will be of great help when you enter the working world and face the .... Of course, if .... hasn't been adapted enough, some workers are incited to attend .... courses.
In fact, whether you have received .... knowledge or acquired your .... on the job, from the lowest-paid jobs to the ...., the key to success today is ....

4 ► Vocabulary

apprenti : apprentice
apprentissage : apprenticeship
aptitude : ability, qualification
avancement (donner de l') : promote, upgrade

boulots (petits) : odd jobs
cadre : executive
carrière : career
chef de bureau : office manager
chef de service : department manager
col blanc : white collar (worker)
col bleu : blue collar (worker)
compétence : skill, qualification, expertise
cours (leçon) : class
cours (série de) : course
cours de remise à niveau : refresher classes
cours du soir : evening classes, continuing education classes
cours par correspondance : correspondence courses

débutant (adj.) : junior
diplôme (obtenu) : degree, qualifications (pl.)
diplôme (document) : diploma
diplômé (être) : graduate
diplômé (pas encore) : undergraduate
diplômé (un) : graduate

échelon : grade
école de commerce : business school
embaucher : hire, take on
emploi (garantie de l') : job guarantee
emploi (l') : employment [U]
emploi permanent : permanent job
emploi saisonnier : seasonal job
emploi (sécurité de) : job security
emploi stable : steady job
emploi temporaire : temporary job
emploi (un) : job
employé de bureau : clerk, clerical worker
engager à l'essai : hire on probation
équipe : team
équipe (travail d') : teamwork
équipe (travail en) : shift work
essai (période d') : probation period
études : studies → study (v.)
études complémentaires : follow-up studies
évaluation : assessment → assess (v.)

formation : training → train (v.)
formation (centre de) : training centre
formation continue : continuing education
formation dans l'entreprise : in-house training
formation du personnel : staff training
formation en alternance : part-time / sandwich course
formation (plan de) : training scheme / programme
formation professionnelle : professional / vocational training
formation (suivre une) : get training, take a training course
formation sur le tas : on-the-job training

maître de stage : tutor
moyen (cadre, etc.) : middle

niveau : level

orientation (scolaire) : guidance / advice on courses and careers
orientation (professionnelle) : careers guidance / advising
orienter vers (s') : specialise in, turn to

perspective d'emploi : job opportunities / prospects
post : post, position
poste libre : vacant post, vacancy
poste sans avenir : dead-end job
potentiel (adj.) : prospective
pourvoir en personnel : staff, man
profession : job, occupation
professions libérales : professions
programme (d'études) : curriculum (pl. curricula)
promotion : promotion
promouvoir : promote, upgrade

qualification : skill, qualification

recherche d'emploi : job hunting / seeking
recyclage : retraining, job training

stage : work experience, work placement, vocational training course, training session / period, internship (US)
stage de formation accélérée : crash course
stagiaire : trainee
supérieur (cadre, etc.) : senior

travailleur occasionnel : casual worker

universitaire (adj.) : academic

Unit 2 Working conditions

A few landmarks

Child labour

- Child labour is the employment of children under a specified legal age. In most western countries children of less than 15 rarely work, except in agriculture.
- In the US, the Fair Labor Standards Act of 1938 set the minimum age for employment in non-manufacturing jobs at 14. In developing countries, millions of children work in mines, quarries, factories. They usually carry out hazardous occupations. They make up more than 10 per cent of the labour force in certain countries of the Middle East, Latin America and Asia.
- **Three historical landmarks**

– **1833** The Factory Act (GB) set the minimum age for employment at 9.

– **1847** The Ten Hours Act (GB) introduced the ten-hour day for children (and women).

– **1989** The United Nations adopted the Convention on the Rights of the Child.

- **Industrial relations**

The Advisory Conciliation and Arbitration Service (ACAS) was created in 1974 to improve industrial relations. It examines abuses of workers' rights under legislation. For example, claims under:

– the Equal Pay Act, 1970,

– the Sex Discrimination Act, 1975,

– the Race Relations Act, 1976.

Warm-up

1 • What are those people doing?

2 • Where and when was the photo taken?

Unit 2

TEXT 1

Annual cost of sick leave rises to £13bn

1. **tackle =** deal (dealt, dealt) with

Sick leave is on the rise and it is costing the economy £13bn a year, a report reveals today. The average employee costs his or her firm £522 each year, according to a survey of 1,300 companies by the Chartered Institute of Personnel and Development (CIPD).

Employees took an average of 10 days off in the past twelve months, up by almost a day from the previous year.

Stress was the most common cause of long-term absence for professional staff, and back pain was the most frequent complaint among manual workers.

Long-term absence – more than four weeks – accounted for a fifth of all time off sick.

Diane Sinclair, policy adviser at CIDP, said; "Our survey suggests organisations need to do more to tackle[1] stress among staff. Reasons for work-related stress and symptoms need to be managed."

© Graham French / Masterfile.

The survey, covering organisations employing 1.7 million workers, showed the most common causes of absence were minor illnesses such as cold or flu. The highest percentage of time lost was in food, drink and tobacco firms, followed by paper and printing and the public sector.

The South-east had lower than average absence levels, while Wales and the North-east showed the highest rates.

Employers said they maintained contact with staff off sick for long periods and often offered reduced hours to help people return to work.

From *The Independent*, 30 July 2002.

► Check your pronunciation

A • Choose between [ɪ] and [iː].

1 • sick
2 • leave
3 • reveal
4 • employee
5 • each
6 • fifth
7 • East
8 • with

B • Can you stress the right syllabe in the following words?

1 • economy
2 • average
3 • companies
4 • development
5 • professional
6 • frequent
7 • illnesses
8 • tobacco
9 • employers

► Words

Find the appropriate word from the text for each definition.

1 • Written or spoken account of an event or situation.
2 • Detailed investigation of something, for example people's behaviours or opinions.
3 • Preceding.
4 • Statement expressing dissatisfaction.
5 • Unimportant.
6 • Winter epidemic

► Meaning

A • Sum up the problem raised in the text. (in English, about 10 words)

B • Fill in the grid below.

Problem raised by sick leave	....
Sort of sick leave	....
Two causes	1) .... 2) ....
Sectors concerned	....
Geographic areas	– lower rates than average: .... – highest rates: ....

C • What is the employers' attitude to employees on sick leave?

D • Reformulate the following sentences in your own words.

1 • "sick leave is on the rise" (l. 1)
2 • "up by almost a day" (l. 5-6)
3 • "long-term absence [...] accounted for a fifth of all time off sick" (l. 9)
4 • "organisations need to do more to tackle stress among staff" (l. 10-11)
5 • "Employers said they [...] offered reduced hours" (l. 22-24)

E • Translate into French.

1 • long-term absence
2 • back pain
3 • work-related stress
4 • staff off sick for long periods

F • Translate into English. (see T&T: Comparatives / superlatives)

1 • *Inférieur à la moyenne.*
2 • *De plus en plus de jours de congé maladie.*
3 • *De moins en moins de temps.*
4 • *Le pourcentage le plus bas.*
5 • *Le taux d'absence le plus élevé des deux entreprises.*
6 • *Notre personnel est souvent malade pour de plus longues périodes qu'autrefois.*
7 • *Les plaintes les plus fréquentes.*
8 • *Les causes les plus faciles à déterminer.*
9 • *Moins de congés de maladie que dans le nord est.*

► Group work

One group represents management within a firm, the other group represents the workers. They are trying to find solutions to tackle stress among staff. Imagine their dialogue.

► Food for thought

Home-based work is often thought to be a solution to reduce stress. Don't you think this new form of work could give rise to new forms of stress?

TEXT 2

Long march to save the world's children

1. quarrying: *travail dans les carrières*

2. bondage = slavery

3. stitch = sew

4. garments = clothes

5. sweatshop: *atelier où l'on exploite les travailleurs*

A shocking number of children – about 170 million – are engaged in hazardous work: in construction, quarrying[1], mining, in jobs exposing them to chemicals, or other conditions likely to harm them because of the hours or their age. Of these, 111 million are children under 15 whom the International Labour Organisation (ILO) says need to be taken out of such work immediately. A further 59 million are youths aged 15-17 who may need, for example, greater protection in the workplace rather than removal from it.

Some 8.4 million children are trapped in appalling kinds of labour, those which the ILO says are "unconditionally the worst forms," likely to lead to irreversible physical and psychological damage: these include slavery, trafficking, debt bondage[2] and other forms of forced labour, forced recruitment for armed conflict, prostitution, pornography, and other illicit activities. By definition these forms of child labour are hidden and hard to quantify, so the figures are likely to be underestimates. [...]

In fact, the vast majority are engaged in domestic service that is hidden from view, or in farming and fishing (70% of child labour in developing countries is in these primary sectors). Only 5% of child workers are involved in the export sector, according to Save the Children Fund.

Liberal instincts may be to use the power of boycott to rescue children from the cruelty of stitching[3] footballs or garments[4] for hours on end, but plucking them out of work before providing alternatives may only aggravate their situation. Well-intentioned, high-profile campaigns against child labour in Bangladesh and Pakistan have had the effect of closing down underage sweatshops[5] but, according to local reports, some of the children simply ended up in even worse forms of labour.

© Gilles Saussier / Gamma.

Work by a Bangladeshi NGO in conjunction with Save the Children in 2000 found that where children were working they contributed about 30% of the family income and that by and large girls were only allowed to work in domestic service, prostitution, brick breaking and the garment industry. Taking them away from the garment factories inevitably forces them into less salubrious forms of labour.

For the first time also, those campaigning against child labour have recognised that short-term solutions may have to be different from long-term ones. One may not be able to remove children from work immediately but their conditions can be improved, combining their work with education while aiming to provide higher adult wages in the long term so that children do not have to work at all.

From *The Guardian,* June 12, 2002.

► Check your pronunciation

Make sure you can read the following words.

1 • [ˈhæzədəs]
2 • [ˈkwɒriiŋ]
3 • [bæŋgləˈdeʃ]
4 • [ˈkemɪklz]
5 • [əˈpɔ:lɪŋ]
6 • [pa:kisˈta:n]
7 • [kənˈdʒʌŋkʃn]
8 • [səˈlu:brɪəs]

► Words

Choose the right meaning for each of the words below.

1 • hazardous (l. 1) means: tedious / dangerous / curious
2 • harm (l. 3) means: heat / hit / hurt /
3 • trapped (l. 8) means: caught / bought / sought
4 • appalling (l. 8) means: careful / hopeful / dreadful
5 • unconditionally (l. 9) means: really / miserably / totally
6 • pluck out (l. 19-20) means: tear from / catch from / come from
7 • provide (l. 20) means: apply / supply / reply

► Meaning

A • Answer the questions in your own words.

1 • Give examples of "worst forms" of child labour.
2 • What is the radical solution that sounds logical to reduce child labour?
3 • Why isn't it a good solution?
4 • What are the short-term solutions that are being proposed?

B • What do the following figures from the text correspond to?

1 • 170 million
2 • 111 million
3 • 59 million
4 • 8.4 million
5 • 70%
6 • 5%
7 • 30%

C • Translate into French from "Well-intentioned" (l. 20) to "forms of labour" (l. 23).

D • Explain the underlined words in the following sentences in your own words.

1 • "Some 8.4 million children are <u>trapped</u> in appalling kinds of labour" (l. 8)
2 • "domestic service that is <u>hidden from view</u>" (l. 14)
3 • "to rescue children from <u>the cruelty of stitching footballs or garments</u>" (l. 18-19)

E • Using all the information collected from questions A to D, make a summary of the text. (in French, about 70 words)

F • Turn the following sentences into the future. (see T&T: Modals)

1 • Under the new law this factory may not open.
2 • We can save the children.
3 • Those children have to work.
4 • Higher adult wages may be a solution.
5 • This form of work must lead to irreversible damage.
6 • We must find a way to stop child labour.
7 • Some youths must work in domestic service.

G • Transform the sentences below according to the following pattern.

Ex.: I've bought this garment for you to wear at the party.
– I've bought this garment so that you can wear it at the party.

1 • We have published this report for the whole world to be informed.
2 • The police will be sent for the factory to be closed down.
3 • Those footballs have been brought for the children to stitch.
4 • We'll use our power of boycott for sweatshops to stop hiring young children.
5 • Drastic steps must be taken for chemicals not to harm the young employees.

► Group work

Divide the class into two groups. Group **A** wants to campaign in favour of a boycott of every garment made in underage sweatshops. Group **B** strongly disagrees. Imagine the conversation.

► Food for thought

The ILO report says that the worst forms of child labour are "likely to lead to irreversible physical and psychological damage". Comment on this sentence. (about 150 words)

1. **slaughter:** *abattoir*
2. **welfare =** well-being
3. **corrugated-iron:** *tôle ondulée*

Fowl play

Grampian, supplier of fresh chicken and nuggets to all the main British supermarkets, has just closed down a factory in Scotland while buying two huge factories outside Bangkok.

In many ways, Thai chicken factories are just like English ones – equipped with vast stainless-steel production lines to take the birds from slaughter[1] to finished product. They are inspected for hygiene and welfare[2] standards by EU inspectors. It is in the lives of those who work in them that the gulf becomes apparent. Some of the 3,500 workers at Grampian Foods Siam live on the factory sites in huge dormitories under corrugated-iron[3] roofs. Others spend hours each day travelling in from miles around. [...] Most of them are paid by the day, and earn the statutory minimum wage of 165 baht (£2.50) a day, six days a week, for a nine-hour day which includes a one-hour break. They work in two shifts, dawn till mid-afternoon or mid-afternoon into the night, depending on the orders. Overtime, which can be two or three hours a day, pays more, and they work it and days off whenever they can to send more money home. Most of them are the first of their families to go into the factories; their parents were rice farmers. [...] The company doesn't like to take on anyone over 40, and the supervisors are very quick to give you warnings – two and you lose seven days' work, any more after that and it's the sack. But Grampian's a good place to work, they say.

From *The Guardian*, 8 July 2002.

► Words

Match the words from the text with their synonyms.

1 • gulf (l. 7)
2 • statutory (l. 10)
3 • shift (l. 12)
4 • dawn (l. 12)
5 • overtime (l. 13)
6 • take on (l. 16-17)
7 • supervisor (l. 17)

a • set period of working time
b • extra working hours
c • legal
d • hire
e • gap
f • daybreak
g • overseer

► Meaning

A • Explain in your own words the following expressions from the text.

1 • "they work it and days off" (l. 14)
2 • "any more after that and it's the sack" (l. 18)

B • Complete the sentences using *not as … as.* (see T&T: Comparatives / superlatives)

Ex.: The room is big but that one is bigger
– This room is not as big as that one.
1 • His salary is low but hers is lower.
2 • It's cold in the slaughterhouse but it is colder in the cutting room.
3 • Hygiene is strict in our factory, but it's stricter at Grampian's.
4 • The factory I work in is a good place, but Grampian is better.
5 • The working conditions are bad here, but they are worse outside Bangkok.

C • Translate into French from "The company doesn't like" (l. 16) to the end.

Checkup Unit 2

1 ► Test

"Change law to make bullying bosses pay"

Bullying bosses who terrorise colleagues should be forced to pay substantial compensation, according to a leading employment pressure group.

The Work Foundation is calling this week for a change in the employment laws to make bullying in the workplace an offence.

It will insist that bullying laws should be brought into line with legal protection against sex discrimination and harassment, complete with the financial penalties for the perpetrators.

According to Angela Ishmael from the Work Foundation 15 per cent of professionals, 11 per cent of skilled workers and 9 per cent of unskilled workers are bullied at work.

In 84 per cent of the cases, the perpetrator has bullied staff before and while management knew of the problem in three out of four instances they did nothing about it.

Research also shows that the problem, which leads to stress, sickness and in the most extreme cases suicide, is costing business between £5bn and £12bn a year. And even that figure is believed to be much higher when the cost of recruiting and retraining to fill the posts of victims as well as funding legal action and tribunals is taken into account.

"What we are trying to do is get an amendment to the employment laws to outlaw bullying and make it an offence," Ms Ishmael said. "We have been campaigning in this area for years but have made very little headway in persuading employers in particular that bullying is an issue they must take seriously."

As part of the proposed legislative change, the Work Foundation is calling for all employers to be forced to draw up proper guidelines for behaviour and structures to deal with complaints. They insist that people should be given strong legal protection but where bullying allegations do arise they must be dealt with quickly so the problem is not allowed to fester.

From *The Independent on Sunday*, 26 May 2002.

A • Answer the questions in English.

1 • Why is bullying at work an important financial issue? (give two reasons)

2 • What are the laws that already exist so as to protect the workers' dignity?

3 • What can the consequences of bullying be for the bullied workers?

4 • What are the two solutions proposed by the Work Foundation?

B • Sum up the text in French. (about 70 words)

C • Translate the last paragraph into French.

D • What does bullying consist of exactly? Can you give examples? (about 150 words)

2 ► Skills in practice

You are welcoming a French employee who has just been hired by Rugby Borough Council. You try to explain to him / her why the No-Smoking Policy is being implemented at work.

The document entitled *Policy to Discourage Smoking in Work Areas / Offices* should help you find arguments to talk him / her out of smoking.

RUGBY BOROUGH COUNCIL

Policy to Discourage Smoking in Work Areas/Offices

As an employer

The Council will endeavour to protect the health of its employees, members and visitors from the effects of tobacco smoke by:

1. Providing a healthy workplace that is unpolluted by tobacco smoke as far as is reasonably practicable.
2. Ensuring all its employees and Council members are informed of the health risks of smoking and passive smoking.
3. Ensuring smokers in its employ and Council Members receive encouragement and help to stop smoking.

Objectives

- To encourage employees not to smoke for their own sake and for the sake of others.
- To allow the Council to protect the health and safety of employees under Section 7 of the Health and Safety at Work Act.
- To reduce illness, absenteeism, death and disability.
- To reduce the fire risk.
- To uphold the rights of the non-smoker to clean indoor air.
- To promote awareness of the effects of smoking on health and to assist smokers who want to stop.
- To set an example to the public.
- To establish a "non-smoking" norm.

From *Rugby Borough Council, Employee Handbook*

3 ► The right word

A • Crossword

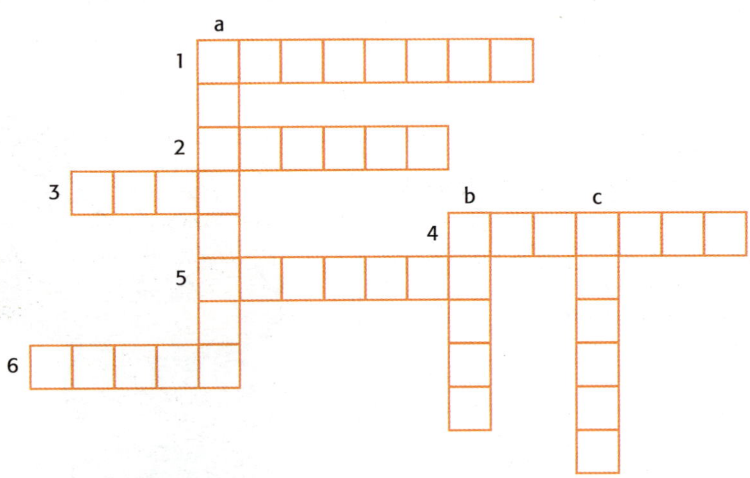

Across

1 • Scab.
2 • A worker cannot be dismissed without it.
3 • Pay As You Earn system.
4 • Someone who refuses to continue working.
5 • Examine.
6 • Groups of people working together.

Down

a • Money given by government to help sick people, for example.
b • Employees.
c • An industrial one may lead to days off.

B • Fill in the blanks with words from the following list.

assembly line / shiftwork / break / involvement / white collar / schedules / resume / bank holiday / clocking in / incentives

1 • Flexitime will considerably alter .... within our firm.
2 • Efficiency bonuses are good .... for our workers.
3 • .... is widespread in iron and steel industry.
4 • The management is ready to negotiate with us as long as we .... work at once.
5 • There has been a new trend toward employee .... in this company.
6 • .... work is performed in offices.
7 • .... work is depicted by Charlie Chaplin in *Modern Times*.
8 • After working two hours on end in front of a computer screen, employees should be given a 15-minute ....
9 • If you are late ...., you will lose pay.
10 • In Great Britain Good Friday is a ....

4 ► Vocabulary

absentéisme : absenteeism
accident du travail : industrial / work injury
ancienneté (à l') : according to seniority
arrêt de travail : stoppage of work
avantages en espèces : cash benefits
avantages en nature : perks, fringe benefits

base (à la) : on the shop floor
bulletin de salaire : pay slip

caisse de retraite : pension scheme
comité d'entreprise : works committee
conflit : dispute
congé : leave, time off
congé de maladie : sick leave
congé de maternité : maternity leave
congé (en) : on leave
congé (prendre un) : take time off, take some leave
congés payés : paid holiday (GB), paid vacation (US), paid leave
cotisations sociales : social contributions

débrayer : walk out
délégué syndical : shop steward

équipe : team, shift
État providence : Welfare State
exécuter des tâches : perform / carry out tasks

flexibilité : flexibility

grève : strike → striker
grève (se mettre en) : go on strike

heures supplémentaires : overtime [U]
horaire mobile : flexitime [U]
horaire de travail : schedule

impasse : deadlock
indemnité : allowance
inspecteur du travail : factory inspector
intérim : temping

jour de fête légal : bank holiday (GB), public holiday (US)
jour ouvrable : working day

maladie : sickness
maladie (assurance) : health insurance
maladie (prestation) : sick benefit
maladie professionnelle : industrial disease
manifestation : demonstration
muter : transfer

négocier : bargain, negotiate
norme de sécurité : safety standard

participation aux résultats de l'entreprise : profit-sharing scheme
patron : boss, employer
patronat : employers
pause : break
pension de retraite : retirement pension
pension d'invalidité : disability pension, industrial disablement benefit
pointer : clock in / out
poste : position, job, occupation
poste sans avenir : dead-end job
préavis (donner un) : give notice
préavis (sans) : without notice
prestations sociales : social insurance benefits
prime : incentive, bonus
prime d'ancienneté : seniority pay
prime d'encouragement : incentive bonus
prime de rendement : efficiency bonus
promouvoir : promote

rappel de salaire, de traitement : back pay
rémunération : earnings
rémunérer : remunerate, pay
reprendre le travail : resume work
représentant du personnel : staff representative
responsable syndical : union representative
retenir sur le salaire : deduct from a salary
retenue : deduction
retenue à la source : Pay As You Earn, PAYE
revendication : claim, demand
revenu : earnings, income
revenu imposable : taxable income
risque du métier : occupational hazard

sécurité : safety
somme forfaitaire : lump sum
stressant : stressful
stressé : stressed
surmené : overworked
syndicat : Trade Union, TU, union

taux horaire : hourly rate
temps partiel : part-time
travail posté : shift work
travail posté (pratiquer le) : be on shift work

usine : factory, plant

Unit 3 Women

A few landmarks

Women's suffrage movement

- In Britain, the first women's suffrage committee was formed in Manchester in 1865. In the 1870s suffragists submitted petitions with almost 3 million signatures. Despite growing support, suffrage bills were continually defeated; in frustration, some suffragists became militant activists under the leadership of Emmeline and Christabel Pankhurst. Parliament finally passed the Representation of the People Act in 1918. Women had already won voting rights in New Zealand (1893), Australia (1902), Finland (1906), Norway (1913), and the Soviet Union (1917). They were followed by Poland (1918), Sweden (1919), Germany (1919), the USA (1919) and Ireland (1922); France, Italy, India and Japan passed women's suffrage laws after World War II.

From *The Britannica Concise.*

- **Sex discrimination**

It is the discrimination on the grounds of sex, which is an offence under the following acts:

– **The Equal Pay Act, 1970**, which forbids having different terms for men and women in their contracts of employment.

– **The Sex Discrimination Act, 1975**, which prohibits discrimination when offering a contract of employment. It also prohibits discrimination in employment on the grounds of marital status.

- **Equal Opportunities Commission**

It is a body which was established by the Sex Discrimination Act, 1975, to work towards the elimination of discrimination and to promote equality of opportunity between the sexes.

- **Sexual harassment**

– **Sexual harassment** is unsolicited verbal or physical behaviour of a sexual nature.

– Under **the Protection from Harassment Act, 1997**, a person guilty of harassment is liable to imprisonment for a term not exceeding 5 years or a fine, or both.

Warm-up

1 • Where was this photo taken?

2 • What are those women doing?

3 • Can you read what is written on their banners?

TEXT 1

Earnings of women still lag[1] by 18%

1. lag = trail, drag
2. patchy = irregular
3. snapshot = photograph

British women can celebrate 50 years of progress in the workplace, but still lack sufficient childcare, are concentrated in particular jobs, and earn on average 18% less than men, according to the equal opportunities commission.

Its statistics show that over the 50 years improvements in employment have been patchy[2], though significant. The pay gap has narrowed, the proportion of female managers has doubled to 30%, and the proportion of women working in the professions has rocketed from 8% to 42%.

Women have also gained ground in education: the proportion of female students has more than doubled, from 23% to 51%.

© Roy Ooms / Masterfile.

"These figures offer a fascinating snapshot[3] of how our lives have changed since the Queen's accession," said Julie Mellor, chair of the commission. "We should be celebrating, because women do have more choices in being able to choose to work, or stay at home, or combine both. But although women have made great strides towards equality in education and in the workplace, there are still inequalities. There's still an 18% difference between the hourly rate that men and women receive for full-time work, and the gap between women working part time and men working full time is a horrendous 41% per hour."

From *The Guardian*, June 3, 2002.

► Check your pronunciation

Read the following words.

1 • [ɒpə'tju:nətɪz]
2 • ['fɪgəz]
3 • [tʃu:z]
4 • [straɪdz]
5 • ['aʊəlɪ]
6 • [hɒ'rendəs]

► Words

Match each word from the text with its equivalent.

1 • lack (l. 1)	a • president
2 • sufficient (l. 2)	b • considerable
3 • significant (l. 5)	c • suddenly increase
4 • rocket (l. 7)	d • shocking
5 • chair (l. 13)	e • shortage
6 • stride (l. 20)	f • enough
7 • horrendous (l. 28)	g • advance

► Meaning

A • Choose between *still* and *always*. (see T&T: Adverbs)

1 • The 1950s model, which assumes every employee has a wife at home, is .... too common.
2 • It is .... difficult for women to balance work and family life.
3 • There has .... been a pay gap between men and women.
4 • Women have .... said that the pay gap could be narrowed.
5 • Even if there have been some significant strides, there are .... too few women working in the professions.
6 • Figures show women are .... concentrated in a few occupations.

B • "women working in the professions" (l. 6-7): what professions can you think of?

C • Reformulate the following sentences from the text.

1 • "improvements in employment have been patchy, though significant" (l. 4-5)
2 • "the pay gap has narrowed" (l. 5)

D • *For* or *since*? (see T&T: Present perfect / Preterite)

1 • The working world has been dramatically evolving .... 50 years.
2 • Our lives have changed .... the death of George VI.
3 • Queen Elizabeth has been in power .... over 50 years.
4 • The percentage of females in sales has risen from 52% to 70% .... the end of WWII.

E • Translate into English.

1 • *Le salaire des femmes reste en retard sur celui des hommes.*
2 • *Les femmes peuvent maintenant choisir de travailler ou bien de rester au foyer.*
3 • *Des inégalités subsistent bien que les femmes aient fait de gros progrès en matière d'instruction.*
4 • *La différence de salaire entre hommes et femmes reste importante.*
5 • *Les progrès ont été considérables sur les 50 dernières années.*

F • Translate into French.

1 • The title.
2 • "the proportion of female managers has doubled to 30%, and the proportion of women working in the professions has rocketed from 8% to 42%." (l. 5-7)

G • Everything has been mixed up. Put the words below in the correct order.

progress / women / there / men / made / and / although / has / significant / still / too / remain / many / between / been / inequalities

► Pair work

Should women celebrate 50 years' improvements at work or should they still be complaining about inequalities?

► Food for thought

"British women [...] are concentrated in particular jobs": try to list those jobs.

TEXT 2

All we need is a break

1. **sheer =** total
2. **fish fingers:** *bâtonnets de poisson*

What do working mothers want? The simple answer is – to be happy.
Why do working mothers want to be happy? It seems, because they are not.

A Bupa-commissioned survey of 5,000 women found that nine out of 10 feel permanently stressed, and eight out of 10 would not be in full-time careers if they had the choice. The reason? Sheer[1] exhaustion.

Women who work are finding that they have three lives – the office, the children and the housework. The school run, followed by the dash to the desk, has no moment of welcome relief at the end of the day. Instead of nipping down to the pub on the way home – like so many of their male colleagues – women are finding their way around the supermarket, throwing a few fish fingers[2] at the kids, helping with homework, cleaning up, oh, and making themselves sexy for bedtime.

The trouble is, bedtime is never sexy when you are exhausted, and six hours' sleep is no relaxation and not enough rest.

Some women have help, many don't. According to the survey, 77% of working women still do all the housework.

© Getty Images / Taxi.

Women are saying loud and clear that they can't cope with the way things are, but is anybody listening? Perhaps. The employment bill, currently going through parliament and due to become law early next year, says that working mothers and fathers with children under the age of six will have the legal right to ask for changes to their working hours. They will also be able to submit a proposal for working from home. [...]

Time to breathe is what women want. Time is what women want. Happiness is not about possessions; happiness is about freedom – freedom to be yourself and to enjoy your life. Freedom to love others and take some pleasure in each day.

From *The Guardian*, 12 July 2002.

► Check your pronunciation

Can you read the following words?

1 • [sə'veɪ]
2 • ['pɜːmənəntlɪ]
3 • [rɪ'liːf]
4 • ['kʌrəntlɪ]
5 • [briːð]
6 • [pə'zeʃnz]

► Words

A • Select the right meanings.

1 • "the dash to the desk" (l. 7) means:
when they rush to their place of work / when they use washing powder / when they rush to school

2 • "no moment of welcome relief" (l. 7-8) means:
no time for welcoming friends / no time for a happy break / no time for a happy trip

3 • "nipping down to the pub" (l. 8-9) means:
avoiding the pub / popping in the pub / staying in the pub

4 • "they can't cope with the way things are" (l. 17-18) means:
they can't stand the way things are / they are not able to face reality as it stands / they can't deal with this state of things

5 • "due to become law" (l. 20-21) means:
is to become law / may become law / could become law

B • Think of at least five adjectives, turn them into adverbs of manner and translate them. (see T&T: Word formation)

Ex.: permanent → permanently, current → currently

► Meaning

A • Put the verbs in brackets in the correct form. (see T&T: Conditional clauses)

1 • If I .... (have) the choice, I would not be in full-time career.

2 • If she had decided to resume work, she .... (find) a job quite easily.

3 • If my colleague .... (have / not) three lives, she would not have broken down.

4 • If she had been stronger, she .... (be able to) cope with her life.

5 • It .... (be) great if I had a moment of relief each day.

B • Give a short answer contradicting each of the following statements.

1 • You really think I am happy, well I ....

2 • Some women have help but many ....

3 • I am glad you can cope with the children, I ....

4 • You desperately need a break but your boss ....

5 • You will have enough time tomorrow, unfortunately I ....

C • Answer the following questions by using ONE word.

1 • What do working mothers want?

2 • What do 9 out of 10 women suffer from?

3 • What do working women still have to do when they go back home?

4 • What do women desperately want?

D • Reformulate the following sentences in your own words.

1 • "Women who work are finding they have three lives" (l. 6)

2 • "Instead of nipping down to the pub on the way home [...] women are finding their way around the supermarket" (l. 8-10)

E • What is the employment bill about?

F • Translate into French.

1 • "Women are saying loud and clear" (l. 16) to "Perhaps". (l. 18)

2 • "The employment bill, currently going through parliament"(l. 19) to "from home". (l. 26)

► Pair work

A supports the idea that women have to cope with too many things, B is a male chauvinist. Imagine their dialogue.

► Food for thought

"Happiness is not about possessions; happiness is about freedom". What do you think of such a statement? (about 200 words)

Unit 3

TEXT 3

1. **secretary:** *ministre*
2. **deputy chairwoman:** *vice-présidente*

Women still barred from frontline military duties

Women will continue to be barred from close combat roles in the armed forces because it would be too risky to find out how their presence would affect operations, Geoff Hoon, the defence secretary[1], said yesterday. A long awaited report on women in the forces refers to their lower physical capacity and psychological differences from men, including a "gap in the capacity for aggression". [...] Differences between women and men in their capacity to develop muscle strength and aerobic fitness were such that only about 1% of women could equal the performance of the average man, said a report. When exposed to the same physical workload, women had to work up to 80% harder than men to achieve the same results. The report also found that "capacity for aggression was generally lower for women, who required more provocation and were more likely to fear consequences of aggressive behaviour". [...] The decision was criticised by the equal opportunities commission. Jenny Watson, the deputy chairwoman[2], said the EOC still believed that "automatically excluding women from armed combat posts is not the right approach and that mixed units would not have a negative impact on operational effectiveness".

From *The Guardian*, May 23, 2002.

► Words

Match the following words from the text with their synonyms.

1 • barred (title)
2 • risky (l. 2)
3 • gap (l. 5)
4 • workload (l. 9)
5 • achieve (l. 9)
6 • likely (l. 11)
7 • opportunity (l. 13)
8 • effectiveness (l. 16)

a • dangerous
b • forbidden
c • succeed in doing
d • probable
e • success
f • difference
g • amount of work
h • prospect

► Meaning

A • Fill in the following blanks.

1 • The decision of the defence secretary: ....
2 • Reasons for this decision: ....
3 • Reaction of the EOC deputy chairwoman: ....

B • Turn the following sentences into reported speech.

1 • "Women will continue to be barred from close combat roles," the secretary said.
2 • "It will be too risky," he added.
3 • The report concluded: "Differences between men and women are too important."
4 • "Capacity for aggression has always been lower for women," the secretary remarked.
5 • "It is not right to exclude women from armed combat posts," the EOC declared.
6 • "Women have already been used in close combat roles but the practice has been abandoned," the journalist pointed out.

C • Translate into English (use compound words only). **(see T&T: Compound nouns)**

1 • *Le ministre de la défense.*
2 • *La force musculaire.*
3 • *La vice-présidente.*
4 • *Des postes de combat.*

Checkup Unit 3

1 ► Test

Going solo

[…] Compared with Canada and western Europe, the U.S. is in the middle range in births to unmarried women, but among adolescents U.S. rates are much higher. Teenage motherhood is particularly problematic because most girls lack parenting skills and don't have the resources to bring up children properly. In most western countries, but not the U.S., there is a strong consensus that adolescents should not bear children. American adolescents are less apt than those in other countries to use contraceptives and may not use them as effectively. Western Europeans and Canadians generally provide better access to family-planning programs for teenagers. In France, for example, nurses in public and parochial high schools dispense the "morning-after pill," a practice unheard of in the U.S.

In Japan, where nonmarital births are extremely rare, unwed mothers and their children are severely stigmatized, even to the point of denying them benefits available to married mothers. In Europe, countries with large Catholic populations tend to have fewer nonmarital births, although France is a major exception. In Scandinavia, a traditionally strong Protestant region, the rate of nonmarital childbearing is the highest in Europe.

Percent of all nonmarital births accounted for by women aged 15 to 19

U.S.	29%
Canada	15%
Great Britain	15%
Italy	10%
Germany	9%
France	4%
Sweden	2%

From *Scientific American*, January 2002.

A • Answer the following questions in French.

1 • What is the main topic of this article?
2 • Why is teenage motherhood a big problem?
3 • Why are U.S. rates higher for teenage girls?
4 • What is specific about France?
5 • What is specific about Japan?
6 • Explain the difference between Catholic Europe and Protestant Europe.
What is the exception?

B • What does the chart confirm? Answer in English. (about 30 words)

C • Translate into French from "In Japan" (l. 18) to "married mothers" (l. 21).

D • A U.S. survey showed that two thirds of births among unmarried teenagers were unintended. Can you try to explain why?

© Mingasson / Liaison-Gamma.

2 ► Skills in practice

What is Domestic Violence ?
US National Statistics

- Nearly one third of American women (31%) report being physically or sexually abused by a husband or boyfriend at some point in their lives.
- While women are less likely than men to be victims of violent crimes overall, women are 5 to 8 times more likely than men to be victimized by an intimate partner.
- Violence by an intimate partner accounts for about 21% of violent crime experienced by women and about 2% of the violence experienced by men.
- In 92% of all domestic violence incidents, crimes are committed by men against women.
- Of women who reported being raped and/or physically assaulted since the age of 18, three quarters (76%) were victimized by a current or former husband, cohabitating partner, date or boyfriend.
- Forty percent of teenage girls aged 14 to 17 report knowing someone their age who has been hit or beaten by a boyfriend.
- One in five female high school students reports being physically or sexually abused by a dating partner.

From *National Domestic Violence Hotline*, www.ndvh.org

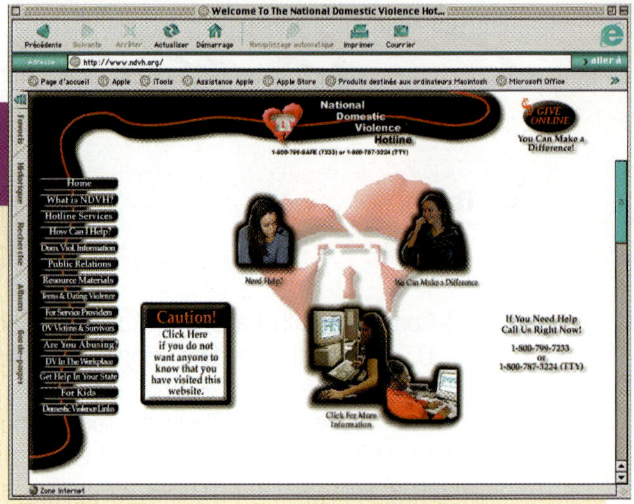

Carefully read the US national statistics and then answer the following questions:

1 • Are there as many victims of violent crimes among women as among men?
2 • Who do women experience violence from?
3 • Among women who have been raped what is the percentage of women who know their rapists?
4 • Are teenagers familiar with domestic violence?
5 • Who generally abuses female high school students?

3 ► The right word

A • Crossword

Across

1 • Something difficult to achieve between men and women.
2 • Period of time when a woman is pregnant.
3 • They are not often shared between husband and wife.
4 • Legal union.
5 • Opposite of death.
6 • End of marriage.

Down

a • An alternative to marriage.
b • Unlawful at work.
c • It can be a maternity or a sick one.

B • Fill in the blanks with words from the following list.

female / equal / part-time / discrimination / crèche / maternity leave / maternity pay / marital status / sexual harassment / Equal Opportunities Commission

1 • .... is the practice of unfairly treating someone worse or better than other people.
2 • In the US mothers are not entitled to any ....
3 • A .... is a place where small children are looked after while their parents are working.
4 • It is prohibited to discriminate against a woman on the grounds of ....
5 • In order to promote equality of opportunity between the sexes the .... was created.
6 • In England .... is nine-tenths of a week's pay, less than the amount of the National Insurance maternity allowance.
7 • A law was recently passed in the US to protect women against ....
8 • In industrialised countries, women are more likely to work .... than men.
9 • Faced with men and women of .... ability, bosses will hire men.
10 • Most of the increase in .... workers reflects a change in the way married women arrange their lives.

4 ► Vocabulary

accouchement : childbirth, delivery
accoucher : give birth to, deliver
allocations : allowances
allocations de maternité : maternity allowances, maternity benefits
allocations familiales : child benefits
avortement : abortion

briser (se) (mariage) : break up

célibataire : single
chance : opportunity
concubinage : cohabitation → cohabit (v.)
concubins : cohabiting couple
congé de maternité / paternité : maternity / paternity leave
crèche : crèche

discrimination sexuelle : sexual discrimination → discriminate against sb, be prejudiced against sb
dispositif de garderie : childcare facilities
divorce : divorce → divorce (v.)
divorcé(e) : divorced

éducation : upbringing
égalité : equality
égalité des chances : equality of opportunity, equal opportunity
égalité des salaires : equal pay
élever des enfants : bring up / raise children

enceinte : pregnant
enfant : child (pl. children)
enfant (sans) : childless
épouser qqn : marry sb
époux, épouse : spouse

féminin : female
femme au foyer : housewife
femme (épouse) : wife, (pl. wives)
foyer : household
foyer (au) : at home
foyer familial : two-parent family
foyer monoparental : single-parent family

grossesse : pregnancy

harcèlement sexuel : sexual harassment
horaire mobile : flexitime, flextime

instruction : education
interrompre (grossesse) : terminate

mari : husband
mariage (institution) : marriage, matrimony
mariage (cérémonie) : wedding
marié(e) : married → get married to sb
masculin : male
maternité : motherhood

naissance d'un enfant : childbirth
né hors mariage : born out of wedlock
nourrice : nanny

parent unique : single parent
partenaire : partner
pension alimentaire : alimony
phallocrate : male chauvinist
pied d'égalité (être sur un) : be on an equal footing
pillule : pill
plein-temps (à) : full-time
préjugé : préjudice
préservatif : condom

rapport sexuel : sexual intercourse

salaire perçu au cours de la maternité : maternity pay
sévices : abuse → abuse (v.)
sexe (différenciation sexuelle) : gender
sexiste : sexist
situation familiale : marital status

tâches ménagères : chores, housework [U] → do the housework
temps partiel : part-time

veuf(ve) (adj.) : widowed
vie de famille : family life
vivre seul(e) : live on one's own

Unit 4 Employment and unemployment

A few landmarks

- When you belong to **the working population** you can either be a **blue-collar** worker, i.e. a manual industrial worker, or a **white-collar** worker, i.e. a non-manual worker employed in professional or clerical occupations. If you work in **the professions** it means that you have a job in law or medicine. Another possibility is being your own boss; in that case you are **self-employed**.

  You may opt for a **full-time** or **part-time** job and be a full-timer or part-timer. You can also choose between a **permanent** job or a **temporary** job. However, these types of employment are not necessarily a matter of choice.

  Lastly, in some unfortunate cases, you may be **on the dole** (GB), that is to say you may receive money from the state while out of work, and you will be part of the figures of the **unemployment rate**.

- So as to improve their wages and working conditions, workers are represented by **trade unions** (U.S. = labor unions) for negotiations with management and the government. Their members are called **trade unionists**.

  In Great Britain, trade unions were created in the 19th century to improve working conditions in mines and factories. The most important trade union is the TUC (Trade Union Congress), the major association of British trade unions. Linked with the Labour Party, unions cooperate with management.

  In the U.S., the biggest labor union is the AFL-CIO (American Federation of Labor and Congress of Industrial Organizations), a confederation of unions. Unions are linked with the Democratic Party, yet they are not political forces as European unions are.

  In both countries, when a meeting is organised within a company, the negotiation talks are called **collective bargaining**.

Inland Revenue — *Details of employee leaving work* — **Copy for employee ★** — P45 Part 1A

1 PAYE Reference — Office number: 671 — Reference number: R566

2 Employee's National Insurance number: TN 28 11 82 M (Mr Mrs Miss Ms Other)

3 Surname: LEVI — MR.

First name(s): CHARLES

4 Leaving date: Day 27 Month 07 Year 2001

5 Continue Student Loan Deductions(Y)

6 Tax Code at leaving date. *If Week 1 or Month 1 basis applies, write 'X' in the box marked* Week 1 or Month 1 — Code: NT

7 Last entries on *Deductions Working Sheet* (P11) *If there is an 'X' at item 6, there will be no entries here*

- Week or month number: Month 4
- Total pay to date: £ 760 . 36 p
- Total tax to date: £ p

8 This employment pay and tax. *If no entry here, the amounts are those shown at item 7*

- Total pay in this employment: £ p
- Total tax in this employment: £ p

★ To the employee . . . Detach this Part 1A and keep it safe. Copies are not available

This form is important to you, so take good care of it. You may need the information shown on Part 1A when completing any Tax Return you are sent at the end of the tax year. Please also read the notes on Part 2 attached to this Part 1A. Those notes give some important information about what you should do next and what to do with Parts 2 and 3.

Employer's name, address and Postcode: RUGBY BOROUGH COUNCIL, P.O. BOX 16, TOWN HALL, RUGBY. CV21 2LA 20-7-2001

To the new employer

If your new employee gives you this form please detach this Part 1A and return it to the employee. Deal with Parts 2 and 3 normally.

P45

Inland Revenue — *Details of employee leaving work* — Copy for new employer — P45 Part 2

1 Previous PAYE Reference — Office number: 671 — Reference number: R566

2 Employee's National Insurance number: TN 28 11 82 M (Mr Mrs Miss Ms Other)

3 Surname: LEVI — MR

First name(s): CHARLES

4 Leaving date: Day 27 Month 07 Year 2001

5 Continue Student Loan Deductions(Y)

6 Tax Code at leaving date. *'X' in the box means Week 1 or Month 1 basis applies* — Code: NT

7 Last entries on *Deductions Working Sheet* (P11) *If there is an 'X' at item 6, there will be no entries here*

- Week or month number: Month 4
- Total pay to date: £ 760 . 36 p
- Total tax to date: £ p

To the employee

This form is important to you, so take good care of it. Copies are not available. Keep Parts 2 and 3 of the form together and do not alter them.

Going to a new job
Give this form (Parts 2 and 3) to your new employer, or you will have tax deducted using the emergency code and may pay too much tax. If you do not want your new employer to know the details on this form, send it to your Tax Office immediately with a letter saying so and giving the name and address of your new employer. The Tax Office can make special arrangements, but you may pay too much tax for a while as a result.

Becoming self-employed
Let your local Tax Office know and ask for *Starting your own business* (leaflet CWL1).

Going abroad
If you are going abroad or returning to a country outside the UK ask for *Income Tax form for those Leaving the United Kingdom* (form P85) from any Tax Office or Tax Enquiry Centre.

Claiming Jobseeker's Allowance
Take this form to the Benefit Office. They will pay you any tax refund you may be entitled to when your claim ends, or at 5 April if this is earlier.

Not working and not claiming Jobseeker's Allowance
If you have paid tax and wish to claim a refund ask for *Claim for income tax repayment* (form P50) from any Tax Office or Tax Enquiry Centre.

To the new employer

Check this form, complete items 8 to 17 in Part 3 and prepare a *Deductions Working Sheet* (form P11). Follow the instructions in the *Employer's Quick Guide to PAYE and NICs* (cards CWG1).

Detach Part 3 of this form and send it to your Tax Office immediately. Keep Part 2.

P45

Warm-up

1 • **Read the copy for employee.**

a • What does this form correspond to?
b • Who did Mr Charles Levi work for?
c • How long did he work for them?
d • When did he stop working for them?
e • How much did he earn?
f • Can he ask for a copy of this form?
g • In what case could he need this form?

2 • **Read the copy for the new employer.**

a • Who is this part for?
b • What may happen if the employee doesn't give this form to his new employer?
c • What should the employee do if he doesn't give this form to his new employer? What could the consequences be?
d • What other advice is given to the employee?

TEXT 1

Working-class graduates kept out of highly paid jobs

1. **academic** = from university or college
2. **attend** = go to

An old boys' network is preventing working-class graduates with excellent academic[1] records from being appointed to highly paid jobs, according to new research. [...]

Graduates from lower social classes earned significantly less than their fellow students of higher social status, no matter which university they attended[2], a report commissioned by the Council for Industry and Higher Education (CIHE) found.

Oxford and Cambridge graduates from poorer families earned an average of 16 per cent less than equally well-qualified students from professional backgrounds, the study, by academics from the London School of Economics, concluded. [...]

Ministers have tried to open "top universities" to students from a wider range of backgrounds, assuming that this would give them access to high status jobs, they argue. [...]

[Mr Brown, chief executive of CIHE] said: "Employers should consider their recruitment policies; the business benefits of having a diverse labour force that can relate to an equally diverse range of customers; the ethics of discriminating, however unwittingly, against older graduates or those from different social groups. There is a danger that some employers just recruit in their own image."

He said that students from poorer backgrounds may be losing out to their better-connected classmates because they lacked the confidence and social skills to impress at job interviews.

"Employers want to recruit individuals who have confidence and social skills as well as academic capabilities," he said. "Individuals from non-traditional backgrounds need help to improve how they learn, to plan how they acquire the skills needed and how they present their experiences and capabilities."

From *The Independent*, 20 May 2002.

► Check your pronunciation

Read these words aloud.

1 • sig'nificantly
2 • 'social
3 • 'equally
4 • co'mmissioned
5 • 'qualified
6 • a'cquire
7 • pro'fessional

► Words

Find the opposites (in the text) to the words below.

1 • smaller (§ 4)
2 • intentionally (§ 5)
3 • inaptitude (§ 7)

► Meaning

A • Translate into English.

1 • *On empêche les étudiants issus de la classe ouvrière d'accéder à des postes à forte rémunération.*
2 • *Ils sont victimes de discrimination sociale.*

B • Rephrase the sentences using *whatever, whoever, whenever, wherever, however*.

Ex.: They earned less "no matter which university they attended" (l. 4)
– They earned less whatever the university they attended.

1 • You can get a high level diploma, no matter what your social background is.
2 • No matter whom he meets, it will be difficult for him to get this job.
3 • I am ready for the interview, no matter when the appointment is.
4 • She will improve her language skills, no matter where she travels.
5 • No matter how long it takes, they will succeed.

C • Choose the correct answer and quote the text to justify it.

1 • Employers:
– enable any good graduate to get highly paid jobs.
– stop good lower-class graduates from getting highly paid jobs.
– discourage good lower-class graduates from getting highly paid jobs.

2 • – It all depends on the universities they went to.
– The universities they went to aren't taken into account.
– It only concerns those who went to Oxford and Cambridge.

3 • – All the former Oxbridge graduates earn the same wage.
– The former Oxbridge graduates from the upper class get better qualified jobs.
– Former, lower-class Oxbridge graduates are less paid than their upper-class counterparts.

4 • The government have created high level universities for students:
– from varied social backgrounds.
– from any social background.
– from less varied social backgrounds.

► Group work

Draw up a questionnaire for the CIHE report, enquiring about your town's graduates.

D • What does the article deal with? Choose the best answers (one in each series).

1 • Discrimination / Academic discrimination / Social discrimination…
2 • … against low-level graduates / against high-level graduates / against graduates…
3 • … from any social class / from lower social classes / from higher social classes.

E • Based on your answers to exercises C and D, give an account in English of the current situation. (70 words) Don't forget to add link words.

F • Explain Mr Brown's viewpoint.

1 • Is he satisfied with employers' recruitment policies?
2 • What can the danger of such policies be?
3 • What advantages can a varied workforce bring to business?

G • Sum up the difficulties lower-class graduates often face. Use the following words in the appropriate order.

fail / personal and academic skills / self-confident / job interviews / bring out

H • Which phrase clearly indicates the journalist's viewpoint? Explain it.

I • Translate into French from "He said" (l. 19) to "capabilities" (l. 28).

► Food for thought

Write a letter to Mr Brown.
– You feel you have been discriminated against for a work placement.
– Give the reasons for this feeling.
– Ask him if he can give you the references of a behavioural training organisation.

TEXT 2

Tesco workers stack up[1] £38m

1. **stack up:** *amasser*
2. **payout =** sum of money
3. **checkout workers =** cashiers
4. **shelf stacker:** *gondolier / gondolière*
5. **be put in trust:** *être mis en gestion*
6. **save-as-you-earn schemes:** *plan d'épargne par prélèvement automatique*

More than 100,000 Tesco employees were this weekend sharing a £38m payout[2] from a three-year scheme that matured last week.

The checkout workers[3], shelf stackers[4] and other store employees are receiving shares worth just under 4% of their salaries.

When the shares were put in trust[5] three years ago they were worth £1.88 each and they had risen to £2.58 by last Friday, though they are about 30p below their peak last year.

Every Tesco employee who has completed two years' service receives the free shares, in addition to opportunities to join save-as-you-earn schemes[6]. This year Tesco put the equivalent of £48m into a new scheme that will run for another three years.

About 104,000 employees – out of a payroll of 195,000, the largest of any private company – received payout this year.

Sir Terry Leahy, chief executive of Tesco, said: "The profit share scheme is a great way for us to say a big thank you for everyone's hard work."

It might also help to deflect any criticism of boardroom pay at Tesco, where last year eight of its directors, including Sir Terry, received more than £1m. Sir Terry received a 53% pay rise last year after his total pay packet reached £2.4m, mainly as a result of performance-related deals.

© Jez Couslon / Insight-Réa.

With him at the helm, Tesco has secured a place as the country's biggest and most profitable supermarket group. It reported a 14% rise in profits to £1.2bn last year. […]

Other retailers have been highlighting pay deals for their staff at a time when their bosses' paypackets are also being disclosed. Marks & Spencer, whose chairman Luc Vandevelde was paid £1.4m, said its 6,000 employees shared a £60m bonus last year.

From *The Guardian,* June 3, 2002.

► Check your pronunciation

Can you pronounce these words properly?

1 • share
2 • shelf
3 • scheme
4 • checkout

► Words

Find the equivalents in the text of the following words.

1 • staff
2 • board of directors
3 • wage
4 • at the command
5 • revealed
6 • SAYE
7 • CEO

► Meaning

A • Complete with *each, every* or *all.* (see T&T: Quantifiers)

1 • .... employee with two years' experience with us is entitled to receive shares.
2 • They are paid more than £1m ....
3 • .... employees can open a SAYE plan provided they have worked for two years in this company.
4 • .... of them want to know their bosses' wages.
5 • These two workers don't have the same point of view; .... of them gives their arguments.

B • Translate with a genitive or a compound. Sometimes both are possible. (see T&T: Genitive / Compound nouns)

1 • *Les employés de Tesco.*
2 • *Le salaire des directeurs.*
3 • *Une augmentation de salaire.*
4 • *Les bénéfices de l'entreprise.*
5 • *Un montant de 4 %.*
6 • *Un plan de trois ans.*
7 • *Deux ans d'expérience.*

C • Fill in Tesco profile and specify dates when possible.

1 • Number of employees: ....
2 • Size compared with other companies: ....
3 • Profits: ....
4 • 8 directors' wages: ....
5 • Sir Terry's wage and reward: ....

D • Complete the grid on Tesco's scheme.

1999	Creation of the scheme	• amount invested = ... • .... = £1.88
....	Ø	share price = £2.88
2002	.... employees shared £38m, which represents a little less than .... of their wages.	share price = ...
....	Tesco opened a new 3-year scheme	amount invested = ...
Conditions	Employees have worked in the company for at least	
Advantages	Possibility of opening a	

E • Compare Marks & Spencer's boss's wage and staff payout with Tesco's. (see T&T: Comparatives)

1 • Tesco invested a .... amount in their new scheme .... in the first one.
2 • Tesco's share price was .... in 2002 .... it was in 1999, but .... in 2001.
3 • Mr Vandevelde has about .... wage .... the average Tesco boss but he earns .... than Sir Terry.
4 • Sir Terry's wage is about .... other Tesco directors'.
5 • Marks & Spencer's staff shared .... payout .... Tesco's.
6 • So Marks & Spencer offered .... payout.

F • Translate the first two sentences into French.

► Pair work

Unlike **B, A** considers bosses often earn too much. Imagine their dialogue. (See T&T: Agreement, Disagreement, Preference, Suggestions)

► Food for thought

What are the advantages and drawbacks of profit-sharing schemes for employees?

Unit 4

TEXT 3

Job seekers may score points with "nonabusive" networking

1. **scope out** = examine carefully
2. **self-pacing** = time management
3. **beyond:** *au-delà*
4. **acknowledge** = confess

One of the best avenues for exploring the hidden job market is networking – using your friends, acquaintances and referrals to scope out[1] unadvertised job opportunities. [...]

Abuse of the networking process can be as simple as contacting the same person too frequently or overstaying one's welcome at an appointment. In many cases, abuse is simply overuse that results from poor planning and inadequate self-pacing[2] in the job search. Successful networkers pace themselves to arranging calls and meetings at an easily managed tempo. [...]

Recognizing that networking is part of the "job" of looking for a job is a good stimulus to do it, and do it correctly.

One way to learn to network well is to begin with those people with whom you feel most relaxed. Start with someone you know on a first-name basis and are certain will respond.

Remember to keep your interviews brief. When you make the appointment, mention that it won't take more than 10 minutes. Then stick to that. If you find the interview going beyond[3] that time, acknowledge[4] that you are running over and give your contact the option of continuing.

From *The Wall Street Journal Europe*, June 11, 2002.

► Words

A • The particle "over" (+ n. or v.) means "more than expected / usual".

Ex.: overwork = have too much work;
overtime = work extra hours;
overmanned = with too many staff.

Can you explain the meaning of "overstay" (l. 5) and "overuse" (l. 6)?

B • Match the words from the text with their equivalents.

1 • acquaintances (l. 2)
2 • referrals (l. 2)
3 • poor (l. 6)
4 • pace themselves (l. 7)
5 • tempo (l. 8)

a • organise their time
b • bad
c • rhythm
d • referees
e • relations

► Meaning

A • Present be + V-*ing* or gerund? Make two lists with all the V-*ing* forms of the text.

B • Choose the correct answer.

1 • "someone you know on a first-name basis" (l. 12) means: someone you have just seen once / someone you know well / the person who gave you a first job.
2 • "Then stick to that" (l. 15) means: stick a note indicating your time limit / allow yourself to go beyond that time / don't go beyond that time.

C • Answer the questions in your own words.

1 • What does networking mean?
2 • Efficient networking: list what shouldn't be done and what should be done.

D • Translate the title and the first paragraph.

1 ► Test

Employers dismayed by EU proposals on temps

Temporary workers could lose up to 160,000 job placements every year as a result of European plans to grant increasing rights to employees.

The CBI[1] claims the EU draft directive on temporary agency work would lead to more than half the companies using temps cutting back significantly.

The UK has about 770,000 temporary workers, far more than any other EU country. Under the terms of the directive, they would be entitled to the same pay and conditions as full-time staff. It would also force host companies to negotiate temps' contractual terms.

The CBI survey suggests that 10% of employers would stop using temps altogether if the directive came into force, with just 1% saying it would encourage them to take on permanent staff.

Deputy director-general John Cridland said: "These proposals would deliver a serious blow to the UK. Most large firms use agencies to meet unexpected upturns in demand while small firms use them to cover for absence. We must prevent these proposals from harming our labour market."

At present, the rights would only apply after a temp has worked at a company for six weeks but Mr Cridland said any time limit of less than 12 months would be unacceptable.

Bruce Warman, director of personnel at Vauxhall, described the directive as "ludicrous". He said: "If the boss's PA goes on maternity leave after working their way up and developing a wealth of skills and experience, why should the company pay a temp who doesn't have the same amount of experience the same money?"

He argued that the reason Britain had low unemployment compared with Germany was because of the relative flexibility of the labour market, which the directive would erode. "No one is trying to deny temporary workers fundamental rights on safety or health grounds but this directive would add costs and red tape[2] to companies, which would discourage them from taking on temps. They would prefer to just muddle on."

Julia Stones of recruitment agency Carlisle Staffing Services argued that the directive would hurt those it is trying to help by removing choice from workers who do not want a permanent job and creating barriers to permanent work to those who find it through the agency system.

From *The Daily Telegraph*, August 8, 2002.

1. **CBI:** Confederation of British Industry ≈ MEDEF
2. **red tape:** time-consuming bureaucracy

A • Sum up the article in English. (190 words)

B • Translate into French.

– The title.
– From the beginning to "contractual terms." (l. 12).

C • Whom would you side with, the EU commissioners or managers and temp agencies? Develop your arguments.

2 ► Skills in practice

Unemployment in the regions of the European Union 2001

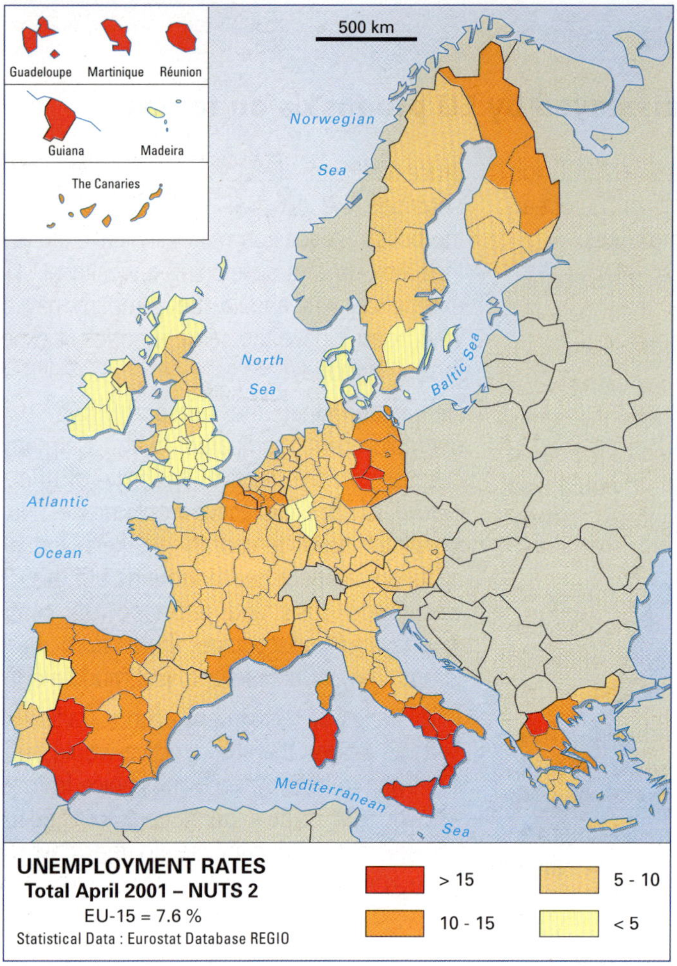

In April 2001, the unemployment rate in the NUTS-2* regions of the European Union varied between 1.2% and 33.3%. Breakdowns by gender and age highlight even greater regional differences. The rate of unemployment among women, for example, ranged from 1.1% to 36.4%, while between 2.1% and 59.9% of under-25s were out of work. [...]
The youth unemployment rate decreased in 139 of the 207 regions under consideration from April 2000 to April 2001.

*** NUTS:** nomenclature of territorial units for statistics (Eurostat classification)

From *Eurostat, Statistics in Focus*, completed on 07/2002. © European Communities, 2002.

Look at the map and answer the questions.

1 • Which regions have the lowest unemployment rate?
2 • Where can the highest unemployment rates be found?
3 • What's the average EU unemployment rate?
4 • How is France situated?

3 ► The right word

A • Crossword

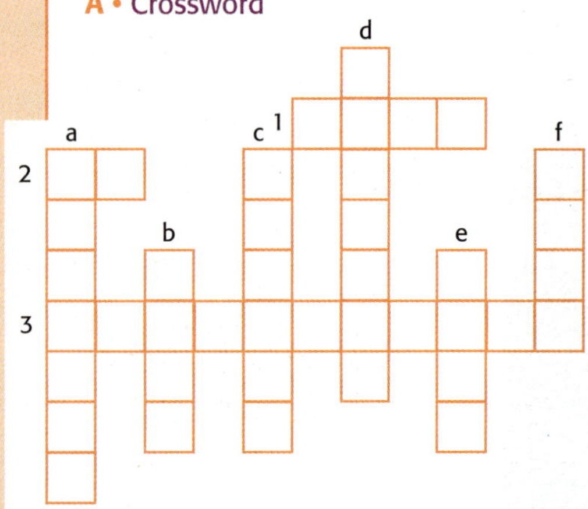

Across
1 • Take on.
2 • Trade union.
3 • They concern jobs in law or medicine.

Down
a • Working temporarily.
b • Opposite of leisure.
c • Plan.
d • Fire.
e • When people receive money for being out of work, they are on the … .
f • Occupations.

B • How many equivalents of each of these words do you know?

1 • lay off
2 • unemployed
3 • employ
4 • employees

4

► Vocabulary

agence pour l'emploi : job centre
allocation chômage : unemployment benefit
augmentation de salaire : pay rise, wage increase
avancement (donner de l') : promote

blocage des salaires : wage control, wage freeze
bloquer les salaires : freeze (froze, frozen) salaries
bourse du travail : employment agency, labour exchange
bulletin de salaire : payslip

carrière : career
certificat de travail : attestation of employment
chômage : unemployment
chômage de longue durée : long-term unemployment
chômage (être au) : be jobless / unemployed / out of work
chômage partiel : short-time / unemployment
chômage (recevoir des allocations de) : be on the dole
chômage structurel : structural unemployment
chômage (taux de) : jobless rate, unemployment rate
chômage technique (mettre au) : lay off (laid, laid)
chômage technique (travailleurs mis au) : lay-offs
contrat : contract
contrat à durée déterminée (CDD) : fixed-term contract
contrat à durée indéterminée (CDI) : permanent contract
convention collective : collective agreement
coût de la main-d'œuvre : labour costs
couverture sociale : cover

dégraissage : streamlining
dégraisser : streamline
délocalisation : relocation → relocate (v.)
démission : resignation
démission (remettre sa) : tender / hand in / send in one's resignation
démissionner : resign

embaucher : hire, take on
émoluments : emoluments
emploi (l') : employment
emploi à mi-temps : part-time job
emploi à plein-temps : full-time job
emploi à vie : lifetime employment
emploi (garantie de l') : job guarantee
emploi (plein) : full employment
emploi (sécurité de l') : job security
emploi (sous-) : underemployment
employé (n.) : employee
employeur : employer
engager à l'essai : hire on probation
essai (période d') : probation period

gagne-pain : livelihood
gagner de l'argent : earn money
gagner sa vie : earn one's living

heures supplémentaires (faire des) : work overtime

indemnité de chômage : dole, unemployment benefit
indemnité de licenciement : dismissal payment, redundancy pay, severance pay
indépendants (travailleurs) : the self-employed
interruption de carrière : career break

licencié pour raisons économiques (être) : be made redundant
licenciement : dismissal
licenciement abusif : unfair dismissal
licenciement pour cause de chômage technique : redundancy

main-d'œuvre : labour force, workforce labour, manpower [U]
marché du travail : labour market
masse salariale : payroll
métier : job

négociations salariales : collective bargaining
nomination : appointment
nommer : appoint

partage du travail : job-sharing
patron : boss
patronat : employers
permis de travail : work permit
personnel : staff [U], personnel [U]
population active : working population
poste : position, job, occupation
poste libre : vacancy
poste sans avenir : dead-end job
préavis : notice
préavis (sans) : without notice
prime de licenciement : redundancy payment, severance pay
profession : occupation
professions libérales : professions
promotion : promotion
promouvoir : promote

qualification : skill, qualification
qualifié : skilled
qualifié (non) : (un)skilled

récession : slump
reconversion : retraining → retrain (v.)
renvoyer : dismiss, sack, fire
renvoyer sans préavis : dismiss without notice
réorganiser : reshape
retraite : retirement
retraite anticipée : early retirement
retraite (caisse de) : pension fund, superannuation fund
retraite (pension) : pension
retraite (prendre sa) : retire
retraité : retiree (US), old-age pensioner (GB), senior citizen
retraités (les) : the retired
rétrograder : demote, downgrade

salaire : pay, salary, wage
salaire brut : gross wage
salaire de début : initial / commencing salary
salaire minimum interprofessionnel garanti : guaranteed minimum wage
salaire net : net wage
salaires (blocage des) : wage freeze
salaires (éventail des) : wage range
salaires (indice des) : wage index
spécialisé (ouvrier) : semi-skilled
spécialité (d'un travailleur) : line
syndicat : trade union (GB), labor union (US)
syndicaliste : trade / labor unionist

travail (le) : work [U], labour [U]
travail à la chaîne : assembly line work
travail au noir : moonlighting
travail de bureau (le) : white-collar work
travail en usine (le) : blue-collar work
travail (lieu de) : workplace
travail posté : shift work
travail (télé-) : telecommuting, teleworking
travail temporaire : temporary work
travailleur : worker
travailleur à temps partiel : part-timer
travailleur à temps plein : full-timer
travailleur temporaire : temp → temp (v.)

vie active : working life

The world at stake

PART III

Unit 1 Social issues

A few landmarks

US crime statistics

- **Lifetime likelihood of going to prison**
  - An estimated one of every 20 persons (5.1%) will serve term in prison during their lifetime.
  - Lifetime chances of a person going to prison are higher for:
    * men (9%) than for women (1.1%);
    * blacks (16.2%) and Hispanics (9.4%) than for whites (2.5%).

Violent crime rates
Adjusted victimization rate per 1,000 persons age 12 and over

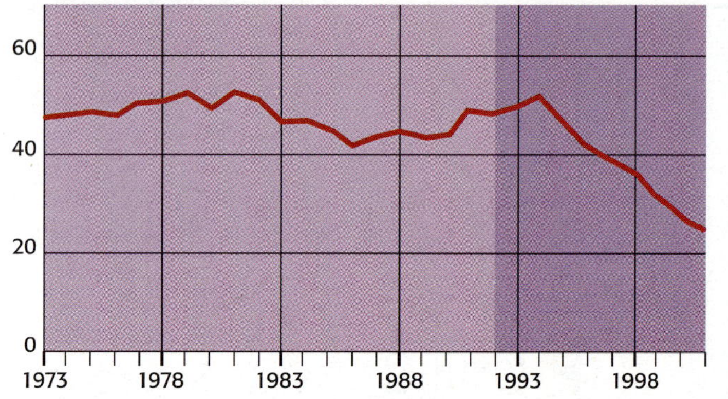

Note: The violent crimes included are rape, robbery, aggravated and simple assault, and homicide.

- **Characteristics of State prison inmates**
  - Women were 6.6% of the State prison inmates in 2001, up from 6% in 1995.
  - 64% of prison inmates belonged to racial or ethnic minorities in 2001.
  - An estimated 57% of inmates were under age 35 in 2001.

- Drug abuse violations are defined as State or local offenses relating to the unlawful possession, sale, use, growing, manufacturing, and making of narcotic drugs including opium or cocaine and their derivatives, marijuana, synthetic narcotics, and dangerous nonnarcotic drugs such as barbiturates.
- Juveniles are defined as persons under 18 years of age.
- Adults are defined as persons 18 years old and older.

- **Death penalty**
  - In 2000, 85 persons in 14 States were executed – 40 in Texas; 11 in Oklahoma, 8 in Virginia, 6 in Florida, 5 in Missouri, 4 in Alabama, 3 in Arizona, 2 in Arkansas, and one each in Delaware, Louisiana, North Carolina, South Carolina, Tennessee, and California.
  - Of persons executed in 2000: 49 were white, 35 were black, one was American Indian.
  - Of those executed in 2000: 83 were men, 2 were women.
  - Eighty of the executions in 2000 were carried out by lethal injection and 5 by electrocution.
  - Thirty-eight States and the Federal government in 2000 had capital statutes.

From US Bureau of Justice.

© Agostini / Gamma Liaison.

Warm-up

- How do you react to those two photographs which were taken in New York City?

© Moyer / Gamma Liaison.

Unit 1

TEXT 1

The needle and the damage done

1. **spree =** long time spent doing something you enjoy
2. **nonce =** offender
3. **charity:** *association caritative*
4. **crime =** offence: *délit*

In and out of prison, thieving and selling sex, Brian was a criminal from the age of 17. Only after he had wasted his twenties on eight prison terms and intermittent crime sprees[1] did anyone bother to address the sickness at the root of it all: he was a drug addict.

Brian, from Manchester, turned to drugs after being sexually abused in his mid-teens. He stole to pay for amphetamines, crack, and heroin – but now, aged 34, he has not taken drugs for over two years and is out of prison.

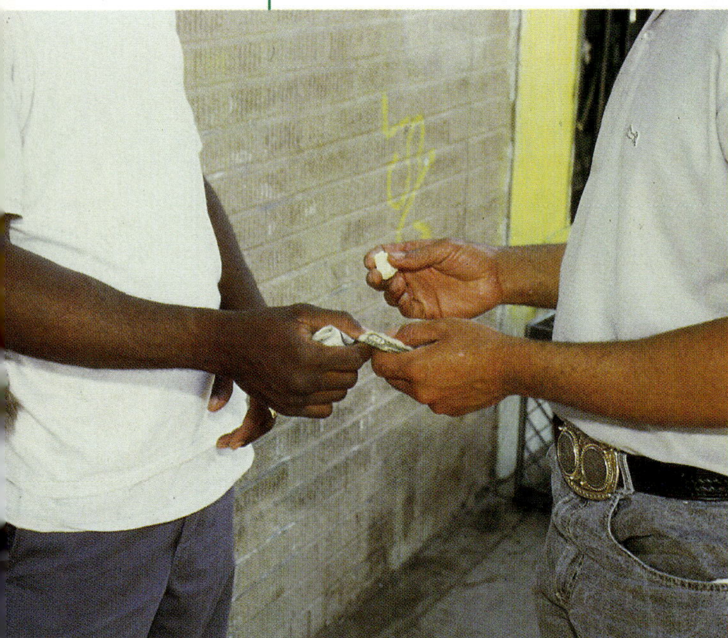

© Gamma-Liaison / Stevens.

Brian was lucky enough to be put in and get through the tough regime of the "therapeutic community" at Channings Wood prison in Devon, sharing his inner feelings with 112 other drug addicts, facing the daily shouts of "Nonce[2]!" as they walked to the treatment centre. He survived several breakdowns.

Brian's early story is typical. "Pretty well all the people we deal with are involved in both criminal behaviour and drug taking," says a spokeswoman for Addaction, Britain's largest drugs and alcohol charity[3].

Not all drug addicts commit crime[4] – but the average problem user spends about £16,500 a year on drugs, of which £13,000 has been obtained illegally.

The response of successive governments has been to punish the crime rather than treat the condition. There is now, however, a growing clamour for that to change. Increasing numbers of experts and people working with drug abusers are suggesting it is time to try helping sick people rather than just locking them up.

From *The Independent on Sunday*, 26 May 2002.

► Check your pronunciation

A • Can you pronounce the following words without making a mistake?

1 • through 2 • tough 3 • thought 4 • thorough 5 • though

B • Can you stress the right syllable in the following adjectives?

1 • intermittent 2 • typical 3 • successive 4 • therapeutic

► Words

A • Match the following words with their definitions.

1 • thieve (l. 1)	a • cruel and violent treatment
2 • term (l. 2)	b • reaction
3 • bother (l. 3)	c • harsh
4 • root (l. 3)	d • depression
5 • abuse (l. 5)	e • period of time
6 • tough (l. 9)	f • participating
7 • breakdown (l. 15)	g • steal
8 • involved (l. 17)	h • trouble
9 • response (l. 25)	i • origin

B • It is generally possible to create a noun by using a verb and adding the suffix *-er*. (see T&T: Word formation)

Look at the following example from the text:
abuse → abuser

Then find five examples using verbs from the text and translate them.

► Meaning

A • Give information on Brian's life.

1 • before the age of 17
2 • at the age of 17
3 • during his twenties
4 • now, at 34

B • Reformulate the sentences from the text.

1 • "intermittent crime sprees" (l. 2-3)
2 • "address the sickness at the root of it all" (l. 3)
3 • "in his mid-teens" (l. 5)
4 • "lucky enough to be put in and get through the tough regime" (l. 8-9)
5 • "there is now, [...] – a growing clamour for that to change" (l. 26)
6 • "just locking them up" (l. 28)

C • Sum up the main idea of the text in French. (about 20 words)

D • Transform the following sentences using the pattern below. (see T&T: Sentence patterns)

Ex.: He had never asked me any information.
→ Never had he asked me any information.

1 • He had hardly been abused when he turned to drugs.
2 • He had no sooner arrived in prison than he was put in the therapeutic community.
3 • He realised only then that he badly needed treatment.
4 • He not only survived several breakdowns but he totally stopped taking drugs.
5 • He had never resumed taking drugs after his treatment.

E • Translate into English.

1 • *Il a eu assez de chance pour être envoyé dans ce centre thérapeutique.*
2 • *À partir de 17 ans il devint voleur.*
3 • *C'est l'association caritative la plus importante de la Grande-Bretagne.*
4 • *Cela fait deux ans qu'il est sorti de prison.*
5 • *De plus en plus de gens pensent qu'il faut aider les toxicomanes.*

F • Translate into French.

1 • The first sentence of the text.
2 • From "Not all drug addicts" (l. 21) to "illegally". (l. 24)

► Pair work

A maintains that drug addicts are sick and in need of help whereas **B** thinks they are dangerous and should be locked up. Imagine their dialogue.

► Food for thought

What are the pros and cons of adopting liberal attitudes, such as in Spain and Portugal, where the possession of drugs is not a criminal offence? (about 200 words)

Unit 1

TEXT 2

A cargo of exploitable souls

1. lure= entice, attract
2. smuggle: *faire de la contrebande*
3. prosecution: *poursuites judiciaires*
4. convicted: *reconnu coupable*

America, a "prime tourist destination", is also a prime destination for much less happy people. One group, impoverished young girls from Mexico, was found earlier this year in a suburban house in New Jersey. They had been lured[1] from their home towns by an international trafficking ring, smuggled[2] to the United States and forced into prostitution. The victims, who were beaten if they resisted, sold their bodies to customers for as little as $35.

Trafficking is distinguished from mere immigrant-smuggling by the degree of coercion, deception and exploitation. Every year, on State Department estimates, about 50,000 people, the vast majority women and children, are forcibly trafficked into the United States from all over the world – Eastern Europe, Asia, Central America, Africa. Once there, most victims disappear among the 8m or so illegal immigrants in the country. They are forced to work as virtual slaves, for the traffickers' profit, in the sex industry, on farms and in factories. The victims, who rarely speak English, exist in a sort of parallel universe with no money, no documents, the threat of beatings and limited contact with anyone but their keepers and other victims.

© Gamma-Liaison / Miami Herald.

Since the passage in 2000 of the Trafficking Victim Protection Act, pioneered by Congressman Chris Smith, both investigations and prosecutions[3] have been stepped up. […] Those convicted[4] of trafficking may now receive up to 20 years in prison and, in some cases, life sentences. […]

The State Department has also created a new class of visas especially for victims of trafficking. Five thousand of the so-called T-visas will be available each year to victims who provide information to the authorities, allowing them to live and work in America while their cases are investigated and prosecuted. Previously, trafficking victims who came forward were deported as illegal immigrants.

From *The Economist*, June 1st, 2002.

► Check your pronunciation

A • **Read the following words aloud:**

1 • [praɪm] 2 • [lʊəʳd] 3 • [ˈsmʌgld] 4 • [ˈvɜːtʃuəl] 5 • [θret] 6 • [ˈkiːpəʳz] 7 • [paɪəˈnɪəʳd]

B • **Read the *-ed* ending words. What conclusion can you come to?**

1 • impoverished 2 • trafficked 3 • forced 4 • limited 5 • created 6 • investigated 7 • prosecuted

► Words

Match the following words from the text with their synonyms.

1 • prime (l. 1)
2 • impoverished (l. 2)
3 • ring (l. 4)
4 • deception (l. 8)
5 • threat (l. 21)
6 • keeper (l. 22)
7 • stepped up (l. 26)
8 • provide (l. 30)
9 • previously (l. 31)
10 • investigate (l. 31)

a • trick
b • warden
c • before
d • intensified
e • main
f • give
g • made poor
h • menace
i • gang
j • inquire into

► Meaning

A • Turn the following sentences into the passive. (see T&T: Passive form)

1 • The investigators found young Mexican girls in a suburban house.
2 • Traffickers had lured them into the US.
3 • "We will beat you if you resist," they said.
4 • This ring is even trafficking children.
5 • The traffickers can force them to work endless hours.
6 • The new Act has stepped up prosecutions.
7 • Authorities will give a visa to victims who provide information on trafficking.
8 • The authorities used to deport the victims.
9 • One must distinguish trafficking from immigrant-smuggling.
10 • The judge has sentenced the smuggler to 10 years' imprisonment.

B • Reformulate the following expressions from the text.

1 • "America, a "prime tourist destination"" (l. 1)
2 • "They had been lured from their home towns" (l. 3)
3 • "forcibly trafficked into the United States" (l. 10)
4 • "virtual slaves" (l. 16)
5 • "trafficking victims who came forward" (l. 31-32)

C • Explain the difference between trafficking and immigrant-smuggling.

D • Why do you think the special visas have been called "T-visas"?

E • Sum up the text by completing the following blanks.

1 • The victims' country of origin: ....
2 • The country they are trafficked into: ....
3 • The jobs they are forced to do: ....
4 • They live in a parallel universe because: ....
5 • Two solutions have been found to fight this exploitation:
– Name, date and content of the recent US Act: ....
– Creation by the State Department of: ....

F • Translate into English.

1 • *Ce visa vous permettra de travailler aux États-Unis.*
2 • *On estime qu'il y a environ 8 millions de clandestins aux États-Unis.*
3 • *Pendant que l'on poursuit l'enquête vous pouvez rester dans notre pays.*

G • Translate into French.

1 • "Once there, most victims disappear among the 8m or so illegal immigrants in the country." (l. 13-15)
2 • From "Since the passage" (l. 24) to "life sentences". (l. 27)

H • Everything has been mixed up. Put the words below in the correct order.

1 • created / new / a / of / has / visas / been / class
2 • the / impoverished / have / US / smuggled / Mexicans / to / been
3 • rarely / the / English / can / victims / speak
4 • immigrant-smuggling / trafficking / different / is / from

► Group work

Group A would like to give a visa to any illegal immigrant coming into our country. Group B totally disagrees. Imagine the discussion.

► Food for thought

Try to find a proper definition of slavery. What do you know about the current state of worldwide slavery? (about 150 words)

TEXT 3

1. curb = limit
2. industrial action = strike
3. spit, spat, spat: *cracher*
4. panel: *commission*

Rate of violent pupils expelled rises for first time since 1996

The number of children expelled from school because of violence and lack of discipline is set to rise for the first time in five years as head teachers take aggressive action to curb[1] high levels of bad behaviour. [...] An internal report by one of the teaching unions also reveals a litany of aggressive behaviour by pupils, which makes teaching in a "supportive" school environment almost impossible. The report reveals that teachers at 71 schools have threatened industrial action[2] in the last 18 months because pupils have proved too difficult to teach. Teachers, who said they were often spat[3] at, kicked and punched by pupils, also claim they are regularly undermined by exclusion appeals panels[4] which try to reinstate pupils rather than educate them elsewhere. On one occasion a pupil required hospital treatment after being beaten up by 10 other pupils. Although two of the pupils responsible were excluded, they were later reinstated on appeal. [...] From September, excluded pupils will be sent to specialist education units where they will receive help with their behaviour and start the process of being reintegrated into mainstream schools. Excluded pupils roaming the streets with little to do is thought to be one of the reasons for the increase in street crime.

From *The Observer*, 19 May 2002.

► Words

What is the right meaning of the following words?

1 • "expel" (title) means:
- throw out
- push
- pull

2 • "lack" (l. 1) means:
- luck
- chance
- shortage

3 • "set to" (l. 2) means:
- sure to
- likely to
- ready to

4 • "mainstream" (l. 15) means:
- special
- ordinary
- rare

5 • "roam" (l. 15) means:
- run
- wander
- stay

► Meaning

A • Reformulate the following sentences in your own words.

1 • "a litany of aggressive behaviour" (l. 4)
2 • "a 'supportive' school environment" (l. 5)
3 • "they are regularly undermined" (l. 9)
4 • "reinstate pupils" (l. 9-10)

B • Complete the following sentences using *although* + a sentence from the box below. **(see T&T: Clauses of contrast)**

1 • We can't go on expelling so many children from school ....
2 • This teacher is often spat at ....
3 • .... violence still continues in schools.
4 • .... they are later reinstated on appeal.
5 • Nobody was really punished ....

a • he has never proved aggressive
b • high levels of bad behaviour must be curbed
c • the number of children expelled from school is on the increase
d • one child was sent to hospital after being beaten up
e • violent pupils are excluded

Checkup Unit 1

1 ► Test

High-tech ID cards planned to curb asylum seekers

Plans to introduce a £1 billion identity card scheme for more than 30m Britons will be unveiled in the next few days amid new evidence of the growing number of asylum seekers entering Britain.

Ministers want every adult to have a high-tech card to help combat benefit fraud and expose bogus asylum seekers and illegal workers. The scheme has already provoked controversy with civil liberties campaigners arguing that identity cards allow the government to track every individual. [...]

United Nations figures published this week show Britain tops a league of 29 industrialised countries, with a monthly average of 6,510 new asylum cases, compared with 6,120 in Germany, the second most popular destination.

The average number of cases has jumped 9% in Britain compared with a year ago. Most other countries saw a fall or no change in number.

The options for new cards include one the size of a credit card showing the holder's name, address, date of birth and photograph, with information about their entitlement to health and welfare benefits stored on a magnetic strip or microchip.

A second option would see information imprinted on cards already in use, such as driving licences or even rail or bus passes. [...]

It will not be compulsory for people to carry the cards; police would not be given powers to stop people and demand their papers.

Critics say that because the scheme is not compulsory it will not deter asylum seekers who want to work and do not need to claim benefits. Some campaigners say an ID system could not work without a vast "Big Brother" database that would carry sensitive information on all card holders.

From *The Sunday Times*, June 30, 2002.

A • Fill in the following blanks (in French).

1 • Problem Britain has to face: ....
2 • Plans to solve the problem: ....
3 • Description of the plan:
– option 1: ....
– option 2: ....
4 • Point of view of those supporting the plan:
....
5 • Point of view of the opponents:
1. ....
2. ....

B • Translate the first paragraph into French.

C • Translate into English.

1 • *Le ministre veut que tous les Anglais aient une carte d'identité.*
2 • *Certains pays ont enregistré une baisse du nombre de demandeurs d'asile.*
3 • *Ce système va-t-il dissuader les gens ?*
4 • *Il faut freiner le nombre d'étrangers qui souhaitent entrer en Angleterre illégalement.*

D • Why do you think the number of asylum seekers is growing in Europe?

2 ► Skills in practice

Carefully study the chart and then answer the following questions.

1 • What are the two kinds of refugees that appear on this chart?
2 • Which continent has the most refugees?
3 • Which continent comes second?
4 • Which country ranks first?
5 • Which country ranks last?
6 • Does Britain rank among the top 10 countries?
7 • Does France appear on the grid?

© Nicolas Cotto / Gamma.

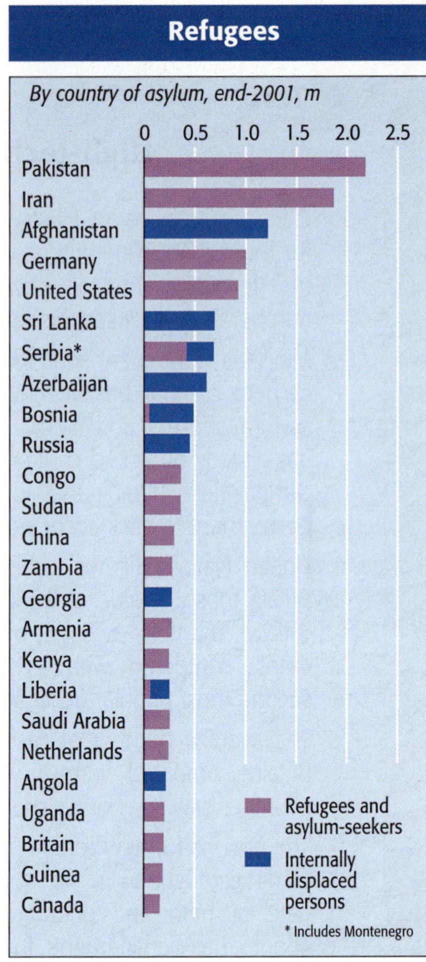

UNHCR

3 ► The right word

A • Crossword

Across
1 • Also called cardboard people.
2 • Inebriated.
3 • "Les Restos du Cœur" is one.
4 • Destitution.
5 • An outcast suffers from it.

Down
a • Disabled.
b • Ask for food or money.
c • Give food.
d • Shanty.

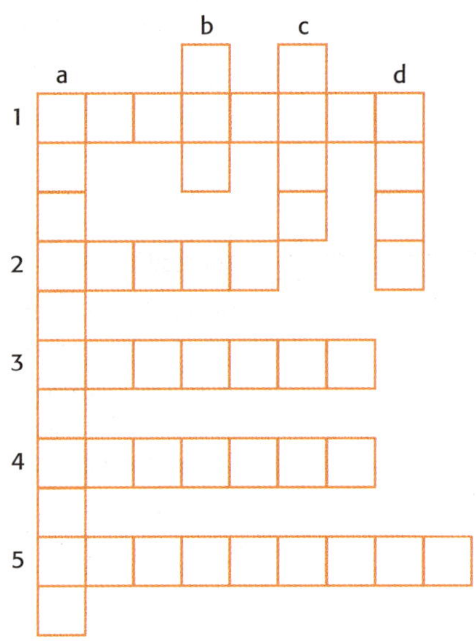

B • Match each of the following words with its definition.

1 • having nowhere to live	a • a plague
2 • not having the things that are essential in life	b • extreme suffering or death caused by lack of food
3 • a lot of unpleasant things that happen at the same time	c • be underfed
4 • shortage	d • be homeless
5 • an organisation which raises money in order to help the poor	e • be deprived
6 • someone who lives by asking people for food or money	f • living standards
7 • disgusting amount of dirt	g • scarcity
8 • not having enough food	h • charity
9 • starvation	i • beggar
10 • the level of comfort in which people live	j • filth

4 ► Vocabulary

alcoolique (adj. et n.) : alcoholic
avenir : future

bidonville : shanty town, slum

charge (être à la) : be supported by
clochard : tramp

défavorisé : underprivileged
dépendre de : depend on, be dependent on
déshérité : deprived
dormir sous les ponts : sleep in cardboard city

échec : failure
échelle sociale : social ladder / scale
en dessous du seuil de pauvreté : below the poverty line
exclus de la société (n.) : social outcasts

faim : hunger, starvation
fléau : plague
frapper : hit (hit, hit)

ghetto social : social ghetto

handicapés (les) : the disabled, the handicapped

ivrogne : drunkard

logement : housing
loi de la jungle : law of the jungle
loi du plus fort : survival of the fittest

malnutrition : malnutrition
mauvais traitements infligés aux enfants : child abuse
mendiant : beggar
mendier : beg
misère (être dans la) : be very badly off
mourir de faim : die of starvation, starve (to death)

niveau de vie : standard of living
nourrir (se) : feed (fed, fed) (oneself)

organisation caritative : charity, charitable organisation
organisme : body

parent isolé : lone parent

pauvre : poor
pauvres (les) : the poor, the have-nots
pauvreté : poverty
pénurie : scarcity, dearth

saleté : dirt, filth
sans abri (adj.) : homeless
sans abri, SDF (n.) : the homeless, cardboard people
services sociaux : social services
sinistre (adj.) : gloomy, bleak
situation difficile : predicament, plight
solitude : loneliness
soulagement : relief
soupe populaire : soup kitchen
sous-alimentation : undernourishment
sous-alimenté : underfed, undernourished
survivre : survive

taudis : slum

vivre au jour le jour : live from hand to mouth

Unit 2 Developing countries

A few landmarks

Fact file

Location: Geneva
Established: 1 January 1995
Created by: Uruguay Round negotiations (1986-1994)
Membership: 144 countries (as of 1 January 2002)
Budget: 43 million Swiss francs for 2002
Secretariat staff: 550
Head: Mike Moore (director-general)

Functions:
- Administering WTO trade agreements
- Forum for trade negotiations
- Handling trade disputes
- Monitoring national trade policies
- Technical assistance and training for developing countries
- Cooperation with other international organisations

- The **World Trade Organisation** (WTO) is the only global international organisation dealing with the rules of trade between nations.

Developing countries

Over three-quarters of WTO members are developing or least-developed countries. All WTO agreements contain special provisions for them, including: longer time periods to implement agreements and commitments, measures to increase their trading opportunities, and support to help them build the infrastructure for WTO work, handle disputes, and implement technical standards.

Least-developed countries

The WTO recognises as least-developed countries (LDCs) those countries which have been designated as such by the United Nations. There are currently 49 LCDs on the UN list, 30 of which to date have become WTO members and nine additional LCDs are in the process of accession to the WTO.

Adapted from www.wto.org

- The **Food and Agriculture Organisation** (FAO) of the United Nations was founded in 1945 with a mandate to raise levels of nutrition and standards of living to improve agricultural productivity and to better the condition of rural populations.
Today, FAO is one of the largest specialised agencies in the UN system and the lead agency for agriculture, forestry, fisheries and rural development. FAO has 183 member countries plus one member organisation, the European Community.
Since its inception, FAO has worked to alleviate poverty and hunger by promoting agricultural development, improved nutrition and the pursuit of food security – defined as the access of all people at all times to the food they need for an active and healthy life.

From www.fao.org

- The **Organisation for Economic Cooperation and Development** (OECD) groups 30 member countries. With active relationships with some 70 other countries, NGOs and civil society, its work covers economic and social issues from macroeconomics, to trade, education, development and science and innovation. Its activities include emerging economies, sustainable development, territorial economy and aid.

Adapted from www.oecd.org

MALAWI
2001 floods followed by drought, lack of seeds and fertilisers, low maize production, depletion of strategic grain reserves, price rises in staple foods.
Population: 11 million
At risk: Nearly 8 million

ZIMBABWE
Drought from late 2001, disruption of commercial farming, high inflation and poor economic performance, tenuous food security, sharp food price rises.
Population: 12 million
At risk: Between 3 million and 7.8 million

ZAMBIA
Floods in some parts, severe drought in others, depletion of strategic grain reserves, sharp rises in food prices.
Population: 10 million
At risk: About 1.3 million

MOZAMBIQUE
Devastating floods in 2000 and 2001, followed by drought, rises in food prices.
Population: 17.5 million
At risk: Over 500,000, expected to rise sharply

LESOTHO
Heavy rains, hailstorms and frost, poor economic performance, food price hikes.
Population: 2.2 million
At risk: Over 1 million

SWAZILAND
Erratic rainfall
Population: About 1 million
At risk: Up to 400,000

ANGOLA
Long civil war has displaced millions of people.
Population: About 12 million
At risk: At least 1 million

Warm-up

1 • Which countries are essentially devastated by climatic disasters?
2 • Give the main consequences of these disasters.
3 • What are the other causes of famine risk? Which countries are concerned?
4 • Where can the most appalling situations be found?
5 • In which countries should it be more difficult to cope with this plight? Why?

Unit 2

TEXT 1

1. brand = label
2. crop: *récolte*
3. steamroller = force
4. tremendous = enormous
5. yield = output
6. seed: *graine*
7. patent: *breveter*

GM firms the only winners at food talks summit

The world food summit ended in recrimination yesterday when it was branded[1] a waste of time for everyone except the United States, which successfully sold genetically modified crops[2] as a solution to famine. [...]

Environmental and agricultural groups accused the US of steamrollering[3] the summit into approving biotechnology, after robust lobbying by Washington.

"The US played very hard and succeeded. They now have the moral authority to use genetically modified food for aid purposes," said Fernando Almansa of Oxfam*. [...]

The US delegation was led by the agriculture secretary, Ann Veneman, and made no secret that its priority was to promote the wider use of biotechnology, an industry dominated by American companies.

"Biotechnology has tremendous[4] potential to develop products that can be more suited to areas of the world where there is persistent hunger," Ms Veneman said. [...]

Another delegate was more forthright: "We're here to sell biotech, and that's what we've done."

Advocates say GM crops with improved yields[5], resistance to drought and tolerance of salt could ease food shortages in stricken areas. But critics say it could destroy biodiversity and force poor farmers to buy seeds[6] from US corporations.

© Gamma / Palmour Hayne.

Fred Kalibwani, an ecology activist from a Zimbabwe-based non-governmental organisation, said that the patented[7] GM seeds in effect placed food security in the hands of a few corporations. "This will be tragic for Africa in the next few years," he said. [...]

Some UN officials said the £1.6m cost of the event would have been better spent on grain for the poor.

From *The Guardian,* June 14, 2002.

***Oxfam** = Oxford Committee for Famine Relief

► Check your pronunciation

A • Divide up the following list of words into [ɪ] sounds and [aɪ] sounds.

1 • summit	7 • biotechnology
2 • United	8 • lobbying
3 • modified	9 • priority
4 • famine	10 • wider
5 • environmental	11 • stricken
6 • agricultural	12 • organisation

B • Can you find the pairs for each of the following sounds? [ɔ], [əʊ], [u:]

1 • only	3 • sold	5 • use
2 • food	4 • crols	6 • modified

► Words

A • Find out their opposites in §7: flood / surpluses.

B • Match the synonyms.

1 • except (l. 2)	a • aims
2 • lobbying (l. 5)	b • regions
3 • purposes (l. 7)	c • but
4 • wider (l. 9)	d • ruined
5 • suited (l. 12)	e • supporters
6 • areas (l. 12)	f • pressures
7 • forthright (l. 13)	g • decrease
8 • advocates (l. 15)	h • bigger
9 • ease (l. 16)	i • straightforward
10 • stricken (l. 16)	j • adapted

► Meaning

A • What do the following words refer to?

1 • "we" (l. 13 and 14)
2 • "it" (l. 16)
3 • "this" (l. 23)
4 • "the event" (l. 27)

B • Make complete sentences with *accuse*, *blame* and *reproach* in the correct form, as shown in the examples.

Ex.: – The Americans are accused of selling GMOs.
– The Americans are blamed for selling GMOs.
– The Americans are reproached for selling GMOs.

1 • The Americans / take advantage of the world food summit to their own profit.
2 • American GMO companies / further impoverish poor farmers.
3 • American GMO companies / threaten health in developing countries.
4 • The USA / make everybody else lose time and money.

C • Answer the questions in your own words.

1 • Which country didn't disapprove of the world summit issue?
2 • What are the benefits of GM crops for impoverished countries according to US officials?
3 • What is the real reason for the selling of GM seeds to these countries?
4 • What arguments are given by those against GM food?
5 • Why was the world food summit both a waste of time and of money?

D • Translate the first three paragraphs.

► Pair work

Student **A** is a GM food backer whereas student **B** strongly opposes it. Imagine their conversation.

► Food for thought

Instead of using GM food, how could the developed world help the developing world as regards food?

Visiting disaster

1. **debt-strapped =** debt-ridden: *criblé de dettes*
2. **manna =** food
3. **headman =** chief
4. **prime =** main
5. **real estate:** *immobilier*
6. **loot:** *piller*

Ecotourism is growing massively around the world and is now backed by governments, world bodies and international banks. [...]

According to many conservationists and tour operators, this "benign" version of tourism offers a way to fund environmental protection, stimulate the incomes of the poor and encourage cultural exchange. Ecotourists are thought to spend considerably more than mass tourists, and for debt-strapped[1] developing countries, having people visit, look at things that require minimal investment and pay lots of money for the privilege, can seem like manna[2] from heaven.

Nature is a money spinner. Ecuador earns more than $100m a year from 60,000 visitors to the Galapagos, for instance, and Kenya as much income from its safari holidays. While ecotourism run by indigenous communities can be a lifesaver in areas where other income sources are being depleted, all too often these very people are being left out of the ecotourism development plans. The dispossession of people from their land is increasingly associated with ecotourism.

The cases are widespread. In the Moulvibaza district of Bangladesh more than 1,000 families of the Khasi and Garoare indigenous groups face eviction from their ancestral lands for the development of a 610-hectare ecopark. "We have been living here for hundreds of years... we will not leave this forest," said a Khasi headman[3], Anil Yang Yung, in a public demonstration during a hunger strike in Dhaka in February. "We cannot survive if we are evicted from the forest." [...]

Governments in developing countries, keen to modernise, often say that "primitive" subsistence activities are incompatible with conservation. These were the arguments given to evict the Masai in East Africa and the Bushmen of Botswana, but the reality is that many indigenous and other poor communities are living on prime[4] areas of ecotourism real estate[5] and speculators want the land.

"There are many cases in Indonesia where whole communities have been evicted, driven out, beaten up and their possessions destroyed or looted[6], to clear land for tourist developments," says Sean Foley, a development consultant who worked in Indonesia during the 1980s and 1990s.

© GettyImages / Image Bank / Guid Rossi.

From *The Guardian Weekly*, June 20-26, 2002.

► Check your pronunciation

A • Is "ge" pronounced [ʒ] or [dʒ] in these words?

1 • encourage 2 • privilege 3 • indigenous

B • Can you pronounce these words correctly?

1 • ecotourism
2 • debt
3 • dispossession
4 • widespread
5 • whole

C • Read the words aloud and focus on the [ʃ] sound.

1 • conservationists
2 • version
3 • protection
4 • disposse<u>ss</u>ion
5 • associated
6 • eviction
7 • demonstration

► Words

A • Find the equivalents in the text (verbs are given in the infinitive).

1 • support (§1)
2 • a gold mine (§3)
3 • use up (§3)
4 • expulsion (§4)
5 • eager to (§5)
6 • expel (§6)

B • What does "subsistence activities" (l. 22) mean? Give examples.

C • From the verb "evict", the noun "eviction" is made. Find as many such patterns as you can with words from the text.

► Meaning

A • Say what the figures and dates correspond to?

1 • $100m (l. 9)
2 • 60,000 (l. 9)
3 • 1,000 (l. 16)
4 • 610 hectares (l. 17)
5 • the 1980s and 1990s (l. 36)

B • What is the subject of "can seem like manna from heaven" (l. 8)?

C • Look at the sentences "income sources are being depleted" (l. 12) and "these very people are being left out" (l. 12).
(see T&T: Present Be + V-ing / Passive form)
Now make your own sentences, using the same pattern, with the following elements.

1 • large areas / cleared for ecoparks
2 • today / many indigenous / expelled from their land
3 • many of them / even beaten up
4 • no measures / taken to protect the native communities

D • What's the difference between ecotourists and mass tourists?

E • What do Ecuador and Kenya have in common?

F • Fill in the grid on ecotourism, in your own words whenever possible.

	In favour	Against
Who?		
Arguments		

G • What does ecotourism mean? Why is it a paradoxical word?

H • Translate the last two paragraphs into French.

► Pair work

A tells **B** about his intention to make a safari tour in Kenya but **B** is strongly against ecotourism. Imagine their conversation. (see T&T: Disagreement / Reproach / Suggestions)

► Food for thought

"Primitive subsistence activities are incompatible with conservation."
Comment.
(about 200 words)

TEXT 3

20 million at risk

1. **stalk** = spread over
2. **wrack** = rack = afflict, ruin

The World Food Programme is warning that it may soon have to feed up to 8 million people in southern Africa as famine stalks[1] a region wracked[2] by drought, floods, economic mismanagement and political instability. [...] A total of 20 million across the region are at risk from famine. [...]

Southern Africa has become a laboratory for the ideas of the Nobel prize-winning economist, Amartya Sen, who argues that countries, however poor, do not suffer famine if they have independence, democracy and a relatively free press. He pointed out that Botswana and Zimbabwe escaped starvation in the early 1980s, despite suffering worse falls in grain production than Ethiopia. Botswana, still democratic, is coping well with the current crisis but Zimbabwe, where President Mugabe is seeking to stamp out all opposition, is one of the worst-affected.

From *The Independent on Sunday,* 26 May 2002.

► Words

Find the synonyms of these nouns in the text.

1 • dryness 2 • inundation 3 • famine 4 • decrease

► Meaning

A • Pick out the equivalent.

1 • "The World Food Programme is **warning** ..." (l. 1): is advising people / is making people aware of danger / is complaining

2 • "Botswana is **coping** well with the current crisis" (l. 10): is managing the current crisis / is facing the current crisis / is starting the current crisis

3 • "the current crisis" (l. 10): the actual crisis / the present crisis / the ordinary crisis

4 • "President Mugabe is seeking to **stamp out** all opposition." (l. 10-11): He is trying to help all opposition. / He is trying to satisfy all opposition. / He is trying to crush all opposition.

B • What do they refer to?

1 • 20 million. (title)

2 • "it" in the first sentence of the text.

3 • southern Africa = a country in the south of Africa / several countries in the south of Africa / a continent.

C • *Still* or *always*?

1 • There have .... been floods and drought in southern Africa.

2 • Even if the situation is better, Botswana .... suffers from a crisis.

3 • A lot of progress is .... to be made.

4 • Please don't say there will .... be problems! There are .... problems but let's hope things will improve.

D • Apart from drought and flood, what are the causes of famine? (in your own words)

E • List the factors that can prevent poor countries from starving.

F • Which countries benefited from at least one of these factors in the 1980s and what was the consequence? (in your own words)

G • Is their situation the same today? Why? (in your own words)

Checkup
Unit 2

1 ► Test

The twin plagues of Brazil: deforestation and slavery

The recruiters gather at the bus station here in this grimy Amazon frontier town, waiting for the weary and the desperate to disembark. When they spot a target, they promise him a steady job, good pay, free housing and plenty of food. A quick handshake seals the deal.

But for thousands of peasants, that handshake ensures a slide into slavery. No sooner do they board the battered trucks that take them to work felling trees and tending cattle deep in the jungle than they find themselves mired in debt, under armed guard and unable to leave.

"It was 12 years before I was finally able to escape and make my way back home," said Bernardo Gomes da Silva, 42. […]

Interviewed recently, […] Mr Gomes da Silva said particularly troublesome workers, especially those who kept asking for their wages, were sometimes simply killed.

"I can't read, so maybe a half-dozen different times I was ordered to burn the identity cards and work documents of workers who I had last seen walking down the road, supposedly on their way out," he said. "We also found heaps of bones out in the jungle, but none of us ever talked about it." […]

Government authorities admit that despite a federal crackdown announced seven years ago, "contemporary forms of slavery" continue to flourish. The reasons range from ranchers in cahoots with[1] corrupt local authorities to ineffective land reform policies and high unemployment.

Perhaps most important, though, is the growing pressure to exploit the Amazon's vast agricultural frontier, in part to supply foreign markets with two prized goods: timber[2] and beef.

In the jungle, fortunes are being made clearing the forest and harvesting mahogany[3] and other tropical hardwoods. The United States is the main importer of Brazilian mahogany […].

In booming mill towns, dealers openly resell, copy or counterfeit the government certificates needed to export timber.

As the trees have fallen, there has also been a huge expansion in cattle ranches that raise grass-fed "green beef". Brazil's commercial cattle herd, the largest in the world, generally does not eat manufactured feed or synthetic supplements.

That makes Brazilian beef especially attractive in Europe and the Middle East. […] Exports of Brazilian beef, fresh and processed, grew 30 percent in 2001, to $1 billion, according to government statistics.

"Slave labour in Brazil is directly linked to deforestation," Claudio Secchin, director of the Ministry of Labour's special anti-slavery Mobile Enforcement Team, said in an interview in Brasilia. "There are more and more cattle ranchers who want to increase the size of their herds, but to do that they need more space, so the clearing of land is a constant."

From *The New York Times* in *Le Monde*, April 7-8, 2002.

1. **in cahoots with:** *de mèche avec*
2. **timber** = wood
3. **mahogany:** *acajou*

© Gamma / Antonio Ribeiro.

A • Explain how people are forced into slavery. (100 words)

B • Develop the causes of "the twin plagues of Brazil". (150 words)

C • Translate paragraphs 7 to 10 into French.

2 ► Skills in practice

Answer the following questions.

1 • What do the black and the white figures stand for?
2 • What is the world population's general trend?
3 • Which countries / continents follow a reverse tendency?
4 • Which group of countries had the lowest population in 2000? Will they have the same position in 2100?
5 • Which group of countries had the lowest population over 60 in 2000? Will they have the same position in 2100?
6 • Which countries / continent had and will have the highest and the oldest populations?
7 • How would you account for the world ageing population?

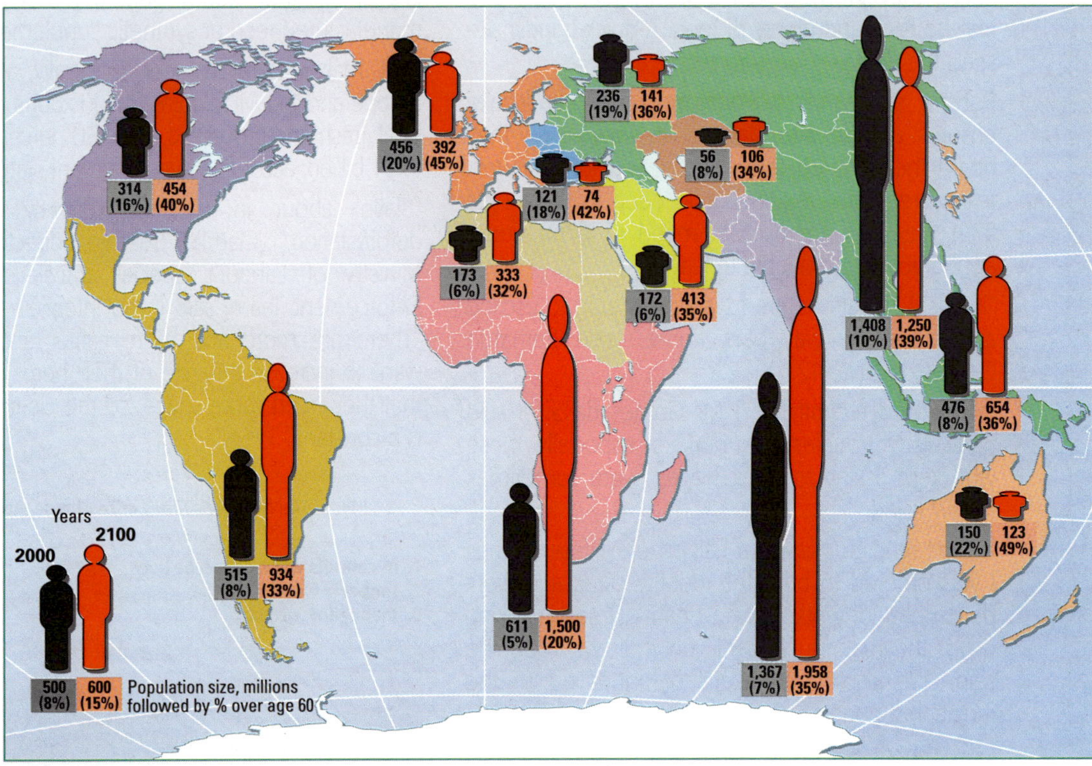

3 ► The right word

A • In the grid, 10 abbreviations of world organisations or of groups of countries are written either across, down, crosswise from left to right or crosswise from right to left. Find them and say what they stand for.

U	D	U	F	A	O
B	N	G	O	L	E
G	N	I	C	H	C
W	W	W	C	S	D
H	T	N	I	E	Y
O	V	L	D	C	F

B • Fill in the blanks with the following words.

birth control / diseases / gap / life expectancy / literacy / poverty line / relief / underfed

1 • The aim of UNICEF is to bring .... to destitute children in the developing world.
2 • .... calculates the average age of death of a population.
3 • Family planning centres provide free information on ....
4 • .... children suffer from physical but also from mental handicaps.
5 • Far too many people live below the ....
6 • Unlike Aids, the mumps, the measles and diphtheria are easily preventable ....
7 • .... assesses the ability to read, write and count.
8 • The widening .... between rich countries and poor countries is more and more alarming.

4

► Vocabulary

affamé : starving, famished
agriculture : farming
aide alimentaire : food aid
aide humanitaire : relief / humanitarian aid
allègement des dettes : debt relief
alphabétisation (degré d') : literacy
analphabète : illiterate
analphabétisme : illiteracy
approvisionnement : supply
autochtone (adj., n.) : native
autonome : self-reliant
auto-suffisant : self-sufficient
auto-suffisance : self-sufficiency

bénévolat : voluntary work
bénévole (adj.) : voluntary
bénévole (n.) : voluntary help / worker, volunteer
bétail : livestock

campagne (d'alphabétisation) : literacy campaign
carence : deficiency
céréales : grain
coefficient d'endettement : debt ratio
contrôle des naissances : birth control
cultiver : grow (grew, grown), cultivate
cultures vivrières : food crops

démographie : demography
désert (adj.) : barren
développement (en voie de) : developing
dilapider : squander
don : donation
donateur : donor → donate (v.)
durée de vie : life span

écart : gap
élever (bétail) : breed, raise, rear
espérance de vie : life expectancy
exode : exodus
exode forcé : forced resettlement
explosion démographique : population explosion

faim : hunger, starvation
famille nombreuse : big family
famine : famine
fléau : plague → plague (v.)
fonds : funds → fund (v.)
fossé : gap

habitant : inhabitant

industrialisé : industrialised
inondation : flood
installations sanitaires : sanitation
installer (s') : settle
irriguer : irrigate

labourer : plough
logement : housing

main-d'œuvre bon marché : cheap labour
maladie : disease, illness
malnutrition : malnutrition
manque : lack → lack (v.)
manquer de nourriture : starve
maternité : childbearing, maternity
matière première : raw material
moisson : harvest → harvest (v.)

niveau de vie : standard of living
nourrir : feed (fed, fed)
nourrisson : new-born infant
nourriture de base : staple diet / food
Nouveaux Pays Industrialisés : Newly Industrialised Countries, NICs

organisation caritative : charity
organisation humanitaire : voluntary organisation
outil : tool

par habitant : per inhabitant, per capita
pâturage : grazing / pasture land
pays d'accueil : host country
pays débiteur : debtor country
pays en voie de développement : developing country
pénurie : shortage, dearth
pilule contraceptive : pill
planification démographique : population planning
point d'eau : water hole
pont aérien : air lift
précipitations (pluie) : rainfall
première nécessité (article de) : staple commodity
préservatif : condom
produits agricoles : farm produce
projet : plan, scheme
puits : well

rareté (pénurie) : scarcity
ration : ratio
récolte : crop → crop (v.)
recueillir (argent) : collect, raise
remboursement : repayment
rembourser : pay back, repay
ressortissant : national

sécheresse : drought
secours : relief
semer : sow
Sida : Aids
soins : care
sous-alimenté : underfed
surpeuplé : overpopulated

tiers monde : third world
troupeau : herd, flock

Unit 3 The environment

A few landmarks

After the 1992 Earth Summit in Rio de Janeiro, the World Summit on **Sustainable Development** (2002 in Johannesburg) brought together thousands of participants including heads of States and Governments, national delegates, NGOs leaders, businesses and other groups to improve people's lives and conserve our **natural resources**.

- Over 6bn people inhabit the earth, an increase of 140% over the past 50 years. By 2050, the earth's population is projected to rise to 9bn.
- One fifth of the world's people must survive on less than one dollar per day.
- About 1.1bn people lack access to **safe drinking water**. Contaminated drinking water and an inadequate supply of water account for 10% of all **diseases** in developing countries.
- **Infant mortality** is ten times higher in developing countries than in the industrialised world.
- In 1996, 25% of the world's 4,630 mammal **species** and 11% of the 9,675 bird species were at significant **risk of extinction**.

Some of the most important challenges facing the world today include:

- alleviating **poverty**, especially in rural communities where the majority of the world's poor live;
- improving the ability of all countries, particularly developing countries, to meet the challenges of **globalisation**, including greater capacity building and the transfer of financing and **environmentally-friendly technologies**;
- promoting responsible **consumption** and **production patterns** to reduce **waste** and over-reliance on natural resources;
- ensuring that all people have access to the **energy sources** needed to improve their lives;
- reducing **environment-related health problems** that account for many of the illnesses in the world today;
- improving access to clean water to reach those who today must rely on unsafe and unsanitary sources to raise their children and maintain their livelihoods.

From *The Johannesburg Summit 2002* brochure
(published by the United Nations department of public information)
and from www.johannesburgsummit.org

Portrait of a Beleaguered Planet

Two centuries of population growth and industrialization have taken a heavy toll on the environment.

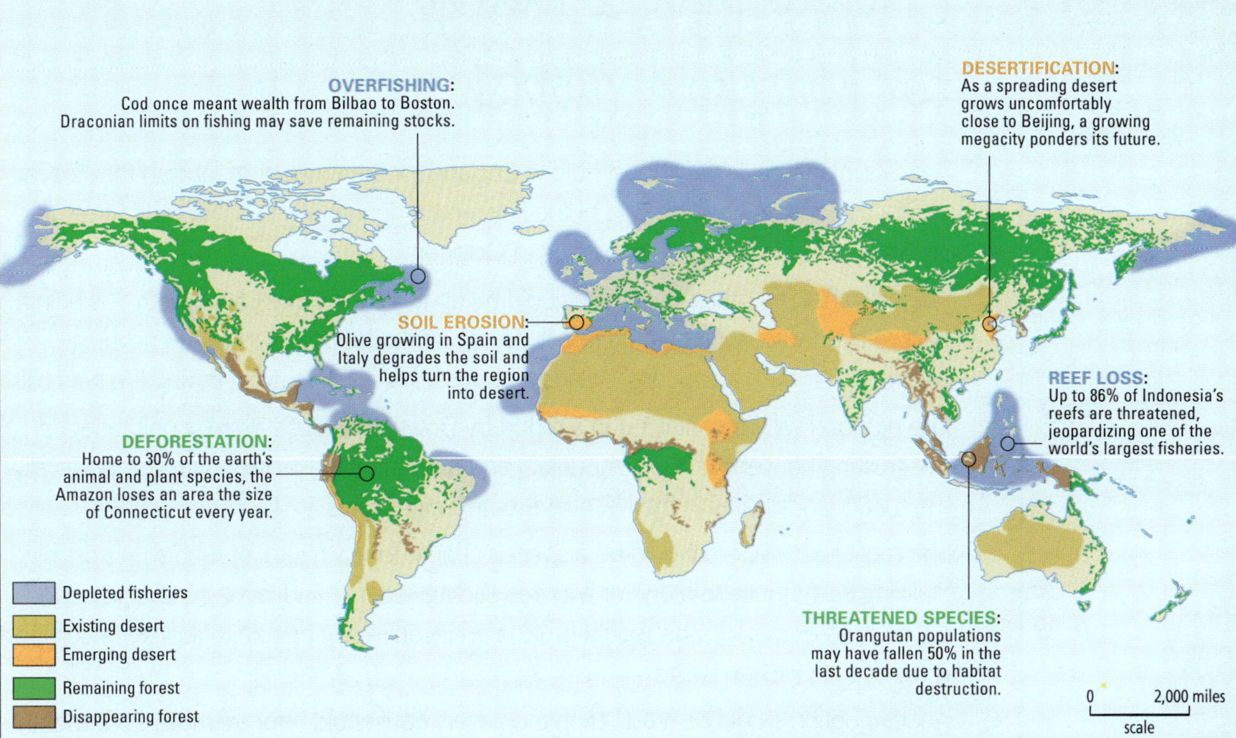

… And Those Who Live on It

Human health is directly related to that of the planet. Respiratory disease is exacterbated by airborne emissions. Millions of people are infected by contaminated water. Loss of arable land leads to malnutrition. Here's look at the trends:

Percentage of population undernourished

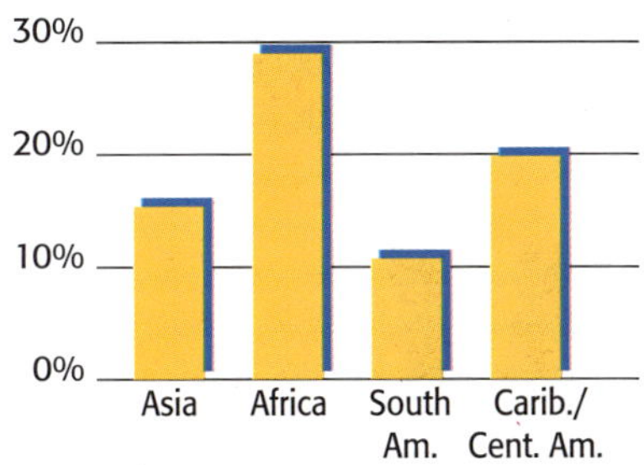

Carbon dioxide emissions per capita in 2000 (in metric tons)

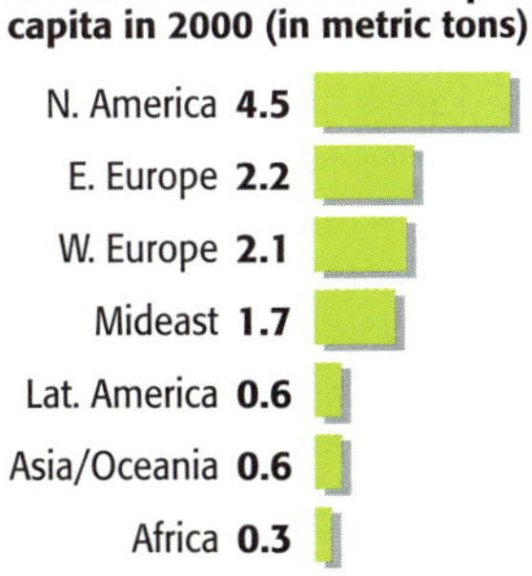

Respiratory deaths from indoor air pollution

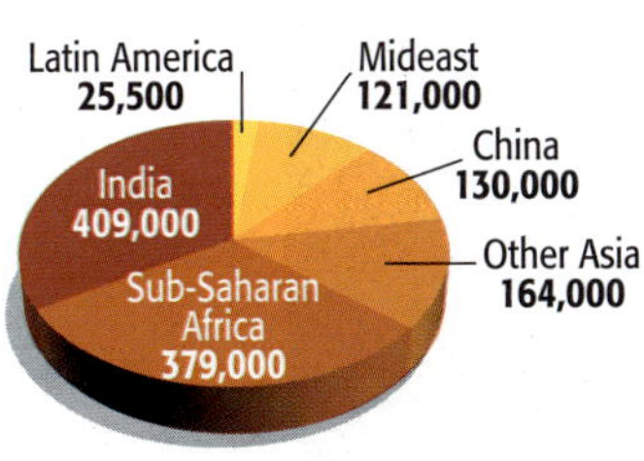

Newskeek, September 2002

Warm-up

Fauna and flora

1 • Name the main hazards Earth is faced with.

2 • Where can 30% of the world's flora and fauna be found?

3 • Is Connecticut about the size of Paris, of Ile-de-France or of France?

4 • In what country is Bilbao located?

5 • Where can we still find one of the biggest amount of fish on Earth?

6 • Which capital city is threatened by an approaching desert?

People

1 • What are the consequences of Earth's bad health on its inhabitants?

2 • Which group of countries is the heaviest polluter?

3 • Is it the hardest hit by pollution?

Unit 3

TEXT 1

1. **flat** = fixed
2. **bogus** = (here) illegal

No. 10 plan to charge for household rubbish

A radical plan to bill every household in England for the amount of rubbish they leave out for the dustman will be one of the key recommendations in a Downing Street report to tackle waste to be published in October.

The new charging scheme – which could be up to £1 a sack or £5 a month – is being backed by the Treasury. It would run alongside a free doorstep service to encourage people to recycle papers, cans, bottles and plastics in order to avoid paying the new bills.

The proposal will be contained in a report by Downing Street's strategy unit to tackle the growing household waste mountain and meet an EU directive to reduce drastically the 1,400 landfill sites in the UK over the next eight years. [...]

The most likely system would be a specific charge for each sack of rubbish – possibly allowing each household one or two free sacks a week – and levying a charge up to £1 on each extra sack. This would provide an incentive for people to recycle or compost more of their kitchen waste.

Another option would be a flat[1] charge on every household – for example, £5 a month – that filled up more than two sacks a week. [...]

A third possibility is to introduce weighing of wheelie bins in dustcarts resulting in charges for excess weight paid by the householder. Similar schemes have been piloted in Europe.

The government also wants tougher powers to discourage illegal dumping [...] involving a bigger role for the Environment Agency. A review of police powers to handle illegal dumping and prosecute people running bogus[2] landfill sites is under way.

From *The Guardian*, July 11, 2002.

© Réa / Tom Craig.

► Check your pronunciation

Which words are these?

1 • [kiː]
2 • [skiːm]
3 • [riːˈsaɪkl]
4 • [ˈjuːnɪt]
5 • [saɪts]
6 • [weɪst]
7 • [weɪɪŋ]
8 • [tʌfəʳ]

► Words

A • Find the equivalents of the verbs from the text.

1 • bill (l. 1)	a • dispose of
2 • tackle (l. 3)	b • collect
3 • back (l. 5)	c • turn rubbish into fertiliser
4 • levy (l. 11)	d • charge
5 • compost (l. 12)	e • take to court
6 • dump (l. 19)	f • control
7 • handle (l. 20)	g • support
8 • prosecute (l. 21)	h • deal with

B • Complete this short paragraph with words from the text.

A .... is somebody who collects .... from household .... with a .... The .... then either goes to a .... where it is buried or to a ....

► Meaning

A • Which is which?

1 • Is 10 Downing Street the equivalent of "l'Élysée" or of "Matignon"?
2 • Is a household a family or the people who live in the same place?
3 • Does "an incentive" (l. 12) mean a sum of money or an encouragement?

B • What word do "they" (l. 1) refer to?

C • Which of the statements are correct?

1 • The British government intends to charge the English for their household waste.
2 • This scheme goes against EU regulations.
3 • The EU wants the UK to cut the number of its landfill sites significantly within 8 years.
4 • The British scheme consists in billing each household for their domestic waste together with making them pay for the door-to-door service.

D • Complete this summary.

The scheme will adopt .... out of three possibilities.
First possibility: each household will pay .... for each sack of rubbish disposed of every .... from the .... sack.
Second possibility: from the third sack a week, each household will be charged £5 ....
Third possibility: dustcarts will be .... with weighing facilities, and if a household wheelie bin ...., the household will ....

E • Fill in a part of this article with *a / an, the* or Ø.

" .... report will also consider whether charging should be introduced at .... household waste tips – except where .... people are dumping .... rubbish for .... recycling – to reduce .... use of landfills. There may be no firm recommendation in favour of charging because of .... fears that it could add dramatically to .... illegal dumping in .... countryside.
.... proposals are likely to receive .... warm welcome from .... environmental groups."

F • Translate the last paragraph into French.

► Group work

Group **A** cares about household rubbish and explains its attitudes and motivations unlike group **B** who finds household recycling boring and time-consuming. Debate the issue.

► Food for thought

Which of the three possibilities given in the article suits you best? Develop your arguments and compare the English proposal with the situation in France or other countries. (250 words)

Unit 3
TEXT 2

Dust from the east plagues Korea

School was called off throughout much of this sprawling city the other day because of inclement weather. [...]

It was an immense cloud of dust that blew in from China's fast-spreading deserts, about 750 miles away.

It hid Seoul from view throughout the morning, obscuring the sunrise just as surely as the heaviest of fogs. Clinics overflowed with patients complaining of breathing problems, drugstores experienced a run on cough medicines and face masks that supposedly filter the air, and parks and outdoor malls were nearly empty of pedestrians. [...]

In Seoul, a measurement of 70 micrograms of dust per cubic meter of air is considered normal during most of the year. At 1,000 micrograms, experts say, serious health warnings are indicated. Earlier this month, in the fourth storm of the season, a record measurement of 2,070 micrograms was reached in this city. [...]

Scientists say the dust storms, which are distinctly visible on regional satellite weather maps as gigantic yellow blobs, are a result of the rapid desertification in China and a prolonged drought affecting that country and other parts of Northeast Asia. [...]

According to China's Environmental Protection Agency, the Gobi grew by 20,000 square miles from 1994 to 1999, and its steadily advancing edge[1] now sits a mere 150 miles north of Beijing. [...] China's environmental changes are accelerating because of overfarming, overgrazing and the widespread destruction of forests. [...]

As a mood of resignation has set in over the persistence of this phenomenon, Koreans have already begun to focus on the economic costs. What was only recently regarded here as a minor nuisance is now seen as posing a serious threat in areas as diverse as public health, travel, retail shopping and even high-tech manufacturing.

From *The New York Times* in *Le Monde*, April 21-22, 2002.

1. edge: *bord*

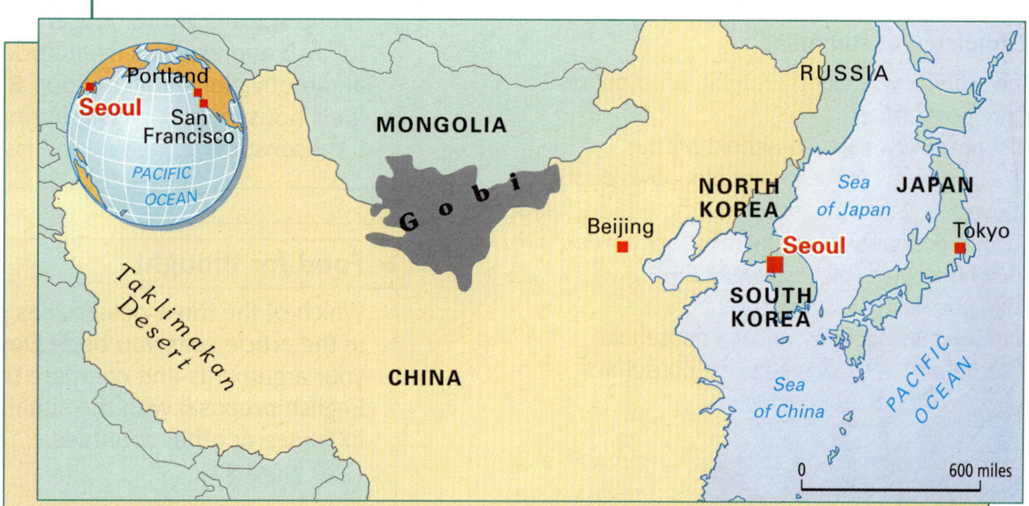

► Check your pronunciation

A • How do you pronounce "th" in the following words: [θ] or [ð]?

1 • throughout
2 • breathing
3 • health
4 • threat

B • Can you read these words aloud?

1 • [kɒf] 2 • [draʊt] 3 • ['nju:sns]

► Meaning

A • Give the correct answer.

1 • Schools were: empty / crowded /closed.
2 • The Korean dust cloud: comes from China / is spreading to China / is going to reach China soon.
3 • The cause(s) of dust storms in Korea is (are): blobs in China / desert-spreading in China / desert-spreading in China plus drought in northeast Asia and China.
4 • China's EPA:
tried to spread the Gobi desert in the late 1990s / said the Gobi desert isn't a threat / noted the threatening development of the Gobi desert.
5 • Which one is affected by these storms? Northeast Asia as a whole. / Only Seoul. / Only China.
6 • Koreans:
are used to dust storms / fight against dust storms every year / think this one is the last one.

B • What do these figures correspond to?

1 • 70 micrograms / m^3 of air
2 • 1,000 micrograms / m^3 of air
3 • 2,070 micrograms / m^3 of air

C • Fill in the blanks with the correct prepositions.

"Unlike West Africa's dust, which is carried ...... the southern United States ...... winds known as the tropical easterlies, dust ...... the Gobi and Taklimakan deserts ...... rapidly industrialising China is binding ...... toxic industrial pollutants, including arsenic, cadmium and lead, increasing the health threat."

D • How can we account for these dust storms? (30 words)

E • Detail the consequences of such storms on Seoul's inhabitants and the country's economy. (100 words)

► Words

Find the equivalents in the text of the following words.

1 • afflict (title)
2 • widespread (§1)
3 • shopping centres (§3)
4 • walkers (§3)
5 • shapeless forms (§5)
6 • regularly (§6)
7 • state of mind (§7)
8 • trouble (§7)

© AFP / STR.

► Pair work

A is a staunch conservationist whereas **B** is not ecologically-minded at all. They have just read the article and are having a conversation about it. Imagine their dialogue.

► Food for thought

After your visit to a friend in Seoul, you've been so shocked by the situation over there that you've decided to write to China's EPA. In your letter you expose the situation, complain about it and ask for drastic measures to be taken.

TEXT 3

Disposal plant opens in Wales

1. **liquid coolant:** *liquide de refroidissement*
2. **insulating casing:** *système d'isolation*
3. **foam:** *mousse*

A specially-designed "fridge eater" will start taking a bite out of the UK's fridge mountain today, with the opening of an advanced recycling plant in Wales.

SimsMetal switches on the country's first fixed plant for the safe disposal of old refrigerators at Newport docks, where 25,000 fridges are awaiting degassing – disposing of liquid coolant[1] – and removal of insulating casings[2].

Up to three million fridges are thrown out in this country each year, with recent European Union regulations imposing tough conditions on the disposal of ozone-depleting chlorofluorocarbon gas-based coolants, as well as insulation foam[3] containing CFCs.

© Dino Fracchia / Réa.

The new rules mean that fridges can no longer be dumped in landfill sites – leading to a stack-up of old ones as the UK lacked the capacity to comply with the EU regulations.

According to Simsmetal, at full capacity, the Newport plant will treat up to 300,000 old domestic and commercial refrigeration units a year. The plant uses special enclosed "fridge eaters" which crush the insulating casing to extract the CFCs in liquid form, so it can be destroyed in an environmentally-friendly manner.

From *The Guardian*, July 1, 2002.

► Words

A • Match the equivalents.

1 • plant (title)
2 • take a bite out of (l. 1)
3 • switch on (l. 3)
4 • await (l. 4)
5 • regulations (l. 7)
6 • tough (l. 7)
7 • stack-up (l. 11)
8 • comply with (l. 12)

a • rules
b • wait for
c • eat
d • factory
e • pile
f • respect
g • open
h • strict

B • Is Wales part of England, Britain and / or the United Kingdom?

► Meaning

A • Give the correct answer when necessary and justify it in your own words.

1 • SimsMetal is located in England.
2 • The plant has already recycled 25,000 old fridges.
3 • The British have thrown away 3 million fridges over the years.
4 • The EU has implemented strict rules on the recycling of CFCs.
5 • This is because they destroy the ozone layer.
6 • The EU encourages the UK to bury their old fridges in landfill sites.
7 • As the UK couldn't be in accordance with the EU rules, the fridges have been piled up in dumping grounds.
8 • SimsMetal's minimum fridge recycling rate will amount to 300,000 a year.
9 • SimsMetal's fridge eaters are environmentally-minded.

B • Consider the following phrases: "a specially-designed fridge eater" (l. 1), "ozone-depleting CFCs" (l. 8) and "gas-based coolants" (l. 8). Then, using these patterns, rewrite the phrases below.

1 • a plant based in Wales
2 • a device that degasses safely
3 • an issue known by everybody
4 • a task that takes time

C • Answer in your own words.

1 • Why do CFC-containing devices need special care for recycling?
2 • Why in your opinion does the EU ban the dumping of fridges in landfill sites?

D • Translate the first two paragraphs into French.

Checkup Unit 3

1 ► Test

In debt to the Earth, and we can't repay

Humanity is overdrawn at the Earth's resource bank and is going further into debt every year, according to research.

A detailed study by environmental experts shows that we are using more of the Earth's resources than is sustainable and have been doing so since the 1980s.

The international experts calculated that while in 1961 we were using only 70 per cent of the Earth's regenerative capacity, we reached parity by the mid-1970s and by 1999 were using 25 per cent more than could be regenerated. The 1999 figure means the Earth needs 15 months to replenish what humans take out of the biosphere every year. "We haven't reached the point of no return yet," said Valerie Kapos, a senior advisor at UNEP-WCMC, the United Nations' conservation monitoring project. "But we're heading that way and have been ever since we crossed that line [in the 1970s]."

The net effect is that natural resources are wearing out because they cannot be replaced by biological processes. That applies to such essentials as arable land, grazing areas, timber, fish, "infrastructure", and fossil and nuclear fuels.

The only solutions are to use less resources or to find "eco-technologies", which can help restock resources more quickly. [...]

Promising technologies to reverse the trend include those to generate renewable energy from biomass or solar power because they do not require fossil fuel, which need land mass to absorb their effects. By far the biggest increase in demand since 1961 has been for energy, which has doubled, while demand for crop land and grazing land has remained almost flat.

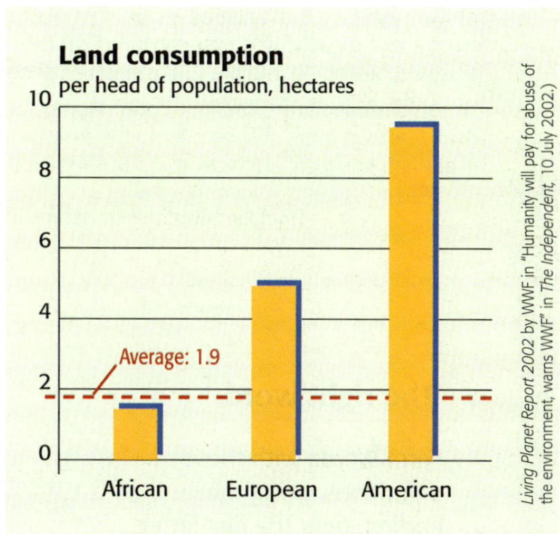

From *The Independent,* 26 June 2002.

A • Which vocabulary register is used in the title and in paragraphs 1 and 3? What for? (30 words)

B • Complete the table with elements from the text.

Dates	Use of ...
....	70%
mid-70s	....
....	over 100%
1999	....

C • Sum up the article. (50 words)

D • Comment on the chart. (60 words)

E • Translate the last two paragraphs.

2 ► Skills in practice

Total daily power usage of inkjet printers

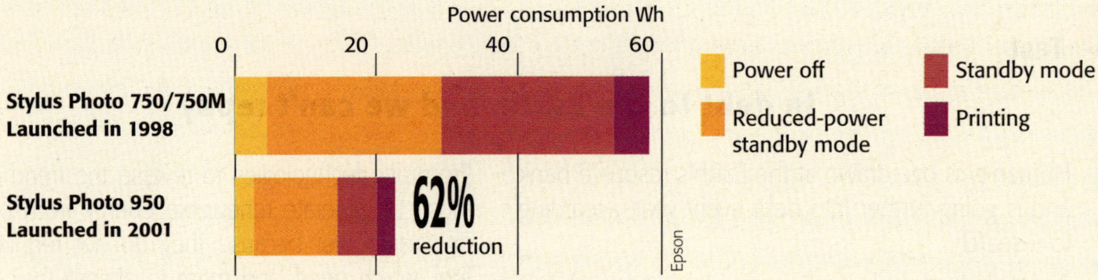

Imai [an engineer] and other engineers started by drawing up a set of criteria for determining how much electricity a typical printer used in a day. They decided to look at a small office/home office (SOHO) setting, where the printer was always plugged into the power but only switched on for eight hours a day. They also decided the ratio of black-and-white to colour printing would be 60:40 and 15 print jobs of two pages each constituted a typical amount of usage. Then they went about measuring power consumption over a full 24-hour period. This was broken up into the four categories shown in [the graph].

"If you think about the saving in Japan alone, it's quite significant. If 1.11 million users change over to the new model, the power saved is enough to supply electricity to 3,200 homes for a month," he says.

From the advertisement section of *Time,* September 2, 2002.

A • What does the graph represent?

B • What does "Wh" stand for?

C • Give the criteria Imai and his team took for their study.

D • Compare the four stages of the two printers.

E • What can the consequences of this technological evolution be?

3 ► The right word

A • Form words with these definitions, using the ending *-tion*; the first letter of each word is given.

1 • planting trees (a)
2 • turning lands into deserts (d)
3 • preserving the environment (c)
4 • purchasing and using goods (c)
5 • clearing forests of trees (d)
6 • building and growing towns in rural areas (u)

B • Fill in the blanks with the following words.

biodiversity / carbon dioxide / environmentalists / exhaust fumes / extinction / greenhouse effect / oil spill / pollutants / preservatives / recycling / scourges / water table

1 • Noise is one of the .... of our civilisation.
2 • Ozone depletion and the .... directly threaten man.
3 • The .... of paper is more and more encouraged.
4 • The variety of plants and animals that exist in nature is called ....
5 • The .... try to fight air pollution and water pollution among others.
6 • Lots of Australian mammals are facing ....
7 • Pesticides and chemical fertilisers are ....
8 • The .... is the level of water in the Earth.
9 • The .... that come from cars are extremely noxious for our lungs as they release ....
10 • This orange juice is without artificial colouring or ....
11 • An .... occurs when an oil tanker has an accident or cleans its tanks in the open sea.

4 ► Vocabulary

articles à jeter après usage : disposables

centrale nucléaire : nuclear power plant (US) / station (GB)
cheminée d'usines : smokestacks
conservateur : preservative
conteneur à verre : glass container
couche d'ozone : ozone layer
couche d'ozone (réduction de la) : ozone depletion

danger : danger, hazard
débarrasser de (se) : dispose of, get (got, got) rid of
déboisement : deforestation
décharge publique : dumping ground, rubbish tip, rubbish heap, rubbish dump
déchets nucléaires : nuclear waste [U]
dégâts : damage (U)
détergent : detergent
déversement de produits toxiques dans l'océan : ocean dumping
durable : sustainable

eau potable : drinking water
eaux usées : servage
écologique (qui a l'esprit) : ecologically-minded
écologiste : ecologist
économie d'énergie : power / energy saving, energy conservation
économique en carburant : fuel-efficient
effet de serre : greenhouse effect
élimination des ordures : waste disposal
emballage à jeter : throwaway packaging
emballages vides : empties
empoisonner : poison
énergie (nouvelles sources d') : alternative sources of energy
enfouir : bury
engrais : fertilizer
environnement (défenseur de l') : environmentalist, conservationist
équilibre : balance
érosion des sols : land erosion
espèce disparue : extinct species
espèce en voie de disparition : species threatened with extinction
essence sans plomb : lead-free petrol (GB), lead-free gas (US), unleaded gasoline (US)

fléau : plague, scourge

gaz carbonique : carbon dioxide
gaz d'échappement : exhaust fumes
gaz toxiques : noxious gases

incinérateur à ordures : garbage-burning incinerator (US), refuse destructor

marée noire : oil spill, black tide
menacer : threaten
mesures préventives : prevention
mettre en danger : endanger, jeopardise
mortel : lethal

nappe phréatique : water table
normes réglementant les rejets : emission standards
nucléaires (anti-) : antinuke people
nucléaires (pro-) : pronuke people
nuire à : harm

ordures : litter [U], refuse [U], rubbish [U], waste [U], garbage (US) [U], trash (US) [U]
ordures (jeter des) : litter
ordures ménagères : household waste / refuse / garbage (US)
ordures (recyclage des) : waste recycling
ordures (traitement des) : waste processing

pesticides : pesticides
pétrol brut : crude oil
pluies acides : acid rains
polluant : pollutant
polluer : pollute
pot catalytique : catalytic converter
poubelle : trash can (US), dustbin, garbage can (US), refuse bin, rubbish bin
produit chimique : chemical

réchauffement de la terre : global warning
récupération des déchets : waste salvage
recyclage : recycling

station d'épuration : sewage works

usine de retraitement : treatment plant

Unit 4

Travelling and tourism

A few landmarks

Whether for **business** or for **leisure**, when we **travel** we have to **book** or reserve a hotel room, a transport ticket or a tour.

Thus, several possibilities are offered. We can:

- go to a **travel agency** whose **travel agent** will arrange **transport** and **tours / trips** for us. The travel agent will usually contact a **tour operator** that will sell him a trip or a **package holiday / tour** with or without transport. If no transport is offered, the travel agent will contact a **carrier**, for example an airline company, a railway company or a ferry company to organise our **journey**, to which can be added **car rental**;
- call on a tour operator directly for a journey only and / or for package holidays;
- contact a carrier directly if we just need a transport ticket;
- make any booking through a **central reservation system** run by travel agencies or tour operators;
- **book online**, i.e. reserve our journey and / or trip or holiday through the web sites of travel agencies, tour operators and carriers.

According to what they do, travellers / travelers (US) on holiday / vacation (US) are called **holidaymakers, tourists, sightseers or visitors**; if they travel for their jobs, they can be called **business trippers** or visitors. That applies to trips in their **home countries** or to a stay in a **host country** for a while.

And remember: **"Travelling broadens the mind,"** as they say.

© Greg Stott / Masterfile.

Warm-up

1 • Try to guess where these photos were taken.

2 • What are the people doing?

3 • Which trip could suit you best? Why?

© C. & A. Purcelle / Corbis.

© GettyImages / Taxi / Kaz Chiba.

© Randy Faris / Corbis.

© GettyImages / Stone / Anthony Cassidy.

Unit 4

TEXT 1

1. **surgery:** *chirurgie*

2. **loose shards of fat** = rolls of fat

Low-cost surgery[1] and safaris draw tourists to South Africa

Nearly 19,000 more tourists visited South Africa in January than did a year earlier, and travel agents, hotel managers, car rental agencies and restaurants have all reported dramatic increases in business since the end of last year.

Visitors from Europe account for the bulk of the increase; overseas arrivals from Britain and Germany have risen by more than 14 percent this year. [...]

Recognising that South Africa was uniquely qualified to capitalise on a niche market, Lorraine Melvill started her company, Surgery and Safari, two years ago. Working with local plastic surgeons, L. Melvill put up a Web site and now organises vacation packages and surgical consultations for five or six well-off professionals from the United States and Europe each week. Several competitors have followed. [...]

Price is what initially piqued the interest of Regina Housley of Southern California. Forty-seven and divorced, the graying biologist was beginning to notice loose shards of fat[2] on her legs and arms, but couldn't bring herself to spend the $10,000 that a surgeon back home estimated it would cost for a facelift and liposuction.

© Gamma / Mark Graham.

Housley read about Melvill's company in a travel magazine and went online to do research. She picked up the phone. Melvill put her in touch with a cosmetic surgeon. For about $11,000, Housley got the facelift and liposuction she wanted, plus airfare, two days on safari and nearly a week of shopping and relaxation, all the while staying at one of Johannesburg's most exclusive hotels.

"It was all first-rate," she said. [...] "The doctors took their time and explained everything to me, and Lorraine caters to your every need. I'm really looking forward to going home. I really want to wear a swimsuit this summer."

Jedeikin, the Cape Town surgeon, said that 50 percent of his patients are from abroad now, compared with less than 10 percent four years ago.

From *The Guardian Weekly*, June 20-26, 2002.

► Check your pronunciation

How do you pronounce letter "a" in the following words: [a:], [æ] or [eɪ]?

1 • sa'f<u>a</u>ris
2 • 'Afric<u>a</u>
3 • 'tr<u>a</u>vel
4 • '<u>a</u>gents
5 • 'm<u>a</u>nagers
6 • c<u>a</u>r
7 • '<u>a</u>gencies
8 • 'm<u>a</u>rket
9 • va'c<u>a</u>tion
10 • 'p<u>a</u>ckages

► Words

Pick out the equivalents in the article of the following words.

1 • major part (§2)
2 • package tours (§3)
3 • wealthy (§3)
4 • return plane ticket (§5)
5 • classy (§5)
6 • provide for (§6)
7 • be eager to (§6)

► Meaning

A • **Translate into French.** (see T&T: **Comparatives / superlatives**)

1 • *Il y a beaucoup plus de touristes qu'il n'y en avait il y a 10 ans.*
2 • *Il y a beaucoup moins de touristes qu'avant.*
3 • *Elle a payé beaucoup plus.*
4 • *Les Européens sont les plus nombreux.*
5 • *Entre les Américains et les Australiens, les Américains sont les moins nombreux.*

B • **With the help of the following elements, make complete sentences using the present, present perfect or preterite tenses.** (see T&T: **Present / Present perfect / Preterite**)

1 • South Africa's "medical tourism" industry / significantly grow recently
2 • He / decide to try his luck last year
3 • The plastic surgeons / be first-rate / and the animals / be exotic
4 • I / feel so much better since I / come back
5 • They / be told to come for the surgery and stay for the scenery.

C • **Right or wrong? Justify in your own words when necessary.**

1 • Fewer tourists went to South Africa in January 2001 than in January 2002.
2 • The tourism industrialists have been alarmed by the sharp decrease in tourists since late 2001.
3 • The rise in tourists is mainly due to Europeans.
4 • However, the British and the Germans are those who mainly stay at home.
5 • The number of Jedeikin's foreign patients has skyrocketed by more than 40% since 1998.

D • **Explain the history of Lorraine Melvill's company in your own words. (60 words)**

E • **Draw up Regina Housley's file.**

– Place of residence: ....
– Age: ....
– Marital status: ....
– Job: ....
– Her problem: ....
– How she got in touch with Lorraine Melvill: ....
– Result: ....
– Personal comment: ....

F • **Translate the title into French.**

► Group work

Student **A** is Regina Housley, student **B** Lorraine Melvill, student **C** Jedeikin the surgeon. Imagine the phone conversation they are having – including the organisation of the stay – just after Regina has found Lorraine's phone number.

► Food for thought

What would your ideal type of holiday be? (250 words)

Fit for DIY?

1. **squeeze:** *coincer*
2. **climb on (to) the bandwagon:** *prendre le train en marche*

Travel agents have been around at least since Thomas Cook organised his first tours abroad in 1855. But today they are under threat. Squeezed[1] on one side by the urgent desire of airlines and hotels to cut costs, and on the other by the enthusiasm of consumers for "disintermediation" – cutting out middlemen by using the Internet – they are between a rock and a hard place. [...]

Both business and leisure travellers are shifting from online browsing to online buying. The low-cost carriers that have become so familiar, particularly at European airports, have pioneered the direct selling of tickets via their websites. For instance, easyJet, a successful British low-cost carrier, now sells 90% of its seats through its own site.

Hotels are also discovering that the web can be a powerful and cheap distribution channel, and not just an online brochure. [...]

Traditional offline agents are themselves struggling to climb on to the Internet bandwagon[2]. [...]

There is no doubt that the travel business is rapidly moving online. More than 15% of all leisure travel in America is already booked online, and a recent survey by Accenture, a consulting firm, found that 60% of American consumers planning to fly this year intend to book their travel electronically. Fewer than a quarter intend to use a traditional agent. [...]

The profusion of online offers leaves plenty of opportunity for intermediaries to add value for corporate and leisure travellers by steering them in the right direction. To do that, though, they need to become more like professional-services firms, rather than second-hand car dealers. The travel-agency system of the future will be based on helping customers to buy what they want, not on helping suppliers to flog what they've got.

From *The Economist,* June 1st, 2002.

D.R.

► Check your pronunciation

Find these words in the text:

1 • [ˈkæriəʳ] 3 • [paɪəˈnɪəʳd] 5 • [ˈvaɪə]
2 • [klaɪm] 4 • [kwɔːtəʳ] 6 • [ˈvæljuː]

► Words

A • What does DIY stand for?

B • Match the equivalents.

1 • fit (title)
2 • middlemen (l. 4)
3 • struggle (l. 13)
4 • move (l. 15)
5 • intend (l. 18)
6 • steer (l. 24)
7 • though (l. 25)
8 • second-hand (l. 28)
9 • flog (l. 32)

a • used
b • try hard
c • intermediaries
d • however
e • sell
f • go
g • guide
h • ready
i • plan

C • Find the opposites in the text of the following words.

1 • package tour
2 • raise
3 • unpopular
4 • expensive
5 • lack
6 • little
7 • cut

D • Make two- word compounds with the following elements. Some elements can be used several times. (see T&T: Compound nouns)

1 • agent
2 • browsing
3 • business
4 • buying
5 • car
6 • dealer
7 • leisure
8 • offer
9 • offline
10 • travel
11 • traveller

► Meaning

A • What do they refer to?

1 • "they" (l. 2)
2 • "Squeezed" (l. 2)
3 • "they" (l. 5)
4 • "have pioneered" (l. 8)
5 • "intend" (l. 18)
6 • "Fewer than a quarter" (l. 18)
7 • "them" (l. 24)
8 • "that" (l. 25)
9 • "they" (l. 25)
10 • "they" (l. 31)
11 • "they" (l. 32)

B • Consider "by" in the article and indicate each time if it introduces the agent of a sentence in the passive form or if it is a preposition of means.

1 • "… by the urgent desire of …" (l. 2)
2 • "… by the enthusiasm of …" (l. 3)
3 • "… by using the Internet" (l. 4)
4 • "… by Accenture" (l. 17)
5 • "… by steering them …" (l. 23)

C • Translate into English.

1 • *J'ai trouvé votre site en surfant sur Internet.*
2 • *J'ai été informé de votre site web par un article de presse.*
3 • *Une nouvelle politique des prix a été lancée par les agences de voyages.*
4 • *Tu gagneras du temps en allant chez un agent de voyages.*
5 • *Que ce soit pour des courtes ou longues distances, elle préfère voyager en avion.*

D • Answer the questions in your own words.

1 • How long have travel agents existed?
2 • What are the two threats travel agents are facing today?
3 • What is the new trend regarding buying travel? Who is concerned?
4 • How is it made easy?

E • Explain in your own words what the figures correspond to.

1 • 90%
2 • 15%
3 • 60%
4 • 1/4

F • Read l. 20 ("The profusion of online offers leaves plenty of opportunity") and say where the subject and the verb are.

G • Translate the last paragraph into French.

► Pair work

A is enthusiastic about online travel booking whereas **B** prefers traditional travel agents. Imagine their conversation. (see T&T: Likes / Dislikes / Agreement / Disagreement / Preference)

► Food for thought

Traditional travel agencies are bound to close down. Comment. (250 words)

Chequing in

1. **doss house:** *asile de nuit*
2. **shareholder:** *actionnaire*

According to the *Which? Hotel Guide 2002,* British hotels are the most expensive in Europe, from the lowliest doss house[1] up (see chart). The situation is especially bad in London, where a shortage of hotel rooms, coupled with strong demand, keeps prices sky-high. "You can find a good individual hotel in the middle of Paris for €60 a night," says Patricia Yates, co-editor of the *Which? Hotel Guide,* "but I wouldn't like to try to find one at that price in London – or to have to stay there."

The strength of the pound is often blamed. VAT is certainly a factor: at 17.5% it is second highest in Europe, after Denmark. Elsewhere it hovers between 3% and 10%. But any independent hotelier will tell you that it is above all the cost of property that accounts for the scarcity of well-designed, moderately priced, owner-run hotels in central London. [...]

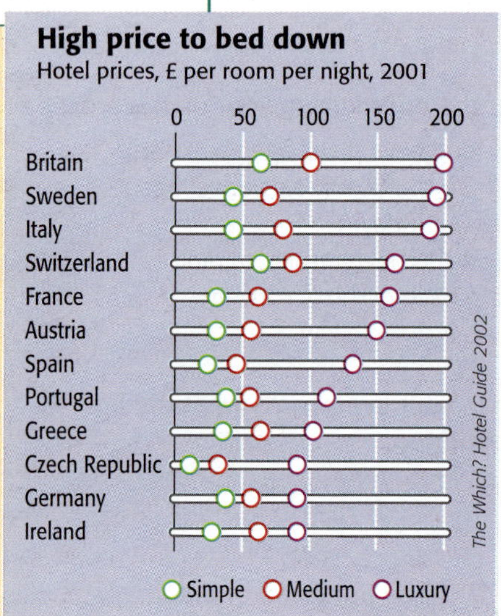

No wonder, then, that most London hotels are run by multinational chains. Continental Europe, by contrast, still has a strong tradition of independent hotels, many of which remain in the same family for generations, and can thus operate with a lot less pressure from bank managers or shareholders[2].

From *The Economist,* July 6th, 2002.

► Words

A • What does VAT stand for?

B • Find the translation of these words in the text.

1 • *pénurie* (2 words): ....
....
2 • *exorbitant :* ....
3 • *accuser :* ....
4 • *osciller :* ....
5 • *avant tout :* ....
6 • *gérer :* ....

► Meaning

A • Which of these statements are false? Justify your answers in your own words.

1 • The dearest European hotels are to be found in Britain.
2 • The cheapest and most uncomfortable British hotels are the most expensive ones in Europe.
3 • The worst area in Great Britain for finding a hotel is London.
4 • The only cause is that there aren't enough hotels there, considering the demand.
5 • A chain hotel room at €60 per night can be found in the centre of Paris.
6 • Patricia Yates doesn't even want to look for such hotels in London.

B • In 100 words, give an account of the situation described in paragraph 1 with the help of exercise A.

C • Explain Ms Yates' remark about hotels in London. (35 words)

D • Translate paragraphs two and three into French.

E • Explain the pun in the title.

F • Make as many varied sentences as you can with comparatives and superlatives to comment on the chart. (see T&T: Comparatives / superlatives)

Checkup Unit 4

1 ► Test

Tour operators fly into low-cost zone

Stung by slackened demand for package tours and a trend toward do-it-yourself vacations, big travel companies are using their massive charter airplane fleets to get a piece of the price-sensitive market so successfully tapped by Europe's booming low-cost carriers. Tour operators are broadening their traditional customer base – purchasers of package vacations – to go after travelers willing to buy "seat only" tickets on charter aircraft. [...]

Low-cost carriers in many ways have beaten the charter companies at their own game. Budget airlines fly to many of the same short-haul destinations and follow a similar mode of operating: pack people in, keep on-board service to a minimum and get aircraft in the skies as often as possible. Marketing themselves as budget alternatives to major airlines, the low-cost carriers rely on tricks pioneered by the charter firms to operate more cheaply than traditional carriers. Specifically, they fly from smaller airports at hours that aren't always the most convenient.

Europe's charter fleets, however, have evolved dramatically since the days of the once-a-week flight in the middle of the night. And now their frequencies and timetables don't differ greatly from those of many scheduled carriers. [...]

Tour operators sell their seat-only tickets much like other airlines – through their own travel agents and through third-party agents – over the Internet and more recently through electronic reservation systems.

Budget airlines see only a minor threat from tour operators moving more aggressively into the seat-only business. "We're not too worried about them. Our customers need the full flexibility and schedule that we can offer and we don't see a tour operator as being able to provide that kind of service," says Samantha Day, a spokeswoman for easyJet.

Some industry analysts say tour operators could do themselves more harm than good by straying too far from their basic business model. The charter-flight model is built for travelers with itineraries structured around a one-week or two-week gap between each leg of a round-trip flight; the model isn't geared to the shorter and more impulsive journeys that the low-cost carriers serve. [...]

[Tour operators] say the seat-only business will never replace their core business. And they say they have learnt plenty about accommodating seat-only clients as demand for more flexible service, and for seat without package tours, has grown in recent years.

In addition to selling their seat-only tickets directly, tour operators have begun working with one of the cornerstones of the broader airline business: central reservation systems. Formerly limited to their own retail-distribution systems – tour operators – by paying standard booking fees that reservations systems charge airlines, they can now sell their charter flights alongside the services offered by bigger carriers.

From *The Wall Street Journal Europe*, June 11, 2002.

A • Translate the first two paragraphs into French.

B • Give an account of this article in English. (150 words)

C • What would you rather book: a package tour or a seat-only plane ticket for DIY holidays? Develop your arguments. (200 words)

2 ► Skills in practice

A • Where do the planes take off?

B • Are the flight prices for single or for return tickets?

C • How much is a return flight to Glasgow?

D • What's the name of the airlines company that will take you to Belfast?

E • How much will it cost you for a night at the Buchanan Hotel in Glasgow with a return flight?

F • You and your boyfriend / girlfriend can afford a £300 trip and you want to go to Edinburgh and stay there one night. Is it possible? If not, is another destination possible?

G • You would like more information on car rental. What do you have to do? Why?

Your Country Needs You!

FLIGHTS

Flights depart London, price including tax from		
Belfast	bmi british midland	£58
Edinburgh	bmi british midland	£68
Glasgow	bmi british midland	£68
Manchester	bmi british midland	£69
Newcastle	British Airways	£68

HOTELS

Hotels per room, per night including tax from			
Belfast	Fitzwilliam International Hotel	4★	£96
Edinburgh	Radisson SAS Airth Castle Hotel	4★	£91
Glasgow	The Buchanan Hotel	3★	£76
London	K&K George Hotel	4★	£96
Manchester	Gardens Hotel	3★	£66
Newcastle	Royal Station Hotel	3★	£82

CAR HIRE

UK car hire from £20.
Plus free cancellation for all rental until the end of the year.

The Expedia Deal Hunter finds great deals.

Expedia.co.uk
Everything for Travel

Flights are return, per person and include pre-paid taxes. Hotel prices are per room and in approx. GBP and include pre-paid taxes. Car hire includes £5 online discount. Offers subject to availability. Terms and conditions apply. See www.expedia.co.uk for details.

© *The Observer*, May 19th 2002.

3 ► The right word

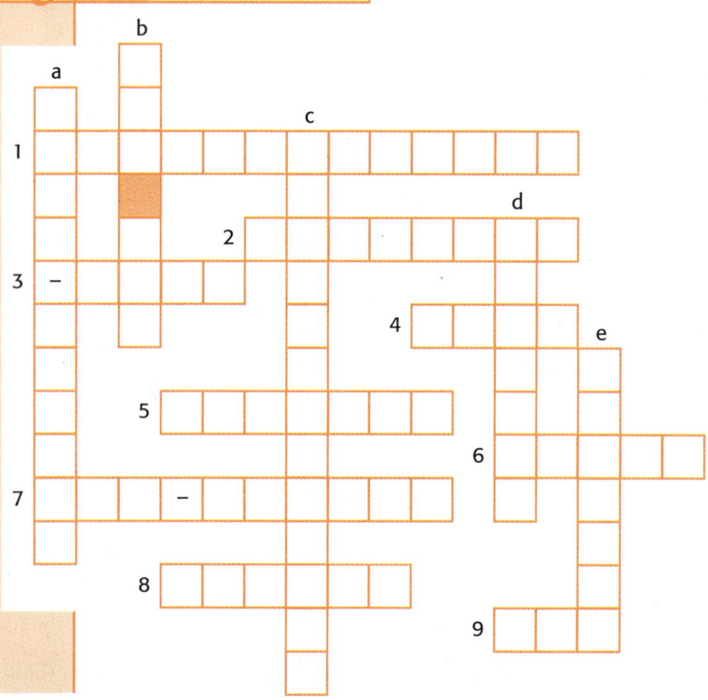

A • Crossword

Across

1 • That provides people with amusement.
2 • List of times.
3 • Excessively developed tourism.
4 • It can be a business or a leisure one.
5 • Places where tourists stay by the sea or for skiing.
6 • Itinerary.
7 • Period when there are few tourists.
8 • Trip by sea with stops.
9 • Arranged by yourself.

Down

a • Period when tourism reaches its climax.
b • Consequence of time difference.
c • Lodging, food and services.
d • Time for relaxation.
e • Distance covered to go somewhere.

B • List six means of transport we can take for travelling quite a long distance.

C • Can you enumerate four types of places to stay the night for low-budget travellers?

4 ► Vocabulary

agence de voyages : travel agency
animation (des loisirs) : entertainment
animaux non admis : no pets
annuler : cancel
arrivée : arrival
atterrissage : landing
autocar : coach

bagage : luggage [U], baggage (US) [U]
billet : ticket
billet aller-retour : return ticket, round-trip ticket (US)
boutique hors taxes : duty-free shop

chambre : (bed)room
chambre à deux lits : double room
chambre à un lit : single room
chambre avec douche : bedroom with shower
chambre avec petit déjeuner / chez l'habitant : bed and breakfast, B&B
circuit touristique : round-trip excursion
classe : class
classe touriste : economy class, tourist class
complet : booked up, fully booked
confort (tout) : with all modern amenities, with all modern conveniences
correspondance : connection
correspondance d'avion : connecting flight
couchette : sleeping berth

décalage horaire : jet lag
décollage : takeoff
départ : departure
douane : customs
douane (passer la) : go through the customs
douanier : customs officer

embarquement : boarding
embarquement (carte d') : boarding card
enregistrement (à l'aéroport) : check-in
équipements : facilities
escale : stopover
escale (faire) : break a journey at, stop over at (US), stop off at (US)

étranger (adj.) : foreign
étranger (n.) : foreigner
étranger (à l') : abroad, overseas
excédent de bagages : luggage excess

facultatif : optional
fuseau horaire : time zone, time belt

guichet : counter, desk
guichet d'enregistrement : check-in counter

heure limite d'occupation d'une chambre : check-out time
horaire : schedule
hôtel : hotel

itinéraire : route, itinerary

ligne aérienne : airline
liste d'attente : stand-by list
location saisonnière : holiday let, vacation rental (US)
logement : accommodation
loisir : leisure [U]
louer : rent, let (let, let)

occupation : occupancy
occupation (taux d') : occupancy rate

passeport : passport
pension complète : full board
pension de famille : guest house, boarding house
place : seat
plate-forme de retrait des bagages : luggage claim, baggage counter (US)
porte (aéroport) : gate
prendre (train, avion, etc.) : catch (caught, caught)
prix forfaitaire : package price

quai (bateau) : quay
quai (train) : platform
quitter (une chambre) : vacate, check out

réservation : reservation
réserver : book, reserve
retard (adj.) : late
retard (n.) : delay
retarder : delay
retarder (pour une montre) : put back

saison : season
saison (basse) : off season
saison (haute) : peak season
saison (morte) : slack season, low season
saison (pleine) : high season
saisonnier : seasonal
situation (emplacement) : location, situation
station balnéaire : seaside resort
station de sports d'hiver : mountain resort, ski resort, winter resort
supplément : extra cost
syndicat d'initiative : tourist information centre, tourist board

tarif : tariff
tarif (demi-) : half terms
tarif (plein) : full fare
tarif tout compris : all-in tariff
taux de change : exchange rate
taxe : tax
traversée maritime : crossing
TVA comprise : VAT included
TVA non comprise : exclusive of VAT

vacances : holidays, vacations (US)
vacances (être en) : be on holiday / vacation
vacancier : holidaymaker
valise : suitcase
visa : visa
visite guidée : sightseeing tour
vol : flight
vol charter : charter flight
vol direct : direct flight
vol régulier : scheduled flight
voyage : journey
voyage à forfait : package tour
voyage d'affaires : business trip
voyage d'agrément : trip
voyage de stimulation : incentive trip
voyage en car : coach tour
voyage organisé : package holiday
voyage sur mer (traversée) : voyage
voyagiste : tour operator

wagon : carriage

Unit 5 The European Union

A few landmarks

- **1951:** The Treaty of Paris establishes the **European Coal and Steel Community (ECSC)**. Britain refuses to take part.
- **25 March 1957: The Treaty of Rome** is signed by Germany, France, Italy, the Netherlands, Belgium and Luxembourg. It adds the **European Atomic Energy Community (Euratom)** and the **European Economic Community (EEC)** to the ECSC.
- **1973: Britain**, along with Ireland and Denmark, formally joins the EEC.
- **February 1992:** Signing of the **Maastricht Treaty** formalises the path to a single currency.
- **January 1, 1999:** The **Euro** comes into effect.

The 15-member European Union's principal institutions are the **European Community**, the **Council of Ministers** (its forum for individual ministries), the **European Commission** (its administrative bureaucracy), the **European Parliament**, and the **European Court of Justice**.

Warm-up

- **The front of each of these one-euro coins has a common design for the 12 countries in the euro area. The reverse side displays different designs. Can you describe them?**

Austria

Belgium

Finland

France

Germany

Greece

Ireland

Italy

Luxembourg

The Netherlands

Portugal

Spain

Unit 5

TEXT 1

Money go round

1. **bland** = dull and uninteresting

[…] Here's a positive thought about the single currency: it can be fun!

The banknotes, it's true, are bland[1], biliously coloured and faceless.

Having 12 different sets of coins in circulation on the other hand makes your small change interesting. […] It was a smart move to put the common symbol on one side and a national image on the flip side of the eight denominations: Ireland's Celtic harp, Italy's Marcus Aurelius, France's Marianne, etc.

Six months since the great E-day changeover, Amsterdam University mathematicians have done some sums. Using purse-content analysis to track patterns of diffusion, they discovered that one in four euro coins in Belgium is already non-Belgian. In a year, half the coins in the Netherlands will be from elsewhere in Euroland.

Geographically peripheral Ireland, Portugal and Greece are likely to remain numismatically homogeneous for longer. But because of Germany's sheer size, its coins will eventually dominate the Eurozone.

From *The Guardian Weekly*, June 20-26, 2002.

► Check your pronunciation

A • Check your pronunciation of the following words.

1 • currency
2 • coins
3 • Celtic
4 • peripheral
5 • numismatically
6 • homogeneous

B • Can you stress the right syllable in:

1 • Belgium
2 • Germany
3 • Greece
4 • Ireland
5 • Italy
6 • the Netherlands
7 • Portugal

► Words

A • **Give the correct definitions.**

1 • "Coins" (l. 3) are:
small pieces of metal used as money / small corners / small banknotes

2 • "The flip side" (l. 5) is:
the side that is depressed / the reverse side / the wrong side

3 • "peripheral" (l. 11) means:
equipped with computing tools / on the edge of the EU / linked with a ring road

4 • "sheer" (l. 12) means:
mere / utter / simple

5 • "eventually" (l. 13) means:
possibly / likely / finally

B • **Find the opposite of the following words (the are all to be found in the text).**

1 • similar 2 • unintelligent 3 • diverse

► Meaning

A • **Choose the right meaning of the following expressions from the text.**

1 • "biliously coloured" (l. 2) means:
coloured with ability / coloured without taste / disgustingly coloured

2 • "a smart move" (l. 4) means:
a good idea / a nice movement / a bad thing

3 • "have done some sums" (l. 8) means:
have made some mistakes / have carried out simple calculations / have thought about the huge sum of money

4 • "using purse-content analysis" (l. 8) means:
studying how happy people were / using analytical tools / studying what was found in purses

5 • "track patterns of diffusion" (l. 8) means:
discover the truth about the patterns of the new currency / try to find out how coins have been circulating in Euroland / investigate forgery

6 • "remain numismatically homogeneous" (l. 12) means:
keep their local euros / be interested in collecting coins / see the introduction of foreign coins

B • **What makes euro coins more attractive than euro banknotes?**

C • **There are 15 EU members and yet only 12 different kinds of coins; can you explain why?**

D • **What was E-day?**

E • **Why do you think one in four euro coins in Belgium is non-Belgian?**

F • **Which coin will dominate Europe? Why? Which ones won't?**

G • **Translate into English.**
(see T&T: Genitive / Articles)

1 • *L'héritage culturel de la France.*
2 • *Le passé de l'Allemagne.*
3 • *La prospérité des Pays-Bas.*
4 • *La pauvreté de la Grèce.*

H • **Translate into French the title and from "Here's a positive thought" (l. 1) to "France's Marianne, etc." (l. 6)**

► Pair work

A is a Briton who is strongly opposed to the single currency, **B** is an Irishman who is glad his country has adopted the single currency. Imagine their dialogue.

► Food for thought

Why do you think there are still people who are strongly opposed to the euro?

Unit 5

TEXT 2

1. **Labour's policy:** *politique du parti travailliste*
2. **betray:** *trahir*
3. **commit to =** promise

Europe ready to outlaw the sale of cosmetics tested on animals

The European Parliament is preparing to vote an EU-wide ban on the sale of all cosmetics tested on animals, dealing a humiliating blow to Labour's policy[1] on animal welfare.

A cross-party coalition of MEPs will back proposals making it illegal for make-up, hairspray, deodorant and other cosmetics tested on animals to be sold in any EU country, regardless of where they are produced. The ban would take effect in five years' time.

Many companies, including Body Shop, already voluntarily refuse to stock products tested on animals. But the British Government opposes an outright ban because it believes it will break World Trade Organisation rules.

MEPs are worried that anything short of a total sales ban in European countries will simply have the effect of driving animal testing of cosmetics to countries outside Europe, while allowing the fruits of that testing to be sold freely within it.

Animal welfare groups accuse ministers of "hypocrisy" over the issue and of having betrayed[2] voters, who were told in 1997 that "Labour is totally committed to[3] stopping cosmetics testing on animals". They believe British ministers have succumbed to lobbying by the animal testing industry and cosmetics companies and have let down the British public, 83 per cent of whom support a sales ban.

Denmark and Austria are likely to support MEPs when they vote next week on the amendment to the EU directive on animal testing. But Britain will use its votes in the Council of Ministers to block the move, despite a compromise exemption proposed by MEPs to allow three tests for which there are no non-animal alternatives to continue for 10 years.

Chris Davies, the Liberal Democrat spokesman on consumer affairs in Brussels, said "there was major public resistance to the idea of testing for vanity products. Any government claim that a ban on animal testing within the borders of the UK will have any effect on the welfare of animals is a pretence," he said.

© Réa / Pierre Bessard.

From *The Independent*, 7 June 2002.

► Check your pronunciation

A • **Make sure you can pronounce the *-ing* endings correctly.**

1 • humiliating
2 • making
3 • testing
4 • allowing
5 • stopping
6 • lobbying

B • **Can you stress the right syllable in the following words?**

1 • cosmetics
2 • policy
3 • voluntarily
4 • government
5 • hypocrisy
6 • amendment
7 • compromise
8 • alternatives
9 • affairs

► Meaning

A • **Which group is in favour of animal testing? Which group opposes it?**

1 • A cross-party of coalition of MEPs.
2 • The current British Government.
3 • The Labour party in 1997.
4 • Animal welfare groups.
5 • Denmark and Austria.
6 • The Liberal Democrats.

B • **Tick the correct meaning of each of the sentences from the text.**

1 • "regardless of where they are produced" (l. 6)
– depending on where they are produced
– no matter where they are produced
– in spite of being produced

2 • "voluntarily refuse" (l. 8)
– refuse without any discussion
– refuse without being asked to
– are willing to refuse

3 • "anything short of a total sales ban" (l. 11)
– unless a total sales ban is decided
– because of a total sales ban
– although a total sales ban is voted

4 • "Any government claim that a ban on animal testing within the borders of the UK will have any effect on the welfare of animals is a pretence" (l. 31)
– The government pretends a ban will be useless on the welfare of animals within the UK.
– All bans will be useless unless measures are taken within the UK.
– It is a lie to pretend that a ban on animal testing will be effective within the UK.

C • **Sum up the text in French. (about 80 words)**

► Words

Match the words from the text with their synonyms.

1 • outlaw (title)
2 • ban (l. 1)
3 • welfare (l. 3)
4 • back (l. 4)
5 • outright (l. 9)
6 • rule (l. 10)
7 • succumb (l. 17)
8 • let down (l. 18)

a • abandon
b • yield
c • make illegal
d • regulation
e • absolute
f • health and comfort
g • interdiction
h • support

D • **Translate into English.**

1 • *Si cette décision était votée, elle prendrait effet dans six mois.*
2 • *Tous les pays de l'Union européenne, y compris le Royaume-Uni.*
3 • *Il est probable que notre pays soutienne le projet.*

E • **Turn the following sentences into the passive.**

1 • The European Parliament is preparing to vote a new law.
2 • A cross-party coalition will back those proposals.
3 • The British Government opposes an outright ban.
4 • Animal welfare groups accused ministers of hypocrisy.
5 • They believe British ministers have succumbed to lobbying.
6 • We can sell those cosmetics freely.
7 • Someone told animal welfare groups that story.

F • **Translate into French from "Denmark" (l. 19) to "10 years" (l. 26).**

► Group work

Group **A** supports animal testing whereas group **B** is against it. Imagine the conversation.

► Food for thought

Does the EU have its own geographical, historical and cultural identity? (about 200 words)

Unit 5

TEXT 3

EU split over plan to curb migrants

European Union governments split publicly on linking aid to developing countries to their cooperation in tackling illegal migration. Proposals by Spain, backed by Britain, to suspend financial assistance to developing countries that fail to crack down on people-smugglers[1] and take back their own nationals were opposed by Sweden, France and Luxembourg. Sweden's foreign minister, Anna Lindh, warned: "It is very important to have a serious partnership with third countries to help them fight the reasons behind the influx of emigrants. Threatening them is not the right way." [...] Twelve of the EU's 15 member states backed the Spanish ideas, which were heavily influenced by Tony Blair's wish to use the two-day summit [in Seville] to make concrete progress in a normally slow-moving area. [...] Britain's Foreign Secretary, Jack Straw, said: "We must send a powerful signal to some third countries that if they want to develop a strong relationship with the EU they must better cooperate in fighting illegal migration and taking back their own nationals." Some 500,000 illegal migrants a year enter the EU.

From *The Guardian Weekly*, June 20-26, 2002.

1. **smuggler:** *contrebandier*

© Gamma / Ian Jones / FSP.

► Words

Match the words from list A with their synonyms in list B.

A	B
1 • curb (title)	a • support
2 • split (l. 1)	b • limit
3 • tackle (l. 2)	c • disagree
4 • warn (l. 5)	d • deal with
5 • back (l. 8)	e • caution

► Meaning

A • Right or wrong? Tick the correct answers.

1 • EU countries all agree on the same policy concerning illegal migration.
2 • Britain supports Spain's proposals.
3 • So do Sweden, France and Luxembourg.
4 • Sweden thinks it's a good idea to have a threatening attitude to third countries.
5 • Great Britain thinks third countries should prove more cooperative.

B • Complete the following sentences with *say* or *tell* in the correct form.

1 • The Prime Minister .... goodbye to his French counterpart.
2 • The Spanish Prime Minister .... he was heavily influenced by Tony Blair's ideas.
3 • "Did the government's spokesman .... the journalist when he could meet him?"
4 • The German foreign minister .... in Seville that a balance must be found.
5 • He couldn't answer my question. He .... me to ask Britain's Foreign Secretary.
6 • He couldn't answer my question. He .... to ask Britain's Foreign Secretary.

Checkup
Unit 5

1 ► Test

Common cause

Forty years after it was forged as a postwar bargain between French farmers and German industry to boost food production, Europe's original redistributive project is coming under closer scrutiny than ever before.

Long pilloried for its butter mountains, wine lakes and fraud-prone bureaucracy, fortress CAP* has been battered by a new set of arguments in recent years. Its staggering cost – currently €41bn (£26.5 bn) or nearly half the entire EU budget – has always grated. Recent reform rounds marked a significant move away from traditional market support to the compensatory direct payments which now make up 70% of CAP expenditure. Still, 20% of the farmers, the biggest, receive 80% of the subsidies. Both the Organisation for Economic Cooperation and Development and the UK Consumers Association say that European and British food is overpriced.

Franz Fischler, the European Commissioner in charge of agriculture, is calling for a 20% shift away from product support to rural development over six to seven years. Each farm would be limited to receiving a maximum of €300,000 in direct aid every year. Small farmers will be less affected than large (good for Greece and Portugal, bad for Germany).

If the concept is approved, the number of sheep raised and of hectares of wheat grown will become less significant than adherence to high standards of environmental protection, animal welfare, food quality and business practice. "It will for the first time float the possibility that direct payments can go down as well as up," says one Brussels diplomat. And beyond the cash shift involved, this also raises the radical idea that farm payments should be decoupled from production. Quality, in short, should replace quantity.

Fischler's watchword is that the consumer matters as much as the farmer. "Without food safety," he warns bluntly, "there is no market." Eurobarometer polling shows that the BSE, dioxin and foot-and-mouth crises have fed a growing appetite for a CAP that ensures that "the food you buy is safe to eat".

Country living

Employment in agriculture, forestry, hunting and fishing, % of population, 2000.

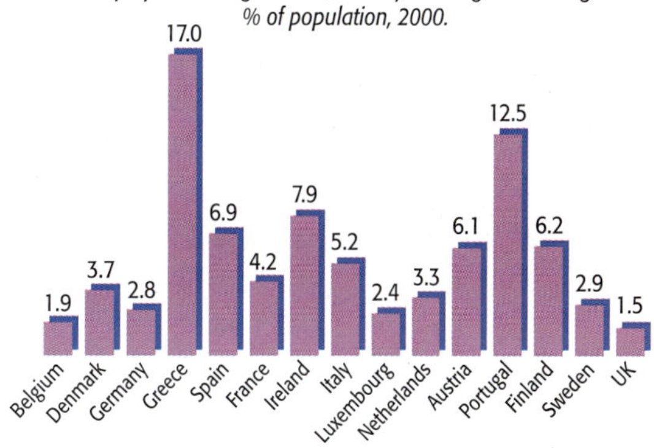

From *The Guardian*, July 5, 2002.

* **CAP:** Common Agricultural Policy

A • Sum up the text in French; you will insist on the following points. (about 80 words)

1 • What CAP used to be.
2 • What CAP has been accused of.
3 • The recent reforms.
4 • Frank Fischler's scheme.
5 • What CAP would be like if this scheme was accepted.

B • Translate into English.

1 • *La PAC coûte actuellement des milliards d'euros.*
2 • *Les montants compensatoires représentent un fort pourcentage des dépenses de la PAC.*
3 • *Les produits agricoles coûtent trop cher en Europe.*
4 • *L'agriculteur ne compte pas autant que le consommateur.*

C • Carefully study the chart above and say what you learn about the agricultural sector in the 15 EU countries. (at least 5 sentences in English)

2 ► Skills in practice

Test your own knowledge on the EU.

1 • On January 1st, 1993, the Single European Market gathered:
a • 4 countries c • 11 countries
b • 12 countries d • 13 countries

2 • The Treaty of Rome was signed in:
a • 1956 b • 1947 c • 1957 d • 1968

3 • The European Court of Justice stands in:
a • Brussels c • Luxembourg
b • Strasbourg d • Paris

4 • The Euro-MPs are elected by universal suffrage for:
a • 5 years c • 10 years
b • 2 years d • 6 months

5 • The EMS stands for:
a • European Man Standard
b • Economic Monetary Satisfaction
c • Economic Monetary System
d • European Monetary System

6 • Comett is a programme on:
a • Astronomy
b • Education and Training Technology
c • Astrology
d • Economy, Technology and Training

7 • The euro notes and coins were introduced on:
a • 1 January 1999
b • 1 January 2000
c • 1 January 2001
d • 1 January 2002

8 • The UK joined the EU in:
a • 1963 b • 1972 c • 1973 d • 1983

9 • The EU has:
a • 380m inhabitants
b • 455m inhabitants
c • 345m inhabitants
d • 155m inhabitants

10 • The Treaty of Rome was signed by:
a • Germany, Belgium, France
b • Germany, Belgium, France, Italy
c • Germany, Belgium, the Netherlands, the UK, Luxembourg
d • Germany, Belgium, France, Italy, Luxembourg, the Netherlands

11 • The EU anthem is:
a • Mozart's *Jupiter Symphony*
b • *The Ode to Joy* from Beethoven's Ninth Symphony
c • Vivaldi's *Four Seasons*
d • Beethoven's *Third Symphony, Eroica*

12 • Europe Day is:
a • 18 April, commemorating the Treaty establishing the European Coal and Steel Community
b • 8 May, commemorating the end of WWII
c • 9 May, commemorating Robert Schuman's declaration in 1950 which is regarded as marking the creation of the EU
d • 1 January, commemorating the day when the Treaty of Rome came into force in 1958

3 ► The right word

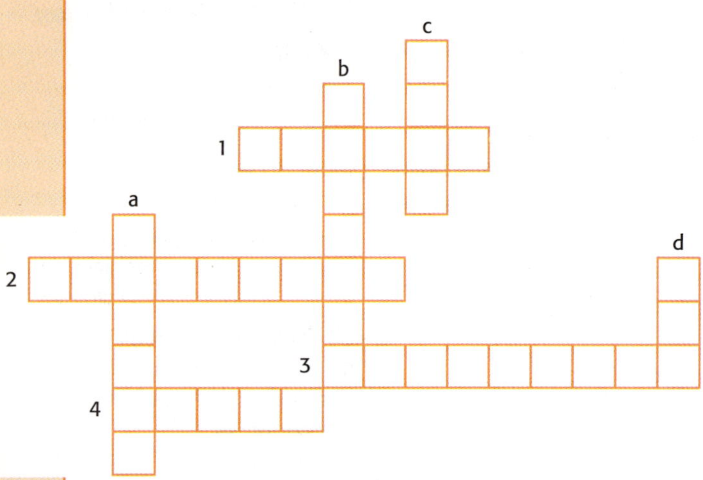

A • Crossword

Across
1 • Written agreement between countries.
2 • That was the case in Germany in 1989.
3 • Measures taken to restrict trade with a country that has broken the law.
4 • Turkey's is a problem.

Down
a • It is discussed every year in Parliament.
b • Countries that have joined the EU.
c • Forbid.
d • Representatives in the EU Parliament.

B • Fill in the blanks with words from the following list.

bill / treaty / unified / chaired / Court of Justice / policy / flow / Council of Europe / citizens / regulations

1 • A .... Europe will make the Europeans stronger competitors.
2 • The European .... has 13 judges who ensure that the .... and decisions are in keeping with the EU constitution.
3 • This .... could have been adopted earlier.
4 • The European flag was adopted in 1986 by the ....
5 • Abolishing border posts will enable people and goods .... more freely.
6 • There is still a lot of anti-European feeling among British ....
7 • Nearly all Europeans agree that they badly need an immigration ....
8 • The .... of Rome was signed in 1957.
9 • The EU is .... by each country in turn for six months.

4 ► Vocabulary

accord : agreement
Acte unique européen : Single European Act
adhérer à l'Union européenne : join the EU
aide : aid
arbitrer : arbitrate

barème : rate-scale
barrières douanières : tariff barrier
budget : budget

chef d'état : head of state
citoyen : citizen
commerce : trade
Communauté européenne : European Community, EC
conflit : conflict
conforme à : in keeping with
Conseil de l'Europe : European Council
consulter : consult
Cour européenne de justice : European Court of Justice

décision : decision
député européen : Euro-MP, MEP
droit de veto : right of veto
droits de douane : customs duties

élu : elected
entrée (dans l'Union européenne) : entry
entrer dans l'Union Européenne : enter / join the EU
État membre : member state

fixer : set (set, set)

harmoniser : harmonise

institution : institution

juge : judge

libre échange : free trade

Marché unique : Single Market
membre : member
mettre en œuvre : implement
monnaie : currency
montant compensatoires : compensatory payments

nommer : appoint
norme : norm, standard

obligatoire : binding
O.C.D.E. : OECD = Organisation for Economic Co-operation and Development
ordre du jour : agenda

pacte : pact
Parlement européen : European Parliament
plan : scheme
Politique Agricole Commune (PAC): Common Agricultural Policy (CAP)
politique (la) : politics
politique (une) : policy
pourparlers : talks, discussions
pouvoir : power
présider : chair
programme : programme
proposition : proposal

règlement : regulation
réunifier : reunify
réunion au sommet : summit meeting

sanctions : sanctions, penalties
sommet : summit
suffrage universel : universal suffrage
Système monétaire européen, SME : European Monetary System, EMS

traité : treaty
TVA : VAT

unification : unification, integration
unifié : unified, united, integrated, consolidated
union économique et monétaire : economic and monetary union, EMU
Union européenne : European Union, EU
union politique européenne : European political union

Key to texts 3

Part I • The business world

Unit 1 Launching, advertising, promoting

"Don't eat too much of our food," warns McDonald's

► Words

Il s'agit d'un mot-valise "advertisement + editorial" = publicité informative.

► Meaning

A • 1 • marketing advice
2 • the fast food giant
3 • health benefits
4 • orange juice
5 • beef meat
6 • the key message
7 • diet food

B • 1 • Because it's quite unusual for a company to disclose negative advertisement on what it produces or commercialises.
2 • Because McDonald's has always declared that its food was nutritious and part of a balanced diet.
3 • First the burgers are 100% meat, then they say no fat is added, and they also underline that orange juice is available for those who are not keen on fizzy drinks such as Coke.
4 • The idea was to publish one point of view which gave rise to a debate. That debate was in itself good advertising for the company.

C • McDonald's France a testé un stratagème mercatique d'une franchise inhabituelle : présenter des publicités conseillant aux gens de ne pas trop consommer ses produits.

Unit 2 Distribution

Carphone sends brighter message

► Words

1 • rise
2 • fallen
3 • doubled
4 • increased

► Meaning

A • 1 • Wrong
2 • Right
3 • Right
4 • Right
5 • Right
6 • Wrong
7 • Wrong

B • 1 • The company is now concentrating on after-sales services.
2 • We have started selling new products such as DVDs.
3 • Europe's largest mobile phone retailer.
4 • A dramatic drop in sales.

Unit 3 Consumption

Billion bottle record for scotch whisky

► Words

A • 1 • alcohol
2 • exploit
3 • ambitious
4 • fashionable

B • 1 • in
2 • to
3 • in
4 • for

► Meaning

A • 1 • Right
2 • Wrong
3 • Right
4 • Right
5 • Right
6 • Right

B • 1 • Whisky is more popular in France than brandy.
2 • The Asian drinkers are increasingly drawn to scotch.
3 • Last year we sold 3 million bottles.
4 • Whisky is the most widely exported spirit in the world.

Unit 4 Big business

Boots plans £100m revamp for stores

► Words

1 • impatiently
2 • old-fashioned
3 • include
4 • apart

► Meaning

A • spruced up / put off / brighten up / brought in / bring in

B • 1 • Other investments were needed by the business.
2 • Shareholders will be given the benefits of future growth prospects.
3 • The group is expected to announce a 9-per-cent increase.
4 • Shoppers are being put off by the dated stores.

Unit 5 World trade

Sri Lanka plans tea venture in Pakistan

► Words

1 • will raise
2 • will create kindness
3 • India feels uneasy
4 • The Pakistani market is big enough to welcome a third supplier

► Meaning

A •
– Country 1: Sri Lanka
Country 2: Pakistan.
– Industry at stake: Tea.
– The plan is: Allowing duty-free imports of tea from Sri Lanka.
– Consequence for country number 1: Boosted tea exports.
– Two major suppliers for country number 2: Kenya and Indonesia.
– Another country is not happy with the decision: India.
– Major advantage of the plan for country number 2: Investment in the country by Sri Lanka.

B • 1 • Pakistan is a big tea importer whereas Sri Lanka is not.
2 • Unlike India, customs duties were cut for Sri Lanka.
3 • Unlike Indonesia, Sri Lanka excels in tea packaging.
4 • The customs waiver will create goodwill for Pakistan in Sri Lanka whereas it won't for India.

Unit 6 Banking

G7 issues warning to Swiss banks

► Words

1 • limiting
2 • there is no time left
3 • following the September 11, 2001 events
4 • supplying a safe place
5 • an accusation
6 • resolved

► Meaning

A • The G7 countries are the US, Canada, Germany, Japan, France, Great Britain and Italy. G stands for "group of countries". We also speak of G8 because Russia now belongs to the group.

B • 1 • Three global blights: Money laundering, tax evasion, the financing of terrorism.
2 • Accusation against Switzerland: providing a haven for terrorist funding.
3 • What the leading economies would like to put an end to: banking secrecy.
4 • What the leading economies are looking forward to: an exchange of information.

C • 1 • unless
2 • if
3 • provided
4 • unless

Unit 7 Accounting and investing

Insurance giants

► Words

1 • Insurance industry
2 • Insurance premiums
3 • Insurance giants
4 • Aviation sector
5 • Trade volumes

► Meaning

A • 1 • insurance premiums / aviation industry
2 • insurance industry
3 • trade volumes
4 • insurance giants

B • 1 • The Twin Towers tragedy
2 • Damaged world economy
3 • Increased insurance costs, increased spending on defence, increased trade barriers
4 • Fall of trade volume
5 • Medium-term consequences
6 • Major bankruptcy
7 • Some companies would go bankrupt
8 • Rise in insurance premiums

Unit 8 Transport

UPS Internet Shipping

► Words

1 • largest = widest (l. 3).
2 • range = array (l. 3)
3 • directly = right (l. 4)
4 • invoicing = billing (l. 5)
5 • shipping = shipments (l. 7)
6 • give (2 verbs = provide (l. 7), hand = (l. 10)
7 • deposit = drop-off (l. 14)
8 • plan = schedule (l. 16)
9 • pick up = collect (l. 16)

► Meaning

A • 1 • Whether you are a regular customer or not, / or a new one, UPS can deal with your packages.
2 • Whether UPS drivers come to your company or you go to an Authorized Shipping Outlet, your packages will be well looked after by UPS.
3 • Whether your packages are sent within the USA or to any other country, you can rely on UPS.

B • 1 • We can either take our packages to an authorized shipping outlet or to a UPS customer counter.
2 • International packages are either dropped in UPS boxes or collected by a UPS driver.
3 • Either you register now or you log in.

C • 1 • UPS is an American company that deals with the shipment of goods. Thanks to UPS Internet Shipping, individuals and companies can prepare their shipment by making their own labels with their computer.
2 • If you're a loyal customer, you just give your parcel to your UPS driver who comes every day in the morning or in the afternoon. If you're not, you have to go to the nearest outlet or counter that you'll have found on the online UPS site.
3 • Either you put your letters and small parcels in special boxes, or you call a UPS driver who will come and collect your goods to be shipped by plane or worldwide. For letters and small parcels, special boxes are to be found.
4 • A new customer has to register with MY UPS.COM on the Internet. In this case, they have to click on "register now!", follow the instructions and give the necessary information. If this customer works with MY UPS.COM again, they will only have to click on "log in" and follow the instructions.

Unit 1 Education and training

Reaching one and all

► Words

1 • information technology: IT
2 • operation: enterprise
3 • day in day out: every day
4 • manage: run

► Meaning

A • 1 • Thompson
2 • "managing his 150 or so staff"
3 • Donc la gestion de son personnel d'environ 150 employés.
4 • – Before diversifying, Rick was a restaurant owner.
– Make a list of the points you want to improve before viewing the video.
– After seeing the video I was again full of hope.
5 • "As the business has grown" =
since, given that + S + V → introduces a cause.
It "acts as a kind of workbook" =
like + N → expresses a comparison.

B • 1 • He manages his training video company for which he himself makes and produces the videos.
2 • After high school, he attended a film school; there, he made videos for courses and obtained his diploma. Then, he did a training course in IT and worked for a management consultancy.
3 • Rick is the owner of an enterprise that includes a restaurant, a café, a delicatessen, a hotel and a cookery school. We understand that he probably started with a restaurant and then opened a café, etc.
4 • It now consists in managing his staff / in being a staff manager.
5 • It is a training method including a video, a guide and a CD-Rom.

C • Thompson uses this method for managers who need to receive training in personnel or company management.

D • There's a pun on "recipe" as the video gives indications on how to manage a company and the example given in the video is that of a cook.

E • La vidéo que Thompson en a fait, *La recette de la réussite*, est accompagnée d'un guide et d'un CD-Rom. Elle joue le rôle d'une sorte de cahier d'exercices qui rappelle aux spectateurs les questions soulevées et comment elles peuvent être mises en relation avec leurs propres situations individuelles.

F • The title may mean that to make his video Thompson reached, i.e. contacted, one person (Rick) and that, thanks to this contact, Thompson reaches managers (many people, "all") with the video, that is to say he gives them the training they need.

Unit 2 Working conditions

Fowl play

► Words

"Fowl" et "foul" se prononcent de la même façon en anglais, d'où un jeu de mot possible entre « jeu de poulet » (fowl play) et « acte criminel » (foul play).

1 • gulf / gap
2 • statutory / legal
3 • shift / set period of working time
4 • dawn / daybreak
5 • overtime / extra working hours
6 • take on / hire
7 • supervisor / overseer

► Meaning

A • 1 • They agree to work overtime even when they are on leave.
2 • The third warning and the worker is fired.

B • 1 • His salary is not as low as hers.
2 • It isn't as cold in the slaughterhouse as it is in the cutting room.
3 • Hygiene is not as strict here as it is at Grampian's.
4 • The factory I work in is not as good a place as Grampian's.
5 • The working conditions are not as bad here as they are outside Bangkok.

C • La société n'aime pas embaucher quelqu'un de plus de 40 ans, et les contremaîtres sont prompts à distribuer des avertissements – deux et on perd une semaine de travail, un de plus et c'est le renvoi. Mais c'est bien de travailler chez Grampian, dit-on.

Unit 3 Women

Women still barred from frontline military duties

► Words

1 • barred / forbidden
2 • risky / dangerous
3 • gap / difference
4 • workload / amount of work
5 • achieve / succeed in doing
6 • likely / probable
7 • opportunity / prospect
8 • effectiveness / success

► Meaning

A • 1 • Women may not participate in close combat in the armed forces.
2 • They are physically and psychologically less strong than men.
3 • She thinks this is a wrong decision.

B • 1 • The secretary said women would continue to be barred from close combat roles.
2 • He added it would be too risky.
3 • The report concluded that differences between men and women were too important.
4 • The secretary remarked capacity for aggression had always been lower for women.
5 • The EOC declared it was not right to exclude women from armed combat post.
6 • The journalist pointed out women had already been used in close combat roles but the practice had been abandoned.

C • 1 • The defence secretary
2 • Muscle strength
3 • The deputy chairwoman
4 • Combat posts

Unit 4 Employment and unemployment

Job seekers may score points with "nonabusive" networking

► Words

A • overstay = stay too long
overuse = more than usual use

B • 1 • acquaintances = relations
2 • referrals = referees
3 • poor = bad
4 • pace themselves = organise their time
5 • tempo = rhythm

► Meaning

A • Present Be + V-ing: going (= If you find the interview is going beyond that time), running.
Gerund: networking / exploring / using / contacting / overstaying / planning / self-pacing / arranging / recognizing / looking / continuing.

B • 1 • Someone you know well.
2 • Don't go beyond that time.

C • 1 • It is the use of one's relations to get a job that is not necessarily advertised.
2 • What shouldn't be done:
– get in touch with the same person too often,
– stay too long at an appointment,
– bad schedule,
– poor time management.
What should be done:
– appropriate time management,
– contact people you know well and are well-at-ease with,
– make the interviews short,
– if the interview is longer than you had planned, say so and ask your interviewer if he / she is willing to go on.

D • Les demandeurs d'emploi peuvent peut-être marquer des points s'ils n'abusent pas de leur réseau de contacts.
L'une des meilleures façons d'explorer le marché du travail caché est le réseau de contacts, c'est-à-dire vous mettre en relation avec vos amis, vos connaissances et les personnes qui peuvent vous recommander afin de passer en revue les possibilités de candidatures spontanées.

Part III • The world at stake

Unit 1 Social issues

Rate of violent pupils expelled rises for first time since 1996

► Words

1 • throw out
2 • shortage
3 • likely to
4 • ordinary
5 • wander

► Meaning

A • 1 • Endless complaints on aggressive behaviour.
2 • A school environment when people prove kind and helpful.
3 • They feel their authority is shaken, subverted by the appeal panels.
4 • Send them back to school.

B • 1 • although high levels of bad behaviour must be curbed.
2 • although he has never proved aggressive.
3 • Although the number of children expelled from school is on the increase.
4 • Although violent pupils are excluded.
5 • although one child was sent to hospital after being beaten up.

Unit 2 Developing countries

20 million at risk

► Words

1 • dryness = drought (l. 2)
2 • inundation = flood (l. 2)
3 • famine = starvation (l. 8)
4 • decrease = fall (l. 9)

► Meaning

A • 1 • is making people aware of danger.
2 • is managing the current crisis.
3 • the present crisis.
4 • He is trying to crush all opposition.

B • 1 • The number of southern Africans who are likely to suffer from starvation soon.
2 • The World Food Programme.
3 • Several countries in the south of Africa.

C • 1 • There have **always** been floods and drought in southern Africa.
2 • Even if the situation is better, Botswana **still** suffers from a crisis.
3 • A lot of progress is **still** to be made.
4 • Please don't say there will **always** be problems! There are **still** problems but let's hope things will improve.

D • The governments don't run their countries' economies well, and these countries suffer from political unrest.

E • The factors that can prevent poor countries from starving are independence, democracy and a relatively free press.

F • The countries which benefited from at least one of these factors in the 1980s are Botswana and Zimbabwe which didn't suffer from starvation although they had a very low grain production.

G • Botswana is in the same situation, but Zimbabwe is in dire straits owing to political problems.

Part III • The world at stake

Unit 3 The environment

Disposal plant opens in Wales

► Words

A • 1 • plant = factory
2 • take a bite out of = eat
3 • switch on = open
4 • await = wait for
5 • regulations = rules
6 • tough = strict
7 • stack-up = pile
8 • comply with = respect

B • Wales is part of Great Britain, itself part of the United Kingdom. (See Passport)

► Meaning

A • 1 • Wrong, it's located in Wales, i.e. in Great Britain.
2 • Wrong, it has to recycle 25,000 old fridges and it only started on July 1, 2002.
3 • Wrong, they discard 3 million fridges every year.
4 • Right
5 • Right
6 • Wrong, the new EU regulations forbid it.
7 • Right
8 • Wrong, this will be the highest rate.
9 • Right

B • 1 • a Wales-based plant
2 • a safely-degassing device
3 • a well-known issue
4 • a time-consuming task

C • 1 • Because CFCs deplete the ozone layer and so are a threat to the environment. Moreover, they are gases that have to be transformed into liquid in order to be recycled.
2 • Because, with time, the CFCs contained in the fridges may spread in the earth and endanger the environment.

D • Un « mangeur de réfrigérateurs » spécialement conçu à cet effet va commencer aujourd'hui à entamer la montagne britannique de réfrigérateurs grâce à l'ouverture d'un centre de retraitement de pointe au pays de Galles. SimsMetal ouvre la première véritable usine britannique de destruction sécurisée de vieux réfrigérateurs aux docks de Newport où 25 000 réfrigérateurs attendent le dégazage – la destruction du liquide de refroidissement – et la suppression des systèmes d'isolation.

Unit 4 Travelling and Tourism

Chequing in

► Words

A • Value added tax.

B • 1 • pénurie (2 words) : shortage, scarcity
2 • exorbitant : sky-high
3 • accuser : blame
4 • osciller : hover
5 • avant tout : above all
6 • gérer : run

► Meaning

A • 1 • True
2 • True
3 • True
4 • False, it's also owing to the dramatically high prices of these hotels.
5 • False, for this price it will be a good, owner-run hotel.
6 • True

► Meaning suite

B • A survey reveals that the dearest European hotels are to be found in Britain.
Indeed, even the cheapest and most uncomfortable British hotels are the most expensive ones in Europe.
The worst area in Great Britain for finding a hotel is London, firstly because there aren't enough hotels, considering the demand, and secondly owing to the dramatically high prices of those hotels.
As a matter of fact, Patricia Yates explains that a good, €60-per-night, owner-run hotel in the centre of Paris can be found whereas she doesn't even want to look for such hotels in London.

C • She clearly points out that if ever you find a hotel for €60 per night in central London, not only will it be in a derelict district but it will also be very dirty and / or maybe unsafe.

D • On accuse souvent la puissance de la livre sterling.
La TVA est certainement un facteur : à 17,5 % elle est au second rang en Europe après le Danemark. Ailleurs, elle oscille entre 3 et 10 %. Mais n'importe quel hôtelier indépendant vous dira que c'est avant tout le prix du foncier qui est responsable de la pénurie dans le centre de Londres d'hôtels bien conçus, aux prix modérés et gérés par des particuliers.
Il n'est alors pas surprenant que la plupart des hôtels londoniens soient gérés par des chaînes multinationales. L'Europe continentale, en revanche, garde une forte tradition d'hôtels indépendants dont beaucoup restent aux mains de la même famille pendant des générations et peuvent ainsi fonctionner avec nettement moins de pression de la part des banquiers et des actionnaires.

E • On the one hand "A cheque" ("check" in American English) is a mode of payment, on the other hand when you arrive in a hotel, you "check in", i.e. you fill in an identity form and give an ID. So here the journalist has played on the two words to show that if you want to stay in a hotel in London you'll have to pay a lot.

F • Here are a few examples:
A luxury hotel in Sweden is about as expensive as a luxury hotel in GB.
The cheapest / The least expensive hotels are to be found in the Czech Republic.
Switzerland's medium hotels are among the dearest but are less expensive / are cheaper than GB's.
etc.

Unit 5 The European Union

EU split over plan to curb migrants

► Words

1 • curb / limit
2 • split / disagree
3 • tackle / deal with
4 • warn / caution
5 • back / support / harsh

► Meaning

A • 1 • Wrong: Eu countries "split publicly" (l. 1)
2 • Right
3 • Wrong: "opposed by Sweden, France and Luxembourg" (l. 4-5)
4 • Wrong: "threatening them is not the right way" (l. 7)
5 • Right

B • 1 • said
2 • said
3 • tell
4 • said
5 • told
6 • said

Sommaire / Contents

1. LE GROUPE VERBAL

1. Présent simple

Formation

Forme affirmative : BV

Ex. : – I / You / We / They work in a bank.
– *Je / etc. travaille dans une banque.*

⚠ **Ne pas oublier le S à la 3e personne du singulier :**

Ex. : – He / She / It helps.
– *Il / Elle / Cela aide.*

Formes interrogative et négative

On utilise DO / DOES, DON'T / DOESN'T

Ex. : – I don't work on Saturdays. Does he work here?
– *Je ne travaille pas le samedi. Travaille-t-il ici ?*

Emploi

Pour exprimer une action habituelle, une vérité générale, une caractéristique attribuée à quelqu'un, une activité mentale.

Ex. : – I usually get up at 7. The sun rises in the East. He loves Spain. I don't agree with you.
– *Je me lève d'habitude à 7 h. Le soleil se lève à l'est. Il adore l'Espagne. Je ne suis pas d'accord avec vous.*

2. Présent en BE + V-ING

Formation

BE (au présent) + V-ING

Emploi

1. Pour exprimer une action qui se déroule au moment où l'on parle.

Ex. : – Oh look! The sun is shining!
– *Oh ! Regarde ! Le soleil brille !*

2. Pour mettre en valeur un point de vue exprimé ou une décision (valeur modale).

Ex. : – Mary! You are being stupid! (point de vue)
– *Mary ! Tu fais l'idiote !*
– My car? But I am not selling it! (décision)
– *Ma voiture ? Mais je ne la vends pas !*

3. Prétérit simple

Formation

Forme affirmative V-ED

Ex. : – I / you / he / we / they listened. – *J'ai / etc. écouté.*

⚠ **Attention aux verbes irréguliers !**

Formes interrogative et négative : DID (NOT) + BV

Ex. : – Yesterday I didn't meet him. Did you see the film?
– *Je ne l'ai pas rencontré hier. Avez-vous vu le film ?*

Emploi

Pour un évènement révolu, c'est-à-dire sans lien avec le présent, qui se situe dans une narration. Souvent accompagné d'un complément de temps (Yesterday, two days ago, last year, when I was at school).
Le prétérit se traduit généralement en français par le passé composé.

⚠ **• « Pendant » se traduit par FOR + durée déterminée ou par DURING + période de temps indéterminée.**

⚠ **• « Il y a » + date se traduit par la date + AGO.**

Ex. : – Last night I met my friend at the pub.
– *Hier soir j'ai rencontré mon ami au pub.*
– She worked in a bank for 2 years.
– *Elle a travaillé dans une banque pendant 2 ans.*
– He relaxed during the holidays.
– *Il s'est détendu pendant les vacances.*
– I went to New York 10 years ago.
– *Je suis allée à New York il y a dix ans.*

4. Prétérit en BE + V-ING

Formation

WAS / WERE + V-ING
(très souvent traduit en français par l'imparfait)

Emploi

Pour le déroulement d'un évènement révolu.

Ex. : – I was sleeping when the phone rang.
– *Je dormais quand le téléphone a sonné.*

5. Present perfect simple

Formation

HAVE / HAS (3e personne du singulier) + V-ED (p. passé)

⚠ **Attention aux verbes irréguliers !**

Emploi

Contrairement au prétérit, le present perfect établit un lien avec le présent.

1. Dans le cas d'une action qui, commencée dans le passé, se poursuit au moment où l'on parle.

⚠ **« Depuis » se traduit par FOR pour exprimer une durée et par SINCE pour un point de départ. Quand SINCE n'est pas suivi d'une date, il est suivi d'un nom ou d'une proposition (impossible pour FOR).**

Ex. : – I have worked here for ten years / since 1995 / since I left university / since his departure.
– *Je travaille ici depuis 10 ans, depuis 1995, depuis que j'ai quitté l'université, depuis son départ.*

2. Dans le cas où l'on envisage le résultat présent d'une action passée.

Ex. : – Oh! You've bought a new car!
– *Oh ! Tu as acheté une nouvelle voiture !*
– I've had a hard day's work.
– *J'ai eu une dure journée de travail.*
– You've improved your accent.
– *Tu as amélioré ton accent.*

On emploie donc le present perfect :
– après l'expression "It's the first time".

Ex. : – It's the first time he has driven a car!
– *C'est la première fois qu'il conduit une voiture !*

– avec les adverbes tels que EVER, ALREADY, NOT… YET.

Ex. : – I've not finished yet!
– *Je n'ai pas encore terminé !*

6. Present perfect en BE + V-ING

Formation

HAVE / HAS BEEN V-ING

Emploi

1. Dans le cas d'une activité qui vient de prendre fin, dont on constate les conséquences.
Ex. : – The ground is wet, it has been raining.
– *Le sol est humide, il a plu.*

2. Dans le cas où l'on veut insister sur l'activité qui se poursuit au moment où l'on parle.
Ex. : – It's been raining since this morning.
– *Il pleut depuis ce matin.*

7. Past perfect

Formation

HAD + V-ED (participe passé)

Emploi

Pour marquer une antériorité par rapport au prétérit.
Ex. : – When I arrived he had already gone.
– *Lorsque je suis arrivé il était déjà parti.*

8. Futur

Formation et emploi

1. WILL + BV **(simple prédiction)**
Ex. : – The plant will employ more staff next year.
– *L'usine recrutera plus de personnel l'an prochain.*

2. WILL + BE + V-ING **(prédiction + intention, décision)**
Ex. : – We will be recruiting more staff next year.
– *Nous recruterons plus de personnel l'an prochain.*

3. AM / IS / ARE GOING TO + BV **(intention de celui qui parle)**
Ex. : – I am going to employ more secretaries.
– *Je vais employer plus de secrétaires.*

4. AM / IS / ARE ABOUT TO + BV **(évènement imminent)**
Ex. : – We are about to recruit an engineer.
– *Nous sommes sur le point de recruter un ingénieur.*

5. AM / IS / ARE TO + BV **(programme fixé d'avance)**
Ex. : – We are to lay off 100 employees as part of our redundancy program.
– *Nous devons licencier 100 employés, cela fait partie de notre programme de licenciement.*

6. AM / IS / ARE + V-ING **(décision prise par celui qui parle)**
Ex. : – I am seeing my boss tomorrow about a pay rise.
– *Je vois mon patron demain pour lui parler d'une augmentation de salaire.*

9. Impératif

Formation et emploi

Forme affirmative

2e personne (sing. et pl.) : BV
Ex. : – Listen! Read it again! Stop moving!
– *Écoute(z) ! Relis(ez)-le ! Arrête(z) de bouger !*

1re personne du pl. : LET'S + BV
Ex. : – Let's start!
– *Commençons !*

Forme négative : DON'T + BV
Ex. : – Don't smoke!
– *Ne fume(z) pas !*

10. Modaux

Emploi

1. Pour exprimer un degré de certitude (il se peut que, il se pourrait, il devrait...).

Degré de certitude	Au présent	Au passé
90 % certain → MUST	He must pass his driving test. *Il doit réussir. (quasi certain)*	He must **have** pass**ed**. *Il a dû réussir.*
↓ → SHOULD	He should pass. *Il devrait réussir. (ce serait normal)*	He should **have** pass**ed**. *Il devrait avoir réussi.*
↓ → CAN	He can pass. *Il peut réussir. (les circonstances le permettent)*	He can **have** pass**ed**. *Il peut avoir réussi.*
↓ → COULD	He could pass. *Il pourrait réussir. (c'est envisageable)*	He could **have** pass**ed**. *Il pourrait avoir réussi.*
≈ 50 % certain → MAY	He may pass. (→ perhaps he'll pass). *Peut-être réussira-t-il.*	He may **have** pass**ed**. *Peut-être a-t-il réussi.*
↓ → MIGHT	He might pass. *Il se pourrait qu'il réussisse. (mais il a peu de chances d'y parvenir)*	He might **have** pass**ed**. *Il se pourrait qu'il ait réussi.*
Presque impossible → CAN'T	He can't pass. *Il ne peut pas réussir. (en toute logique, c'est quasi impossible)*	He can't **have** pass**ed**. *C'est impossible qu'il ait pu réussir.*

2. Pour exprimer la liberté d'action dont jouit quelqu'un (il peut, il doit, il n'a pas besoin de...).

Degré de liberté	Au présent	Au passé
Capacité → CAN	She can swim. *Elle sait nager.*	She could swim. She was able to swim.* *Elle pouvait / savait nager. Elle a pu nager.*
Absence de capacité → CANNOT / CAN'T	She cannot / can't find her hotel room. *Elle n'arrive pas à trouver sa chambre d'hôtel.*	She couldn't / wasn't able to find her hotel room.* *Elle ne pouvait pas / Elle n'a pas pu trouver sa chambre d'hôtel.*
Permission → MAY / CAN	You may drive at 16. *Vous pouvez conduire à 16 ans.* Can I take your pen? *Puis-je prendre votre stylo ?*	You were allowed to** drive. *Vous aviez la permission de conduire.* Could I take your pen? *Pouvais-je prendre votre stylo ?*
Absence de permission → MAY NOT / CANNOT (CAN'T)	You may not smoke. *Vous ne pouvez pas fumer.* You cannot / can't go out alone. *Vous ne pouvez sortir seul.*	You were not allowed to smoke. You were not allowed to go out alone. *Vous n'étiez pas autorisé à fumer / à sortir seul.*
Obligation → MUST	I must pay my income tax. *Je dois payer mes impôts.*	I had to** pay my income tax. *Je devais payer mes impôts.*
Interdiction → MUST NOT	You are drunk, you must not drive. *Vous êtes ivre, vous ne devez pas conduire.*	You didn't have to drive. *Vous ne deviez pas conduire.*
Absence d'obligation → DON'T HAVE TO	I don't have to get up early every day. *Je n'ai pas à me lever tôt tous les jours.*	I didn't have to get up early every day. *Je n'avais pas à me lever tôt tous les jours.*
Absence de nécessité → NEEDN'T / DON'T NEED TO	You needn't / don't need to worry. *Vous n'avez pas besoin de vous inquiéter.* *Vous n'aviez pas besoin de vous inquiéter.*	You needn't have worried / didn't need to worry.
Conseil → SHOULD	He should apply for the job. *Il devrait poser sa candidature pour cet emploi.*	He should have applied for the job. *Il aurait dû poser sa candidature pour cet emploi.*

* Could n'indique pas une action accomplie (on traduit par «pouvait»). Was / were able to indique une action qui a eu lieu (on traduit par «a pu»).
**Be able to / be allowed to / have to étant des verbes à part entière ils peuvent se conjuguer à tous les temps.
Attention, cependant, à la différence entre must (obligation intériorisée) et have to (contrainte extérieure).
Ex. : – I must go home now. *(c'est moi qui impose cette obligation) – Je dois rentrer à la maison à présent.*
– I have to go home now. *(la contrainte est extérieure, s'il n'y avait que moi, je resterais). – Il faut que je rentre à la maison à présent.*

3. Autres expressions modales

Volonté	→ WILL	Will you have some more tea? *Voulez-vous reprendre du thé ?* I'll make some tea. *Je vais faire du thé.*
Conseil	→ HAD BETTER / 'D BETTER	You'd better hurry up. *Vous feriez mieux de vous dépêcher.*
Préférence	→ WOULD RATHER / 'D RATHER	I'd rather rest than work.* *Je préférerais me reposer plutôt que travailler.*
Habitude au présent	→ WILL **(avec valeur de proverbe)**	Boys will be boys. *On ne changera jamais les garçons.*
Habitude passée	→ WOULD	I would get up and make tea. *Je me levais et faisais du thé.*
Habitude passée (idée de contraste avec le présent)	→ USED TO	When I was younger I used to get up early. *Quand j'étais plus jeune, je me levais tôt.*

*cf. aussi prétérit modal.

11. Prétérit modal

Formation

V-ED

Emploi

Dans ce cas, le prétérit ne renvoie pas à du passé, il s'utilise pour des faits présentés comme irréels.

1. Dans le cas d'hypothèse après IF, SUPPOSE (cf. Subordonnées circonstancielles de condition)
Ex. : – If / Suppose he arrived late, I would be furious.
– *Et s'il arrivait en retard ? Je serais furieux.*

2. Dans le cas de l'expression du souhait ou du regret
Ex. : – If only I were in New York! – *Ah si j'étais à New York !*

⚠ Au prétérit modal BE devient WERE à toutes les personnes.
Ex. : – I wish I were you. – *J'aimerais être à ta place.*

3. Dans l'expression de la préférence avec 'D RATHER (= I WOULD RATHER) lorsque le sujet de 'D RATHER est différent de celui de la subordonnée.
Ex. : – She'd rather he decided now.
– *Elle préférerait qu'il décide maintenant.*

NB Lorsque le sujet de 'D RATHER et celui non exprimé du verbe renvoie à la même personne, on utilise BV.
Ex. : – I'd rather stop now.
– *Je préférerais arrêter maintenant.*

12. Passif

Formation

BE + V-EN (participe passé) (+ BY + complément d'agent)

Lorsqu'un verbe est accompagné d'un auxiliaire modal à la forme active, cet auxiliaire ne change pas mais le verbe qui le suit devient BE + participe passé.

Ex. : *Forme active :*
– Our boss has just hired a new secretary.
– *Notre patron vient de recruter une nouvelle secrétaire.*
– People should ask for more information.
– *Les gens devraient / On devrait demander plus de renseignements.*

Forme passive :
– A new secretary has just been hired by our boss.
– *Une nouvelle secrétaire vient d'être recrutée par notre patron.*
– More information should be asked for.
– *Plus de renseignements devraient être demandés.*

NB On omet le complément d'agent introduit par BY lorsqu'il ne fournit aucun renseignement supplémentaire.
Ex. : – She is expected tonight (by someone *est superflu)*
– *On l'attend ce soir.*

Dans le cas d'un verbe à particule, ne pas l'oublier au passif.
Ex. : – The boss will put off the meeting
→ The meeting will be put off by the boss.
– *La réunion va être reportée par le patron.*

⚠ Attention au double passif ! Certains verbes anglais peuvent être suivis de deux compléments d'objet direct, l'un animé, l'autre pas, tels que : ASK, GIVE, OFFER, PAY, SELL, SHOW, TEACH, TELL… Il y a alors deux possibilités de forme passive : (cf. Emploi 3.)
Ex. : – I'll give John a present.
– *Je donnerai un cadeau à John.*
→ John will be given a present.
– *John recevra un cadeau.*
→ A present will be given to John. (Apparition de TO car on dit à la forme active : give something TO somebody.)
– *Un cadeau sera remis à John.*

Emploi

On emploie le passif quand on veut mettre l'accent sur l'objet de l'actif. Le passif est donc souvent utilisé dans les articles de presse.
Ex. : – New measures were taken.
– *De nouvelles mesures ont été prises.*

1. Dans tous les cas où un verbe est transitif (suivi d'un complément d'objet direct).

2. La traduction de « on » en anglais. Penser à utiliser le passif !
Ex. : – *On l'attend ce soir.* She is expected tonight.

NB Quelques formules au passif :
– He IS SUPPOSED to be in Paris. – *Il est censé être à Paris.*
– IT IS SAID THAT he works hard. = He IS SAID TO work hard.
– *On dit qu'il travaille avec acharnement.*
– The strike started a few days ago, IT IS EXPECTED TO end soon. = The strike IS EXPECTED TO end soon.
– *On s'attend à ce que la grève se termine rapidement.*

3. Pour les verbes à deux compléments, on peut choisir de mettre l'accent sur la personne ou sur la chose.
Ex. : – She was offered a promotion. *(C'est à elle qu'on a proposé une promotion et non à une autre personne.)*
– A promotion was offered to her. *(C'est une promotion qui lui a été proposée et non une mutation.)*

13. Discours direct et indirect

Emploi

1. On emploie le discours direct lorsque l'on cite les paroles de quelqu'un textuellement. On utilise les guillemets.
Ex. : – "I'll be back soon," she said. – *« Je reviendrai bientôt », dit-elle.*

2. On emploie le discours indirect lorsque l'on rapporte des paroles. Il y a alors l'apparition d'une subordonnée introduite par THAT (bien que THAT soit souvent omis).
Ex. : – She said (that) she would be back soon. – *Elle a dit qu'elle reviendrait bientôt.*

Formation du discours indirect
Si le verbe introductif de la phrase au discours indirect est au passé, le verbe de la subordonnée va changer de temps.

Discours direct	Discours indirect
Présent "She works well," he said. *« Elle travaille bien », a-t-il dit.*	→ **Prétérit** He said (that) she worked well. *Il a dit qu'elle travaillait bien.*
Prétérit "She worked well," he said. *« Elle travaillait bien », a-t-il dit.*	→ **Past perfect** He said she had worked well. *Il a dit qu'elle avait bien travaillé.*
Present perfect "She has worked well," he said. *« Elle a bien travaillé », a-t-il dit.*	→ **Past perfect** He said she had worked well. *Il a dit qu'elle avait bien travaillé.*
Futur en « will » "She will work well," he said. *« Elle travaillera bien », a-t-il dit.*	→ **Would** He said she would work well. *Il a dit qu'elle travaillerait bien.*
May "She may work well," he said. *« Peut-être va-t-elle bien travailler », a-t-il dit.*	→ **Might** He said she might work well. *Il a dit qu'elle pourrait peut-être bien travailler.*
Can "She can work well," he said. *« Elle peut travailler bien », a-t-il dit.*	→ **Could** He said she could work well. *Il a dit qu'elle pouvait travailler bien.*

Autres modifications

Discours direct	Discours indirect
Questions fermées (YES / NO questions) "Does she work well?" he asked. *« Travaille-t-elle bien ? » a-t-il demandé.*	→ **Subordonnée introduite par IF ou WHETHER + S + V** He asked if / whether she worked well. *Il a demandé si elle travaillait bien.*
Questions ouvertes (WH- questions) "Where does she work?" he asked. *« Où travaille-t-elle ? » a-t-il demandé.* "How long has she been with us?" he asked. *« Depuis combien de temps travaille-t-elle avec nous ? » a-t-il demandé.*	→ **Subordonnée introduite par un pronom interrogatif en WH-** He asked where she worked. *Il a demandé où elle travaillait.* He asked how long she had been with them. *Il a demandé depuis combien de temps elle travaillait avec eux.*
Impératif "Go out and don't come back!" he said. *« Sors et ne reviens pas ! » a-t-il dit.*	→ **Infinitive** He told her to go out and not to come back. *Il lui a dit de sortir et de ne pas revenir.*
Today "You can leave early today," he said to her. *« Vous pouvez partir tôt aujourd'hui », lui a-t-il dit.*	→ **That day** He said to her she could leave early that day. *Il lui a dit qu'elle pouvait partir tôt ce jour-là.*
Yesterday "I met you yesterday," he answered her. *« Je vous ai rencontrée hier », lui a-t-il répondu.*	→ **The day before / the previous day** He answered her that he had met her the day before. *Il lui a répondu qu'il l'avait rencontrée la veille.*
Tomorrow *demain*	→ **The next day / the following day** *le lendemain / le jour suivant*
Next week *la semaine prochaine*	→ **The following week** *la semaine suivante*
Now *maintenant*	→ **Then** *alors*
This *ceci*	→ **That** *cela*
Here *ici*	→ **There** *là*

Verbes introductifs

1. SAY et TELL

SAY peut être suivi ou non d'un complément. Apparition de TO entre SAY et un pronom. TELL est obligatoirement suivi d'un complément.
Au discours direct, SAY peut précéder ou suivre les propos. S'il suit la phrase au discours direct, l'inversion V + S est possible.
SAY TO SB et TELL SB ne peuvent être placés qu'après la phrase au discours direct.

Ex. : – She said: "It's sunny."
– "It's sunny," she said / said she.
– "It's sunny," she said to me / she told me.
– *Elle (m') a dit : « Il y a du soleil ».*

Au discours indirect, on utilise SAY + S + V ou TELL SB + S + V.

Ex. : – She said it was sunny.
– She told me it was sunny.
– *Elle (m') a dit qu'il y avait du soleil.*

2. Autres verbes

N'hésitez pas à utiliser d'autres verbes tels que:

ADD: ajouter	INVITE: inviter
ADMIT: admettre	ORDER: commander
ADVISE: conseiller	POINT OUT: faire remarquer
ANSWER: répondre	REMARK: remarquer
ARGUE: argumenter	REPLY: répondre
DENY: nier	WANT TO KNOW: vouloir savoir
EXPLAIN: expliquer	WARN: avertir
INQUIRE: demander	WONDER: se demander

14. Question tags

Emploi et formation

Ce sont des questions courtes qui permettent de demander l'adhésion de son interlocuteur à ce que l'on vient d'énoncer. Cela correspond souvent au français « n'est-ce pas ? », « hein ? », « non ? ».

1. Si la première partie de l'énoncé ne comporte pas de négation, le tag est négatif.

Ex. : – She's nice, isn't she?
– *Elle est sympathique, non ?*
– They're sleeping, aren't they?
– *Ils dorment, hein ?*

2. Si la première partie de l'énoncé comporte une négation, le tag est positif.

Ex. : – She is not that clever, is she?
– *Elle n'est pas si intelligente que ça, n'est-ce pas ?*
– They aren't working, are they?
– *Ils ne travaillent pas, hein ?*

⚠ Attention aux constructions suivantes :

- EVERYONE, EVERYBODY, SOMEONE, SOMEBODY, ANYONE, ANYBODY, NO ONE, NOBODY sont repris par le pronom THEY.

Ex. : – Everybody had fun, didn't they?
– *Tout le monde s'est bien amusé, n'est-ce pas ?*

- NEVER (jamais), HARDLY (à peine, ne… guère), HARDLY EVER (presque jamais) dans la première partie de l'énoncé nécessitent un tag positif.

Ex. : – He hardly ever watches TV, does he?
– *Il ne regarde presque jamais la télévision, n'est-ce pas ?*

- Après LET'S, le tag est SHALL WE?

Ex. : – Let's go home, shall we?
– *Rentrons à la maison, d'accord ?*

- Après un impératif, le tag est WILL YOU?

Ex. : – Eat up your dinner, will you?
– *Termine ton dîner, veux-tu ?*

- I AM est repris par AREN'T I?

Ex. : – I am hopeless, aren't I? – *Je suis nulle, non ?*

15. Réponses courtes

Emploi et formation

Ce sont des expressions elliptiques qui permettent de demander la confirmation d'un énoncé, de confirmer un énoncé ou bien d'apporter la contradiction.

1. Réponses à des questions fermées (YES / NO questions)

→ Reprise de l'auxiliaire de la question

Ex. : – Are you working? – Yes I am.
– *Es-tu en train de travailler ? – Oui.*
– Can you speak Chinese? – No, I can't.
– *Parlez-vous chinois ? – Non.*

2. Demande de confirmation

Lorsque la première partie de l'énoncé est affirmative, la demande de confirmation est une interrogation qui reprend l'auxiliaire de cette première partie. S'il n'y a pas d'auxiliaire dans la première partie, il faut employer l'auxiliaire DO conjugué.

Ex. : – I'll do the shopping. – Will you?
– *Je ferai les courses. – Ah oui ?*
– She stopped. – Did she?
– *Elle s'est arrêtée. – Ah oui ?*
– He likes shopping. – Does he?
– *Il aime faire les magasins. – Ah oui ?*

Lorsque la première partie de l'énoncé est négative, la demande de confirmation se fait à la forme interro-négative.

Ex. : – I won't do it. – Won't you?
– *Je ne le ferai pas. – Ah bon ?*

3. Confirmation

Ex. : – You were late. – Yes, I was.
– *Tu étais en retard. – Oui, c'est vrai.*
– She spoke to him. – Yes, she did
– *Elle lui a parlé. – Oui, c'est vrai.*

4. Contradiction

Ex. : – You don't like tea. – Yes, I do.
– *Tu n'aimes pas le thé. – Bien sûr que si !*
– I slowed down. – No, you didn't.
– *J'ai ralenti. – Pas du tout !*

2. LE GROUPE NOMINAL

1. Dénombrables / indénombrables

▸ **1.** On appelle dénombrables les noms que l'on peut compter. On peut donc les employer au singulier et au pluriel.

Ex. : – a dog, five cats, not many students, 1,000 employees.
– *un chien, cinq chats, pas beaucoup d'étudiants, 1 000 employés.*

On emploie les dénombrables avec A FEW (quelques), FEW (peu de), MANY, A LOT OF, LOTS OF (beaucoup de). (cf. Quantifieurs)

NB Certains noms collectifs sont suivis d'un singulier lorsqu'ils renvoient au groupe en tant qu'unité mais d'un pluriel lorsqu'ils désignent les éléments du groupe : AUDIENCE, STAFF, CROWD, FAMILY, GOVERNMENT.

Ex. : – The new government is going to cut back on public expenditures. – *Le nouveau gouvernement va réduire les dépenses publiques.*
– My family are coming over for Christmas.
– *Ma famille vient pour Noël. (= les membres de ma famille).*

⚠ PEOPLE (les gens) est un dénombrable : on peut dire TWO PEOPLE, FIVE PEOPLE, MANY PEOPLE. Sa particularité est de ne pouvoir s'employer dans ce sens qu'au pluriel.

▸ **2.** On appelle indénombrables les éléments que l'on ne peut pas compter, qui renvoient à des éléments vus dans leur globalité.

Ex. : – Tea, not much tea; violence, much violence.
– *Le thé, pas beaucoup de thé ; la violence, beaucoup de violence.*

Ils sont donc incompatibles avec A(N), ONE, TWO…
On emploie les indénombrables avec A LITTLE (un peu de), LITTLE (peu de), MUCH, A LOT OF, LOTS OF (beaucoup de).

⚠ Après un indénombrable le verbe est au singulier !

▸ **3.** Certains noms sont dénombrables en français mais indénombrables en anglais. En anglais ils désignent donc un ensemble, une globalité.

Ex. : – advice *(les conseils)*, business *(les affaires)*, evidence *(les preuves)*, furniture *(les meubles)*, hair *(les cheveux)*, information *(les renseignements)*, luggage *(les bagages)*, news *(les nouvelles)*, progress *(les progrès)*, rubbish *(les ordures)*, work *(le travail)*, travel *(les voyages)*, etc.

NB Les dénombrables sont signalés [C] dans les dictionnaires, les indénombrables [U]

▸ **4.** Comment traduire « un bagage », « une nouvelle » ?
Il suffit d'utiliser un dénombreur du type A PIECE OF.

Ex. : – He gave me an excellent piece of advice.
– *Il m'a donné un excellent conseil.*

2. Quantifieurs

Sens	+ Dénombrable	+ Indénombrable
Combien ?	How many? How many dollars? *Combien de dollars ?*	How much? How much money? *Combien d'argent ?*
Trop	Too many Too many people. *Trop de gens.*	Too much Too much time. *Trop de temps.*
Beaucoup trop	Far too many Far too many inhabitants. *Beaucoup trop d'habitants.*	Far too much Far too much fat. *Beaucoup trop de graisse.*
Tant de / tellement de	So many So many jobs. *Tant d'emplois.*	So much So much work. *Tant de travail.*
Tout, tous, toute(s)	→ All / All the All flights have been cancelled. *Tous les vols ont été annulés.* *(= l'ensemble des vols)* All the flights to Miami. *Tous les vols pour Miami. (= groupe défini)* → Every + singulier Every town. *Chaque ville / Toutes les villes.* → Each + singulier Each town. *Chaque ville (envisagée séparément).* → All = the whole + singulier : en entier All the book / The whole book. *Tout le livre.* → Whole + pluriel : se traduit par « entier » Whole towns. *Des villes entières.*	All the All the truth. *Toute la vérité.* All the information. *Tous les renseignements.*

Sens	+ Dénombrable	+ Indénombrable
Tous les deux	**Both** Both secretaries. *Les deux secrétaires.*	**Both** Both wine and whisky. *À la fois le vin et le whisky.*
La plupart	**Most / Most of** Most Japanese. *La plupart des Japonais. (en général)* Most of the Japanese I know. *(un groupe limité)* *La plupart des Japonais que je connais.*	**Most / Most of** Most violence. *La plus grande part de violence.* Most of the violence I meet. *La plus grande part de la violence que je rencontre.*
Beaucoup	**A lot of / Lots of / Many / Plenty of** A lot of people; lots of dollars; many friends; plenty of examples. *Beaucoup de gens / de dollars / d'amis / d'exemples.*	**A lot of / Lots of / Much / Plenty of / A great deal of** A lot of courage; lots of luck; much progress; plenty of meat; a great deal of money. *Beaucoup de courage / de chance / de progrès / de viande / d'argent.*
Assez (suffisamment)	**Enough** Enough apples. *Assez de pommes.*	**Enough** Enough patience. *Assez de patience.*
Plus… que	**More… than** More chairs than tables. *Plus de chaises que de tables.*	**More… than** More bread than butter. *Plus de pain que de beurre.*
Moins… que	**Fewer… than** Fewer people than yesterday. *Moins de gens qu'hier.*	**Less… than** Less coffee than tea. *Moins de café que de thé.*
Une certaine quantité	→ **Some + pluriel** • **Phrase affirmative** Some books. *Des livres.* • **Phrase interrogative** *Questions polies* *(on suppose l'existence de ce dont on parle)* Would you like some cakes? *Est-ce que vous voulez des gâteaux ?* → **Any + phrase interrogative** Any questions? *Des questions ?*	→ **Some** • **Phrase affirmative** Some whisky. *Du whisky.* • **Phrase interrogative** Même remarque que pour les dénombrables. Would you like some coffee? *Voulez-vous du café ?* → **Any + phrase interrogative** Is there any bread left? *Reste-t-il du pain ?*
Une faible quantité	→ **A few: quelques** A few ideas. *Quelques idées.* → **Few: peu de** Few questions. *Peu de questions.*	→ **A little: un peu de** A little time. *Un peu de temps.* → **Little: peu de** Little sleep. *Peu de sommeil.*
Pas de	**Not any / No** Not any problems; no questions. *Pas de problèmes ; pas de questions*	**Not any / No** Not any hope / No hope. *Pas d'espoir.*

⚠ **ALL, A FEW, EACH, BOTH, MANY, MUCH, MOST sont suivis de OF lorsqu'ils portent sur un pronom.**
Ex. : – All of them came. – *Ils sont tous venus.*
– Both of us said… – *Nous avons tous les deux déclaré…*
– A few of them understood. – *Quelques-uns ont compris.*

3. Articles

Article indéfini : a/an

Article A devant un son consonne.
Ex. : – a company, a huge decrease, a university, a European, a young applicant
– *une société, une forte baisse, une université, un Européen, un jeune candidat.*

Article AN devant un son voyelle.
Ex. : – an increase, an affiliate, an hour
– *une augmentaiton, une filiale, une heure*

Fonction

1. Désigne un élément non défini, un élément parmi tous les autres.
Ex. : – I'm looking for a job.
– *Je cherche un emploi.*

2. Présente un élément nouveau qui sera ensuite repris par THE ou par un démonstratif.
Ex. : – He's working for a car manufacturer.
– *Il travaille pour un fabricant de voitures.*

Emploi

1. Devant un nom dénombrable singulier.
Ex. : – a computer, an interview
– *un ordinateur, un entretien*

2. Devant un nom de métier ou de fonction (sauf si cette fonction ne peut être occupée que par une seule personne. Ex. : – He was company manager two years ago. – *Il a été un chef d'entreprise il y a deux ans*).
– He is a sales representative.
– *Il est représentant.*

3. Après une préposition.
Ex. : – As a PA, she should be well-organised.
– *En tant qu'assistante de direction, elle devrait être bien organisée.*
– You can't send this contract without an agreement.
– *Vous ne pouvez pas envoyer ce contrat sans accord.*

4. Dans une apposition.
Ex. : – This customer, a big retailer, has to be contacted.
– *Ce client, important grossiste, doit être contacté.*

5. Devant une unité de temps, de mesure et avec HALF.
Ex. : – Five days a week
– *Cinq jours par semaine*
– £10 a kilo – *10 livres le kilo*
– Half a pint of beer (a half pint of beer *est possible*)
– *une demi pinte de bière*

6. Après SUCH et WHAT.
Ex. : – It was such a long trip!
– *Ce fut un voyage si long !*
– What an amazing country!
– *Quel pays étonnant !*

⚠ **Structure avec SUCH, SO et TOO.**
Ex. : – It's such a hard task! / It's so hard a task!
– *C'est une tâche si difficile !*
– It's too hard a task.
– *C'est une tâche trop difficile.*

Article défini : the

THE se prononce [ðe] devant un son consonne et [ðiː] devant un son voyelle.

Fonction

1. Renvoie à ce qui est connu (proche d'un démonstratif THIS / THESE ou THAT / THOSE).
Ex. : – I'm working for a company. The company is located near London.
– *Je travaille pour une société. Cette société se trouve près de Londres.*

2. Détermine un nom dénombrable défini par une situation, un contexte, un complément de nom, un adverbe ou une proposition.
Ex. : – Can you shut the window, please?
– *Pouvez-vous fermer la fenêtre, s'il vous plaît ?*
– Could you please show me the letter?
– *Pourriez-vous s'il vous plaît me montrer la lettre ?*
– The price of this item is $15.
– *Le prix de cet article est 15 $.*
– The offices upstairs are to be refurbished.
– *Les bureaux à l'étage doivent être refaits.*
– The e-mail that you sent has just been returned.
– *L'e-mail que tu as envoyé vient d'être réexpédié.*

3. Détermine un nom indénombrable défini par une situation ou une proposition relative.
Ex. : – Pass me the sugar, please. *(Le sucre que l'on désigne et non le sucre en général.)*
– *Passez-moi le sucre, s'il vous plaît.*
– I spent the money you gave me. *(Cet argent-là et non l'argent en général.)*
– *J'ai dépensé l'argent que tu m'as donné.*

Emploi

1. Un élément unique
Ex. : – The sun, the sea, the earth, the world, etc.
– *Le soleil, la mer, la terre, le monde, etc.*

2. Un titre
Ex. : – The Queen, the President, etc.
– *La Reine, le Président, etc.*

3. Un adjectif substantivé (cf. Adjectifs)

4. Les noms d'îles, de cours d'eau, de mer et de chaînes de montagne
Ex. : – The Seychelles, the Thames, the Pacific, the Rockies, etc.
– *Les Seychelles, la Tamise, le Pacifique, les Rocheuses, etc.*

5. Les noms d'instruments de musique
Ex. : – She plays the piano. – *Elle joue du piano.*

6. Un nom à valeur générique
Ex. : – The telephone has been through many changes recently.
– *Le téléphone a récemment connu bien des évolutions.*

Absence d'article : Ø

1. On ne met pas d'article devant un nom pluriel (ou un nom indénombrable) lorsque ce nom renvoie à une généralité.

Ex. : – Not enough people know that Ø big companies rule the world.
– *Pas assez de gens savent que les grandes sociétés gouvernent le monde.*
– Ø Prices are still increasing.
– *Les prix continuent d'augmenter.*
– Ø Time is Ø money.
– *Le temps, c'est de l'argent.*

2. Et dans les cas suivants :

Titre + nom
Ex. : – Ø Queen Elizabeth, Ø President Bush, etc.
– *La Reine Élisabeth, le Président Bush, etc.*

Les noms de pays
Ex. : – Ø France, Ø Spain, Ø Germany,
– *La France, l'Espagne, l'Allemagne, etc* (sauf certains qui sont des noms communs à l'origine : the Netherlands = *les Pays-Bas*, the United Kingdom = *le Royaume Uni*, the USA = *les États-Unis*, etc.).

Les noms de langue
Ex. : – Ø French, Ø Spanish, Ø English, etc.
– *Le français, l'espagnol, l'anglais, etc.*

Les noms de sport
Ex. : – He plays Ø golf.
– *Il joue au golf.*

Les noms de maladies
Ex. : – Ø cancer, Ø Aids, etc.
– *Le cancer, le sida, etc.* (sauf quatre : the mumps = *les oreillons*, the measles = *la rougeole*, the flu = *la grippe*, the plague = *la peste*.)

4. Adjectifs

Adjectifs qualificatifs

⚠ **Les adjectifs qualificatifs sont invariables.**

1. Les adjectifs épithètes se placent devant le nom qu'ils qualifient, du plus objectif (1) au subjectif (2).

Ex. : – A brilliant Australian student.
(2) (1)
– *Un brillant étudiant australien.*

L'ordre est le suivant :

jugement (6) taille/forme (5) âge (4) couleur (3) origine/nationalité (2) marque/matière (1)

Ex. : – An interesting, recent survey.
– *Une enquête récente intéressante.*
– An elegant, old, British car.
– *Une vieille et élégante voiture anglaise.*
– A small, new, brown, wooden motel.
– *Un nouveau petit motel en bois marron.*

2. Les adjectifs composés peuvent être formés de différentes façons. Les plus fréquentes sont :

Adjectif + nom
Ex. : – A twenty-year-old applicant, a sixteen-dollar increase.
– *Un candidat âgé de vingt ans, une augmentation de seize dollars.*

Adjectif + nom + -ED
Ex. : – A blue-eyed girl, a London-based company.
– *Une fille aux yeux bleus, une société établie à Londres.*

Adjectif + V-ING
Ex. : – A fast-selling product, an easy-going attitude.
– *Un produit qui se vent bien, une attitude décontractée.*

Adverbe + participe passé
Ex. : – A well-known brand, a well-knit team.
– *Une marque bien connue, une équipe très unie.*

Nom + adjectif
Ex. : – An energy-efficient policy, lead-free petrol.
– *Une politique d'économie d'énergie, de l'essence sans plomb.*

Nom + V-ING
Ex. : – A time-consuming task, a money-saving measure
– *Une tâche prenante, une mesure qui fait gagner du temps.*

NB **Obligation de mettre un trait d'union entre les deux parties composant cet adjectif.**

3. Les adjectifs substantivés – THE + adj. – désignent un groupe de personnes et sont donc suivis du verbe au pluriel.

Ex. : – The poor are more and more numerous.
– *Il y a de plus en plus de pauvres.*
– The unemployed suffer from rejection.
– *Les chômeurs souffrent d'exclusion.*
– The homeless feel hopeless.
– *Les SDF se sentent désespérés.*

C'est aussi le cas des adjectifs de nationalité en -CH, -SH, -ESE et de THE SWISS.

Ex. : – The Dutch, the British, the Japanese, etc.
– *Les Néerlandais, les Britanniques, les Japonais, etc.*

Au singulier, on ajoute MAN / WOMAN aux adjectifs de nationalité en -CH et -SH.

Ex. : – A Irishman, a Frenchwoman,... *mais* a Spaniard.
– *Un Irlandais, une Française, un Espagnol.*

⚠ **Les adjectifs substantivés suivants prennent un « s » :**

Ex. : – The blacks, the whites.
– *Les noirs, les blancs.*

Ex. : – The over-sixties, the under-twenties, the eighteen-year-olds.
– *Les gens de plus de 60 ans, les moins de 20 ans, les jeunes âgés de 18 ans.*

Les adjectifs de nationalité ne se terminant pas par -CH, -SH, -ESE.

Ex. : – The Germans, the Greeks, the Poles, etc.
– *Les Allemands, les Grecs, les Polonais. etc.*

Adjectifs possessifs

MY / YOUR / HIS-HER-ITS / OUR / YOUR / THEIR + N (sing. / pl.)

Ex. : – Let's go to my office / offices!
– *Allons à mon / mes bureau(x) !*
– What's your name? (= one person) / What are your names? (= more than one person)
– *Quel est votre nom ? / Donnez-moi vos noms.*

HIS-HER-ITS s'accordent avec le genre et le nombre du possesseur.

Ex. : – John owns a computer; it's his computer.
– *John a un ordinateur ; c'est son ordinateur.*
– You know where she lives. Could you give me her address / references, please?
– *Tu sais où elle habite. Peux-tu me donner son adresse / ses coordonnées, s'il te plaît ?*
– The company has warehouses; where are its warehouses?
– *La société a des entrepôts ; où sont ses entrepôts ?*

L'adjectif possessif peut être également sujet d'un gérondif.

Ex. : – Do you mind my smoking in the office?
– *Cela vous gêne-t-il que je fume dans le bureau ?*

⚠ **Accords suivants :**

OUR / THEIR + N au singulier si les personnes possèdent une chose en commun.

Ex. : – The workers will show you their factory.
– *Les ouvriers vous montreront leur usine.*

OUR / THEIR + N au pluriel si les personnes possèdent chacune une unité semblable.

Ex. : – We are going to present our companies.
– *Chacun d'entre nous va présenter son entreprise.*

SOMEBODY, EVERYBODY, NOBODY + V au singulier, repris par un adjectif possessif au pluriel.

Ex. : – Will somebody give me their help?
– *Quelqu'un veut-il m'aider ?*

5. Comparatifs / superlatifs

Quel que soit le type de comparaison, deux éléments sont à retenir.

1. Le type d'adjectif

- Adjectif court = une syllabe sauf PLEASED, REAL, RIGHT, WRONG.
- Adjectif long = plus de deux syllabes.
- Adjectif de deux syllabes terminé en -ER, -Y, -LY = adjectif court.
- Adjectif de deux syllabes terminé en -FUL, -ING, -ED, -LESS = adjectif long.
- En cas de doute, considérer l'adjectif comme un adjectif long.

2. Le type de nom

Différencier les noms dénombrables des noms indénombrables (cf. Dénombrables / indénombrables).

⚠ Formes irrégulières

Adjectif / adverbe	Comparatif	Superlatif
good, well	better	the best
bad, ill	worse	the worst
far	farther / further*	the farthest / the furthest
old	elder**	the eldest**
late	later / latter***	the latest***
little + indénombrable (= peu de)	less + indénombrable	the least + indénombrable
many + dénombrable much + indénombrable	more	the most

*outre le sens de « plus loin », further a aussi le sens de « supplémentaire » :
Ex. : – For further information.
– *Pour plus amples renseignements.*
**Elder = *l'aîné (de 2)* ; the eldest = *l'aîné (de plus de 2).*
La forme est régulière (old / older / the oldest) pour dire « âgé / plus âgé / le (la, les) plus âgé(es) ».
***Later = *plus tard.* The latter = le dernier de deux éléments cités.
Ex. : – I met John but not Martin. I think the latter is abroad. (« The latter » reprend Martin.)
– I have worked for small companies and also for multinationals. Working in the latter is quite stressful. (« The latter » reprend « multinationals » mais reste singulier.)
The latest = le dernier dans le temps, donc le plus récent.
Ex. : – The latest survey showed an amazing increase.
– *La dernière étude en date (= la plus récente) a révélé une hausse étonnante.*

Les comparatifs

1. Comparatif d'égalité

Adjectif	Nom
Your office is (not) **as** big **as** mine. *Ton bureau (n')est (pas) aussi grand que le mien.* This task is (not) **as** important **as** the other ones. *Cette tâche (n')est (pas) aussi importante que les autres.*	She's (hasn't) got **as many** children **as** you. *Elle (n')a (pas) autant d'enfants que toi.* He earns (doesn't earn) **as much** money **as** his colleagues. *Il gagne (ne gagne pas) autant d'argent que ses collègues.* She works (doesn't work) in **the same** company **as** her father. *Elle travaille (ne travaille pas) dans la même société que son père.*

Avec un multiplicateur

Ex. : – The sales were **twice as** big in 2003 **as** they were in 2002.
– *Les ventes ont été deux fois plus importantes en 2003 qu'en 2002.*
– They were **three times / four times** … **as** big in 2003 as in 2002.
– *Elles ont été trois fois / quatre fois… plus importantes en 2003 qu'en 2002.*
– There are **three times as many** births in this country **as** in that one.
– *Il y a trois fois plus de naissances dans ce pays que dans celui-là.*
– He earns **twice as much** money **as** her.
– *Il gagne deux fois plus d'argent qu'elle.*
– They consume **half as many** beans **as** you.
– *Ils consomment deux fois moins / moitié moins de haricots que vous.*
– They consume **half as much** bread **as** you.
– *Ils consomment deux fois moins / moitié moins de pain que vous.*

NB En français, on traduit à l'aide d'un comparatif de supériorité / d'infériorité.

Dans l'expression du type : AS SOON AS POSSIBLE / AS SOON AS I CAN (dès que possible, le plus vite possible).

Ex : – Send me a confirmation as soon as possible / as soon as you can.
– *Envoyez-moi une confirmation le plus vite possible / dès que possible.*

2. Comparatif de supériorité

Adjectif	Nom
She is tall**er than** him. *Elle est plus grande que lui.* This company is **more** efficient **than** that one. *Cette société est plus efficace que celle-là.*	She gives **more** details **than** he does. *Elle donne plus de détails que lui.* He's got **more** time now **than** he used to have. *Il a plus de temps maintenant qu'autrefois.*

Beaucoup plus que / de

Ex. : – She is **far / much** tall**er than** him.
– *Elle est bien plus grande que lui.*
– This company is **far / much more** efficient **than** that one.
– *Cette société est bien plus efficace que celle-là.*
– She gives **far / many more** details **than** he does.
– *Elle donne bien plus de détails que lui.*
– He's got **far / much more** time now **than** he used to have.
– *Il a bien plus de temps qu'autrefois.*

De plus en plus

Ex. : – It's getting cold**er and** cold**er**.
– *Il fait de plus en plus froid.*
– It's **more and more** difficult.
– *C'est de plus en plus difficile.*
– There are **more and more** details.
– *Il y a de plus en plus de détails.*
– They've got **more and more** time.
– *Ils ont de plus en plus de temps.*

D'autant plus

Ex. : – It was **all the** funni**er as** he didn't understand.
– *C'était d'autant plus drôle qu'il ne comprenait pas.*
– It's **all the more** essential **as** you'll use it very often.
– *C'est d'autant plus essentiel que vous l'utiliserez très souvent.*

Plus…, plus…

Ex. : – **The** high**er** the prices (are), **the more** difficult it is to sell.
– *Plus les prix sont élevés, plus il est difficile de vendre.*
– **The more** tasks she deals with, **the more** money she gets / **the better** she is paid.
– *Plus elle gère de tâches, plus elle a d'argent / mieux elle est payée.*

⚠ Ordre des mots : adj. / N + S + V.

Le / la / les plus… (comparaison de deux éléments)

Ex. : – Company X and company Y → Company X is **the** bigg**er** / **the more** efficient.
– *L'entreprise X est la plus grande / la plus efficace.*

3. Comparatif d'infériorité

Adjectif	Nom
Her computer is **less** fast **than** theirs. *Son ordinateur est moins rapide que le leur.* His car is **less** reliable **than** hers. *Sa voiture est moins fiable que la sienne.*	She has **fewer** friends **than** them. *Elle a moins d'amis qu'eux.* He's got **less** courage **than** her. *Il a moins de courage qu'elle.*

Trois, quatre … fois moins

Ex. : – They were **three times / four times … less** big in 2003 than in 2002.
– *Ils étaient trois / quatre fois moins importants en 2003 qu'en 2002.*
– There are **three times fewer** births in this country **than** in that one.
– *Il y a trois fois moins de naissances dans ce pays que dans celui-là.*

Beaucoup moins que / de

Ex. : – Her computer is **far less** fast than theirs.
– *Son ordinateur est bien moins rapide que le leur.*
– His car is **far less** reliable than hers.
– *Sa voiture est bien moins fiable que la sienne.*
– She has **far fewer** friends than them.
– *Elle a bien moins d'amis qu'eux.*
– He's got **far less** courage than her.
– *Il a bien moins de courage qu'elle.*

De moins en moins

Ex. : – It's getting **less and less** cold.
– *Il fait de moins en moins froid.*
– It's **less and less** difficult.
– *C'est de moins en moins difficile.*
– There are **fewer and fewer** details.
– *Il y a de moins en moins de détails.*
– They've got **less and less** time.
– *Ils ont de moins en moins de temps.*

D'autant moins

Ex. : – It was **all the less** funny **as** he didn't understand.
– *C'était d'autant moins drôle qu'il ne comprenait pas.*
– It's **all the less** essential **as** you won't use it very often.
– *C'est d'autant moins essentiel que tu ne l'utiliseras pas souvent.*

Moins…, moins…

Ex. : – **The less** high the prices (are), **the less** difficult it is to sell.
– *Moins les prix sont élevés, moins il est difficile de vendre.*
– **The fewer** tasks she deals with, **the less** money she gets.
– *Moins elle gère de tâches, moins elle a d'argent.*

Le / la / les moins… (comparaison de deux éléments)

Ex. : – Company X and company Y → Company X is **the less** big / **the less** efficient.
– *L'entreprise X est la moins grande / la moins efficace.*

Les superlatifs

1. Superlatifs de supériorité

Ex. : – It's **the** short**est** e-mail I have ever received.
– *C'est le mail le plus court que j'ai jamais reçu.*
– This is **the most** interesting meeting I have attended.
– *C'est la réunion la plus intéressante à laquelle j'ai assisté.*
– She has **the most** friends.
– *C'est elle qui a le plus d'amis.*
– He's got **the most** money.
– *C'est lui qui a le plus d'argent.*

Noter les formulations :
– What I **like best / most** is going out.
– *Ce que je préfère / Ce que j'aime le mieux, c'est sortir.*
– I'll **do my best**. – *Je ferai de mon mieux.*

2. Superlatifs d'infériorité

Ex. : – It's **the least** nice view of all the nice views I've gazed at.
– *C'est la vue la moins belle parmi toutes celles que j'ai contemplées.*
– This is **the least** interesting meeting I have attended.
– *C'est la réunion la moins intéressante à laquelle j'ai assisté.*
– She has **the least** friends.
– *C'est elle qui a le moins d'amis.*
– He's got **the least** money.
– *C'est lui qui a le moins d'argent.*

6. Pronoms

Le pronom remplace un déterminant + nom.

Ex. : – Look at that shop window; **it**'s wonderful!
(**It** *remplace « that shop window ».)*
– *Regarde cette vitrine ; elle est magnifique !*

Pronoms personnels

1. Sujets d'un verbe

I / YOU / HE-SHE-IT / WE / YOU / THEY

Ex. : – **He** was satisfied with the meeting.
– *Il était content de la réunion.*
– My colleagues and **I** enjoyed the trip.
– *Mes collègues et moi avons aimé le voyage.*

⚠ Structures suivantes :

Traduction du « on » français

Ex. : – In France, **we** love wine. (**We** *si le locuteur est français ; il s'inclut et s'adresse à des Français.)*
– *En France, on aime le vin.*
– In France, **you** love wine. (**You** *si le locuteur n'est pas français et s'adresse à des Français.)*
– *En France, on aime le vin.*

– In Belgium, **they** love beer. (**They** *si le locuteur n'est pas belge ; il n'est pas inclus dans le groupe et ne s'adresse pas à des Belges.)*
– En Belgique, on aime la bière.

Traduction de la structure impersonnelle « C'est »

• Pronom personnel sujet

Ex. : – Who wrote this fax? **I** did. *(cf. 2. Compléments d'un verbe)*
– Qui a écrit ce fax ? C'est moi.
– **She** is a very efficient receptionist.
*– C'est une réceptionniste très efficace. (**He** si l'on veut parler d'un réceptionniste.)*

• Ø (pas de pronom IT)

Ex. : – Going abroad is beneficial for language skills.
– Aller à l'étranger, c'est bénéfique pour les compétences linguistiques.

Dans une comparaison

Ex. : – He is younger than **she** is. *(cf. 2. Compléments d'un verbe)*
– Il est plus jeune qu'elle.

2. Compléments d'un verbe

ME / YOU / HIM-HER-IT / US / YOU / THEM

Ex. : – I have never met **him**.
– Je ne l'ai jamais rencontré.
– Who wrote this fax? It's **me**.
– Qui a écrit ce fax ? C'est moi.
– He is younger than **her**.
– Il est plus jeune qu'elle.

⚠ Structures suivantes :

Verbes à double complément : V + pronom complément + TO + nom / pronom

Ex. : – I'll show **them** to the rep.
– Je les montrerai au représentant
– Give it to me.
– Donne-le moi.

S + V + pronom + particule

Ex. : – I won't give **it** up!
– Je ne l'abandonnerai pas ! (it = this job, for example)

IT après un verbe d'appréciation + nom / adj. + proposition en THAT ou en TO.

Ex. : – I consider **it** my job **to** check your hours.
– Je considère que contrôler vos horaires fait partie de mon travail.
– I find **it** important **that** we should organise a welcome party.
– Je trouve qu'il est important que nous organisions une fête de bienvenue.

Pronoms possessifs

MINE / YOURS / HIS-HERS-ITS / OURS / YOURS / THEIRS

⚠ **Pas d'article défini THE devant un pronom possessif**

Ex. : – This catalogue is mine.
– Ce catalogue est à moi.
– Is she a friend of yours? (= is she one of your friends?)
– Est-ce une de tes amies ?

7. Génitif

Formation

<u>N1 (possesseur)'s N2 (objet possédé) ou N1s' N2</u>

Ex. : – The secretary's printer.
– L'imprimante de la secrétaire.
– The children's toys.
– Les jouets des enfants.
– The workers' jobs.
– Les emplois des travailleurs.
– The boss's laptop.
– Le portable du patron.

L'adjectif qui précède N1 ou N2 le qualifie.

Ex. : – My manager's new car.
– La nouvelle voiture de mon chef de service.
– My new manager's luxury car.
– La voiture luxueuse de mon nouveau chef de service.

NB **N2 n'est jamais précédé d'un article.**

Si N1 est le sujet d'une proposition relative, on a recours à la structure avec OF.

Ex. : – The request of the applicant who came an hour ago was incredible.
– La demande du candidat qui est venu il y a une heure était incroyable.

Si le nom exprimé en N1 ne comporte pas d'article, il n'en aura pas non plus dans la formation du génitif.

Ex. : – Ø Great Britain's imports.
– Les importations britanniques.
– Ø Employees' working hours.
– Les horaires de travail des employés. (en général)

Comparez avec :

– The employees' working hours.
– Les horaires de travail des employés. (de l'entreprise dont on parle par exemple)

⚠ Structures suivantes :

N1 composé de plusieurs éléments

Ex. : – Harry and Sally's car.
– La voiture de Harry et Sally.
– Fred's and Cat's mobiles.
– Le portable de Fred et celui de Cat.

N2 sous-entendu

Ex. : – Saint Paul's *(sous-entendu* Cathedral*)*
– Saint Paul.
– Harrods' *(sous-entendu* store*)*
– Harrod's.
– McDonald's *(sous-entendu* fast-food restaurant*)*
– McDonald's.
– The baker's *(sous-entendu* shop*)*
– La boulangerie.
– This dictionary is Helen's *(sous-entendu* dictionary*)*
– Ce dictionnaire est à Hélène.

– Next week I'll stay at Henry's. *(sous-entendu* house*)*
– La semaine prochaine, je resterai chez Henri.
– His job is not as well paid as Becky's. *(sous-entendu* job*)*
– Son travail n'est pas aussi bien payé que celui de Becky.
– I am a friend of Mary's. *(sous-entendu* I'm one of Mary's friends*)*
– Je suis une amie de Marie.

Emploi

Quand il y a un rapport de possession entre N1 et N2, N1 peut être :

une personne ou un groupe de personnes

Ex. : – Mr Johnson's company.
– La société de Mr Johnson.
– Somebody's job.
– Le travail de quelqu'un.
– The salesmen's cars.
– Les voitures des vendeurs.
– The governments' policies.
– Les politiques des gouvernements.

une activité humaine

Ex. : – The meeting's beginning.
– Le début de la réunion.

un lieu

Ex. : – The USA's exports.
– Les exportations américaines.
– The world's biggest output.
– La plus grosse production mondiale.

une unité de temps ou une distance

Ex. : – Tomorrow's newspaper.
– Le journal de demain.
– A ten minutes' break.
– Une pause de 10 mn.
– In a week's time.
– Dans une semaine.
– A two thousand miles' journey.
– Un voyage de 2 000 miles.

8. Noms composés

Il s'agit d'une structure du type <u>Nom + Nom</u>.

Ex. : – A bus ticket. (= a ticket for a bus)
– Un billet de bus.

BUS et TICKET sont deux noms, mais BUS, placé devant TICKET a valeur d'adjectif, il est donc normalement invariable.

NB

La traduction en français s'effectue de droite à gauche.

Un nom peut être précédé de plusieurs noms, formant ainsi un très long nom composé.

Ex. : – A business class travel survey.
– Une enquête sur les voyages en classe affaires.

Un nom composé peut être précédé d'un ou de plusieurs adjectifs.

Ex. : – An outdated rail network.
– Un réseau de chemin de fer dépassé.

⚠ **Jamais de pluriel dans le type de noms composés suivants :**

– A three-hour journey. *Un voyage de trois heures.*
– A 10-dollar bill. *Un billet de 10 dollars.*
– A five-year-old child. *Un enfant de cinq ans.*

9. Gérondif

Formation

Tout verbe peut se transformer en nom si l'on ajoute -ING à la base verbale : <u>BV + -ING</u> → <u>Nom</u>.

Ex. : – Read → reading : *la lecture.*
– Sing → singing : *le chant.*

Le gérondif (nom verbal) peut remplir toutes les fonctions du nom.

• **Sujet**

Ex. : – Working on Sundays is no fun.
– Travailler le dimanche n'est pas drôle.

• **Complément**

Ex. : – She likes skiing.
– Elle aime le ski.

Comme un nom, il peut être accompagné d'un adjectif possessif, d'un cas possessif, etc.

Ex. : – I hope you don't mind my smoking.
– J'espère que cela ne vous ennuie pas si je fume.
– Bill's driving is a little erratic.
– La façon de conduire de Bill est un peu imprévisible.

Emploi

Après toutes les prépositions.

Ex. : – I am fond of visiting this museum.
– J'aime bien visiter ce musée.
– I am not keen on cooking.
– Je n'aime pas beaucoup faire la cuisine.
– She went out without taking her bag.
– Elle est sortie sans prendre son sac.

Après certains verbes et expressions.

• **Verbes décrivant une activité : STOP, KEEP, etc.**

Ex. : – He has stopped smoking.
– Il a arrêté de fumer.

• **Verbes décrivant l'intérêt (ou le désintérêt) pour une activité : LIKE, LOVE, ENJOY, DISLIKE, etc.**

Ex. : – I enjoy driving.
– J'aime conduire.

• **Des expressions du type : I CAN'T HELP** *(je ne peux m'empêcher de)*, **I CAN'T STAND** *(je ne supporte pas)*, **IT'S NO USE** *(cela ne sert à rien)*, **BE WORTH** *(valoir la peine de)*.

Ex. : – It's no use talking to her.
– Cela ne sert à rien de lui parler.
– This film is worth seeing.
– Ce film vaut la peine d'être vu.

3. LA PHRASE

1. Structure de la phrase

La phrase simple est composée d'un sujet, d'un verbe et d'un complément (co).

1. Forme affirmative : S + V + co

Ex. : – I like my new computer.
– *J'aime mon nouvel ordinateur.*

⚠ Il n'y a pas d'inversion du sujet et du verbe avec PERHAPS ou MAYBE.

Ex. : – Perhaps / Maybe he will come.
– *Peut-être viendra-t-il.*

2. Forme négative : S + aux. / modal + NOT + V + co.

⚠ L'auxiliaire dépend du temps utilisé (cf. Le groupe verbal).

Ex. : – I didn't like his remarks.
– *Je n'ai pas apprécié ses remarques.*
– You mustn't smoke in the office.
– *Vous ne devez pas fumer dans le bureau.*

Avec NEVER : l'auxiliaire reste à la forme affirmative.

Ex. : – I had never seen that.
– *Je n'avais jamais vu cela.*

3. Forme interrogative

Là encore, l'auxiliaire dépend du temps utilisé.

YES / NO questions : AUX. / MODAL + S + V + CO?

Ex. : – Have you met Mr Fleming?
– *Avez-vous rencontrez M. Fleming ?*
– Can you shut the door, please?
– *Pouvez-vous fermer la porte, s'il vous plait ?*

NB En anglais, toute question doit prendre la forme : Aux. + S + V contrairement au français.

Ex. : – Are you going to the party this evening?
– *Tu vas à la fête ce soir ?*

WH- questions : WH- WORD + AUX. / MODAL + S + V + CO?

NB Les pronoms interrogatifs dits WH- incluent HOW.

Ex. : – What did they answer?
– *Qu'ont-ils répondu ?*
– How can we solve this problem?
– *Comment pouvons-nous résoudre ce problème ?*

⚠ Quand le pronom interrogatif est sujet, on a : WH- + V CONJUGUÉ + CO?

Ex. : – Who phoned an hour ago?
– *Qui a téléphoné il y a une heure ?*

Quelques repères :

who(m)?	*qui ? (indentité)*
whose?	*à qui ? (possession)*
what?	*que ? quel ? (nature)*
which?	*que ? quel ? (choix restreint)*
where?	*où ? (lieu)*
when?	*quand ? (temps)*
why?	*pourquoi ? (cause)*
how?	*comment ? (manière)*

Quand une question porte sur un choix restreint, on utilise WHICH. Dans les autres cas, on utilise WHAT.

Ex. : – Which one do you like best?
– *Lequel (parmi ces quelques éléments) préférez-vous ?*
– What film have you lately seen?
– *Quel film (parmi l'ensemble des films) avez-vous vu récemment ?*

⚠ Ne pas confondre HOW IS HE? = *Comment va-t-il ?* et WHAT IS HE LIKE? = *Comment est-il ?* (apparence physique → description).

Quand HOW est associé à un adjectif ou à un adverbe, la question porte sur le sens de l'adjectif / l'adverbe :
HOW OLD...? → âge
HOW OFTEN...? → fréquence
HOW FAR...? → distance
HOW LONG...? → durée/longueur
HOW MANY / MUCH...? → quantité
etc.

On peut faire suivre HOW d'un adjectif pour demander « Dans quelle mesure... ? ».

Ex. : – How reliable is this tool?
– *Dans quelle mesure cet outil est-il fiable ?*

WHY pose une question sur la cause ; la réponse se formule donc avec BECAUSE ou tout autre connecteur de cause (cf. Les subordonnées circonstancielles).

Ex. : – Why didn't you come?
– I didn't come because I had an appointment.
– *Pourquoi n'êtes-vous pas venu ?*
– *Parce que j'avais un rendez-vous.*

WHAT... FOR porte sur le but et on répond par TO, IN ORDER TO ou SO AS TO.

Ex. : – What did you do that for? I did it to save time.
– *Pour quelles raisons avez-vous fait cela ?*
Pour gagner du temps.

Tags : cf. p. 251.
Réponses courtes : cf. p. 251.

4. Forme interro-négative : Aux. / modal + NOT + S + V + CO

L'auxiliaire dépend du temps utilisé.

Ex. : – Didn't you notice her reaction?
– *N'avez-vous pas remarqué sa réaction ?*
– Couldn't he put off the appointment?
– *Ne pouvait-il pas remettre le rendez-vous ?*

5. L'exclamative

Quelle que soit l'expression utilisée, la forme exclamative est affirmative, donc S + V, sauf dans certains cas comme : ISN'T IT NICE! ***Comme c'est charmant !***

Pour former la phrase exclamative, il faut prendre en compte ce sur quoi porte l'exclamation.

L'exclamation porte sur un adjectif.

Ex. : – It's **so** strange! What I have seen is **so** strange!
– *C'est / Ce que j'ai entendu est tellement bizarre !*
– It's **so** strange **a** story!
– *C'est une histoire si étrange !*
– **How** surprising (to see you)!
– *Comme c'est surprenant (de vous voir) !*

NB **Jamais de nom pluriel avec so.**

L'exclamation porte sur un groupe nominal.

Ex. : – It's **such an** interesting job!
– *C'est un travail si intéressant !*
– These are **such** amazing remarks!
– *Ces remarques sont si curieuses !*
– He has **such** courage!
– *Il a tellement de courage !*
– **What an** idea (to say that)!
– *Quelle idée (de dire cela) !*
– **What** beautiful views!
– *Quelles belles vues !*
– **What** terrible weather!
– *Quel temps épouvantable !*
– **How** time flies!
– *Comme le temps passe !*

NB **WHAT + A + indénombrable pour certaines expressions comme WHAT A PITY / A SHAME!**

6. L'inversion

Certains adverbes à sens négatif ou restrictif peuvent être placés en début de phrase pour marquer une forme d'insistance. C'est le cas notamment de NEVER, NOT ONLY, HARDLY… WHEN, et NO SOONER… THAN. On a alors l'ordre suivant : ADV. + AUX. + S + V + CO. Dans la proposition qui suit, l'ordre S + V + CO. est respecté.

Ex. : – Never will he forget the day when he first saw her.
– *Jamais il n'oubliera le jour où il l'a vue pour la première fois.*
– Not only did they call him but they also sent him a fax.
– *Non seulement ils l'ont appelé mais ils lui ont également envoyé un fax.*

HARDLY et NO SOONER sont suivis du past perfect et la deuxième proposition est au prétérit.

Ex. : – Hardly had he arrived when the phone rang = No sooner had he arrived than the phone rang.
– *À peine était-il arrivé que le téléphone sonna.*

2. Subordonnée relative

Il faut prendre en compte la nature de l'antécédent (humain ou non humain), la fonction du pronom relatif (sujet, complément ou génitif) et la nature de la subordonnée relative (déterminative ou appositive).

1. La relative déterminative

Elle détermine l'antécédent et est donc indispensable.

	Sujet	Complément	Génitif
Humain	who (*ou* that)	whom (*ou* that *ou* Ø)	whose*
Non humain	which (*ou* that)	which (*ou* Ø *ou* that)	whose*

NB **WHOM est de moins en moins utilisé au profit de WHO.**

* Pas de déterminant après WHOSE.

Antécédent humain

Ex. : – I don't know the man **who** phoned yesterday.
– *Je ne connais pas l'homme qui a téléphoné hier.*
– I met the PA **who(m) / that** you've just taken on.
– *J'ai rencontré l'assistante que vous venez d'embaucher.*
– I've called the woman **whose** car has been bumped into.
– *J'ai appelé la femme dont la voiture a été percutée.*

Antécédent non humain

Ex. : – This is the office **which** has been refurbished.
– *C'est le bureau qui a été réaménagé.*
– This is the order **which / that** you asked for.
– *C'est la commande que vous avez demandée.*
– This is the CD **whose** jacket I can't find.
– *C'est le CD dont je ne trouve pas la jaquette.*

2. La relative appositive

Elle donne un complément d'information sur l'antécédent ; elle n'est donc pas indispensable et est précédée et suivie de virgules.

	Sujet	Complément	Génitif
Humain	who	who(m)	whose*
Non humain	which	which	whose*

NB **Même remarque sur WHOM.**

* Pas de déterminant après WHOSE.

Antécédent humain

Ex. : – This customer, **who** is very friendly, would like to see you.
– *Ce client, qui est très sympathique, aimerait vous voir.*
– My main supplier, **who(m)** you've already met, will come tomorrow.
– *Mon principal fournisseur, que vous avez déjà rencontré, viendra demain.*
– My neighbour, **whose** wife works with you, is having a party this evening.
– *Mon voisin, dont la femme travaille avec vous, donne une réception ce soir.*

Antécédent non humain

Ex. : – My printer, **which** broke down last night, should be repaired.
– *Mon imprimante, qui est tombée en panne hier soir, devrait être réparée.*
– That Chinese restaurant, **which** you recommended, is really delicious.
– *Ce restaurant chinois, que vous avez recommandé, est vraiment délicieux.*
– My car, **whose** windshield was broken, is being serviced at the garage.
– *Ma voiture, dont le pare-brise a été brisé, est en réparation au garage.*

3. Traduction de « ce qui, ce que » et de « tout ce qui, tout ce que »

Quand le relatif reprend toute la proposition précédente, on utilise WHICH précédé d'une virgule. Dans les autres cas, on utilise WHAT.

Ex. : – He didn't tell me anything about his trip, **which** hasn't helped me much with my account.
– *Il ne m'a rien dit sur son voyage, ce qui ne m'a pas beaucoup aidé pour mon compte rendu.*
– They don't always understand **what** they are told.
– *Ils ne comprennent pas toujours ce qu'on leur dit.*

« Tout ce qui », « tout ce que » se traduit par ALL (THAT).

Ex. : – **All (that)** we saw was exciting.
– *Tout ce que nous avons vu était passionnant.*

4. Traduction de « dont »

WHOSE quand « dont » est complément de nom.

Ex. : – The report, **whose** details you gave me, is to be typed by tomorrow morning.
– *Le rapport dont vous m'avez donné les détails doit être tapé pour demain matin.*

WHO / THAT / Ø + PRÉPOSITION quand « dont » est complément d'objet indirect.

Ex. : – The meeting Ø you told me about has been cancelled.
– *La réunion dont vous m'avez parlé a été annulée.*

3. Subordonnées nominales

1. Les subordonnées en Ø / THAT

Fonction complément d'objet

On préfèrera Ø à THAT (surtout à l'oral) lorsque la subordonnée est précédée d'un verbe exprimant une opinion comme THINK, IMAGINE, SUPPOSE, ADMIT, etc.

Ex. : – I think Ø they're on holiday.
– *Je pense qu'ils sont en vacances.*

Mais THAT doit apparaître dans la structure suivante :

Ex. : – I find it amazing that he should refuse the contract.
– *Je trouve surprenant qu'il refuse le contrat.*

⚠ **Apparition obligatoire de IT dans la structure correspondant au français « je trouve + adj. + que ».**

NB **Utilisation de SHOULD pour le présent et SHOULD HAVE + PARTICIPE PASSÉ pour le passé pour les structures I FIND IT + ADJ. + THAT + S + V, IT'S + ADJ. + THAT + S + V, et après les verbes exprimant un ordre ou une suggestion.**

Ex. : – She finds it strange that he shouldn't cope with it.
– *Elle trouve étrange qu'il ne fasse pas face à cela.*
– It's normal that you should need some time to adapt.
– *Il est normal que vous ayez besoin d'un temps d'adaptation.*
– He insisted that she should have sent a fax.
– *Il a insisté sur le fait qu'elle aurait dû envoyer un fax.*

Fonction attribut

Dans ce cas, on utilise THAT.

Ex. : – The positive point is **that** I enjoy teamwork.
– *L'aspect positif, c'est que j'aime le travail d'équipe.*

2. Les subordonnées en WH-

Les interrogatives indirectes (cf. aussi Discours direct / indirect)

Ne s'agissant pas d'une question, l'ordre des mots est S + V + CO.

Ex. : – He wondered whether she would come.
– *Il se demanda si elle viendrait.*
– They asked where I came from.
– *Ils demandèrent d'où je venais.*
– He told me when the plane would arrive.
– *Il m'a dit quand l'avion arriverait.*

Les exclamatives indirectes

HOW + ADJ. + S + V + CO

WHAT + NOM + S + V + CO

Ex. : – I saw how disappointed she felt.
– *J'ai vu combien elle était déçue.*
– He told me what a pity it was.
– *Il m'a dit à quel point c'était dommage.*

4. Subordonnées circonstancielles

1. Les circonstancielles de cause

Principales conjonctions de subordination

AS: comme
BECAUSE: parce que
FOR: car
GIVEN THAT: étant donné que
INASMUCH AS: vu que
INSOFAR AS: dans la mesure où
SINCE: puisque

Ex. : – **Since** it's raining, I'll stay inside.
– *Puisqu'il pleut, je resterai à l'intérieur.*
– They were satisfied **for** it was good bargain.
– *Ils étaient satisfaits car c'était une bonne affaire.*
– They are going to stop the production **insofar as** the sales have plummeted.
– *Ils vont arrêter la production dans la mesure où les ventes ont fortement chuté.*

2. Les circonstancielles de but et de conséquence

Principales conjonctions de subordination

FOR ME / YOU / HIM / HER / US / THEM TO: pour que je / tu / etc.
IN ORDER TO: afin de
SO AS TO: afin de
SO THAT: afin que
TO: pour

Ex. : – I brought it **for you to** give him.
– *Je te l'ai apporté pour que tu lui offres.*
– I applied **in order to** be promoted.
– *J'ai posé ma candidature afin d'être promu.*

⚠ Place de la négation : IN ORDER NOT TO, SO AS NOT TO, NOT TO.

Ex. : – He spoke quietly **in order not to** disturb her.
– *Il parla doucement afin de ne pas la déranger.*

NB Les deux sujets étant différents, on pourrait également dire :
He spoke quietly **so that** she wouldn't be disturbed.
Dans ce deuxième cas, on utilise CAN ou WILL si la proposition principale est au présent ou au present perfect, et COULD ou WOULD si elle est au prétérit ou au past perfect.

Ex. : – He speaks quietly to her so that she won't get nervous / so that she can stay calm.
– *Il lui parle doucement pour qu'elle ne s'énerve pas / pour qu'elle reste calme.*
– He spoke quietly to her so that she wouldn't get nervous / so that she could stay calm.
– *Il lui a parlé doucement pour qu'elle ne s'énerve pas / pour qu'elle reste calme.*

⚠ Traduction de « pour »

– FOR, s'il s'agit de la cause (cf. aussi Les circonstancielles de cause).

Ex. : – He was dismissed for making serious mistakes.
– *Il a été licencié pour avoir commis de graves fautes.*

– TO, s'il s'agit du but.

Ex. : – She had a look at all the files to update them.
– *Elle a parcouru tous les dossiers pour les remettre à jour.*

3. Les circonstancielles de manière et de comparaison

Principales conjonctions de subordination

AS: comme
AS IF / AS THOUGH: comme si

Ex. : – Do **as** you like!
– *Faites comme vous voudrez !*
– She was acting **as if / as though** he wasn't there.
– *Elle agissait comme s'il n'était pas là.*

4. Les circonstancielles de concession et de contraste

Principales conjonctions de subordination

ADJ. + AS + S + V: aussi… que
ALTHOUGH / THOUGH: bien que
EVEN IF: même si
EVEN THOUGH: bien que
HOWEVER + ADJ. / ADV. + S + V: avoir beau faire qqch
WHEREAS: alors que
WHILE: tandis que

Ex. : – **Surprising as** it may seem, the two companies didn't merge.
– *Aussi étonnant que cela puisse paraître, les deux entreprises n'ont pas fusionné.*
– **Although** he was exhausted, he kept driving.
– *Bien qu'il fût épuisé, il continua à conduire.*
– **However hard** he tried, he didn't succeed.
– *Il avait beau essayer, il ne réussit pas.*
– I didn't like the atmosphere over there **whereas** here the colleagues are nice.
– *Je n'aimais pas l'atmosphère là-bas alors qu'ici les collègues sont sympathiques.*

⚠ WHEREAS est toujours précédé d'une proposition.

5. Les circonstancielles de condition

Principales conjonctions de subordination

FOR FEAR: de peur que
IF: si
IN CASE: au cas où
ON CONDITION THAT: à condition que
PROVIDED: à condition que
SUPPOSE: à supposer que
UNLESS: à moins que

Ex. : – I'll accompany you **for fear** you should miss your train.
– *Je t'accompagnerai de peur que tu rates ton train.*

– Can you please leave a message **in case** he drops in?
– *Pouvez-vous laisser un message, s'il vous plait, au cas où il passerait ?*
– You can come to the party **provided** you have an invitation card.
– *Vous pouvez venir à la réception à condition que vous ayez un carton d'invitation.*
– **Suppose** he didn't come?
– *À supposer qu'il ne vienne pas ?*
– You won't go out **unless** you tidy up your room.
– *Tu ne sortiras pas à moins que tu nettoies ta chambre.*

NB **FOR FEAR est suivi de SHOULD, MAY ou MIGHT.**
Dans un style soutenu (littéraire), on peut remplacer FOR FEAR par LEST + SHOULD.
Ex. : – He will leave lest she should come.
– *Il partira de peur qu'elle ne vienne.*

If

• **L'hypothèse est possible / réalisable :**
WILL + V, IF + PRÉSENT
Ex. : – You will improve your English if you speak more often. (→ you can)
– *Vous améliorerez votre anglais si vous parlez plus souvent.*

• **L'hypothèse n'est pas réalisée dans le présent :**
WOULD + V, IF + PRÉTÉRIT MODAL
Ex. : – You would improve your English if you spoke more often. (→ you don't)
– *Tu améliorerais ton anglais si tu parlais plus souvent.*
– If I were you, I would react. (→ I'm not)
– *À ta place je réagirais.*

• **L'hypothèse n'a pas été réalisée dans le passé :**
WOULD HAVE + PARTICIPE PASSÉ, IF + PAST PERFECT
Ex. : – You would have improved your English if you had spoken more often. (→ you didn't)
– *Tu aurais fait des progrès en anglais si tu avais parlé plus souvent.*

6. Les circonstancielles de temps

⚠ **Ne jamais employer WILL ni WOULD dans les circonstancielles de temps.**

Principales conjonctions de subordination

AFTER: **après que**
AS: **comme**
AS LONG AS: **tant que**
AS SOON AS: **dès que**
BEFORE: **avant que**
HARDLY… WHEN: **à peine… que**
NO SOONER… THAN: **à peine… que**
ONCE: **une fois que**
SINCE: **depuis que**
UNTIL / TILL: **jusqu'à ce que**
WHEN: **quand**
WHENEVER: **à chaque fois que**
WHILE: **pendant que**

Quand l'action de la subordonnée porte sur du présent ou du futur, on emploie le présent (jamais SHALL ou WILL).
Ex. : – I'll call them **as soon as I arrive** home.
– *Je les appellerai dès que j'arriverai à la maison.*

Quand l'action de la subordonnée est antérieure à celle de la principale, on emploie le present perfect.
Ex. : – She will go out **once she has finished** her work.
– *Elle sortira une fois qu'elle aura fini son travail.*

Quand l'action de la subordonnée porte sur du conditionnel, on emploie le prétérit (jamais WOULD).
Ex. : – He explained that he would show it to them **when he was** back.
– *Il a expliqué qu'il le leur montrerait quand il serait de retour.*

5. Subordonnée infinitive

Les verbes ci-dessous sont suivis soit de TO + V, soit de CO + TO + V* :
ASK: **demander**
BEG: **supplier**
EXPECT: **s'attendre à**
WANT: **vouloir**
Et aussi : WOULD LIKE, WOULD LOVE, WOULD HATE, WOULD PREFER
Ex. : – I **would like to have** a short break.
– *J'aimerais faire une petite pause.*
– I **would like** her **to apply** for this job.
– *J'aimerais qu'elle pose sa candidature pour cet emploi.*
– They **want to go** on strike.
– *Ils veulent se mettre en grève.*
– They **want** their boss **to accept** their conditions.
– *Ils veulent que leur patron accepte leurs conditions.*

Les verbes ci-dessous sont suivis de CO + TO + V* :
ADVISE: **conseiller**
ALLOW: **permettre (donner la permission)**
ENABLE: **permettre (donner la possibilité)**
FORBID: **interdire**
FORCE: **forcer**
INVITE: **inviter**
PERMIT: **permettre**
PERSUADE: **persuader**
REMIND: **rappeler**
TEACH: **enseigner**
TELL: **dire, raconter**
WARN: **avertir**
Ex. : – He **advised** Mary **to attend** the meeting.
– *Il a conseillé à Mary d'assister à la réunion.*
– This will **enable** the company **to increase** its turnover.
– *Cela va permettre à l'entreprise d'augmenter son chiffre d'affaires.*

▸ **Les verbes ci-dessous sont suivis de TO + V* :**
AGREE: **être d'accord pour**
CHOOSE: **choisir**
DECIDE: **décider**
HOPE: **espérer**
MANAGE: **parvenir à**
REFUSE: **refuser**
Ex. : – They **agreed to** sign the contract.
– *Ils se sont mis d'accord pour signer le contrat.*
– They **have decided to** wait until Monday.
– *Ils ont décidé d'attendre jusqu'à lundi.*

⚠ **Place de la négation : NOT/NEVER + TO.**
Ex. : – He **decided never to** see her again.
– *Il a décidé de ne jamais la revoir.*

*** Ces listes ne sont pas exhaustives.**

6. V + V ou V + V-ING ?

1. V + nom / pronom + V

Les verbes LET, MAKE, HAVE, HELP et les verbes de perception sont suivis de la base verbale.
Ex. : – **Let me show** you.
– *Laissez-moi vous montrer.*
– **He made them** laugh.
– *Il les a fait rire.*
– She **had him repair** her car.
– *Elle lui a fait réparer sa voiture.*
– He will **help Susan rewrite** the letter.
– *Il aidera Susan à réécrire la lettre.*
– He **saw them take** the plane.
– *Il les a vus prendre l'avion.*

NB **Pour MAKE et HAVE, voir aussi les Subordonnées causatives et résultatives.**

2. V + V ou V + V-ing?

▸ **Les verbes de perception peuvent être suivis de V ou de V-ING.**
Ex. : – I saw her **chatting** on the Internet.
– *Je l'ai vue qui chattait sur Internet. (Je l'ai vue pendant qu'elle le faisait.* She was chatting on the Internet and I saw her doing it.)
– I saw her **chat** on the Internet.
– *Je l'ai vue chatter sur Internet. (J'en fait le constat.)*

▸ **Quand les verbes REGRET et REMEMBER sont suivis de V-ING, il s'agit d'un évènement passé.**
Ex. : – I **regret to** say that I didn't appreciate it.
– *Je suis au regret de dire que je n'ai pas apprécié. (Je l'avoue.)*
– I **regret** tell**ing** him that he was wrong.
– *Je regrette de lui avoir dit qu'il avait tort. (Je le lui ai dit ; c'est fait mais je le regrette.)*
– **Remember to** post the letters.
– *N'oublie pas de poster les lettres.*
– She **remembers** mak**ing** an appointment with them.
– *Elle se souvient d'avoir pris rendez-vous avec eux.*

▸ **Quand les verbes NEED, REQUIRE et WANT sont suivis de V-ING, ils sont proches d'un sens passif.**
Comparez :
– You **need to** relax.
– *Tu as besoin de te détendre.*
– This machine **needs** fix**ing**.
– *Cette machine a besoin d'être réparée.* (It needs to be fixed.)
Ex. : – The company **requires** the applicants **to** be computer literate.
– *La société demande aux candidats d'être initiés à l'informatique.*
– This task **requires** supervis**ing**.
– *Cette tâche nécessite d'être supervisée.*
– She **wants to** travel.
– *Elle veut voyager.*
– Our offices **want** clean**ing**.
– *Nos bureaux ont besoin d'être nettoyés.*

7. Les subordonnées causatives-résultatives

Elles sont appelées ainsi car une cause et un résultat sont associés.

MAKE, HAVE et GET sont utilisés pour « faire faire quelque chose à quelqu'un » et se construisent différemment selon que leurs compléments font ou subissent l'action.

1. Le complément fait l'action

MAKE + NOM / PRONOM + V
HAVE + NOM / PRONOM + V
GET + NOM / PRONOM + TO + V

NB **MAKE est le plus neutre ; HAVE insiste plus que les deux autres sur le résultat ; GET implique une notion d'effort.**
Ex. : – He still **makes her laugh**.
– *Il la fait encore rire.*
– She **had him look** after the children.
– *Elle lui a fait s'occuper des enfants.*
– They **got him to resign**.
– *Ils l'ont fait démissionner.*

2. Le complément subit l'action

HAVE + NOM / PRONOM + PARTICIPE PASSÉ
GET + NOM / PRONOM + PARTICIPE PASSÉ
Ex. : – He **had his plant visited**.
(*sous-entendu* by the quality controller *par exemple*).
– *Il a fait visiter son usine.*
– They **got their company relocated**.
– *Ils ont fait délocaliser leur entreprise.*

4. ANNEXES

1. Adverbes

⚠ **Contrairement au français, en anglais on ne sépare jamais le verbe de son complément sauf pour le verbe BE.**

Ex. : – I **often** have a coffee break.
– *Je fais souvent une pause-café.*
– I was tired and I was **also** hungry.
– *J'étais fatigué et j'avais également faim.*

1. Les adverbes de lieu, de manière et de temps sont généralement placés en fin de phrase.

Ex. : – The warehouse is **over there**.
– *L'entrepôt est là-bas.*
– This product sells **well**.
– *Ce produit se vend bien.*
– The boss addressed his staff **reassuringly**.
– *Le patron s'est adressé à son personnel de manière rassurante.*
– What are you doing **now**?
– *Que fais-tu en ce moment ?*
– I haven't decided **yet**.
– *Je n'ai pas encore décidé.*

NB **Lorsque deux adverbes se trouvent dans une même proposition, l'ordre est le suivant :**
V + complément + adv. lieu + adv. temps

Ex. : – I met him there yesterday.
– *Je l'ai rencontré là-bas hier.*

2. Les adverbes de fréquence se placent entre le sujet et le verbe (après le verbe BE aux temps simples, après le premier auxiliaire pour les verbes composés).

Ex. : – You are **always** late.
– *Tu es toujours en retard.*
– I **usually** drive back home at 6.
– *Je rentre généralement chez moi à 6 h.*
– They don't **often** go on holiday.
– *Ils ne vont pas souvent en vacances.*
– She has **never** been to Ireland.
– *Elle n'est jamais allée en Irlande.*
– Have you **ever** travelled alone?
– *As-tu déjà voyager seul ?*

3. Les adverbes de degré se placent devant l'élément qu'ils modifient.

Ex. : – I **really** appreciated what you did.
– *J'ai vraiment apprécié ce que tu as fait.*
– You look **very** tired.
– *Tu as l'air vraiment fatigué.*
– Wasn't it **extremely** surprising?
– *N'était-ce pas extrêmement surprenant ?*
– I know him **quite** well.
– *Je le connais assez bien.*
– **Almost** nobody knows her.
– *Presque personne ne la connaît.*

⚠ Pièges pour les francophones

Hard / hardly

Ex. : – It's a hard job.
– *C'est un travail difficile.*
– He works hard.
– *Il travaille avec acharnement.*
– He hardly works. *(adv. : presque pas)*
– *Il ne travaille presque pas.*

Pretty

Ex. : – What a pretty suit! *(adj. : joli)*
– *Quel beau complet !*
– It was pretty good. *(adv. : assez, plutôt)*
– *C'était assez bien.*

Ever / already

Ex. : – Have you ever been to the USA?
– *Es-tu déjà / jamais allé aux États-Unis ? (« ever » dans le sens de « l'occasion de ».)*
– Have you already been to the USA?
– *Es-tu déjà allé aux États-Unis ? (« already » dans le sens de « plus tôt que prévu ».)*

EVER dans les phrases affirmatives = jamais

Ex. : – It's the most interesting course I have ever attended.
– *C'est le cours le plus intéressant auquel j'ai jamais assisté.*
– If you ever come across him, tell him to email me.
– *Si jamais tu le croises, dis-lui de m'envoyer un mail.*

Still / always

Ex. : – Are you still working?
– *Est-ce que tu travailles encore ? (l'action de travailler continue)*
– The sales have still increased recently.
– *Les ventes ont encore augmenté récemment.*
– You're always working late!
– *Tu travailles toujours tard ! (l'action se répète)*

Les structures suivantes

- **Adjectif + ENOUGH :**
  You're not old **enough**. *Tu n'es pas assez âgé.*
- **TOO + adjectif + A / AN + nom singulier :**
  It's **too** easy an answer. *C'est une réponse trop facile.*
- **QUITE + A / AN + nom singulier :**
  It's **quite** a difficult task. *C'est une tâche assez difficile.*
- **PERHAPS / MAYBE + S + V :**
  Perhaps / Maybe they'll come. *Peut-être viendront-ils.*
- **Adverbe + auxiliaire + S + V, quand HARDLY… WHEN, NO SOONER… THAN, NOT ONLY et NEVER sont en début de phrase.**

Ex. : – Hardly had she arrived when the phone rang.
– *À peine était-elle arrivée que le téléphone sonna.*

– No sooner had he left than he remembered he had forgotten his IDs.
– À peine était-il parti qu'il se souvint qu'il avait oublié ses papiers d'identité.
– Not only should you be more dynamic but it would also be better to be smiling.
– Non seulement vous devriez être plus dynamique mais il serait également préférable d'être souriant.
– Never before had there been such an increase.
– Jamais auparavant il n'y avait eu une telle augmentation.

4. Adverbes de liaison

d'adjonction

ALSO: **également**
AS WELL (en fin de phrase): **également**
BESIDES: **en outre**
FURTHERMORE: **de plus**
IN ADDITION: **en plus de cela**
LIKEWISE: **de même**
MOREOVER: **de plus**
SIMILARLY: **de même**

de conséquence

CONSEQUENTLY: **par conséquent**
HENCE: **d'où**
SO: **donc**
THEREFORE: **par conséquent**
THUS: **ainsi**

de contraste

ALL THE SAME: **quand même**
HOWEVER: **cependant**
NEVERTHELESS: **néanmoins**
OTHERWISE: **sinon**
STILL: **cependant**
YET: **pourtant**

2. Prépositions et particules adverbiales

Verbes prépositionnels

Il s'agit de verbes qui sont reliés à leur complément par une préposition, tels que LOOK **(regarder) →** LOOK AT SB / STH **(regarder qqn / qqch).**

⚠ **Le complément ne peut pas être placé entre le verbe et sa préposition.**

Ex. : – Look at him!
– Regarde-le !

⚠ **La préposition accompagne son verbe :**

Phrases interrogatives

Ex. : – What is she looking at? – *Que regarde-t-elle ?*

Relatives

Ex. : – This is what I was looking at.
– C'est ce que je regardais.

Voix passive

Ex. : – The child was looked at.
– On a regardé l'enfant.

1. Liste de verbes + préposition

about	care about talk about	*se faire du souci au sujet de* *parler de*
against	discriminate against react against	*exercer une discrimination contre* *réagir contre*
at	aim at laugh at	*viser* *rire de*
by	live by oneself	*vivre seul*
for	account for apologise for ask for wait for	*expliquer* *s'excuser* *demander* *attendre*
from	hear from suffer from	*avoir des nouvelles de* *souffrir de*
in	consist in succeed in	*consister en qqch / à faire qqch* *réussir à*
of	approve of consist of think of	*approuver* *consister en (plusieurs éléments)* *penser à*

on	agree on call on depend on rely on	*être d'accord sur* *rendre visite à* *dépendre de* *faire confiance à*
out of	run out of	*se trouver à court de*
over	preside over	*présider*
to	apologise to sb belong to complain to listen to object to speak to	*s'excuser auprès de qqn* *appartenir à* *se plaindre auprès de* *écouter* *protester contre* *parler à*
through	come through	*se tirer de*
with	agree with sb argue with sb	*être d'accord avec qqn* *se disputer avec qqn*

2. Liste de verbes + complément + préposition

accuse sb of sth ask sb for sth blame sb for sth forgive sb for sth introduce sb to sb else prevent sb from V-ing sth remind sb of sth warn sb of sth	*accuser qqn de qqch* *demander qqch à qqn* *reprocher qqch à qqn* *pardonner qqch à qqn* *présenter qqn à qqn* *empêcher qqn de faire qqch* *rappeler qqch à qqn* *avertir qqn de qqch*
borrow sth from sb buy sth from sb exchange sth for sth else expect sth from sb prefer sth to sth steal sth from sb	*emprunter qqch à qqn* *acheter qqch à qqn* *échanger qqch contre* *attendre qqch de qqn* *préférer qqch à qqch* *voler qqch à qqn*

3. Autres prépositions

de cause

BECAUSE OF: à cause de
CONSIDERING: étant donné
DUE TO: en raison de
GIVEN: étant donné
IN VIEW OF: vu
ON ACCOUNT OF: à cause de
OWING TO (mauvaise nouvelle) : en raison de
THANKS TO: grâce à

de contraste

CONTRARY TO: contrairement à
DESPITE: malgré
IN SPITE OF: malgré
INSTEAD OF: au lieu de

Verbes à particule adverbiale (Phrasal verbs)

Ce sont des verbes qui sont suivis d'une particule telles que : AWAY, DOWN, IN, OUT, etc.

Rôles de ces particules

- Elles indiquent une direction lorsqu'elles suivent un verbe de mouvement.

Ex. : – Come in!
– *Entrez !*
– He came back.
– *Il est rentré.*
– I am going away.
– *Je pars.*

- Elles modifient le sens des verbes.

Ex. : – Get over: *se remettre.*
– Make up: *se maquiller.*
– Fall for: *tomber amoureux.*
– Go under: *faire faillite.*

⚠ Place du complément

- Si le complément est un nom, il peut se placer entre le verbe et la particule ou après le verbe et la particule.

Ex. : – The police broke up the crowd. = The police broke the crowd up.
– *La police a dispersé la foule.*

- Si le complément est un pronom personnel, il se place obligatoirement entre le verbe et la particule.

Ex. : – Could you pick me up?
– *Peux-tu venir me chercher ?*

Quelques verbes à particule

answer back	*répondre avec insolence*
break down	*échouer, s'effondrer*
bring about	*provoquer, causer*
bring up	*élever (enfant)*
carry on	*continuer*
carry out	*effectuer (tâche)*
cut in	*interrompre (conversation)*
draw up	*rédiger (contrat)*
drop in	*faire une petite visite*
get by	*se débrouiller*
get through	*réussir (examen par exemple)*
give in	*céder*
give up	*abandonner, renoncer*
go up	*augmenter*
hurry up	*se presser*
lay sb off	*licencier qqn*
let sb down	*laisser tomber qqn*
look out	*être sur ses gardes*
make out	*comprendre*
make sth up	*inventer de toutes pièces*
pick sth / sb up	*ramasser qqch / passer prendre qqn*
pick out	*choisir*
pull up	*s'arrêter (véhicule)*
put off sth	*remettre à plus tard*
put sb up	*héberger qqn*
see sb off	*accompagner qqn (à son départ)*
set out	*exposer (idées, plans)*
set up	*monter (une affaire)*
speed up	*accélérer*
slow down	*ralentir*
stand up	*se lever*
stay up	*ne pas aller se coucher*
take off	*décoller (avion par exemple)*
try sth out	*mettre qqch à l'essai*
turn out to be	*se révéler être*
turn up	*se présenter, arriver*
wake up / wake sb up	*se réveiller / réveiller qqn*
wear out	*user / s'user*
work out	*résoudre*
work sth out	*réussir*

3. Dérivations

Préfixes

Préfixes	Sens	Exemples
Sens négatif		
un-	le contraire de	unhappy
in-	le contraire de	incredible
il-	le contraire de	illiterate
ir-	le contraire de	irregular
de-	le contraire de	decentralise
dis-	le contraire de	disgrace
mis-	le contraire de	misunderstand
non-	le contraire de	non-smoker
anti-	le contraire de	anti-American
Temps		
pre-	avant	prepack
fore-	avant	forecast
post-	après	post-war
ex-	ancien	ex-President
Degré, taille		
super-	très grand	superintendent
hyper-	très grand	hypermarket
maxi-	très grand	maximise
out-	dépassement	outnumber
sur-	dépassement	surtax
over-	trop	overpopulated
under-	pas assez	underfed
mini-	très petit	mini-cab
Divers		
pro-	en faveur de	pro-American
re-	répétition	remake
mono-	unique	monoski
poly-	multiple	polytechnic

Suffixes

Suffixes	Transformations	Exemples
-ness	adjectif → **nom**	madness
-en, -ify, -ise / -ize	adjectif → **verbe**	darken, simplify, popularize
-ly	adjectif → **adverbe de manière**	stupidly
-able	verbe → **adjectif**	understandable
-er, -or, -ant	verbe → **nom (auteur de l'action)**	teacher, administrator, inhabitant
-ee	verbe → **nom (subit l'action)**	employee
-less	nom → **adjectif à sens négatif**	homeless
-ful	nom → **adjectif à sens positif**	careful
-like	nom → **adjectif, sens de « semblable à »**	childlike
-dom, -hood	nom → **autre nom indiquant un statut, une condition**	kingdom; womanhood
-ship	nom → **autre nom indiquant un état, une relation**	friendship

4. Verbes irréguliers

Infinitif	Prétérit	Participe passé	Traduction
abide	abode	abode	*demeurer, supporter*
arise	arose	arisen	*s'élever*
awake	awoke	awaken	*(s')éveiller*
be	was / were	been	*être*
bear	bore	borne	*supporter*
beat	beat	beaten	*battre*
become	became	become	*devenir*
begin	began	begun	*commencer*
behold	beheld	beheld	*contempler*
bend	bent	bent	*courber*
bereave	bereft	bereft	*priver*
beseech	besought	besought	*supplier*
bet	bet	bet	*parier*
bid	bade	bidden	*ordonner*
bid	bid	bid	*enchérir*
bind	bound	bound	*lier*
bite	bit	bitten	*mordre*
bleed	bled	bled	*saigner*
blow	blew	blown	*souffler*
break	broke	broken	*casser*

Infinitif	Prétérit	Participe passé	Traduction
breed	bred	bred	*élever*
bring	brought	brought	*apporter*
build	built	built	*construire*
burn	burnt	burnt	*brûler*
burst	burst	burst	*éclater*
buy	bought	bought	*acheter*
cast	cast	cast	*lancer*
catch	caught	caught	*attraper*
choose	chose	chosen	*choisir*
cleave	cleaved / clove	cloven / cleft	*fendre*
cling	clung	clung	*s'accrocher*
come	came	come	*venir*
cost	cost	cost	*coûter*
creep	crept	crept	*ramper*
cut	cut	cut	*couper*
deal	dealt	dealt	*distribuer*
dig	dug	dug	*creuser*
do	did	done	*faire*
draw	drew	drawn	*tirer*
dream	dreamed / dreamt	dreamed / dreamt	*rêver*
drink	drank	drunk	*boire*
drive	drove	driven	*conduire*
dwell	dwelt	dwelt	*habiter*
eat	ate	eaten	*manger*
fall	fell	fallen	*tomber*
feed	fed	fed	*(se) nourrir*
feel	felt	felt	*ressentir*
fight	fought	fought	*se battre, combattre*
find	found	found	*trouver*
flee	fled	fled	*fuir*
fling	flung	flung	*lancer*
fly	flew	flown	*voler (ailes)*
forbid	forbade	forbidden	*interdire*
forget	forgot	forgotten	*oublier*
forgive	forgave	forgiven	*pardonner*
forsake	forsook	forsaken	*abandonner*

Infinitif	Prétérit	Participe passé	Traduction
freeze	froze	frozen	*geler*
get	got	got	*obtenir*
give	gave	given	*donner*
go	went	gone	*aller*
grind	ground	ground	*moudre*
grow	grew	grown	*pousser*
hang	hung	hung	*pendre*
have	had	had	*avoir*
hear	heard	heard	*entendre*
hide	hid	hidden	*cacher*
hit	hit	hit	*frapper*
hold	held	held	*tenir*
hurt	hurt	hurt	*blesser*
keep	kept	kept	*garder*
kneel	knelt	knelt	*s'agenouiller*
know	knew	known	*savoir*
lay	laid	laid	*poser*
lead	led	led	*mener*
lean	leaned / leant	leaned / leant	*se pencher*
leap	leaped / leapt	leaped / leapt	*bondir*
learn	learned / learnt	learned / learnt	*apprendre*
leave	left	left	*quitter, laisser*
lend	lent	lent	*prêter*
let	let	let	*louer ; laisser*
lie	lay	lain	*être allongé*
light	lighted / lit	lighted / lit	*éclairer*
lose	lost	lost	*perdre*
make	made	made	*faire*
mean	meant	meant	*signifier*
meet	met	met	*rencontrer*
mistake	mistook	mistaken	*se tromper*
mow	mowed	mown / mowed	*faucher*
overcome	overcame	overcome	*surmonter*
pay	paid	paid	*payer*
put	put	put	*mettre*
read	read	read	*lire*

Infinitif	Prétérit	Participe passé	Traduction
rend	rent	rent	*déchirer*
rid	rid	rid	*débarrasser*
ride	rode	ridden	*aller à cheval*
ring	rang	rung	*sonner*
rise	rose	risen	*se lever*
run	ran	run	*courir*
saw	sawed	sawn / sawed	*scier*
see	saw	seen	*voir*
seek	sought	sought	*chercher*
sell	sold	sold	*vendre*
send	sent	sent	*envoyer*
set	set	set	*poser*
sew	sewed	sewn	*coudre*
shear	shore	shorn / sheared	*tondre*
shed	shed	shed	*verser (larmes)*
shake	shook	shaken	*secouer*
shine	shone	shone	*briller*
shoe	shod	shod	*chausser, ferrer*
shoot	shot	shot	*tirer (fusil)*
show	showed	shown	*montrer*
shrink	shrank	shrunk	*rétrécir*
shut	shut	shut	*fermer*
sing	sang	sung	*chanter*
sink	sank	sunk	*s'enfoncer, sombrer*
sit	sat	sat	*être assis*
slay	slew	slain	*tuer*
sleep	slept	slept	*dormir*
slide	slid	slid	*glisser*
sling	slung	slung	*lancer*
slink	slunk	slunk	*se dérober*
slit	slit	slit	*fendre*
smell	smelled / smelt	smelled / smelt	*sentir (odorat)*
smite	smote	smitten	*frapper*
sow	sowed	sown	*semer*
speak	spoke	spoken	*parler*
speed	sped	sped	*(se) hâter*

Infinitif	Prétérit	Participe passé	Traduction
spell	spelled / spelt	spelled / spelt	*épeler*
spend	spent	spent	*dépenser*
spill	spilled / spilt	spilled / spilt	*répandre*
spin	spun	spun	*filer*
spit	spat	spat	*cracher*
split	split	split	*(se) fendre*
spoil	spoiled / spoilt	spoiled / spoilt	*gâter*
spread	spread	spread	*(s')étaler*
spring	sprang	sprung	*sauter, jaillir*
stand	stood	stood	*être debout*
steal	stole	stolen	*dérober*
stick	stuck	stuck	*coller*
sting	stung	stung	*piquer*
stink	stank	stunk	*sentir mauvais*
strew	strewed	strewn / strewed	*joncher*
stride	strode	stridden	*aller à grands pas*
string	strung	strung	*enfiler*
strive	strove	striven	*s'efforcer*
swear	swore	sworn	*jurer*
sweep	swept	swept	*balayer*
swell	swelled	swelled / swollen	*gonfler*
swim	swam	swum	*nager*
swing	swung	swung	*(se) balancer*
take	took	taken	*prendre*
teach	taught	taught	*enseigner*
tear	tore	torn	*déchirer*
tell	told	told	*raconter*
think	thought	thought	*penser*
thrive	throve	thriven	*prospérer*
throw	threw	thrown	*jeter*
thrust	thrust	thrust	*pousser brusquement*
tread	trod	trodden	*fouler aux pieds*
understand	understood	understood	*comprendre*
upset	upset	upset	*renverser*
wake	woke	woken	*(s')éveiller*
wear	wore	worn	*porter (vêtements)*

Infinitif	Prétérit	Participe passé	Traduction
weave	wove	woven	*tisser*
weep	wept	wept	*pleurer*
win	won	won	*gagner*
wind	wound	wound	*remonter*
withdraw	withdrew	withdrawn	*retirer*
withstand	withstood	withstood	*résister*
wring	wrung	wrung	*tordre*
write	wrote	written	*écrire*

5. OUTILS DE COMMUNICATION

1. Prononciation

⚠ Par consonnes et voyelles, il faut comprendre « sons » consonnes et « sons » voyelles.

1. Prononciation des terminaisons -*s* ou -*es*
(3e personne du singulier au présent / pluriel des noms)
On prononce le son :
- [s] après les consonnes sourdes [f], [k], [p], [t]
Ex. : – laughs, thinks, hopes, sits
- [z] après les consonnes sonores [b], [d], [g], [l], [m], [ŋ], [r], [v] et les voyelles
Ex. : – dreads, comes, decisions, belongs, cars, receives, plays, tomatoes
- [ɪz] après [s], [ʃ], [z], [dʒ]
Ex. : – kisses, catches, quizzes, manages

2. Prononciation des terminaisons en -ed
On prononce le son :
- [t] après les consonnes sourdes [f], [k], [s], [ʃ], [p], [θ]
Ex. : – laughed, kicked, kissed, rushed, stopped, frothed
- [ɪd] après [t], [d]
Ex. : – waited, succeeded
- [d] dans tous les autres cas (après les consonnes sonores et les voyelles)
Ex. : – changed, called, stayed

3. Non-prononciation de la lettre (liste non exhaustive)
- **b** dans *comb, debt, doubt, thumb, climb*
- **k** dans *know, knowledge, knee, kneel, knit*
- **l** dans *calm, half, could, would, should, talk, walk*
- **p** dans *psychology, psychiatrist*
- **t** dans *listen*
- **u** dans *guard, guardian, vanguard*
- **w** dans *answer, who, whom, whose, whole*

2. Chiffres

nought, zero, O (the letter)	0
1st / the first	le premier
2nd / the second	le deuxième
3rd / the third	le troisième
4th / the fourth	le quatrième
13 / thirteen	treize
30 / thirty	trente
210 / two hundred and ten	210
1,005 / one thousand and five	1 005
10,000 / ten thousand	10 000
12,620 / twelve thousand six hundred and twenty	12 620
5,000,000 / 5m / five million	5 000 000 / 5 m / 5 millions
7,000,000,000 / 7bn / seven billion	7 000 000 000 / 7 milliards
.08 / point nought eight	0,08
3.45 / three point forty-five	3,45
4.6m / four point six million	4,6 millions
2.3bn / two point three billion	2,3 milliards
6.8% / six point eight per cent	6,8 %
9.5‰ / nine point five per thousand	9,5 ‰
1/2 / one half	1/2
2 1/2 / two and a half	2 1/2
1/3 / one third	1/3
3/4 / three quarters	3/4
1/12 / one twelfth	1/12
1,234 is a four-digit number	1 234 est un nombre à 4 chiffres

3. Graphiques

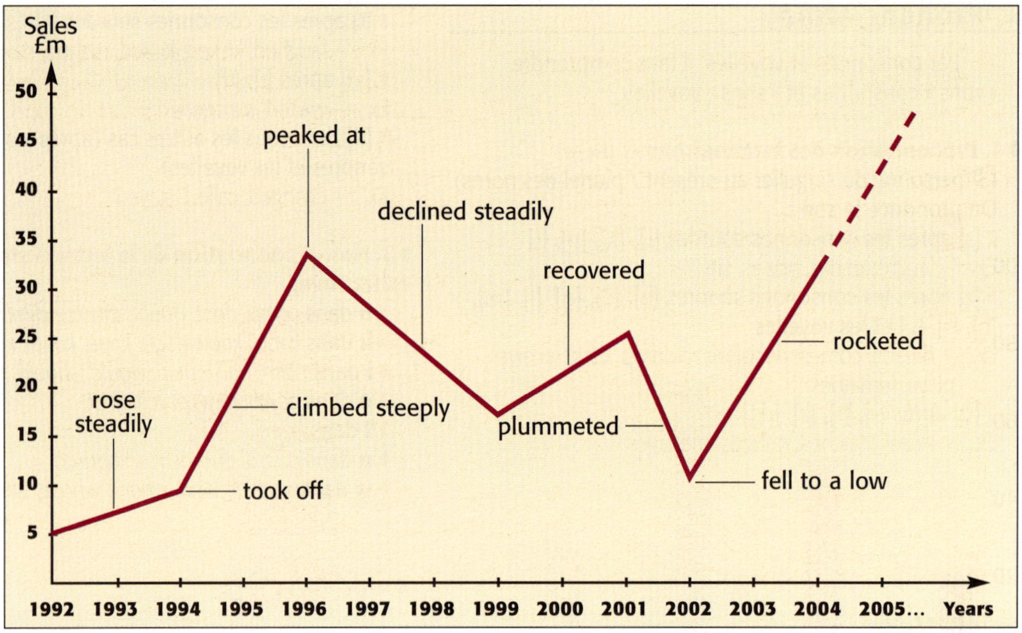

1. Comment lire un graphique

Pensez à présenter le graphique dans une introduction et à terminer avec une conclusion qui en donne la synthèse.

Ex. : – This graph represents the evolution of X company sales from 1992 to 2003 with sales estimates / forecasts in 2004.

– Ce graphique représente l'évolution des ventes de l'entreprise X de 1992 à 2003 et les prévisions de ventes en 2004.

– The vertical line indicates sales in million pounds and the horizontal line the years.

– L'ordonnée indique les ventes en millions de livres sterling et l'abscisse les années.

– Sales rose / increased steadily between 1992 and 1994.

– Les ventes ont régulièrement augmenté entre 1992 et 1994.

– They took off from £10m in 1994 and climbed steeply until 1996 when they peaked at £33m.

– Elles ont décollé à partir de 10 millions de livres sterling en 1994 en augmentant rapidement jusqu'en 1996 où elles ont culminé à 33 millions de livres sterling.

– Then, they declined / decreased / dropped / went down / fell steadily but recovered from 1999 to 2001.

– Puis elles ont connu une baisse régulière mais ont repris de 1999 à 2001.

– Over the next year, they plummeted and fell to a low of £10m in 2002.

– Au cours de l'année suivante elles se sont effondrées et sont descendues à 10 millions de livres sterling en 2002.

– From 2002, they rocketed / soared and it is estimated that this trend will go on for a few years.

– À partir de 2002, elles sont montées en flèche et on estime que cette tendance va se poursuivre pendant quelques années.

– To conclude we can say that sales don't seem to level off but are recovering well.

– En conclusion, nous pouvons dire que les ventes ne semblent pas se stabiliser mais qu'elles effectuent une bonne reprise.

2. Les différentes formes de graphiques

From the following table, different graphs can be made.

	1st quarter	2nd quarter	3rd quarter	last quarter
Computers	20	50	70	30
Peripherals	30	60	90	70
Telecom	25	80	45	30

Units sold

Ex. : – This table represents the quarterly sales of computers, peripherals and telecom equipment over a whole year.

– Ce tableau représente les ventes trimestrielles d'ordinateurs, de périphériques et d'équipement en télécommunication sur une année.

– There was a 50% increase in peripherals sales between the first and the second quarters. / Peripherals sales increased by 50% between the first and second quarters. / Peripherals sales doubled between the first and second quarters.

– Les ventes de périphériques ont connu une augmentation de 50 % / ont doublé entre le premier et le second trimestre.
– In the last quarter, as many computers as telecom equipment were sold.
– Au cours du dernier trimestre, autant d'ordinateurs que d'équipement en télécommunication ont été vendus.
Etc.

NB Pour commenter tableaux et graphiques, pensez à utiliser un vocabulaire varié (cf. Graphiques) et n'oubliez pas de revoir les comparatifs et les superlatifs (cf. p. 257-259).

Bar charts

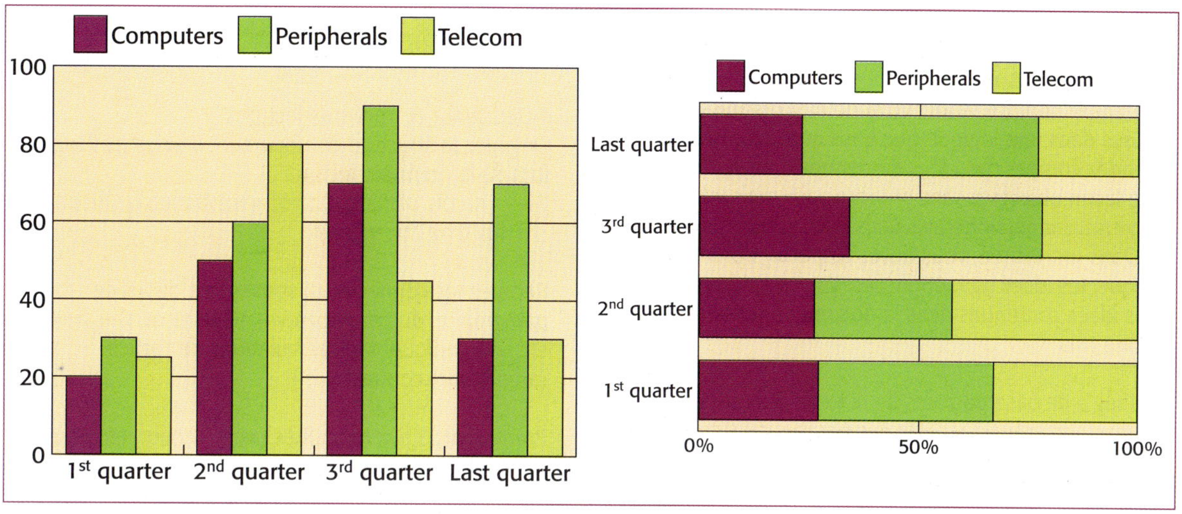

Line charts

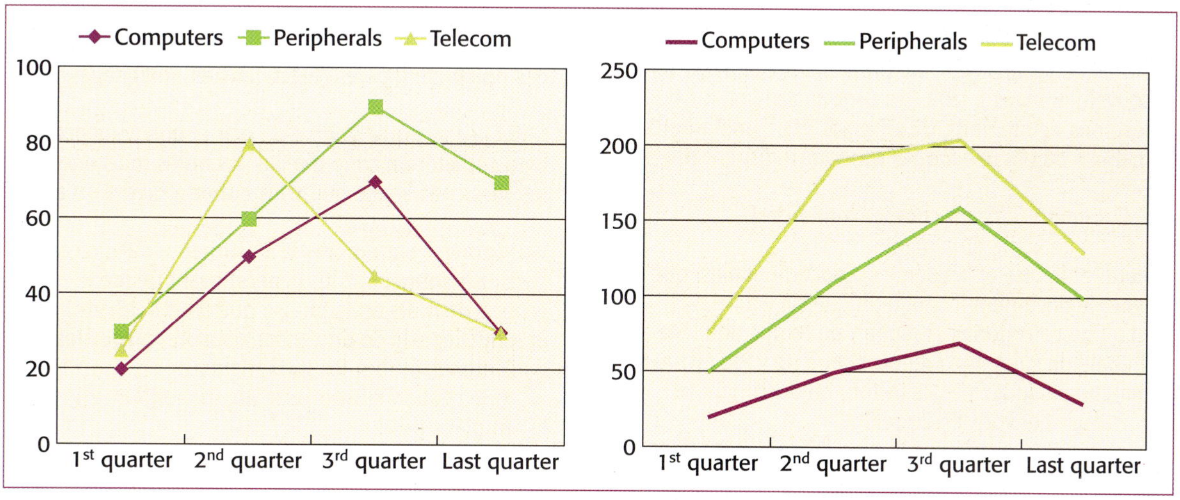

A pie chart

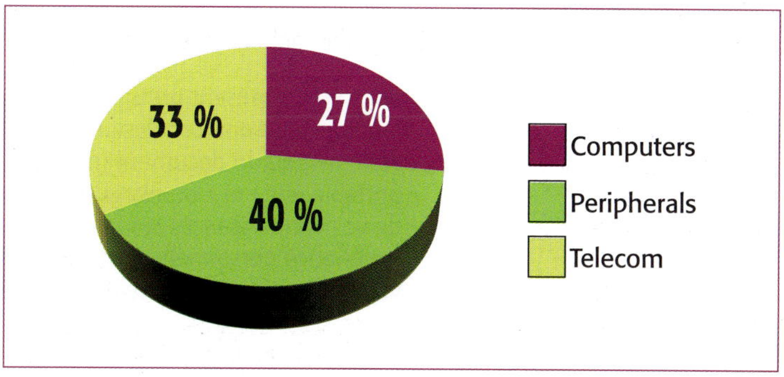

4. Comment faire un compte rendu et un résumé

1. Remarques générales pour l'examen

Qu'il s'agisse de l'oral ou de l'écrit, le support est le plus souvent un article de presse ou une page de site web (présentation d'une entreprise, d'un produit, etc.) qui peuvent être assortis d'un document iconographique (graphique, photo, logo, etc.).

La différence essentielle entre un compte rendu et un résumé est la suivante :
• Dans le compte rendu, vous pouvez organiser les idées dans une logique que vous aurez choisie. Vous rendez compte des idées contenues dans le document de façon objective, sans prendre parti mais vous pouvez donner votre avis dans la conclusion.
• Dans un résumé, vous devez respecter l'ordre dans lequel les idées sont énoncées. Vous ne donnez que les idées contenues dans le document sans donner votre avis.

La règle de base pour ces deux exercices est de ne jamais recopier ou répéter des phrases du support mais de reformuler les idées en utilisant vos propres mots.

N'oubliez pas que ces exercices exigent de la méthode et de la rigueur et que seul un entraînement régulier vous apportera les meilleures conditions pour réussir à l'examen.
Par ailleurs, dans votre vie professionnelle, vous serez souvent amenés à faire des compte rendus et / ou des résumés de réunions, de rapports, etc. ; une bonne maîtrise de ces techniques est donc indispensable.

2. Comment faire un compte rendu oral

<u>Avant de lire le document</u>

Repérez le titre et la source du document ainsi que le type de document iconographique s'il y a lieu.
• Le titre vous donne la plupart du temps une idée globale du sujet. Si toutefois le titre ne vous évoque rien, ne paniquez pas, la lecture du document va certainement vous l'élucider.
• La source vous indique le type de document dont il s'agit (article de journal, de magazine, extrait d'un site web, etc.) et sa date.
• Le document iconographique illustre le texte ou une partie du texte.
À ce stade, nul n'est besoin de rédiger.

<u>Première lecture</u>

Soulignez / Surlignez les mots clefs afin de pouvoir répondre aux questions WHO? WHERE? WHEN? WHAT?

WHO? = Who is concerned?
Ex. : – Employers and their staff / X company versus Y company
WHERE? = a particular country, a continent, the whole world, etc.?
WHEN? = very recent? comparison between ten years ago and now? etc.
WHAT? = What does the document deal with? / is about?
Ex. : – working conditions, evolution of the mobile, etc.
Lors de cette première lecture, prendre des notes suffit.

<u>Deuxième et troisième lectures</u>

Dégagez la structure du document si vous ne l'avez fait lors de la première lecture.
Ex. : – history of X and Y companies + merger *(fusion)* + future of this merger

Repérez les connecteurs, souvent en début de paragraphe, du type MOREOVER, HOWEVER, BUT, IN SPITE OF, etc., qui indiquent les articulations de l'article (adjonction, contraste, ...).

Prenez garde aux modalités (MUST, SHOULD, etc.) qui nuancent certaines affirmations.

Reprenez chacune des parties et reformulez leur développement. Lors de cette étape il vous sera peut-être nécessaire de rédiger quelques phrases mais faites attention à espacer ce que vous rédigez et à indiquer des points de repères (tirets, flèches, surlignage, etc.).

N'oubliez pas qu'il s'agit d'un oral et que vous pouvez bien sûr jeter un coup d'œil à vos notes mais que vous ne devez pas lire ce que vous auriez rédigé de A à Z !

Vous pouvez parfois citer le document ; dans ce cas, pensez à donner la / les ligne(s) avant de lire le groupe de mots ou la phrase que vous souhaitez citer et n'oubliez pas de dire QUOTE, UNQUOTE (ouvrez les guillements, fermez les guillemets).
⚠ Une citation illustre votre argumentation, elle ne la remplace pas !

Votre exploitation du document iconographique doit venir à un moment opportun. Ainsi le logo peut être commenté lors de la présentation de l'entreprise.

Vous êtes à présent prêts pour votre oral mais il vous faut penser à une conclusion. Vous pouvez donner votre avis sur le document (mesures prises, utilité du portable, etc.) et / ou élargir les idées en faisant part de vos connaissances sur le sujet ou de votre expérience personnelle (comparaison avec la France, votre utilisation personnelle du portable, etc.)

Pensez à lier votre propos à l'aide de connecteurs (voir T&T: Prépositions / Adverbes / Subordonnées circonstancielles) et à utiliser un vocabulaire et des structures variés. N'hésitez pas à vous auto-corriger si vous vous rendez compte d'une erreur lors de votre prestation orale.

NB Si lors de l'entretien vous êtes vous-même amené à poser une / des question(s), n'oubliez pas de le faire en anglais !

3. Quelques expressions à connaître

THIS DOCUMENT IS AN EXTRACT FROM / AN EXCERPT FROM
→ Ce document est un extrait de

IT COMES FROM → Il est tiré de

IT WAS WRITTEN BY → Il a été écrit par

IT WAS PUBLISHED IN (OCTOBER) 2003 / ON 20 OCTOBER 2003
→ Il a été publié en (octobre) 2003 / le 20 octobre 2003

IT IS DATED (OCTOBER) 2003 → Il date de

IT DATES BACK TO / IT DATES FROM → Il remonte à

IT DEALS WITH / ACQUAINTS US WITH / INFORMS US ABOUT
→ Il traite de / nous fait prendre connaissance de / nous informe de

IT TACKLES THE QUESTION OF / THE ISSUE OF
→ Il aborde la question de / le problème de

TO BEGIN WITH → Pour commencer

FIRST / FIRSTLY / FIRST OF ALL
→ Premièrement / Tout d'abord

SECONDLY / THIRDLY → Deuxièmement / Troisièmement

THEN / AFTERWARDS → Puis

AT LAST / FINALLY / EVENTUALLY → Finalement

TO CONCLUDE / IN CONCLUSION / ALL IN ALL / TO SUM UP / TO PUT IT IN A NUTSHELL → Pour conclure / En conclusion

RELATE → relater

EXPLAIN → expliquer

DESCRIBE / DEPICT → décrire

UNDERLINE → souligner

BRING OUT / STRESS / LAY A STRESS ON / EMPHASIZE / LAY EMPHASIS ON → mettre en valeur

WE LEARN THAT → Nous apprenons que

WE ARE ACQUAINTED WITH / WE ARE INFORMED ABOUT
→ On nous fait part de / On nous informe de

IT HAS BEEN EXPLAINED TO US THAT → On nous explique que

IT IS CLEARLY MENTIONED THAT → Il est clairement dit que

WHAT IS STRIKING IS THAT / WHAT STRIKES ME IS THAT
→ Ce qui est frappant / Ce qui me frappe, c'est que

IT CONVEYS THE IDEA THAT → Cela exprime l'idée que

IT SHEDS A NEW LIGHT ON
→ Cela apporte un nouvel éclairage sur

THE JOURNALIST MAKES IT CLEAR THAT
→ Selon le journaliste, il est clair que

IT'S INTERESTING TO NOTE THAT
→ Il est intéressant de remarquer que

THIS BRINGS US TO THE QUESTION OF
→ Cela nous amène à la question de

WE ARE GIVEN THE IMPRESSION THAT → On a l'impression que

WE CAN'T HELP THINKING THAT / OF
→ Nous ne pouvons nous empêcher de penser que / à

WE COULD EVEN SAY / STATE / ASSERT THAT
→ Nous pourrions même dire / affirmer que

IT STANDS TO REASON THAT → Il va sans dire que

IN OTHER WORDS → En d'autres termes

LITTLE BY LITTLE, WE REALISE THAT
→ Petit à petit, nous nous rendons compte que

4. Comment faire un compte rendu écrit

Le principe est le même que pour le compte rendu oral :
– identification du document,
– reformulation des idées dans vos propres mots et dans un ordre logique que vous aurez choisi (le respect de l'ordre du texte n'est pas obligatoire).

Les différences sont les suivantes :
Le compte rendu écrit peut :
– être à faire en anglais ou en français ; c'est toujours indiqué très clairement dans l'énoncé !
– porter sur tout ou partie du support (quelques paragraphes seulement, l'avis d'une personne, etc.). Lisez donc attentivement l'énoncé.
Par ailleurs, un nombre de mots est toujours indiqué : 200 WORDS signifie que votre compte rendu devra faire entre 180 et 220 mots ; 150-200 WORDS signifie qu'il devra faire de 150 à 200 mots. Vous devez écrire le nombre de mots que vous avez rédigés à la fin de votre compte rendu ; habituez-vous donc à les compter rapidement afin de ne pas perdre de précieuses minutes.

5. Comment faire un résumé écrit

Les indications ci-dessus sur les différences entre le compte rendu oral et écrit s'appliquent aussi au résumé écrit (langue / tout ou partie du support / nombre de mots).

<u>Dans un résumé, vous devez</u>
– respecter l'ordre des idées du document,
– être « objectif » ; ne donnez donc pas votre avis !
– aller à l'essentiel ; n'indiquez pas de détails, de chiffres, etc. mais généralisez.
Ex. : – X company sales skyrocketed over the last decade.
– *Les ventes de l'entreprise X sont montées en flèche au cours de la dernière décennie.*

<u>Vous ne devez pas</u> recopier des phrases du document. Vous devez résumer les idées avec vos propres mots.
Donner la source n'est pas nécessaire ; il est préférable d'entrer tout de suite dans le vif du sujet.

5. Principaux procédés de traduction

1. Le mot à mot

Aucun problème !

Ex. : – On the sea.
– *Sur la mer.*

2. La transposition

Procédé par lequel on traduit un mot appartenant à une autre catégorie grammaticale que le mot anglais.

Nom en anglais → verbe en français

Ex. : – This is not my first visit.
– *Ce n'est pas la première fois que je viens.*

Verbe en anglais → nom en français

Ex. : – Translating is not easy.
– *La traduction, ce n'est pas facile.*

Adjectif en anglais → nom en français

Ex. : – Medical studies.
– *Des études de médecine.*

Préposition en anglais → verbe en français

Ex. : – This is an extract from *Time*.
– *C'est un extrait tiré du* Time.

3. Le chassé-croisé

Du verbe à la préposition

Considérez l'exemple suivant où 1 est la *manière* dont a été accomplie l'action et 2 le mouvement :

Ex. : – John swam across the river.
(swam = 1, across = 2)
– *John a traversé la rivière à la nage.*
(*a traversé* = 2, *à la nage* = 1)

Il faut donc d'abord traduire la préposition par un verbe, puis le verbe.

Adjectif postposé

Ex. : – You are going to read yourself blind.
(read = 1, yourself blind = 2)
– *Tu vas te rendre aveugle à force de lire.*
(*te rendre aveugle* = 2, *à force de lire* = 1)

4. La modulation

Procédé qui consiste à traduire en voyant les choses sous un angle différent.

Ex. : – Remember the guide.
– *N'oubliez pas le guide*
– The water is shallow here.
– *L'eau est peu profonde ici.*
– It's cheap.
– *C'est bon marché.*
– On the top floor.
– *Au dernier étage.*

5. L'étoffement

Ex. : – The plane from New York.
– *L'avion en provenance de New York.*
– The girl in red trousers.
– *La fille qui porte un pantalon rouge.*
– We'll have to phone for a taxi.
– *Il va falloir que nous appelions un taxi.*
– It's still a debate.
– *Cela reste un débat.*

6. L'équivalence

Il s'agit parfois de trouver en français une expression globalement équivalente.

Ex. : – Staff only.
– *Réservé au personnel.*
– Keep off the grass.
– *Défense de marcher sur les pelouses.*
– Birds of a feather flock together.
– *Qui se ressemble s'assemble.*

6. Quelques expressions pour communiquer

Advice (cf. Le groupe verbal : Modaux / Prétérit modal)

- – I **advise you to** be on time.
  not to smoke.
  – *Je vous conseille d'être à l'heure / de ne pas fumer.*
- – You **should watch** your manners.
  not arrive late.
  have listen**ed** to him.
  – *Vous devriez faire attention à vos manières.*
  – *Vous ne devriez pas arriver en retard.*
  – *Vous auriez dû l'écouter.*
- – You'**d** (= **had**) **better hurry**.
  not wear jeans.
  – *Vous feriez mieux de vous dépêcher / de ne pas porter de jeans.*
- – **Why not put** on this blue shirt?
  – *Pourquoi ne pas porter cette chemise bleue ?*
- – **Why don't you phone** them?
  – *Pourquoi ne leur téléphonez-vous pas ?*
- – **It's in your interest to** go to this meeting.
  – **It would be in your interest to** go to this meeting.
  – *Il est / serait dans votre intérêt d'aller à cette réunion.*
- – You **could move** to town.
  – *Vous pourriez aller habiter en ville.*
- – You **ought to** tell her you are back.
  not to let him wait.
  to have help**ed** her.
  – *Vous devriez lui dire que vous êtes revenu.*
  – *Vous ne devriez pas le laisser attendre.*
  – *Vous auriez dû l'aider.*
- – **Take my advice: go** and speak to him!
  don't accept it!
  – *Suivez mon conseil : allez lui parler ! / ne l'acceptez pas !*

- **– It's (about / high) time you took** a decision.
  you didn't swear.
  – Il est (bientôt / grand) temps que vous preniez une décision / que vous ne juriez pas.
- **– Don't you think you should pay** them a visit?
  you shouldn't send them this letter?
  you should(n't) have phon**ed** them?
  – Ne pensez-vous pas que vous devriez leur rendre visite ? / que vous ne devriez pas envoyer cette lettre ? / que vous auriez dû (n'auriez pas dû) leur téléphoner ?
- **– Don't you think you had better**
  fetch him at the airport?
  not send this fax?
  – Ne pensez-vous pas que vous feriez mieux d'aller le chercher à l'aéroport ? / de ne pas envoyer ce fax ?
- **– I suggest you should(n't) go** to the conference.
  – Je suggère que vous alliez (n'alliez pas) à la conférence.
- **– I suggest he go** to the conference.
  he not go to the conference.
  ⚠ **2ᵉ sujet suivi de BV**
  – Je suggère qu'il aille / qu'il n'aille pas à la conférence.
- **– I (would) recommend you to** listen carefully.
  not to stay too long.
  – Je vous recommande(rais) d'écouter attentivement / de ne pas rester trop longtemps.
- **– It would be a good idea to** recruit this candidate.
  not to refuse this offer.
  – Ce serait une bonne idée de recruter ce candidat / de ne pas refuser cette offre.

Agreement

- – She likes travelling. – So do I.
  – Moi aussi.
- – They can't come. – Neither can I.
  – Moi non plus.
- – Will you go to the meeting? – Yes, I will.
  – Oui
  – I suppose I will.
  – Je suppose que oui.
  – I think I will.
  – Je crois que oui.
- – They'll probably argue again. – I think so.
  – J'en ai bien l'impression.
  – I suppose so.
  – Je suppose.
- – I approve of his decision.
  – J'approuve sa décision.
- – That's how I see it too.
  – C'est également comme cela que je vois les choses.
- – I (quite / totally) agree with you.
  – I couldn't agree more.
  – I'm in full agreement with you.
  – I see eye to eye with you.
  – Je suis (entièrement) d'accord avec vous.
- – That's just what I was thinking.
  – C'est exactement ce que je me disais.
- – I have the same opinion.
  – I share the same opinion.
  – I am of the same opinion.
  – Je partage cette opinion.
- – Whether you agree or not, you can't deny that + S + V
  – Que vous soyez d'accord ou pas, vous ne pouvez pas nier que…
- – What you say is all the truer as + S + V
  all the more relevant as + S + V
  – Ce que vous dites est d'autant plus vrai / pertinent que…
- – As you have (so rightly) pointed out, S + V
  – Comme vous l'avez (si justement) fait remarquer,…
- – There is no (shadow of a) doubt that + S + V
  – Il ne fait aucun doute que… (Il n'y a pas l'ombre d'un doute que…)
- – It goes without saying that + S + V
  – Il va sans dire que…
- – You're right.
  – Vous avez raison.
- – Doubtlessly!
  – Of course!
  – Exactly!
  – Naturally!
  – (Quite) true!
  – That's it!
  – Absolutely!
  – Definitely!
  – (All) right! (coll.)
  – Sure! (coll.)
  – Exactement ! / C'est certain !

Disagreement

- – She enjoys meeting people. – I don't.
  – Moi pas.
- – He's going to be late again. – I don't think so.
  – Je ne pense pas.
  – I don't suppose so.
  – Je ne crois pas.
- – I disapprove of your attitude.
  – I don't approve of your behaving this way.
  – Je n'approuve pas / Je désapprouve votre attitude / votre façon de vous comporter.
- – I don't agree with you.
  – I disagree with you.
  – Je ne suis pas d'accord avec vous.
- – I'm not (quite) sure I agree with you.
  – Je ne suis pas (tout à fait) certain d'être d'accord avec vous.
- – I'm afraid I don't agree with you.
  – J'ai bien peur de ne pas être d'accord avec vous.
- – I'm afraid I can't support that view.
  – J'ai bien peur de ne pouvoir soutenir cette idée / adhérer à cette idée.

- – I don't / can't share your views on this.
  – Je ne partage pas / Je ne peux pas partager votre point de vue sur cette question.
- – I don't see eye to eye with you about it.
  – Je ne vois pas cela sous le même angle que vous.
- – I don't see it that way.
  – Je ne vois pas les choses de cette façon.
- – Unlike you, I consider that + S + V
  – Contrairement à vous, je considère que…
- – My point of view is different.
  – Our views differ.
  – Nos points de vue sont divergents.
- – I can't go along with that.
  – Je ne suis pas du tout d'accord avec cela.
- – It doesn't seem right to me.
  – Cela ne me paraît / semble pas vrai / juste.
- – There is no reason why I shouldn't interfere.
  – Il n'y a aucune raison que je n'intervienne pas.
- – The problem is not to + BV but to + BV
  – Le problème n'est pas de … mais de …
- – It's one thing to + BV, it's another to + BV
  – … est une chose, … en est une autre.
- – I object to this measure / to taking this measure / to your taking this measure.
  – Je m'oppose à cette mesure / Je refuse de prendre cette mesure / Je refuse que vous preniez cette mesure.
- – That's not the point.
  – That's beside the point.
  – Là n'est pas la question.
- – I see no point in + V-ing
  – Je ne vois aucun intérêt à + V
- – It's totally irrelevant!
  – Cela n'a rien à voir avec la question !
- – Count me out!
  – Ne comptez pas sur moi !
- – (That's) ridiculous!
  – (That's) nonsense!
  – It's nonsensical!
  – C'est ridicule ! / Cela n'a pas de sens !
- – Certainly not!
  – Certainement pas !
- – You're wrong.
  – Vous avez tort.
- – You can't be serious!
  – Vous n'êtes pas sérieux !
- – You must be joking!
  – Vous plaisantez !
- – No way!
  – Pas question !

Dislikes

- – I don't **like** sleep**ing** late in the morning.
  – Je n'aime pas dormir tard le matin.
- – She **dislikes** tak**ing** the tube.
  – Elle n'aime pas prendre le métro.
- – They **are not keen** on drink**ing** alcohol.
  – Ils n'aiment pas beaucoup boire de l'alcool.
- – She **can't stand / bear / abide** be**ing** disturbed when she works.
  – Elle ne supporte pas d'être dérangée quand elle travaille.
- – He **resents** go**ing** to parties.
  – Aller à des soirées lui deplaît fortement.
- – I **hate** wait**ing**.
  – Je déteste attendre.
- – I **loathe** see**ing** a bad film.
  – J'ai horreur de voir un mauvais film.

NB Ces groupes verbaux peuvent être suivi de V-ING, d'un nom, d'un pronom ou d'un adjectif possessif.

Ex. : – She is not keen on **sports**.
– Elle n'aime pas beaucoup le sport.
– I hate **it**.
– Je déteste cela.
– I don't like **you** / **your** sleeping late in the morning.
– Je n'aime pas que vous fassiez la grasse matinée.

Likes

- – He **would like to** have an appointment.
  – Il aimerait avoir un rendez-vous.
- – I **would like you to** get an appointment.
  – J'aimerais que tu obtiennes un rendez-vous.
- – She **is interested in*** work**ing** for a multinational.
  – Travailler pour une multinationale l'intéresse. / Cela l'intéresse de travailler pour une multinationale.
- – I **like*** go**ing** to the pictures. *J'aime aller au cinéma.*
- – I **sometimes like to** go dancing. *Parfois, j'aime aller danser.*
- – They **enjoy** learn**ing** English.
  – Ils aiment apprendre l'anglais.
- – You **are keen on*** go**ing** abroad.
  – Aller à l'étranger vous passionne.
- – He **is fond of*** driv**ing** a racing car.
  – Il aime beaucoup conduire une voiture de course.
- – Team work **appeals to** me very much.
  – Le travail d'équipe m'attire beaucoup.
- – She **is enthusiastic about*** travell**ing**.
  – Voyager l'enthousiasme.
- – I **relish** the challenge of starting a new job.
  – Débuter dans un nouvel emploi est un défi qui me ravit.
- – I **dote on**** Marilyn Monroe.
  – Je raffole de Marilyn Monroe.
- – They **are crazy about*** listen**ing** to hard rock music.
  – Ils sont fous de hard rock.
- – She **loves*** walk**ing** in the woods.
  – Elle aime beaucoup marcher dans les bois.
- – I **love to** jog **from time to time**.
  – J'aime faire du jogging de temps en temps.

* **Ces groupes verbaux peuvent être suivis de V-ING, d'un nom, d'un pronom ou d'un adjectif possessif :**
Ex. : – He is fond of **books**.
– *Il aime les livres.*
– I adore **you**.
– *Je t'adore.*
– She loves **his** coming back early.
– *Elle adore quand il rentre tôt.*
** **DOTE ON + N uniquement.**

Personal opinion

- – I (do / really / just / don't) think / feel / suppose / consider / believe that…
  – *Je pense que / J'ai le sentiment que / Je suppose que / Je considère que / Je crois que…*
  – *Je pense etc. vraiment / simplement que / Je ne pense pas que…*
- – In my view,…
  – In my opinion,…
  – To my mind,…
  – As for me,…
  – From my point of view,…
  – As far as I'm concerned,…
  – *À mon avis,…*
- – As far as I know,…
  – *À ce que je sache,…*
- – According to him / her,…
  – *D'après lui / elle,…*
- – It seems to me that…
  – It doesn't seem to me that…
  – *Il me semble que / Il ne me semble pas que…*
- – I should(n't) say that…
  – *Je dirais / ne dirais pas que…*
- – I must confess / admit that…
  – *Je dois avouer / admettre que…*
- – My (view)point is that…
  – *Mon point de vue est que…*
- – What I mean is…
  – *Ce que je veux dire c'est…*
- – My feeling is that…
  – *Mon sentiment est que…*
- – I'm convinced that…
  – *Je suis convaincu que…*
- – I would tend to think that …
  – *Je serais tenté de penser que…*
- – I find it surprising / interesting… that he / people… should complain about / approve of this.
  – *Je trouve surprenant / intéressant… qu'il / que les gens… se plaigne(nt) de / approuve(nt) ceci.*
- – There is no / There can be no (shadow of a) doubt that…
  – *Il ne fait / Il ne peut y avoir aucun doute que… / pas l'ombre d'un doute que…*
- – Doubtlessly,…
  – *Sans aucun doute,…*
- – What we have to realise is that…
  – *Ce dont nous devons nous rendre compte c'est que…*
- – I have the feeling that…
  – I'm under the impression that…
  – *J'ai l'impression que…*
- – I wonder if / whether or not / why…
  – *Je me demande si / si oui ou non / pourquoi…*
- – It's hard to imagine that…
  – *Il est difficile d'imaginer que…*
- – I think it's natural / normal… that he / they… should accept it.
  – I guess it's natural / normal… for him / for them to accept it.
  – *Je pense qu'il est naturel / normal… qu'il(s) l'accepte(nt).*
- – I would like to add / point out… that…
  – *J'aimerais ajouter / faire remarquer… que…*
- – This brings me to the question of knowing whether or not he's right.
  how / when… he did it.
  – *Cela m'amène à la question de savoir s'il a raison ou pas / comment / quand… il l'a fait.*
- – I'd (= would) like to make it clear / to specify that…
  – *J'aimerais préciser que…*

Preference

- – I **like** read**ing better than** watch**ing** TV.
  – *Je préfère lire plutôt que de regarder la télé.*
- – He **prefers** desktops (**to** laptops).
  – *Il préfère les ordinateurs de bureau (aux ordinateurs portables).*
- – She **prefers to** / She **would prefer to** be dismissed (**rather than accept** his conditions).
  – *Elle préfère / Elle préfèrerait être licenciée (plutôt que d'accepter ses conditions).*
- – I**'d prefer not to** come.
  – *Je préfèrerais ne pas venir.*
- – We(**'d**) **prefer you to** travel by plane (**rather than to** waste your time by car).
  – *Nous préférons / préfèrerions que vous preniez l'avion (plutôt que de perdre votre temps en voiture).*
- – They**'d** (= would) **rather leave** early (**than drive** in the traffic jams).
  – *Ils préfèreraient partir tôt (plutôt que de conduire dans les embouteillages).*
- – I**'d rather you** typ**ed** this letter first.
  you didn't type this letter first.
  – *Je préfèrerais que vous tapiez / ne tapiez pas d'abord cette lettre.*
- – She**'d** (= would) **sooner get** a low-paid job (**than remain** unemployed).
  – *Elle préfèrerait obtenir un emploi mal rémunéré (plutôt que de rester au chômage).*
- – I**'d sooner you** finish**ed** your work before going out.
  you didn't answer the phone.
  – *Je préfèrerais que tu finisses ton travail avant de sortir / que tu ne répondes pas au téléphone.*

- – He'**d** (= would) **as soon eat** out **as have** his meal at the canteen.
  – *Il préfèrerait manger à l'extérieur plutôt que de prendre son repas à la cantine.*
- – **I'd as soon go** on holiday next winter.
  – *J'aimerais autant partir en vacances cet hiver.*
- – **My favourite hobby is to** go to the pictures.
  – *Mon passetemps préféré c'est d'aller au cinéma.*
- – **What he likes best is to** look for new markets abroad.
  – *Ce qu'il préfère c'est chercher de nouveaux marchés à l'étranger.*

Probability (cf. Le groupe verbal : Modaux)

1. Modal + BV = action future

⊖
- – He can't phone.
  – *Il est impossible qu'il appelle.*
- – He might phone.
  – *Il se pourrait qu'il appelle.*
- – He may phone.
  – *Peut-être va-t-il appeler.*
- – He could phone.
  – *Il pourrait peut-être appeler.*
- – He can phone.
  – *Il peut appeler.*
- – He should phone.
  – *Il devrait appeler.*
- – He must phone.
  – *Il doit appeler.*

⊕

2. Modal + be + V-ing = action présente

- – He might be phoning. *(et les modaux précédents)*
  – *Il se pourrait qu'il soit en train de téléphoner.*

3. Modal + have + participe passé = action passée

- – He might have phoned.
  – *Il se pourrait qu'il ait appelé.*
- – He may have phoned.
  – *Peut-être a-t-il appelé.*
- – He can have phoned.
  – *Il se peut qu'il ait appelé.*
- – He must have phoned.
  – *Il a sûrement appelé.*

4. Autres expressions

- – **Perhaps / Maybe** he'll come.
  – *Il va peut-être venir.*
- – He **is (most) likely to** sign the contract.
  – He **is not likely to** sign the contract.
  – He **is unlikely to** sign the contract.
  – *Il est (fort) probable qu'il signe le contrat / qu'il ne signe pas le contrat.*
- – He **is liable to** refuse it.
  – *Il risque de le refuser.*
- – **It looks as if** she is going to come.
  – *Il semblerait qu'elle va venir.*
- – He (**most**) **probably / certainly** decided it.
  – *Il l'a (très) probablement décidé.*

Regrets

- – I **regret** telling him this.
  – **I'm sorry I told** him this.
  – *Je regrette de lui avoir dit ceci.*
- – **I regret she didn't phone.**
  – **I'm sorry she didn't phone.**
  – *Je regrette qu'elle n'ait pas téléphoné.*
- – **I regret to say that** he lied.
  – *Je regrette d'avoir à dire qu'il a menti.*
- – **I wish he had** listen**ed** to her.
  – **If only he had** listen**ed** to her.
  – *Je regrette qu'il ne l'ait pas écoutée / J'aurais souhaité qu'il l'écoute / Ah, si seulement il l'avait écoutée !*
- – **What a pity / a shame** you weren't free!
  – *Quel dommage que vous n'ayez pas été libre !*
- – **It's a pity / a shame** you couldn't hear them.
  – *C'est dommage que vous n'ayez pas pu les entendre.*
- – **If I had known, I would(n't) have given** him my phone number.
  – *Si j'avais su, je lui aurais donné / je ne lui aurais pas donné mon numéro de téléphone.*
- – **I should(n't) have said** it. (imposé par le sujet)
  – *J'aurais dû / Je n'aurais pas dû le dire.*
- – **I ought to have** prov**ed** more tactful. *(imposé par l'extérieur)*
  – *Il aurait fallu que je fasse preuve de plus de tact.*
- – **I used to** be more enthusiastic.
  – *Autrefois, j'étais plus enthousiaste.*
- – **Why didn't I try** to persuade them?
  – *Pourquoi n'ai-je pas essayé de les persuader ?*

Reproach

- – I **reproach him for** exaggerat**ing**.
  not listen**ing**.
  – *Je lui reproche d'exagérer / de ne pas écouter.*
- – I **blame her for** talk**ing** too much.
  not invit**ing** them.
  – *Je lui reproche de trop parler / de ne pas les inviter.*
- – They **accuse him of** work**ing** alone.
  not work**ing** enough.
  – *Ils l'accusent de travailler seul / de ne pas assez travailler.*
- – **I wish you** contact**ed** them / **didn't** contact them.
  – *J'aimerais que vous les contactiez / que vous ne les contactiez pas.*
  – **If only you** contact**ed** them! / **didn't** contact them!
  – *Si seulement vous les contactiez ! / ne les contactiez pas !*
- – **You could have** talk**ed** to them.
  – *Vous auriez pu leur parler.*
- – **You should have** talk**ed** to them.
  – *Vous auriez dû leur parler.*
- – **You ought to have** talk**ed** to them.
  – *Il aurait fallu que vous leur parliez.*

- – **Why didn't you** call him back?
  – *Pourquoi ne l'avez-vous pas rappelé ?*
- – **Did you have to** phone them?
  – *Deviez-vous absolument leur téléphoner ? / Étiez-vous obligé de leur téléphoner ?*
- – **Couldn't you** insist?
  – *Ne pouviez-vous pas insister ?*
- – **I'd** (= would) **rather you had** succeed**ed**.
  – *J'aurais préféré que vous réussissiez.*
- – **Instead of** hesitat**ing**,
  you'd (= had) **better be** more self-confident.
  you should have prov**ed** self-confident.
  – *Au lieu d'hésiter, vous auriez mieux fait d'être plus sûr de vous / vous auriez dû vous montrer plus sûr de vous.*
- – **Who do you think you are to** talk to me like that?
  – *Pour qui vous prenez-vous pour me parler sur ce ton ?*
- – That isn't done!
  – *Cela ne se fait pas !*
- – I don't like the way you do this.
  – *Je n'aime pas la façon dont vous faites ceci.*
- – The way you dress is appalling!
  – *La façon dont vous vous habillez est épouvantable !*
- – How dare you!
  – *Comment osez-vous !*
- – What a cheek! / How cheeky!
  – *Quel toupet !*
- – You'd better mend your ways!
  – *Vous feriez mieux de changer vos façons de faire.*

Suggestions / Proposals

- – **I suggest she should accept** his offer.
  she accept his offer. ⚠ **2e sujet + BV**
  – *Je suggère qu'elle accepte son offre.*
- – **Why not reduce** its price?
  – *Pourquoi ne pas réduire son prix ?*
- – **Why don't you** read the ads?
  – *Pourquoi ne lisez-vous pas les petits annonces ?*
- – **What about / How about** invit**ing** her?
  – *Et si on l'invitait ?*
- – **You could sign** the contract, **couldn't you?**
  – *Vous pourriez signer le contrat, non ?*
- – **Wouldn't it be wise to** sell it quickly?
  – **Don't you think it would be a good idea to** sell it quickly?
  – *Ne serait-il pas sage de / Ne pensez-vous pas que ce serait une bonne idée de le vendre rapidement ?*
- – **Can't / Couldn't we ask** the personnel manager?
  – *Ne pouvons-nous pas / Ne pourrions-nous pas demander au chef du personnel ?*
- – **Shall we meet** her? – *On va la rencontrer ?*
- – **Let's** (= us) **see** him! – *Allons le voir !*

Wishes

- – **I wish the situation would** improve (= it may).
  ⚠ **I wish I would = impossible**
  – *J'aimerais que la situation s'améliore.*
- – **I wish they took** measures. (= they don't)
  they didn't take measures.
  – *J'aimerais / Je souhaiterais qu'ils prennent des mesures / qu'ils ne prennent pas de mesures.*
- – **I'd** (= would) **like to** go abroad.
  you to concentrate.
  – *J'aimerais aller à l'étranger / que vous vous concentriez.*
- – **It would be nice / great to** try it.
  if he accept**ed**.
  – *Ce serait génial de l'essayer / si il acceptait.*
- – **I'd** (= would) **give my eyeteeth for** a job / **to** know the results.
  – *Je donnerais cher pour avoir un emploi / connaître les résultats.*
- – **I feel like** travell**ing**.
  – *J'ai envie de voyager.*
- – **I'm dying for** a walk.
  – *J'ai une envie folle de marcher.*
- – **I hope to** see you soon.
  he is right / **he can** do it, …
  – *J'espère vous voir bientôt / qu'il a raison / qu'il peut le faire,…*
- – **I'm looking forward to** visit**ing** your new flat.
  – **I'm eager to** visit your new flat.
  – *J'attends avec impatience de / J'ai hâte de visiter ton nouvel appartement.*

7. Faux amis

abuse	*insulter*	***abuser***	take advantage of
accommodate	*loger*	***accommoder***	prepare
achieve	*réaliser, effectuer*	***achever***	complete, finish
actually	*en fait*	***actuellement***	at present, currently
affluence	*richesse*	***affluence***	rush
caution	*prudence*	***caution***	guarantee
character	*personnage*	***caractère***	nature, personality
charge	*faire payer*	***charger***	load

commodity	*marchandise*	***commodité***	convenience
comprehensive	*complet, exhaustif*	***compréhensif***	understanding
conductor	*contrôleur*	***conducteur***	driver
confection	*confiserie*	***confection***	ready-made clothes
contemplate	*envisager*	***contempler***	gaze (at)
copy	*exemplaire*	***copie***	reproduction
deceive	*tromper*	***décevoir***	disappoint
delay	*retard*	***délai***	time limit, deadline
dispute	*conflit*	***dispute***	quarrel, argument
distracted	*fou*	***distrait***	absent-minded
engaged	*fiancé, occupé (téléphone)*	***engagé***	committed
eventually	*finalement*	***éventuellement***	possibly
expertise	*compétence*	***expertise***	expert's report
grand	*grandiose*	***grand***	tall, big
hazard	*danger*	***hasard***	chance
indulgence	*laisser-aller*	***indulgence***	leniency
lecture	*conférence*	***lecture***	reading
location	*emplacement*	***location***	renting, lease
mechanic	*mécanicien*	***mécanique***	engineering, mechanics
medicine	*médicament*	***médecin***	doctor
notice	*avis, préavis*	***notice***	note, instructions
partition	*séparation*	***partition***	score
petrol	*essence*	***pétrole***	oil
phrase	*expression*	***phrase***	sentence
positive	*catégorique, sûr*	***positif***	positive
prevent	*empêcher*	***prévenir***	warn, tell
recover	*se rétablir*	***recouvrir***	cover
refuse	*déchets, ordures*	***refus***	refusal
regard	*considérer*	***regarder***	look (at)
relieve	*soulager*	***relever***	raise
rest	*repos*	***rester***	stay, remain
resume	*reprendre*	***résumer***	sum up, summarise
route	*itinéraire*	***route***	road
rude	*grossier*	***rude***	rough, hard
sensible	*raisonnable*	***sensible***	sensitive
survey	*examiner*	***surveiller***	supervise
sympathetic	*compatissant*	***sympathique***	nice, friendly
touchy	*susceptible*	***touché***	moved
tour	*voyage, circuit*	***tour***	stroll, turn
vacation	*vacances*	***vacation***	session, sitting
valid	*valable*	***valide***	fit, well
waggon	*chariot*	***wagon***	carriage, car

8. Anglais britannique et américain

British English	American English	French
autumn	fall	*automne*
bill	check	*addition*
biscuit	cookie	*gâteau sec*
bonnet	hood	*capot de voiture*
bumper	fender	*pare-chocs*
car park	parking lot	*parking*
chemist's	drugstore	*pharmacie*
chips	French fries	*frites*
engaged	busy	*occupé (téléphone)*
ex-directory	unlisted	*sur liste rouge*
film	movie	*film*
flat	apartment	*appartement*
floor	storey	*étage*
form	class	*classe (scolaire)*
ground floor	first floor	*rez-de-chaussée*
holiday	vacation	*vacances*
hoover	vacuum cleaner	*aspirateur*
letter box	mail box	*boîte à lettres*
lift	elevator	*ascenseur*
lorry	truck	*camion*
motorway	freeway, throughway	*autoroute*
number plate	license plate	*plaque minéralogique*
off-licence	liquor store	*magasin de vins et spiritueux*
pavement	sidewalk	*trottoir*
petrol	gas	*essence*
postcode	zipcode	*code postal*
postman	mailman	*facteur*
queue	line	*file d'attente*
railway	railroad	*chemin de fer*
roundabout	traffic circle	*rond-point*
rubbish	garbage, trash	*ordures ménagères*
shop	store	*magasin*
shop assistant	clerk	*vendeur*
tin	can	*boîte de conserve*
trolley	cart	*chariot (supermarché)*
trousers	pants	*pantalon*
underground	subway	*métro*

Passport to English-speaking countries

Passport

1• Phonetics and stresses

► Vowels

[iː]	s**ee**, l**ea**f
[ɪ]	sh**i**p
[e]	b**e**d
[æ]	c**a**t
[ɑː]	c**ar**, c**al**m
[ɒ]	b**o**x, w**a**sh
[ɔː]	f**or**, b**or**n
[ʊ]	p**u**t, c**oul**d
[uː]	f**oo**l
[ʌ]	b**u**t
[ɜː]	b**ir**d, w**or**k
[ə]	**a**gain, employ**er**

► Diphthongs

[eɪ]	s**ay**
[əʊ]	n**o**
[aɪ]	b**uy**, l**ie**
[aʊ]	**ou**t, n**ow**
[ɔɪ]	**oi**l, c**oi**n
[ɪə]	b**eer**, h**ear**
[eə]	**air**
[ʊə]	t**our**

► Consonants

[p]	**p**it, **p**o**pp**y
[b]	**b**ed, **b**a**b**y
[t]	**t**ea, **t**o**t**al
[d]	**d**og, men**d**e**d**
[k]	**k**iss, **ch**ord, **c**a**k**e
[g]	**g**ot, bi**g**
[f]	**f**eel, **f**ul**f**il
[v]	**v**ery, cle**v**er
[s]	**s**it, me**ss**, thank**s**
[z]	bu**zz**, cloth**es**, hall**s**
[θ]	**th**umb, ma**th**s
[ð]	**th**is, **th**en
[ʃ]	**sh**e, fi**sh**
[ʒ]	u**s**ual, plea**s**ure
[tʃ]	**ch**ance, **ch**ur**ch**
[dʒ]	**j**ust, **j**ump
[l]	**l**eg, p**l**ace
[r]	**r**oad, emba**rr**assing
[m]	**m**an, fro**m**
[n]	**n**o, fu**n**
[ŋ]	ri**ng**, ba**n**k
[h]	**h**at, be**h**ave
[j]	**y**es, bill**i**on
[w]	**w**in, q**u**iet
[x] Scottish pronunciation for [k]	lo**ch**

[ʳ] Indicates a possible *r*-link before a following vowel.

► Here are a few rules of word stresses

Stress on the last syllable

-ee	trai'nee
-eer	engi'neer
-ese	Chi'nese
-esque	gro'tesque
-ette	launde'rette

Stress on the third from last syllable

-ety	so'ciety
-ity	se'curity
-itive	com'petitive
-itude	'attitude
-ate	a'ppreciate
-ify	'specify
-ise / -ize	'realise / 'realize

Stress on the next to last syllable

-ial	secre'tarial
-ian	poli'tician
-ic / -ics (suffixes in -ical and -ically don't change the place of the stress)	eco'nomic / eco'nomics eco'nomical / eco'nomically
-ion	infor'mation
-ish	di'minish

2• Measures, weights and temperatures

1 ► Linear measures

1 inch (in)	2.54 cm
1 foot (ft)	30.48 cm
1 yard (yd)	0.914 m
1 (statute) mile (mi)	1.609 km
1 nautical mile (nm)	1.852 km

2 ► Square measures

1 square inch (sq in / in^2)	6.45 cm^2
1 square foot (sq ft / ft^2)	0.09 m^2
1 square yard (sq yd / yd^2)	0.83 m^2
1 acre (a)	0.40 ha
1 square mile (sq mi / m^2)	2.59 km^2

3 ► Cubic measures

1 cubic inch (cu in / in^3)	16.38 cm^3
1 cubic foot (cu ft / ft^3)	28.317 cm^3
1 cubic yard (cu yd / yd^3)	0.76 m^3

4 ► Weights

1 grain (gr)	0.064 g
1 ounce (oz)	28.35 g
1 pound (lb)	0.450 kg
1 stone (st)	6.348 kg

5 ► Liquid measures

GB

1 gill (gi)	0.14 l
4 gills = 1 pint (pt)	0.57 l
2 pints = 1 quart (qt)	1.14 l
8 pt = 4 qt = 1 gallon (gal)	4.54 l

US

1 US liquid gill	0.118 l
4 gills = 1 US liquid pint	0.473 l
2 pints = 1 US liquid quart	0.946 l
4 quarts = 1 US gallon	3.785 l

6 ► Crude oil

1 barrel = 42 US gal = 1.59 hl

7 ► Temperatures

32° Fahrenheit = 0° C

212° Fahrenheit = 100° C

3• The United Kingdom

The United Kingdom / the UK = England + Wales + Scotland + Northern Ireland / Ulster
Britain = Great Britain = England + Wales + Scotland
The British Isles = the UK + the Republic of Ireland / Eire

Region	Population	Main city	Language	Adjective	People
England	49,100,000	London	English	English	the English
Wales	2,900,000	Cardiff	English / Welsh	Welsh	the Welsh
Scotland	5,000,000	Edinburgh	English / Scots / Gaelic	Scottish	the Scots
Northern Ireland	1,600,000	Belfast	English / Irish / Gaelic	northern Irish	the northern Irish

4• The British Empire

Worldwide system of dependencies – colonies, protectorates, and other territories – that over a span of three centuries came under the British government. Territorial acquisition began in the early 17th century with a group of settlements in North America and West Indian, East Indian, and African trading posts founded by private individuals and trading companies. In the 18th century the British took Gibraltar, established colonies along the Atlantic seacoast, and began to add territory in India. With its victory in the French and Indian War (1763), it secured Canada and the Mississippi Valley and gained supremacy in India. From the late 18th century it began to build power in Malaya and acquired the Cape of Good Hope, Ceylon and Malta.
The English settled in Australia in 1788, and subsequently in New Zealand. Aden was secured in 1839, and Hong Kong in 1842. Britain went on to control the Suez Canal 1875-1956. In the 19th-century European partition of Africa, Britain acquired Nigeria, Egypt, the territories that would become British East Africa, and part of what would become the Union (later Republic) of South Africa. After World War I, Britain secured mandates to German East Africa, part of Cameroon, part of Togo, German South-West Africa, Mesopotamia, Palestine, and part of the German Pacific islands.
Prior to 1783, Britain claimed full authority over colonial legislatures; after the U.S. gained independence, Britain gradually evolved a system of self-government for some colonies, as set forth in Lord Durham's report of 1839. Dominion status was given to Canada (1867), Australia (1901), New Zealand (1907), the Union of South Africa (1910), and the Irish Free State (1921). Britain declared war on Germany in 1914 on behalf of the entire Empire; after World War I the dominions signed the peace treaties themselves and joined the League of Nations as independent states. In 1931 the Statute of Westminster recognized them as independent countries "within the British Empire", referring to the "British Commonwealth of Nations".

In the dominions the Queen is Head of State even if a governor rules the country (Australia, for instance). The former colonies have their own head of state since they are independent, the Queen is Head of the Commonwealth for them.

At the time of its founding, the Commonwealth consisted of the United Kingdom, Australia, Canada, the Irish Free State (withdrew in 1949), Newfoundland (became a Canadian province in 1949), New Zealand, and the Union of South Africa (withdrew in 1961).
After World War II, with "British" no longer officially used, the Commonwealth was joined by the following countries: India, Pakistan (1947); Pakistan withdrew in 1972, but rejoined in 1989; Ceylon (1948; now Sri Lanka); Ghana (1957); Nigeria (1960); Cyprus, Sierra Leone (1961); Jamaica, Trinidad and Tobago, Uganda, Western Samoa (1962); Kenya, Malaysia (1963); Malawi, Malta, Tanzania, Zambia (1964); Gambia, Singapore (1965); Barbados, Botswana, Guyana, Lesotho (1966); Mauritius, Nauru (special status); Swaziland (1968); Tonga (1970); Bangladesh (1972); Bahamas (1973); Grenada (1974); Papua New Guinea (1975); Seychelles (1976); Solomon Islands, Tuvalu (special status), Dominica (1978); St. Lucia, Kiribati, St. Vincent and the Grenadines (1979); Zimbabwe, Vanuatu (1980); Belize, Antigua and Barbuda (1981); Maldives (1982); St. Kitts-Nevis (1983); Brunei (1984); South Africa (rejoined 1994); Cameroon, Mozambique (1995). The last significant British colony, Hong Kong, was returned to Chinese sovereignty in 1997.

From *Encyclopedia Britannica.*

5• World table

Country	Population (millions)	Capital city	Inhabitants	Official language	Currency (+ the)
Algeria	30,291	Algiers	the Algerians	Arabic	Algerian dinar
Argentina	37,032	Buenos Aires	the Argentinians	Spanish	Argentinian peso
Australia	19,138	Canberra	the Australians	English	Australian dollar
Austria	8,08	Vienna	the Austrians	German	Austrian schilling
Bangladesh	137,439	Dhaka	the Bengalis	Bengali	Bangladesh taka
Belgium	10,249	Brussels	the Belgians	Flemish / French	euro
Botswana	1,541	Gaborone	the Botswana	English	pula
Brazil	170,406	Brasilia	the Brazilians	Portuguese	cruzeiro
Bulgaria	7,949	Sofia	the Bulgarians	Bulgarian	Bulgarian lev
Cambodia	13,104	Phnom Penh	the Cambodians	Khmer	riel
Canada	30,757	Ottawa	the Canadians	English / French	Canadian dollar
Chile	15,211	Santiago	the Chileans	Spanish	Chilean peso
China*	1,282,437	Beijing	the Chinese	Chinese	renminbi
Colombia	42,105	Bogota	the Colombians	Spanish	Colombian peso
Cyprus	784	Nicosia	the Cypriots	Greek / Turkish	Cyprus pound
Czech Republic	10,272	Prague	the Czech	Czech	Czech koruna
Denmark	5,32	Copenhagen	the Danes	Danish	Danish krone
Egypt	67,884	Cairo	the Egyptians	Arabic	Egyptian pound
Estonia	1,393	Tallinn	the Estonians	Estonian	kroon
Finland	5,172	Helsinki	the Finns	Finnish / Swedish	euro
France	59,238	Paris	the French	French	euro
Germany	82,017	Berlin	the Germans	German	euro
Greece	10,61	Athens	the Greeks	Greek	euro
Hungary	9,968	Budapest	the Hungarians	Hungarian	forint
India	1,008,937	New Delhi	the Indians	Hindi / English	Indian rupee
Indonesia	212,092	Jakarta	the Indonesians	Bahasa Indonesia	Indonesian rupiah
Iran	70,33	Teheran	the Iranians	Farsi	Iranian rial
Iraq	22,946	Baghdad	the Iraqis	Arabic	Iraqi dinar
Ireland	3,803	Dublin	the Irish	Irish / English	euro
Israel	6,04	Tel Aviv	the Israelis	Hebrew / Arabic	new shekel
Italy	57,53	Rome	the Italians	Italian	euro
Ivory Coast (the)	16,013	Yamoussoukro	the Ivorians	French	CFA franc
Japan	127,096	Tokyo	the Japanese	Japanese	yen
Kenya	30,669	Nairobi	the Kenyans	Swahili / English	Kenyan shilling
Korea (Dem. People's Rep. of)	22,268	Pyongyang	the North Koreans	Korean	won
Korea (Rep. of)	46,74	Seoul	the South Koreans	Korean	won

*includes Hong Kong and Macao

Country	Population (millions)	Capital city	Inhabitants	Official language	Currency (+ the)
Latvia	2,421	Riga	the Latvians	Latvian	lat
Lebanon	3,496	Beirut	the Lebanese	Arabic	Lebanese pound
Lithuania	3,696	Vilnius	the Lithuanians	Lithuanian	Lithuanian litas
Luxembourg	437	Luxembourg	the Luxembourgers	French / German / Letzeburgisch	euro
Malaysia	22,218	Kuala Lumpur	the Malays	Malay	ringgit / Malaysian dollar
Malta	390	Valletta	the Maltese	English / Maltese	Maltese pound / lira
Mexico	98,872	Mexico City	the Mexicans	Spanish	Mexican peso
Morocco	29,878	Rabat	the Moroccans	Arabic	Moroccan dirham
Myanmar	47,749	Rangoon	the Burmese	Burmese	kyat
Netherlands (the)	15,864	Amsterdam	the Dutch	Dutch	euro
New Zealand	3,778	Wellington	the New Zealanders	English / Maori	New Zealand dollar
Nigeria	113,862	Abuja	the Nigerians	English / French	naira
Norway	4,469	Oslo	the Norwegians	Norwegian	Norwegian krone
Pakistan	141,256	Islamabad	the Pakistanis	Urdu	Pakistan rupee
Peru	25,662	Lima	the Peruvians	Spanish	new sol
Philippines (the)	75,653	Manila	the Filipinos	Pilipino / English	Philippine peso
Poland	38,605	Warsaw	the Poles	Polish	Polish zloty
Portugal	10,016	Lisbon	the Portuguese	Portuguese	euro
Romania	22,438	Bucharest	the Romanians	Romanian	Romanian leu
Russian Federation	145,491	Moscow	the Russians	Russian	ruble
Singapore	4,018	Singapore	the Singaporeans	Chinese / English / Malay / Tamil	Singapore dollar
Slovakia	5,399	Bratislava	the Slovakians	Slovak	Slovakian koruna
Slovenia	1,988	Ljubljana	the Slovenians	Slovene	Slovenian tolar
South Africa	43,309	Pretoria	the South Africans	Afrikaans / English	rand
Spain	39,91	Madrid	the Spanish	Spanish	euro
Sri Lanka	18,924	Colombo	the Sri Lankans	Sinhalese	Sri Lanka rupee
Sweden	8,842	Stockholm	the Swedes	Swedish	Swedish krona
Switzerland	7,17	Bern	the Swiss	French / German / Italian	Swiss franc
Thailand	62,806	Bangkok	the Thais	Thai	Thai baht
Tunisia	9,459	Tunis	the Tunisians	Arabic	Tunisian dinar
Turkey	66,668	Ankara	the Turks	Turkish	Turkish lira
United Kingdom (the)	59,415	London	the British	English	pound sterling
USA (the)	283,23	Washington DC	the Americans	English	American dollar
Vietnam	78,137	Hanoi	the Vietnamese	Vietnamese	dong

The United Kingdom

The USA

Federal capital
State capital
Important city
International boundary
State boundary
C A N A D A
ATLANTIC OCEAN
GULF OF MEXICO
PACIFIC OCEAN
MEXICO
CUBA
BAHAMA ISLANDS
500 miles
500 km
MAINE
Augusta
NEW HAMPSHIRE
Montpelier
Concord
VERMONT
MASSACHUSETTS
Boston
RHODE ISLAND
Providence
CONNECTICUT
Hartford
NEW YORK
Albany
New York
NEW JERSEY
Trenton
Newark
DELAWARE
Dover
MARYLAND
Annapolis
WASHINGTON D.C.
PENNSYLVANIA
Harrisburg
Philadelphia
Pittsburgh
Buffalo
Lake Ontario
Lake Erie
Lake Huron
Lake Michigan
Lake Superior
St Lawrence
WEST VIRGINIA
Charleston
VIRGINIA
Richmond
NORTH CAROLINA
Raleigh
2 038 m Mt Mitchell
SOUTH CAROLINA
Columbia
GEORGIA
Atlanta
FLORIDA
Tallahassee
Tampa
Miami
OHIO
Cleveland
Columbus
Cincinnati
KENTUCKY
Frankfort
Louisville
Ohio
TENNESSEE
Nashville-Davidson
Memphis
Tennessee
ALABAMA
Montgomery
MISSISSIPPI
Jackson
Mississippi
LOUISIANA
Baton Rouge
New Orleans
MICHIGAN
Lansing
Detroit
INDIANA
Indianapolis
ILLINOIS
Chicago
Springfield
WISCONSIN
Madison
Milwaukee
MINNESOTA
Minneapolis
St. Paul
IOWA
Des Moines
MISSOURI
St. Louis
Jefferson City
Kansas City
Missouri
ARKANSAS
Little Rock
NORTH DAKOTA
Bismarck
SOUTH DAKOTA
Pierre
NEBRASKA
Lincoln
Platte River
KANSAS
Topeka
Arkansas
OKLAHOMA
Oklahoma City
TEXAS
Dallas
Houston
Austin
San Antonio
Rio Grande
MONTANA
Helena
2 661 m Snowy Mt
WYOMING
4 196 m Grand Teton
Cheyenne
COLORADO
Denver
4 401 m Mt Elbert
NEW MEXICO
Santa Fe
3 652 m Sierra Blanca
3 444 m Mt Taylor
IDAHO
Boise City
Snake
UTAH
Salt Lake City
Colorado
ARIZONA
Phoenix
Tucson
Grand Canyon
NEVADA
Carson City
Las Vegas
CALIFORNIA
Sacramento
San Francisco
San José
Death Valley
Los Angeles
San Diego
Sacramento
OREGON
Salem
Portland
WASHINGTON
Olympia
Seattle
Mt Rainier 4 392 m
Columbia
HAWAII
4 206 m Mauna Kea
Honolulu
PACIFIC OCEAN
250 miles
250 km
ALASKA
CANADA
Juneau
Fairbanks
Anchorage
6 187 m Mt McKinley
Yukon
Bering Strait
RUSSIAN FEDERATION (former USSR)
PACIFIC OCEAN

Passport

The English-speaking countries

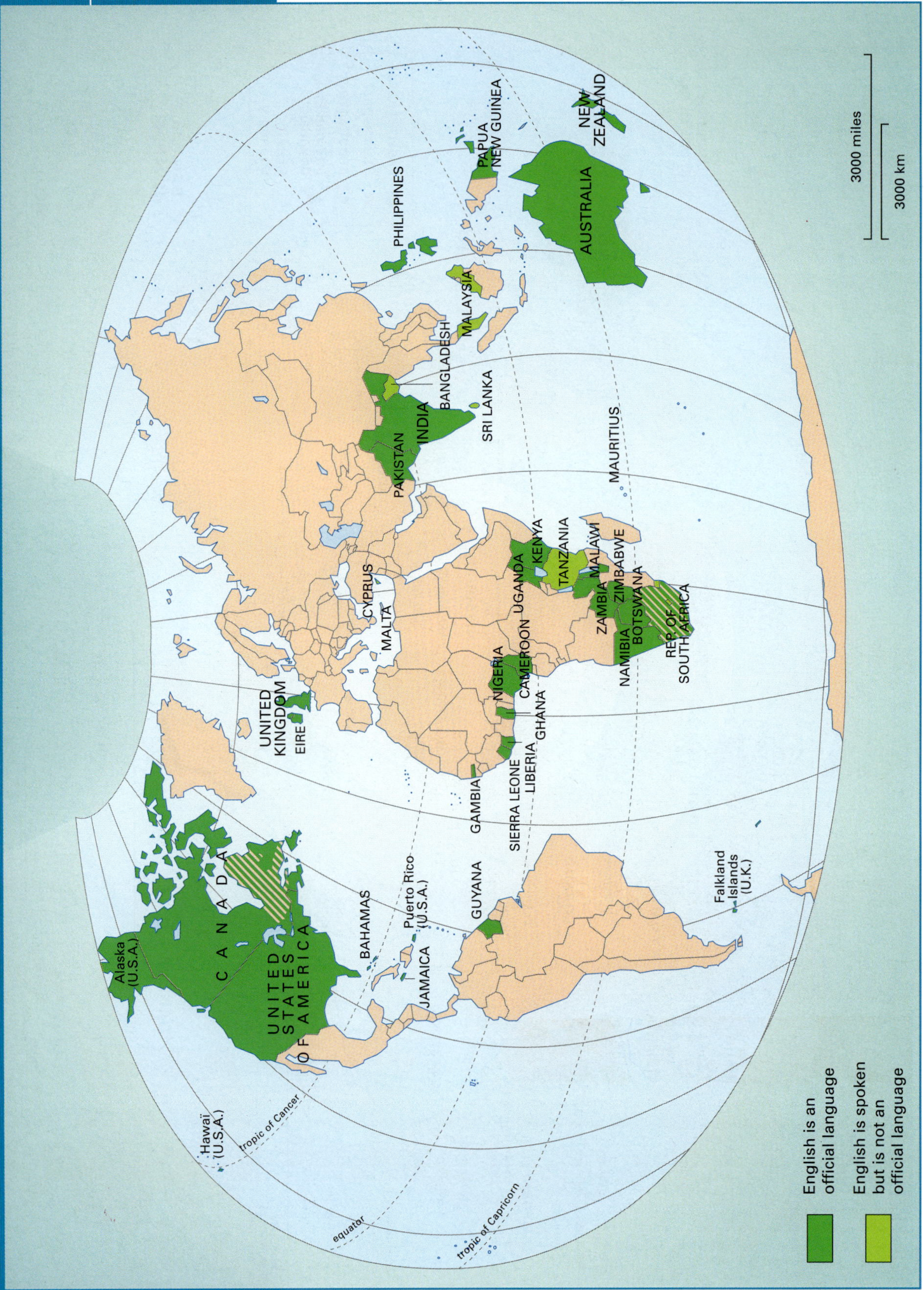

India and southeast Asia

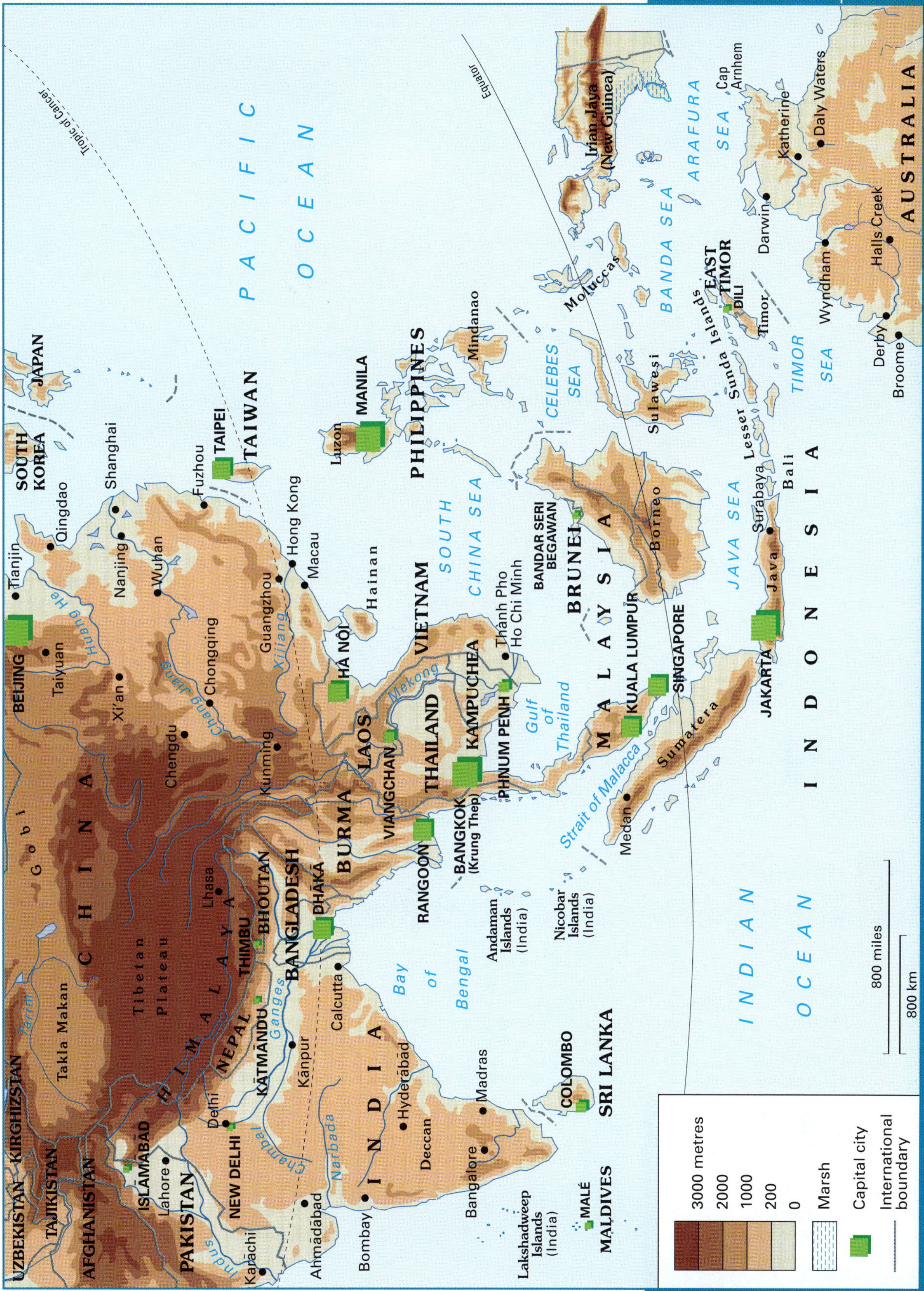

Africa

E U R O P E
A S I A
Arabian Peninsula
Strait of Gibraltar
ALGIERS
TUNIS
RABAT
Oran
Casablanca
Atlas Saharien
Madeira I.
(Portugal)
MOROCCO
TUNISIA
MEDITERRANEAN SEA
TRIPOLI
Alexandria
Suez Canal
Canary Islands
(Spain)
Anti Atlas
Tripolitania
Benghazi
Cyrenaica
Sinai
ALGERIA
CAIRO
LIBYA
Libyan Desert
EGYPT
Tropic of Cancer
Hoggar
Fezzan
Assouan
Tanezrouft
Lake Nasser
RED SEA
MAURITANIA
Ténéré
Nubian Desert
SAHARA
Aïr
Tibesti
CAPE VERDE
NOUAKCHOTT
MALI
Nile
DAKAR
PRAIA
NIGER
SUDAN
SENEGAL
Niger
CHAD
KHARTOUM
ASMERA
Socotra
(Yemen)
GAMBIA
BANJUL
NIAMEY
Lake Chad
ERITREA
BISSAU
BAMAKO
BURKINA FASO
OUAGADOUGOU
Kano
Blue Nile
DJIBOUTI
Gulf of Aden
GUINEA-B.
GUINEA
BENIN
NIGERIA
N'DJAMENA
Darfur
Bab el Mandeb
Cape Guardafui
CONAKRY
FREETOWN
SIERRA LEONE
IVORY COAST
TOGO
ABUJA
Chari
White Nile
Ethiopian Plateau
DJIBOUTI
Ibadan
ADDIS ABEBA
MONROVIA
LIBERIA
YAMOUSSOUKRO
GHANA
Lagos
Benue
CENTRAL AFRICAN REPUBLIC
ETHIOPIA
ACCRA
Abidjan
PORTO-NOVO
CAMEROON
Douala
BANGUI
SOMALI REP.
LOMÉ
MALABO
YAOUNDÉ
Uele
UGANDA
Lake Turkana
EQUAT. GUINEA
Gulf of Guinea
SÃO TOMÉ AND PRÍNCIPE
Congo
Ubangi
Kisangani
KAMPALA
MUQDISHO
Equator
LIBREVILLE
GABON
DEM. REP. OF THE CONGO
RWANDA
KIGALI
Lake Victoria
KENYA
NAIROBI
INDIAN OCEAN
CONGO
BUJUMBURA
BURUNDI
BRAZZAVILLE
SEYCHELLES
Cabinda
(Angola)
KINSHASA
TANZANIA
Pemba I.
Zanzibar I.
VICTORIA
Lake Tanganyika
ATLANTIC OCEAN
Kananga
DODOMA
Dar es-Salaam
Amirante I.
(S.)
Kasai
Shaba Plateau
Aldabra I.
(S.)
LUANDA
Lunda Plateau
Lake Malawi
COMOROS
Cerf I.
(S.)
Mayotte
(F.)
MALAWI
MORONI
ANGOLA
ZAMBIA
LILONGWE
LUSAKA
MOZAMBIQUE
Lake Kariba
Zambezi
HARARE
Mozambique Channel
ANTANANARIVO
NAMIBIA
ZIMBABWE
Beira
MAURITIUS
PORT-LOUIS
Namib Desert
BOTSWANA
MADAGASCAR
WINDHOEK
Kalahari
Limpopo
Réunion
(F.)
Tropic of Capricorn
GABORONE
PRETORIA
MAPUTO
Johannesburg
MBABANE
SWAZILAND
MASERU
LESOTHO
Orange
REP. OF SOUTH AFRICA
Durban
Cape Town
Port Elizabeth
Cape of Good Hope
2000 metres
1000
500
200
0
Depression
Marsh
Capital city
International boundary
800 miles
800 km

CENTRAL AMERICA
1 BELIZE
2 HONDURAS
3 JAMAICA
4 ANTIGUA & BARBUDA
5 DOMINICA
6 SAINTE-LUCIA
7 SAINT-VINCENT
8 TRINIDAD & TOBAGO

EUROPE
9 DENMARK
10 THE NETHERLANDS
11 BELGIUM
12 LUXEMBOURG
13 GERMANY
14 LITUANIA
15 SWITZERLAND
16 CZECH REPUBLIC
17 SLOVAKIA
18 AUSTRIA
19 HUNGARY
20 SLOVENIA
21 CROATIA
22 BOSNA-HERCEGOVINA
23 SERBIA-MONTENEGRO
24 BULGARIA
25 MOLDAVIA
26 MACEDONIA
27 ALBANIA
28 MALTA

AFRICA
29 GAMBIA
30 GUINEA-BISSAU
31 LIBERIA
32 BURKINA FASO
33 GHANA
34 TOGO
35 BENIN
36 EQUATORIAL GUINEA
37 UGANDA
38 RWANDA
39 BURUNDI
40 MALAWI
41 SWAZILAND
42 LESOTHO

ASIA
43 CYPRUS
44 LEBANON
45 ISRAEL
46 AUTONOMOUS TERRITORIES OF PALESTINIA
47 JORDAN
48 GEORGIA
49 ARMENIA
50 AZERBAIJAN
51 UZBEKISTAN
52 TURKMENISTAN
53 KIRGHIZSTAN
54 TAJIKISTAN
55 KUWAIT
56 BAHRAIN
57 QATAR
58 UNITED ARAB EMIRATES

Imprimé en Espagne par MATEU CROMO
Dépôt légal n° 31132 - 04/2003
Collection n°80 - Edition n°01
16/8841/5